Reformed C... of the Sixteenth Century

EDITED, WITH HISTORICAL INTRODUCTIONS

BY

Arthur C. Cochrane

NEW INTRODUCTION BY

Jack Rogers

Westminster John Knox Press

LOUISVILLE • LONDON

© 2003 Westminster John Knox Press

Originally published in Great Britain in 1966 by SCM Press
First published in the United States in 1966 by The Westminster Press

Cover design by Pam Poll Graphic Design

Published by Westminster John Knox Press
Louisville, Kentucky

This book is printed on acid-free paper that meets the American National Standards Institute Z39.48 standard. ∞

PRINTED IN THE UNITED STATES OF AMERICA

03 04 05 06 07 08 09 10 11 12 — 10 9 8 7 6 5 4 3 2 1

Library of Congress Cataloging-in-Publication Data

Reformed confessions of the sixteenth century / Arthur C. Cochrane ; with
   new introduction by Jack Rogers
      p. cm
   Includes bibliographical references.
   Originally published: London : SMC Press, 1966.
   ISBN 0-664-22694-9
   1. Reformed Church—Creeds.   I. Cochrane, Arthur C.

   BX9428.A1C6   2003
   238'.42—dc21   2003050094

CONTENTS

NEW INTRODUCTION

Jack Rogers

IN 1966, THE WESTMINSTER PRESS PERFORMED AN IMPORTANT
service for American readers by publishing Arthur Cochrane's collection of the principal Reformed Confessions of the sixteenth
century.[1]

Publication occurred just at the time that the United Presbyterian Church in the U.S.A. (northern) was debating the adoption of
a *Book of Confessions* intended to free the denomination's understanding of the Reformed tradition from exclusive dependence on
the Anglo-Saxon Westminster Standards.[2]

The Reformed tradition is that stream of the Protestant Reformation that generally emanated from Zurich and Geneva in distinction to the Lutheran, Anabaptist, and Anglican expressions of
reformation.[3]

Cochrane's collection was thus both broader than the Presbyterian *Book of Confessions* in containing twelve Reformed Confessions and more narrow in scope by focusing only on the sixteenth
century. His choice of confessions was notable in that all came
from that yeasty period of development when the Reformation
impulse was fresh. Only two overlapped the selections in the *Book
of Confessions:* The Scots Confession of 1560 and the Second Helvetic Confession of 1566. Cochrane provided a translation into

---

[1] This introduction is meant to supplement the excellent introduction that
Cochrane provided in the original edition: Arthur C. Cochrane, ed., *Reformed Con-
fessions of the 16th Century: Edited, with Historical Introductions by Arthur C. Cochrane*
(Philadelphia: Westminster Press, 1966).

[2] Cochrane added the Nicene and Apostles' Creeds, the Heidelberg Catechism,
and the Theological Declaration of Barmen in an appendix, but omitted the Westminster Standards, and does not have A Brief Statement of Faith added to the *Book
of Confessions* in 1991.

[3] The Anglican confessions evidence many of the characteristics of Reformed
theology. The Anglican tradition, historically, had a very different origin and development. See Jack Rogers, *Presbyterian Creeds: A Guide to the Book of Confessions*
(Louisville, Ky.: Westminster/John Knox Press, 1991), 148.

English of the Second Helvetic Confession at a time when the
UPCUSA was considering it but no complete translation was readily available. His collection contained two confessions more directly
influenced by Calvin than any in the UPCUSA *Book of Confessions:*
the French Confession of 1559 and the Belgic Confession of 1561.[4]

Adoption of the *Book of Confessions,* including the new Confession
of 1967, for Presbyterians in the United States of America, opened
an era of interest in the broader Reformed tradition that has
extended to the present time. Significant actions regarding Confessions have occurred since the publication of Cochrane's work.[5]

NEW CONFESSIONS IN THE TWENTIETH CENTURY

In 1976, the General Assembly of the Presbyterian Church in
the United States (southern) sent to its presbyteries *The Proposed
Book of Confessions of the Presbyterian Church in the United States.*[6]

It included the Geneva Catechism of 1541 and a newly prepared
contemporary statement, "A Declaration of Faith."[7]

The proposal did not receive the necessary three-fourths vote of
the presbyteries to become constitutional. It did, however, awaken
interest in the confessions and caused "A Declaration of Faith" to
be widely used in the southern Presbyterian churches.

In 1983, the northern and southern streams of Presbyterianism
united to form the Presbyterian Church (U.S.A.). Part of the Arti-

---

[4] The 209th General Assembly (1997) instructed the General Assembly Council,
through its Office of Theology, Worship and Discipleship, to develop means to
introduce the French Confession of 1559 throughout the church. That Office in
1998 produced an excellent booklet containing a new translation, a historical and
theological introduction to the confession, and two study guides.

[5] Several North American creeds came into being in the early part of this
period. All of them were presented with modest intentions of giving witness, or
making a testimony, but not of having the status of the older Reformation confessions. In 1959, the General Synod of the United Church of Christ, a union two
years before of the Congregational Christian Churches and the Evangelical and
Reformed Church, adopted a one-page statement of faith. In 1968, the United
Church of Canada, with conscious reference to the United Church of Christ creed,
adopted an even briefer creed, which was revised in 1980 to make the language
more inclusive. In 1974, the General Synod of the Reformed Church in America
approved *Our Song of Hope* for study, and in 1978 received it as an official statement
of faith, but not as a "Standard" equal to the Belgic Confession, the Heidelberg Catechism, and the Canons of Dort that continued to be the doctrinal standards of the
denomination. See Lukas Vischer, ed., *Reformed Witness Today* (Bern: Evangelische
Arbeitsstelle Oekumene Schweiz, 1982), 193–200, 219–27.

[6] Atlanta: General Assembly of the Presbyterian Church in the United States,
1976.

[7] The other documents included were the Apostles' Creed, the Nicene Creed,
the Scots Confession, the Heidelberg Catechism, the Westminster Confession of
Faith, the Larger Catechism, the Shorter Catechism, and the Theological Declaration of Barmen.

cles of Agreement of the reunion was that the Moderator of the reunited church should appoint a committee "representing diversities of points of view and groups within the reunited Church to prepare a Brief Statement of the Reformed Faith for possible inclusion in the *Book of Confessions*."[8]

For the first time in Reformed confessional history, a group was chosen specifically for its diversity and then expected to produce a document evoking unity. The activity of the committee initiated a period of intense discussion regarding the content and function of confessions. After seven years of interaction, the reunited denomination adopted "A Brief Statement of Faith—Presbyterian Church (U.S.A.)" in 1991. A Brief Statement became the eleventh document in the *Book of Confessions*.[9]

Soon after the creation of the Special Committee on a Brief Statement of the Reformed Faith, an agency of the denomination created a committee on "The Confessional Nature of the Church." The committee's report dealt with the nature and purpose of confessions, the character of confessions in the Reformed tradition, and gave rationale for the content—and guidance for the function—of the *Book of Confessions* of the Presbyterian Church (U.S.A.). The 198th General Assembly (1986) commended the report for study. The 209th General Assembly (1997) mandated that this document, as well as another brief paper intended to provide criteria for future additions to the *Book of Confessions*, be included in future editions of the *Book of Confessions*.[10]

THEMES IN THE SIXTEENTH-CENTURY REFORMED CONFESSIONS

How are the sixteenth-century confessions alike and different from those of the twentieth century? How may Reformed Confessions of the twenty-first century will be different still? Despite the conflicts over doctrine and practice within contemporary Reformed churches, their confessional documents remain uniformly orthodox with regard to the central affirmations of the Christian faith. The differences in twentieth-century confessions from those in the sixteenth century arise from the differences in sociopolitical context. All of the

---

[8] Cited in Jack Rogers, *Presbyterian Creeds: A Guide to the Book of Confessions*, rev. ed. (Louisville, Ky.: Westminster/John Knox Press, 1991), 231.

[9] For a commentary prepared by two members of the committee, see William C. Placher and David Willis-Watkins, *Belonging to God: A Commentary on "A Brief Statement of Faith"* (Louisville, Ky.: Westminster/John Knox Press, 1992).

[10] *The Constitution of the Presbyterian Church (U.S.A.), Part I: Book of Confessions*, study ed. (Louisville, Ky.: Geneva Press, 1999), 353–78. The additional document is entitled, "The Assessment of Proposed Amendments to the *Book of Confessions*."

confessions' writers have attempted to apply the Reformed Christian
faith to the problems of their time. The times are simply different.

The twelve doctrinal statements written in the forty-three years
from 1523 to 1566 illustrate the inception, the development, and the
maturation of Reformed theology. The writers were all presenting
their beliefs to the civil authorities. For most of the period, the magistrates were still allied with the Roman Catholic Church. A common
assumption of that era was that any state should have its own religion, or at worst, officially tolerate one or two faiths. To counteract
this assumption, Reformed Christians needed to affirm openly what
they believed in order to convince the governmental authorities that
they were not seditious, nor intending to overthrow civil authority.

Convincing the governmental authorities meant that most of
the confessions were initially debated in the presence of some
regional or city council. Others were presented to an imperial
ruler. In many cases, the consequence was that the civil government ordered that their region was to become Reformed Protestant instead of Roman Catholic. In other instances, where no
change of mind took place in the government, persecution of
Protestants sometimes resulted. In every instance, the Reformed
confessors affirmed the necessity of obedience to the civil magistrate, as long as that authority did not violate the law of God.

Reformed Christians all agreed that the civil authority's duty was
to defend the true religion and to suppress heresy. Thus, the early
Reformed Christians were compelled to convince the people in
power that they, the Reformed, believed and practiced the orthodox Christian faith. Later, some of the confessions were comprehensive statements of the Reformed faith presented to already
Protestant governments to provide a theological foundation for
both the state and the church.

All of these Reformed Confessions asserted that their beliefs
were based on the teachings of Holy Scripture. They connected
themselves to the early church, usually by explicitly affirming their
adherence to the earliest ecumenical councils and to the ancient
creeds, which they often named as the Nicene, the Apostles', and
the Creed of Athanasius.[11]

They developed fully orthodox beliefs in one God, manifested
in three persons of Father, Son, and Holy Spirit. They affirmed

---

[11] "The attribution of the formula to Athanasius, the 4th-century patriarch of
Alexandria, seems to have been a gradual process beginning in the 7th century and
continuing uncontested until the 17th century. This attribution is now generally
abandoned." *New Catholic Encyclopedia*, 2d ed. (Detroit: Gale, 2003, in Association
with the Catholic University of America), s.v., Athanasian Creed.

Jesus Christ as both Divine and Human and often detailed their rejection of the ancient heresies that denied these beliefs. Confession writers evidenced their training in Renaissance scholarship by their reference to philosophers and other authorities of antiquity.

The Reformers' chief opposition was to the reigning Roman Church. They defined their faith over against this extension of the culture of the Middle Ages. Certain non-Roman doctrines necessarily were asserted by all of the Reformed Confessions. These doctrines included that humans are dead in sin and require God's sole saving action in Christ to redeem them. No human cooperation is required. Christ's death on the cross is a once-for-all sacrifice for human sin. Thus, the Reformers rejected as false the Roman claim that, in the Mass, Christ is continually resacrificed. They rejected seven sacraments as claimed by Rome. The Reformers identified only two sacraments instituted by Jesus Christ—baptism and the Lord's Supper—which replaced the Old Testament sacraments of circumcision and the sacrifice of the Paschal Lamb.

With regard to the sacraments, the Reformed Confessions clarified their differences not only with Rome, but also with the Lutherans and the Anabaptists. The Reformed developed a very sophisticated theory of the relation of symbols to reality. They maintained, versus the Roman Catholics, that the symbols of bread and wine are not transformed into Christ's physical body and blood. Neither did they believe, as did the Lutherans, that Christ's physical body was united with the symbols of bread and wine. Yet, versus the Anabaptists, who saw the Lord's Supper only as a memorial feast, the Reformed claimed that the symbols communicate to the believer the real spiritual presence of Christ. Half of the collected Reformed Confessions contain specific rejections of the Anabaptists.

Regarding the symbols, the Reformed continually tried to resolve their differences with the Lutherans, usually without success. While the Reformed Confessions failed to bring about ecumenical unity, they often served to solidify the bonds of the participating Reformed partners. The Reformed were harsh in their criticism of the Anabaptists, and not solely because the Anabaptists believed that only adults could be baptized. The Anabaptists refused obedience to the civil government and were generally viewed as anarchists. The Reformed wished to avoid guilt by association. Bullinger's attitude in the Second Helvetic Confession was characteristic: "We therefore are not Anabaptists and have nothing in common with them."[12]

---

[12] Chapter XX, Cochrane, 283.

In the case of the French Confession, we see a remnant of Calvin's antipathy to Servetus. The Reformed movement, politically, needed not only to set itself off from the Anabaptists, but also from the radical anti-Trinitarianism that all of the Christian states condemned. The French Confession of 1559 is very explicit: "In this we detest all the heresies that have of old troubled the Church, especially the diabolical conceits of Servetus."[13]

Servetus had been condemned to death in Roman Catholic Vienne, but escaped to Geneva. When the City of Geneva discovered him, he was put to death there with Calvin's consent.

Two marks of the true church in the Reformed Confessions are the true preaching of the Word of God and the right administration of the sacraments. In some confessions, most notably the Scots Confession of 1560, a third mark is added: "ecclesiastical discipline uprightly ministered, as God's Word prescribes, whereby vice is repressed and virtue nourished."[14]

While the goal of church discipline is the restoration of the offender, all of the Reformed Confessions accept the necessity of excommunication for persistent, scandalous unbelief or misbehavior.

The Reformed Confessions state that all church members are priests. However, these confessions recognize ministers who have been gifted and called by God and who are recognized as lawful leaders by the elders of the church (and sometimes the civil magistrate). The Belgic Confession clearly specifies the election of office bearers in the church: "We believe that the Ministers of God's Word, and the Elders and Deacons, ought to be chosen to their respective offices by a lawful election of the Church, with calling upon the name of the Lord, and in that order which the Word of God teacheth."[15]

The elders and deacons, together with the ministers, "form the council of the Church . . . By these means every thing will be carried on in the Church with good order and decency."[16]

The power of the keys to the heavenly kingdom does not belong to the priests of Rome, but to lawfully called ministers who preach the gospel from the Word of God.

A commonly expressed opinion since the adoption of the Confession of 1967 has been that it was the first Reformed Confession to speak directly to social issues. Social issues in the sixteenth century were different from ours. We must, however, recognize how

---

[13] Article XIV, Cochrane, 149.
[14] Chapter XVIII, Cochrane, 177.
[15] Article XXXI, Cochrane, 212.
[16] Article XXX, Cochrane, 211.

radically the sixteenth-century Reformers changed their society. Rejection of Roman Catholic traditions that had long molded society was as dramatic as American Presbyterian pleas to end racial segregation in the Confession of 1967 and to recognize the equality of women in A Brief Statement of Faith.

The Reformed Confessions explicitly rejected beliefs and ecclesiastical structures that denied a person's direct access to God: the authority of the pope; the efficacy of the Mass; saints' intercession between God and humans; punishment in purgatory (i.e., seven years for each mortal sin); and veneration of pictures, images, or relics of the saints. Thus people were freed from layers of tradition that denied their full value as persons created for personal relationship with God.

The Reformed Confessions also denounced as unbiblical and unnecessary certain common Roman Catholic practices: fasting during Lent, prohibition of certain foods, festivals and pilgrimages, and observing saints' days. All of these changes had economic impact. People were free to work more often and buy the food they wished without artificial constraints.

The Reformed also wanted simplification of worship and thus rejected Roman practices of private confessions ("murmuring them in his ears"); rote chants or prayers; exorcism; and the use of burning lights, oil, salt, spittle, and such other things with ceremonies. Worship was centered in hearing the Word of God. Reformed worship was designed to enable people to enter directly into God's holy, just, and loving presence.

The Reformed Confessions discarded traditions regarding the clergy that the Reformed believed were unscriptural, impractical, and led to abuses: cloisters, religious orders of monks or nuns, forbidding marriage, and vows of celibacy. The Reformed Confessions are uniform in asserting that celibacy is a gift of God, given to few. Recognizing the powerful human need for sexual expression, the Reformed insisted that marriage is intended by God to answer that need. The notion that a class of people must refrain from marriage in order to please God was labeled false and subject to abuse. Bullinger, in the Second Helvetic Confession, gives specific advice in regard to marital relationships. He recommends, "Let lawful courts be established in the Church, and holy judges who may care for marriages, and may repress all unchastity and shamefulness, and before whom matrimonial disputes may be settled."[17]

---

[17] Chapter XXIX, Cochrane, 298.

Our human problems, in principle, are similar to those of sixteenth-century people, and the confessions' central guidance is still sound.

THE REFORMED CONFESSIONS IN AMERICA

American Presbyterian Confessions also display the marks of their sociopolitical environment. The first Reformed confessional activity in the New World came in 1729, even before there was a Presbyterian General Assembly. The Synod of Philadelphia was wrestling with the issue of whether ministers had to subscribe to the Westminster Confession and Catechisms. People were deeply divided over that issue. The solution was a classic Presbyterian compromise. Yes, all candidates and ministers did have to affirm their loyalty to the Westminster Standards. However, subscription was only to the "essential and necessary" articles. The test of what was "essential" took place if a minister or candidate presented a "scruple" (a disagreement) with some article of the Confession. Then the presbytery, or the synod, decided whether the matter was of sufficient consequence to require adherence. All participants in the discussion were exhorted to civility toward those with whom they disagreed on nonessentials.[18]

That synod meeting in 1729 amended the Westminster Confession in a manner that showed the most notable difference from the sociopolitical context of the sixteenth-century confessions. The Synod of Pennsylvania voted to remove from the Westminster Standards statements that allowed the magistrate to defend the faith, to suppress heresy, or to call ecclesiastical assemblies.[19]

Church and state were now decisively separated.

From 1729 to 1967, the world changed and the church endured conflicts over the confessions. Yet for all of those 238 years, the Westminster Confession of Faith and Catechisms formed the primary confessional standards for Presbyterian churches in America.[20]

---

[18] For the original statement, see Maurice W. Armstrong, Lefferts A. Loetscher, and Charles A. Anderson, eds., *The Presbyterian Enterprise: Sources of American Presbyterian History* (Philadelphia: Westminster Press, 1956), 30–32.

[19] See Westminster Confession, Chapter XXIII, "Of the Civil Magistrate," note on the 1647 edition. Cf. Armstrong et al., *Presbyterian Enterprise*, 32.

[20] The United Presbyterian Church of North America adopted a contemporary confessional statement in 1925, which was set aside at the merger in 1958 of the UPCNA with the Presbyterian Church in the U.S.A. to form the United Presbyterian Church in the U.S.A. The Westminster Standards then prevailed as the doctrinal standard until the adoption of the *Book of Confessions* in 1967.

The United Presbyterian Church in the U.S.A.'s adoption of a *Book of Confessions* with ten documents, including the contemporary Confession of 1967, marked a dramatic shift in confessional thinking. The perspective shifted from only seventeenth-century English standards to include two ancient, ecumenical creeds; sixteenth-century confessions from Scotland, Germany, and Switzerland; and two twentieth-century documents. More importantly, the publication marked a leap of 320 years from the Westminster Confession to the Confession of 1967. By 1991, the *Book of Confessions* contained three twentieth-century theological statements. Their emphases illustrated the different sociopolitical world in which Reformed theology was being applied.

COMMON AND CONTRASTING THEMES
IN THE TWENTIETH-CENTURY REFORMED CONFESSIONS

All three of the twentieth-century confessions begin not with God, nor creation, nor Scripture, but with Jesus Christ. This christological focus reflected the protest in the early twentieth century against an optimistic natural theology that had permitted injustice in society and church to go unchallenged. The Theological Declaration of Barmen protested the errors of the German Evangelical Church that had permitted the Nazi government to impinge on the life and witness of the church. The answer of the Confessing Church at Barmen in 1934 was clear: "Jesus Christ, as he is attested for us in Holy Scripture, is the one Word of God which we have to hear and which we have to trust and obey in life and in death."[21]

Essentially, Adolf Hitler was not Lord.

The Preface to the Confession of 1967 sets a similar tone: "The church confesses its faith when it bears a present witness to God's grace in Jesus Christ."[22]

Its theme of reconciliation in Jesus Christ was applied to the presenting social issues of the 1960s in the United States: racial discrimination, the search for world peace, and enslaving poverty in a world of abundance. In the amending process, a fourth, and more personal, issue was added: "anarchy in sexual relationships."[23]

Both Barmen and the initial three emphases of the Confession of 1967 reflected a modern concern for the sinful structures of society, rather than simply the personal sins of individuals.

---

[21] II. 1, Cochrane, 334.
[22] *Book of Confessions* 9.01.
[23] II.A.4, "Reconciliation in Society." *Book of Confessions* 9.44–9.47.

A Brief Statement of Faith, adopted in 1991, was intended as a creed for liturgical and educational use.[24]

As such, the authors designed it as a short statement, in contemporary language, of the basic elements of the Christian faith. They did, however, address one sinful structure that still prevailed in society: the subordination of women to men. They self-consciously contradicted the statements in the Scots Confession and the Second Helvetic Confession that women could not be ministers.[25]

For the first time in a Reformed Confession, female as well as male images of God were used. In addition, the authors specifically stated that the Holy Spirit "calls women and men to all the ministries of the Church."[26]

All three of these twentieth-century confessions reflect the late-twentieth-century outlook that to be authentically Reformed is to be ecumenical. They stress the humanity of Christ in ways not previously explored, without denying Christ's deity. They assume a scholarly interpretation of Scripture that takes its human character fully into account.[27]

In their concept of the marks of the church, the twentieth-century confessions differ most from their sixteenth- and seventeenth-century predecessors. The sixteenth-century confessions identify the authentic church by its true preaching of the Word, upright administration of the sacraments, and, for the Scots, personal discipline. The Second Helvetic Confession declares: "The Church is an assembly of the faithful called or gathered out of the world; a communion . . . of those who truly know and rightly worship and serve the true God in Christ the Savior, by the Word and Holy Spirit."[28]

The church is depicted as an ark of salvation into which believers are gathered from the world.

In the twentieth century, a new confessional mark of the church appears: to be in mission in and to the world. The Theological Declaration of Barmen evidences this shift in emphasis. The church "has to testify in the midst of a sinful world, with its faith as with its obedience."[29]

In the Confession of 1967, mission in the world has become a clear mark of the true church. "To be reconciled to God is to be sent into the world as his reconciling community."[30]

---

[24] See Rogers, *Presbyterian Creeds,* chap. 11.
[25] Scots Confession, chap. XXII, Cochrane, 181; Second Helvetic Confession, chap. XX, Cochrane, 283.
[26] II. 64. *Book of Confessions* 10.4.
[27] See Stotts, in Rohls, xii.
[28] Chapter XVII, Cochrane, 261.
[29] II.3., Cochrane, 335.
[30] *Book of Confessions* 9.31.

The stress is no longer solely on the salvation of the individual, but also on the activity of the corporate church in the world.[31]

Speaking of church members, the Confession of 1967 declares: "Their daily action in the world is the church in mission to the world."[32]

A true church in the twentieth century was an agent not only of personal, but also of societal change.

Reformed Christians in the sixteenth and seventeenth centuries challenged and changed the world in which they lived. Their attention, however, was on the creation of a true church that would be the church of a Christian nation. In the twentieth century, a self-conscious emphasis emerged on looking outward, on changing the sinful structures of a society that was culturally diverse and not identifiably Christian. Action, as well as belief, had become a mark of the true church.[33]

ISSUES FOR CONTEMPORARY AND COMING CONFESSIONS

In each era in which Reformed Confessions have been written, there were personal and social issues that were "occasions" that called forth confession. At the same time, Reformed Christians, in each era, now seem to us to have been blind and oblivious to sins that now call us to urgent application of the Christian gospel. Our sixteenth-century predecessors in the faith accepted a social and economic class system that, at its worst, fostered the enslavement of African Americans and the oppression of women. The Confession of 1967, reflecting its times, totally overlooked the issue of the equality of women, including using masculine language for all people. A Brief Statement of Faith focused on affirming the equality of women and men. Still, this most recent statement made no mention of the primary issue convulsing the Church in the 1980s and 1990s, namely whether homosexual persons should have the right to hold ordained office in the church.[34]

---

[31] See Jack Rogers, *Claiming the Center: Churches and Conflicting Worldviews* (Louisville, Ky.: Westminster John Knox Press, 1995), 52–53.

[32] II.A.2. *Book of Confessions* 9.37.

[33] Eberhard Busch also notes this difference between the older and new Reformed Confessions. He wrestles critically with this phenomenon in David Willis and Michael Welker, eds., *Toward the Future of Reformed Theology* (Grand Rapids: Wm. B. Eerdmans Publishing Co., 1999), 525–31.

[34] See *Book of Order* G-5.0202 on the rights of membership. Unfortunately, Cochrane, like the Presbyterian Church (U.S.A.) *Book of Confessions,* uses the 1962 translation of the Heidelberg Catechism by the Reformed Church in America, which advocates a position on this contemporary issue by inserting the phrase, "homosexual perversion," at Answer 87 where no such reference appears in the original.

What will be the issues that Reformed Christians will need to address in the early twenty-first century? How to speak about and with persons of other religions will certainly be an imperative as in no previous Reformed statement. Some believe that the christological emphasis, so characteristic of twentieth-century Reformed Confessions, will make interfaith dialogue more difficult. Concern for how we deal with the ecology of our planet will no doubt grow since, as A Brief Statement of Faith states, we "threaten death to the planet entrusted to our care."[35]

We may need to recover concerns from our earlier confessions that we have too easily overlooked: the destructive nature of greed and our responsibility to discern whether the civil government is acting in accordance with the mandate of the gospel.

In the late twentieth and early twenty-first centuries, a dissatisfied minority of members of the Presbyterian Church (U.S.A.) called for a definition of the "essential tenets of the Reformed faith as expressed in the confessions of our church." This phrase comes from the third of nine vows that deacons, elders, and ministers of the Word and Sacrament take at their ordination.[36]

The response to this call was usually twofold. First, the practice of American Presbyterianism, since the Adopting Act of 1729, has been to allow the governing body, usually presbytery or synod, to define what is essential only when a particular case was presented. Second, people pointed to chapter 2 of the *Book of Order*, which lists doctrines characteristic of the Christian, Protestant, and Reformed traditions to which Presbyterians adhere. This listing was not intended to be comprehensive or definitive, but rather exemplary, indicating the kind of doctrines that are characteristic of the Reformed family of churches since the Reformed tradition has never had a definitive list of doctrines.

Some people who asked for a precise definition of "essential tenets" apparently desired to use the confessions juridically. Here the Presbyterian confessional tradition offers helpful advice. The Westminster Confession, which some think of as the most legalistic in its approach, offers a warning. "All synods or councils since the apostles' times, whether general or particular, may err, and many

---

[35] II.38. *Book of Confessions* 10.3.

[36] The entire vow reads: "Do you sincerely receive and adopt the essential tenets of the Reformed faith as expressed in the confessions of our church as authentic and reliable expositions of what Scripture leads us to believe and do, and will you be instructed and led by those confessions as you lead the people of God?" *The Constitution of the Presbyterian Church (U.S.A.), Part II: Book of Order, 2000–2001* (Louisville, Ky.: Office of the General Assembly, 2000), G-14.0405, (3).

have erred; therefore they are not to be made the rule of faith or practice, but to be used as a help in both."[37]

To use confessions from previous centuries as contemporary laws fails to recognize that humans not only applied the gospel to their situation, but that they did so with the assumptions of their time and culture.[38]

Other issues that the Reformed Confessions will address in the future are, of course, not known. New Reformed Confessions will continue to speak to these issues as they arise. Another reason for writing new confessions is so the whole church can be involved in thinking about what Reformed people most deeply believe. Every generation will present occasions that call the church to a fresh statement of faith. These occasions should become the opportunity for serious, healthy theological reflection among the whole people of God.

A creed states the basic elements of the Christian faith, the facts of the Christian story. Creeds have arisen in connection with teaching people the meaning of the sacraments in which they were to participate. Creeds become part of the liturgy of worship and a basis for education in the church.

A confession is an elaborated interpretation and application of those creedal facts to the issues and concerns of a particular people in a particular time and place. We can learn from the sixteenth-century confessions in Cochrane's collection how to hold on to the basic facts of the gospel message. We can be encouraged as well to interpret and apply that saving message to the perplexing problems and seemingly intransigent issues of a new time and culture. The sixteenth-century reformers were faithful, biblical Christians. They also bravely lived out their faith in a world that needed to be changed for the sake of Christ. That twofold challenge is ours as well.

---

[37] *Book of Confessions* 6.175. John Leith noted, "Members of the Westminster Assembly had themselves strenuously opposed the imposition of creeds on the believing community," in Jack L. Stotts and Jane Dempsey Douglass, eds., *To Confess the Faith Today* (Louisville, Ky.: Westminster/John Knox Press, 1990), 44.

[38] A present instance of the problem of using the confessions juridically is the addition to the Presbyterian Church (U.S.A.) *Book of Order* of G-6.0106b, the last sentence of which reads, "Persons refusing to repent of any self-acknowledged practice which the confessions call sin shall not be ordained and/or installed as deacons, elders, or ministers of the Word and Sacrament." If taken literally, this statement would likely prohibit all twenty-first-century Presbyterians from being ordained to church office, since the *Book of Confessions* mentions approximately 250 sins, many of which contemporary Christians no longer considered sinful.

RECENT LITERATURE ON THE REFORMED CONFESSIONS

Regarding the confessions and the Reformed tradition, a considerable literature has appeared since the publication of Cochrane's work in 1966 that both interprets and extends the Reformed tradition. In 1987, the Lilly Foundation awarded a sizeable grant to Louisville Presbyterian Seminary for a study of American Presbyterianism in the twentieth century. Presbyterianism was only a part of a larger study sponsored by the Lilly Foundation of what had been called "Mainstream Protestantism." Six denominations were studied: American (northern) Baptists, two Congregationalist bodies (United Church of Christ, Disciples of Christ), Episcopalians, Methodists, and Presbyterians. Some shared characteristics of the six denominations were that while they had helped shape American religion and culture in the nineteenth century, they had all been "displaced—religiously and culturally— to a significant degree." All had suffered severe losses of membership. All had experienced "significant theological tensions." Yet all continued to be "influential voices" in a rapidly changing culture.[39]

The research on American Presbyterians yielded essays by more than sixty scholars. These essays were published in seven volumes between 1990 and 1992 under the series title: "The Presbyterian Presence: The Twentieth-Century Experience."[40]

The first volume of the series dealt specifically with issues regarding the function of confessions. This volume was entitled *The Confessional Mosaic: Presbyterians and Twentieth-Century Theology*. James Moorhead's article, "Redefining Confessionalism," noted that the Presbyterian *Book of Confessions* came into being just at the time that the neo-orthodox consensus shared by its framers was giving way to a host of "contextual theologies." He asked, therefore, whether an unintended consequence of having multiple confessional authorities was that it "cleared the ground for various efforts to 'do theology'—the verb is significant—in an ad hoc fashion, responding to particular issues raised by contemporary culture."[41]

Westminster John Knox Press and Columbia Theological Seminary have furthered interest in confessions by creating the Columbia Series in Reformed Theology. Two recent volumes, both

---

[39] Series foreword to *The Confessional Mosaic: Presbyterians and Twentieth-Century Theology*, ed. Milton J Coalter, John M. Mulder, and Louis B. Weeks (Louisville, Ky.: Westminster/John Knox Press, 1990), 7–8.

[40] A retrospective after a decade was produced in *Presbyterian Outlook* 184, no. 38 (November 11, 2002).

[41] Moorhead, in *The Confessional Mosaic*, 83.

translations from German, have focused on the theology of the Reformed Confessions. First was *Reformed Confessions: Theology from Zurich to Barmen* by Jan Rohls.[42]

Jack L. Stotts, chair of the Special Committee on a Brief Statement of the Reformed Faith, provided a stimulating introductory essay, "Confessing after Barmen." Rohls discusses "The Development of the Old Reformed Confessional Writings," and then organizes the theological contents of the confessions under traditional *loci,* or topics. His final section deals with "Conciliatory Theology, Toleration, and the Development of Neo-Reformed Confessional Writings."

Another in the Columbia Series in Reformed Theology of significant interest is the first translation into English of *The Theology of the Reformed Confessions* by Karl Barth.[43]

The English translation is from a new, critical German edition produced in 1998 by a research team at the Institute for Barth Studies at the University of Göttingen. It presents Barth's lectures in Göttingen in the summer of 1923. He had in 1921 taken up the chair of Reformed Theology and was, for the first time, dealing systematically with the theology of the Reformed Confessions. Barth expounded the significance and content of the Reformed Confessions in contrast with the Lutheranism and the modern Christianity of his day.

The Columbia Series has produced other specialized studies that illumine our understanding of the Reformed confessional tradition. For example, see I. John Hesselink's *Calvin's First Catechism: A Commentary.*[44]

John W. Riggs's *Baptism in the Reformed Tradition: An Historical and Practical Theology* offers considerable insight into the Reformed Confessions on this issue.[45]

In addition to new studies that look back at the Reformation era are collections that show the openness of the Reformed movement to the future. In the early 1980s, Lukas Vischer edited *Reformed Witness Today: A Collection of Confessions and Statements of Faith Issued by Reformed Churches.*[46]

---

[42] John Hoffmeyer, trans. (Louisville, Ky.: Westminster John Knox Press, 1998).

[43] Columbia Series in Reformed Theology, trans. and annotated Darrel L. Guder and Judith J. Guder (Louisville, Ky.: Westminster John Knox Press, 2002).

[44] Columbia Series in Reformed Theology. Featuring Ford Lewis Battles's translation of the 1538 Catechism (Louisville, Ky.: Westminster John Knox Press, 1997).

[45] Columbia Series in Reformed Theology (Louisville, Ky.: Westminster John Knox Press, 2002).

[46] Bern: Evangelische Arbeitsstelle Oekumene Schweiz, 1982.

This collection of thirty-three Reformed statements includes confessions from Asia, Africa, Latin America, Australasia, Europe, and North America. Vischer's collection shows that Reformed thinking has developed many indigenous statements of faith outside the Euro-American context.[47]

Never has only one, universally recognized Reformed Confession or group of doctrinal statements been commonly acknowledged as a single confessional standard. This distinguishes Reformed Confession writers from Lutherans who continue to adhere to the Augsburg Confession of 1530 and other writings in the *Book of Concord* (1580) as their definitive unifying documents.[48]

However, in 1581, Reformed theologians Beza, Daneau, and Salnar produced a compilation, or harmony, of the Reformed Confessions and included, for comparison, the Lutheran Augsburg Confession. The structural outline used for the whole was the Second Helvetic Confession, the most comprehensive Reformed statement. Topics taken from the Second Helvetic Confession, usually in the order presented there, were arranged in the left-hand margin, and statements from each confession on that subject were then presented in parallel columns. Thus the agreements among the various confessions could easily be seen. This *Harmony of the Protestant Confessions* was translated into English and most recently published in 1842.[49]

In the late twentieth century, some additional harmonies were produced. Following adoption of the Confession of 1967 and the *Book of Confessions* by the United Presbyterian Church in the U.S.A., the chair of the drafting committee, Edward A. Dowey Jr., published a commentary on these documents. In an appendix, Dowey produced "A Harmony of *The Book of Confessions*."[50]

In 1999, Joel R. Beeke and Sinclair B. Ferguson edited a book entitled *Reformed Confessions Harmonized*. Their scope was more narrow, utilizing only the Belgic Confession, the Heidelberg Cate-

---

[47] Eberhard Busch, in a review of Vischer's volume, notes that "it contains no confessions from the Reformation's countries of origin, Switzerland and Germany, and also none from other 'classically' Reformed countries such as France, Scotland, Holland, or Hungary." See Eberhard Busch, "The Closeness of the Distant: Reformed Confessions after 1945," in *Toward the Future of Reformed Theology*, Willis and Welker, eds., 519.

[48] Hans J. Hillerbrand, ed. in chief, *The Oxford Encyclopedia of the Reformation*, vol. 1 (New York: Oxford University Press, 1996), s.v. "Book of Concord."

[49] John H. Leith, "A Brief History of the Creedal Task: The Role of Creeds in Reformed Churches," in *To Confess the Faith Today*, Stotts and Douglass, eds., 42.

[50] Edward A. Dowey Jr., *A Commentary on the Confession of 1967 and an Introduction to "The Book of Confessions"* (Philadelphia: Westminster Press, 1968).

chism, the Canons of Dort, the Second Helvetic Confession, and the Westminster Confession and Catechisms.[51]

In 1999, Jean-Jacques Bauswein and Lukas Vischer edited a comprehensive volume entitled *The Reformed Family Worldwide: A Survey of Reformed Churches, Theological Schools, and International Organizations.*[52]

They catalogued the churches and institutions of the Reformed movement in 750 communities worldwide. In an initial essay, they pointed to bonds of unity amidst the great and sometimes conflicting variety of the Reformed Confessions.

Several books for Presbyterian ministers and office bearers were also published, in the late twentieth century, to help people understand both the diversity and the continuities within the new *Book of Confessions.* My book, *Presbyterian Creeds: A Guide to the Book of Confessions,* was designed to meet this need.[53]

Harry W. Eberts's *We Believe: A Study of the Book of Confessions for Church Officers* followed.[54]

In 1999, Geneva Press published my *Reading the Bible and the Confessions: The Presbyterian Way.* It applies guidelines for interpreting Scripture in times of controversy to the interpretation of the *Book of Confessions.* The guidelines are those adopted by the United Presbyterian General Assembly in 1982.[55]

Hopefully this body of work will stimulate further understanding and application of this vital sixteenth-century embrace of the gospel into the twenty-first century.

JACK ROGERS
EPIPHANY 2003

---

[51] Joel R. Beeke and Sinclair B. Ferguson, eds. (Grand Rapids: Baker Books, 1999). They use the Belgic Confession as the outline for the whole. An extensive annotated bibliography of works on the topics of the Belgic Confession is given at the end. The annotations are quite polemical and evidence the commitment of the editors to a Reformed scholasticism as the proper understanding of the confessions.

[52] Jean-Jacques Bauswein and Lukas Vischer, comps. and eds. (Grand Rapids: Wm. B. Eerdmans, 1999).

[53] Jack Rogers, *Presbyterian Creeds.* By 1985, Dowey's commentary was out of print.

[54] Harry W. Eberts, *We Believe: A Study of the Book of Confessions for Church Officers* (Louisville, Ky.: Geneva Press, 1987; rev. ed., Westminster John Knox Press, 1994).

[55] Jack Rogers, *Reading the Bible and the Confessions: The Presbyterian Way* (Louisville, Ky.: Geneva Press, 1999).

PREFACE

THIS BOOK IS THE FIRST COLLECTION IN ENGLISH OF THE twelve principal Confessions of Faith of the Reformed Churches of the sixteenth century. Heretofore English readers have been dependent upon Philip Schaff's great work, *The Creeds of Christendom*, Vol. III, for the largest compilation of Reformed symbols; but it contained translations of only three from the sixteenth century — four if one includes the Scottish Confession of 1560, which Schaff printed in the original Scottish dialect. Accordingly, translations have been made of Zwingli's Sixty-seven Articles, the Ten Theses of Berne, and of the First and Second Confessions of Basel from the original Swiss dialect, and a modern English version of the Confession of the English Congregation at Geneva (1556) and of the Scottish Confession of Faith of 1560 has been provided. In addition, a new translation of the last and most important of the sixteenth-century Reformed Confessions — the Second Helvetic Confession of 1566 — has been made from the Latin text as found in the collection edited by Wilhelm Niesel, *Bekenntnisschriften und Kirchenordnungen der nach Gottes Wort reformierten Kirche* (Munich, 1938). Thus, together with the collection of the catechisms of the Reformed Churches in *The School of Faith* (1959), translated and edited by Thomas F. Torrance, there is now available to English readers the rich confessional literature of the Reformed Churches of which they have been deprived.

When the Report of the Special Committee on a Brief Contemporary Statement of Faith recommended to the 177th General Assembly of The United Presbyterian Church in the United States of America, at Columbus, Ohio, May 20–26, 1965, that the Form of Government of that Church be amended in various places to include the sentence that " this Church, under the authority of the Scriptures, and in the tradition of the one catholic and universal Church, accepts and is guided by the Nicene and Apostles' Creeds, the Scots Confession, the Heidelberg Catechism, the Second Helvetic Confession, the Westminster Confession and Shorter Catechism, the Theological Declaration of Barmen, and the Confession of 1967," it was suggested that it would be timely and useful to include in an appendix to this volume the Nicene and Apostles' Creeds, the Heidelberg Catechism, and the Theological Declaration of Barmen. With this suggestion I readily concurred, inasmuch as I have explained in the introduction that although " there is a marked difference between the early creeds and the Confessions," the Reformation Confessions were based upon the creeds, and sought to unfold and safeguard a proper understanding of them. The Barmen Theological Declaration of May, 1934, deserves a place, because, like the Confession of the Free Reformed Synod in Barmen-Gemarke, January, 1934, it purported to be an " explanation concerning the right understanding of the Reformation Confessions of Faith in the German Evangelical Church of the present." The justification for the inclusion of the Heidelberg Catechism of 1563 in the Appendix is simply that, of all Reformed catechisms, it is the most widely accepted doctrinal standard among Reformed Churches. The Westminster symbols are easily available elsewhere, and their inclusion here would have made the book unduly long.

An editor of a collection such as this is naturally indebted to a host of scholars who have gone before. Many of these are indicated in the bibliographies and notes. Special thanks are due to Prof. Edward A. Dowey, Jr., of Princeton Theological Seminary, who read the historical introductions and offered helpful criticisms, and contributed the introduction to the Second Helvetic Confession. I also wish to acknowledge the assistance of a former colleague on the faculty of the University of Dubuque, Prof. Carl Geffert, now head of the German Department of St. Andrews Presbyterian College, Laurinburg, North Carolina, in the translation of Zwingli's Sixty-seven Articles and the First Confession of Basel from the Swiss dialect.

The appearance of a new translation of the Second Helvetic Confession in this year 1966 coincides with the four hundredth anniversary of its original publication. Grateful as we are to Almighty God for its testimony to the gospel of God's free grace which, as we believe, was rediscovered at the Reformation, yet we sorrow that the great schism in the Western Church, which was sealed, as it were, by its publication, has not yet been healed. All the more do we rejoice that theologians of the Roman Catholic and Protestant Churches, after four centuries of virtual isolation, have now entered into genuine dialogue and are seeking to understand not only their respective traditions, but also their present-day witness to Jesus Christ as the only Lord and Savior of mankind. How fitting it is, then, that I am able to record my gratitude to my friend, Father Richard T. A. Murphy, O.P., of the Aquinas Institute, Dubuque, Iowa, for carefully reading my translation of the Second Helvetic Confession. Even so, I must accept responsibility for any inaccuracies that remain in this particular translation and in the rest of the volume.

Finally, I wish to express my thanks to Miss Mary Haywood for her painstaking typing of the entire manuscript.

ARTHUR C. COCHRANE

Dubuque Theological Seminary
Dubuque, Iowa

ACKNOWLEDGMENTS

Acknowledgment is due to the following publishers for permission to use the material specified: to Miss Mary L. Schaff, for the translation of the French and Belgic Confessions of Faith in Philip Schaff, *The Creeds of Christendom*, Vol. III (1919), copyright by Harper & Row, Publishers, Inc.; to The Westminster Press for the translation of the Lausanne Articles and the Geneva Confession in The Library of Christian Classics, Vol. XXII, and of the Barmen Theological Declaration in Arthur C. Cochrane, *The Church's Confession Under Hitler;* to The Saint Andrew Press, Edinburgh, for Dr. James Bulloch's modern English version of the Scots Confession of Faith 1560, published 1960; to the United Church Press for *The Heidelberg Catechism,* translated by Allen O. Miller and M. Eugene Osterhaven (Philadelphia, 1962), published 1962. The translation of the Tetrapolitan Confession is by Henry E. Jacobs in *The Book of Concord,* Vol. II, published by G. W. Frederick, Philadelphia, 1883.

Introduction

Concerning Collections
of Reformed Confessions

IT IS AN EXTRAORDINARY FACT THAT THERE IS NO COLLECTION of Reformed Confessions of Faith available in English to-day. It is true that there have been such collections dating from the eighteenth and nineteenth centuries, but these now have the character of rare books and are unobtainable except in a few large libraries. The best of these is Dunlop's *A Collection of Confessions of Faith, Catechisms, Directories, Books of Discipline, etc., of Public Authority in the Church of Scotland. With a large preface, containing a full account of the several ends and uses of Confessions of Faith, the just foundations of their authority as a public standard of orthodoxy, and a vindication of the equity, usefulness, and the excellency of such composures.* This comprehensive work appeared in two volumes (1719, 1722).[1] But because it was a compilation of those Confessions which had enjoyed public authority in Scotland, it did not contain the Confessions of the Swiss and German Churches, though it did include Calvin's Geneva Catechism and the Heidelberg Catechism.

Of lesser pretensions might be mentioned, *The Scriptural Unity of Protestant Churches exhibited in their published Confessions,* edited by the Rev. D. Stuart, D.D., Dublin (1835). It contained: (1) Articles of the Irish Church; (2) Articles of the Church of England; (3) The Confession of Faith of the Church of Scotland; (4) Declaration of Faith of the Congregational or Independent Dissenters.

Two harmonies of Reformed Confessions have appeared in

---

[1] This rare and valuable collection contains in the first volume the Westminster standards, and in the second, the Confession of Faith of the English Congregation at Geneva (1558), the Scottish Confession of 1560, the National Covenant of 1638, Calvin's Catechism, the Heidelberg, and some other catechisms, and not least, the Books of Discipline.

English: (1) *The Unity of Protestantism, being Articles of Religion from the Creeds of the Reformed Churches,* edited by the Rev. John Cumming, M.A., London (1837). This brief harmony contained extracts from the Thirty-nine Articles of England, the Latter Helvetic Confession, the Württemberg, the Bohemian, the Augsburg, the Belgic, the Scottish, and the Westminster Confessions. (2) *The Harmony of Protestant Confessions,* familiarly known as Salnar's *Harmony.* This harmony, which of course is in no sense a collection, was originally published in Latin at Geneva in 1581 under the title, *Harmonia confessionum fidei orthodoxarum et reformatarum ecclesiarum.*[2] A first edition of an English translation of this appeared at Cambridge in 1586; the second and last in London in 1643. Each of the English editions has the Confession of the Church of Scotland, issued the same year, with the Latin edition of the *Harmony* annexed, that is, the Second Scottish Confession, or the National Covenant of 1580. A new edition of the translation of the *Harmony,* revised and considerably enlarged, was published by Peter Hall, M.A. (London, 1842). Since a collection of Reformed Confessions of Faith has never been produced, these translations of the *Harmony* have served " as a manual the most convenient for general reference." But these two have now become exceedingly scarce.

The hymn writer Horatius Bonar issued *Catechisms of the Scottish Reformation* (London, 1866), and these have been republished by Thomas F. Torrance in *The School of Faith: The Catechisms of the Reformed Faith* (London, 1959). Torrance has added an extremely valuable introduction in which he discusses the content and form of the catechisms, the catechetical method of instruction, the dialogical nature of theology, and leading doctrinal tendencies in the Reformed doctrines of God, Christ, and the Holy Spirit. What has been needed is a companion volume to Torrance's: a collection of the Reformed Confessions.

The largest selection of Reformed Confessions in English is to be found in a section of Philip Schaff's great work, *Creeds of Christendom,* Vol. III. But it contains only nine Confessions,

---

2 A German reproduction of the *Harmonia* was published by Aug. Ebrard in 1887 under the title Salnar's *Harmonia confessionum fidei.* The author is not Salnar or Salnart, but Francesco Salluardo, a preacher in Frankfurt. See Otto Weber, *Vorerwägungen zu einer neuen Ausgabe Reformierter Bekenntnisschriften* in *Hören und Handeln* (Chr. Kaiser Verlag, Munich, 1962), p. 389. Cf. P. F. Geisendorf, *Théodore de Bèze* (Geneva, 1949), pp. 337–339.

and three of these were not translated — four, if one includes the Scottish Confession of Faith of 1560 which was printed in the original Scottish dialect. In the recently published *Creeds of the Churches: A Reader in Christian Doctrine from the Bible to the Present* (Doubleday & Company, Inc., 1963), edited by John H. Leith, three Reformed Confessions are included — four, if the Barmen Theological Declaration of 1934 is counted among official Reformed symbols — and of these only an abridged version of the Second Helvetic Confession. In *The Faith of Christendom: A Source Book of Creeds and Confessions,* edited by B. A. Gerrish (The World Publishing Company, 1963), the Gallic Confession of 1559 is the only Reformed Confession in the collection. Thus, except for Schaff's incomplete assemblage, the English-speaking Church has had virtually no information about the extraordinarily rich and varied Reformed confessional literature.

From time to time collections of Reformed Confessions have been issued in their original Latin, German, and French texts. The earliest of these is the *Corpus et syntagma confessionum fidei* of 1612 in which some thirteen Confessions were gathered together by the editor Gaspar Laurentius. These included four of the early church creeds and the Lutheran Augsburg, Saxon, and Württemberg Confessions.[3] A new edition of the same work, but with considerable alterations, appeared in Geneva in 1654. " In this edition the Confession of Helvetia is printed from the edition of Zurich, 1651; and the Confession of Belgia, as it was revised, corrected, and approved by the Synod of Dort in 1619. At the end are also given (1) the Confession of Basel; (2) the Judgment of the Synod of Dort; (3) the Confession of Cyril, Patriarch of Constantinople; and (4) The General Confession of the Reformed Churches in Polonia, Lithuania, and the provinces annexed." [4]

A more complete collection was published in Elberfeld in 1827 under the title: *Corpus librorum symbolicorum qui in ecclesia reformatorum auctoritatem publicam obtinuerunt. Novam collectionem instituit dissertationem historicam et*

---

[3] The Lutheran *Book of Concord* contains all the Lutheran symbols which are still in force. The Saxon Confession and the Württemberg Confession, both written in 1551, were superseded and now enjoy only historical importance. See Philip Schaff, *The Creeds of Christendom*, with a History and Critical Notes, 3 vols. (Harper & Brothers, 1877), Vol. I, pp. 340–344.
[4] Peter Hall, *The Harmony of Protestant Confessions of Faith* (1842), p. xviii.

litterariam subjunxit et indices rerum verborumque adjecit, Jo. Christ.Guil.Augusti. This in turn was superseded by an even more satisfactory collection, that of H. A. Niemeyer, *Collectio confessionum in ecclesiis reformatis publicatarum* (Leipzig, 1840). It contained twenty-eight listings. Sixty-three years later and twenty-five years after Philip Schaff's three-volume work was published in America, E. F. K. Müller published the most comprehensive collection extant. It bears the title *Die Bekenntnisschriften der reformierten Kirche* (Leipzig, 1903). Unfortunately, Müller's edition has long been out of print and can scarcely be acquired, even in German antiquarian bookstores. During the Church struggle in Germany under Hitler, Wilhelm Niesel edited a selection of Reformed Confessions and Church Orders, *Bekenntnisschriften und Kirchenordnungen der nach Gottes Wort reformierten Kirche* (Munich, 1938). Thus since Müller's work appeared no edition of Reformed Confessions has been published that is comparable to the two-volume work, *Die Bekenntnisschriften der evangelisch-lutherischen Kirche,* published by a committee of the German Evangelical Church in 1930 in celebration of the four hundredth anniversary of the Augsburg Confession. However, this same committee planned to issue a similar collection of Reformed Confessions and appointed A. Lang, Hans Lietzmann, and Otto Weber as editors to carry out the project. But for a number of reasons, outlined by Otto Weber, the goal has not yet been reached.[5] However, before we consider these reasons — which shed considerable light upon the Reformed understanding of the nature of a Confession — we should take note of collections of the Reformed standards in the German language.

F. A. Beck published *Die symbolischen Bücher der ev. reformierten Kirche* in two parts in 1830 at Neustadt an der Orla. A second edition appeared in 1845 with brief introductions and notes. Two years later followed E. G. Adolf Böckel's *Die Bekenntnisschriften der evangelisch-reformierten Kirche* (Leipzig, 1847). It is the best German collection, containing thirty-two Reformed symbols, including the Anglican Catechism and the Arminian Confessions, which Niemeyer had omitted. It is also furnished with illuminating introductions and notes. Next in importance is *Die Bekenntnisschriften der reformierten Kirchen Deutschlands,* edited by Heinrich Heppe (Elberfeld, 1860). It contains the Confession of Elec-

---

[5] *Vorerwägungen,* pp. 389 ff.

tor Frederick III of the Palatinate (1577), the *Repetitio Anhaltina* (1581), *Aufrichtige Rechenschaft von Lehr und Ceremonien* (1593), *Consensus Ministerii Bremensis Ecclesiae* (1595), the Confession of the General Synod held at Cassel (1608), a Report on the Faith of the Reformed Churches in Germany (1607), the Confession of John Sigismund of Brandenburg (1614), another Confession of the same (1615), and the Emden Catechism (1554), all in German. Finally, we might mention a partial translation by P. Jacobs of the collection edited by W. Niesel and P. Jacobs, *Reformierte Bekenntnisschriften und Kirchenordnungen* (1949).

Otto Weber has observed that there are special impediments to making a collection of Reformed Confessions that do not pertain to Lutheranism.[6] With the *Book of Concord* the Lutheran Church has a canon of confessional literature that is widely acknowledged and was officially approved by certain state governments. Nothing similar is to be found among Reformed Churches. There is no such thing as a Reformed *corpus doctrinae*. It is true that even in the sixteenth century the Reformed Churches compiled synopses and harmonies, the earliest being the Geneva *Harmonia confessionum* of 1581. The *Harmonia,* as well as the *Corpus et syntagma* of 1612, were conceived as Reformed counterparts to the Lutheran *Book of Concord.* With their inclusion of the Augsburg, Saxon, and Württemberg Confessions they reveal their unionist tendencies. But neither collection ever achieved ecclesiastical or political sanction. They remained private collections with a more or less limited sphere of influence. This is in keeping with the nature of the Reformed Churches.

It might be well if we quote here at some length from the preface of Niemeyer's *Collectio confessionum* concerning the origin of the *Harmonia.*

"At the time when the Lutheran divines, at the command of Augustus, Elector of Saxony, had just collected their symbolical books, and were beginning to publish their collection under the title of *Concordia,* there were also certain, in the Reformed Church, men of the greatest influence who must needs compose a Harmony of Confessions of Faith, in the name of the French and Belgian Churches. And this for two reasons: of which the one lay in the reproaches urged

---

[6] *Ibid.,* pp. 389 f.

(and lately repeated with wrath and vehemence) by the Roman Catholics, about the multitude and discordancy of these Confessions; the other in the hope (vain and deceitful as it proved, yet sincerely entertained by those who suggested the expedient) that they might succeed in reconciling the minds of dissentients, and uniting all the churches, distracted and separated as they were, in one common bond." [7] Basing his conclusions upon earlier authorities,[8] Niemeyer stated that the origin of the *Harmonia* was as follows: "The assembly held at Frankfort, in the year 1577, under the auspices of Joh. Casimir, the Count Palatine, entertained the thought of receiving a new Confession of Faith, if not from all, at least from many parts of the Evangelical Church. Such a project found acceptance chiefly with a number of French divines: for the Synods which met in France in the years 1578 and 1579, fell into the sentiments of that assembly, and consulted diligently how a new Confession might be composed. But the churches of Zurich and Geneva, fearing lest a new Confession might give occasion to new disturbances, instead of following their opinion, obtained a respite; and at length entered into a most seasonable arrangement with Salvart (or Salnar) for the construction of a Harmony. The work was accordingly undertaken, in the year 1581, by the principal divines (among whom Salvart, Beza, and Daleau [9] are mentioned), in the name of the French and Belgian Churches; and was so accomplished as to issue from the press with public authority, accruing yet further to the French from the Synod of Vitré in 1583." [10]

The foregoing account of the origin of the *Harmonia* brings out two things: (1) the failure or inability of the Reformed Churches to draw up a general Confession of Faith; (2) the *Harmonia* was a sort of weak substitute for such a union document. These points suggest that any collection of Reformed Confessions must serve the purpose of illustrating the variety and diversity of Reformed Confessions, depending upon the time, place, and circumstances in which they

---

[7] Peter Hall, *Harmony of Protestant Confessions*, p. xv.

[8] Hospinian, *Concordia, Tigurina*, p. 92; Koecher, *Bibliotheca Theologiae Symbolicae*, pp. 320–321; D. Clement, *Bibliothèque Historique et Critique*, Vol. VII, p. 257; Lückius, *Annales Gottingenses*, p. 1.

[9] Probably a misprint for Lambert Daneau (Danaeus).

[10] *Praefatio in Collectionem Confessionum*, pp. v, viii, ix. Translation from Peter Hall, *Harmony of Protestant Confessions*, pp. xvi f. Cf. P. F. Geisendorf, *Bèze*, pp. 337–339, and John T. McNeill, *Unitive Protestantism* (John Knox Press, 1964), pp. 215 f.

arose, rather than of demonstrating their complete uniformity. A collection of Reformed Confessions will attest the freedom with which many particular Churches have confessed Jesus Christ quite independently of the others. Anything like a universal Confession imposed on all congregations and Churches is foreign to the genius of Reformed Churches. Although Reformed Churches are concerned about union and ecumenical relations with other Churches, they do not wish this to be achieved at the expense of the particularity and concreteness of a church's Confession.

Weber has also reported that at one time Hans Lietzmann expressed the wish that there were an organ which was in a position to speak authoritatively for all the Reformed Churches in Germany and this could determine the selection of Reformed Confessions that should go into an official collection.[11] "Lietzmann," Weber writes, "had in mind the situation of the Lutheran Church in 1580. At that time the civil magistrates, who permitted the *Book of Concord* to be issued, guaranteed its limits and therefore its contents. Even documents like Luther's catechisms and the Schmalkald Articles, which were originally personal statements, acquired official authority in this way, *post festum*. On the Reformed side, it is true, there obtained the *usus* of mutual recognition of Confessions that were not directly authoritative in both Churches. But there has never been a universal authoritative body that could make doctrinal decisions binding for all."[12] Moreover, right down to the present time Reformed Churches have produced *new* Confessions. The Lutherans, on the other hand, seem to imply by their stand that the confessional decisions were made once and for all and with completeness in the six-

---

[11] Weber, *Vorerwägungen*, pp. 390 f.

[12] *Ibid.*, p. 390. " The specific local or national church makes its Confession of Faith: the church of Berne, of Basel, of Bremen, or Bentheim, of France or of Scotland. Each looks for his direction first in direct appeal to the Bible. They greet one another, back and forth, as from one island to another, from Basel to Strassburg, from Geneva to Zurich, rejoicing over every possibility of mutual understanding. But every church lives its own life; and with surprising independence, each church, marked off by the accidental boundaries of the authority of the various states, goes its own way, even in the matter of creed-making. So there results that diversity of formulae which led Luther to judge that the doctrine of South Germany was certainly from Satan (Enders, *Luthers Briefwechsel* 5, p. 294) ," Karl Barth, *Theology and Church: Shorter Writings, 1920–1928*, tr. by Louise Pettibone Smith, with an introduction by T. F. Torrance (Harper & Row, Publishers, Inc., 1962), p. 120. See also pp. 120–126 on the particularity of the Reformed Church and its Confession.

teenth century.[13] From time to time efforts have been made to produce a universal Reformed Confession in the World Presbyterian Alliance. But they have never been too successful. Thus there is no individual and no body that is able to say what Confession of Faith is to be regarded as "Reformed" and therefore should be included in a collection. All collections are to that extent arbitrary, and it is no accident that all vary with respect to their tables of contents.

The basis upon which Otto Weber proposes to determine what confessional documents should be included in a collection is their historical effect. That is to say, those confessional documents are accepted which either determine the historical character of certain Churches for a significant period of time or which have proved to be lasting because of the historical strength inherent in them. History is the criterion for the inclusion or exclusion of a Confession.

For the above reasons, Weber urges that the title of a new collection cannot be the one E. F. K. Müller gave to his edition, namely, *The Confessions of the Reformed Church.* Niemeyer's title comes closer to the truth: *Collectio confessionum in ecclesiis reformatis publicatarum.* Today, Weber would prefer: "Confessions of Reformed Churches." That is to say, neither all Reformed Churches nor all their Confessions are given a place. For if history is the criterion, then it can happen that pronouncements of proportionately small Churches will be included because of their historical importance, such as Zurich and Berne, whereas the documents of quite large Churches are omitted or are only permitted to be heard in part. This is true, according to Weber, of the Confessions of the ancient Hungarian Church that Müller had included in his collection but that possessed only a very independent character.

The question has been raised in Germany whether a collection should contain only Confessions that had arisen in that country. Heinrich Heppe had indeed gathered all such documents into a single volume, but it in no sense purported to be a collection of all Reformed Confessions. Weber argues against such a nationalistic collection for the following rea-

---

13 Reformed Confessions, on the other hand, are held to be in force only from time to time and in a given historical place. The Lutheran tendency to endow their sixteenth-century Confessions with finality and completeness doubtless accounts for the fact that many Lutherans have been unable to look upon the Barmen Theological Declaration of May, 1934, as a genuine Confession.

sons: (1) Although the Reformed Confessions each have their own place and time, yet the Reformed Churches of all lands, because of the conception of Reformed catholicity, have maintained that even those Confessions which are not literally in force among them are to be respected as valid expressions of the one Church. (2) The Lutheran Confessions all arose in Germany. But very early they had their effect upon other countries, notably the Scandinavian countries, and today their authority extends far beyond Germany. Conversely, Confessions that arose outside Germany have had an influence upon Reformed Churches and congregations within Germany — one thinks of the French Confession of Faith which achieved formal recognition first among the Huguenot congregations and then in Germany, and the Belgic Confession which became a subordinate standard in the county of Bentheim. Above all, one thinks of the confessional writings of Zwingli and Calvin which have to a large extent determined the nature of Reformed Churches throughout the world. (3) For all their diversity and variety, the Reformed Confessions as a whole constitute a real " Harmonia " in which the voice of the Lutheran Augsburg Confession has and should still be heard. Weber claims that if it were not for the fact that the Confessions of the Lutheran Church are already contained in an excellent collection, it would be necessary to include the Augsburg in a new edition of Reformed Confessions in the interest of a proper understanding of the nature of a Reformed Confession.[14]

Professor Weber's suggestion that the Lutheran Augsburg Confession might well be included in a collection of Reformed Confessions raises the question whether the Anglican Thirty-nine Articles of 1563 and 1571, as well as the Twenty-five Methodist Articles of Religion drawn up by John Wesley for the American Methodists and adopted at a Conference in 1784, might not be included. It is interesting to note that Schaff included the Thirty-nine Articles, as well as the Anglican Catechism (1549, 1662), and the Lambeth Articles (1595) and the Irish Articles (1615) under a section entitled "The Creeds of the Evangelical Reformed Churches." But strangely enough, Schaff does not include here the Congregational Savoy Declaration of 1658,[15] which is simply a modification of

---

[14] The Augsburg *variata* had in fact been included in Salnar's *Harmonia*.
[15] This was also adopted by American Congregationalists in the Synod of Boston, 1680, and in the Synod of Saybrook, 1708.

the Westminster Confession of Faith with respect to the chapters on "Christian Liberty and Liberty of Conscience," the "Civil Magistrate," and the addition of a chapter, " Of the Gospel, and the Extent of the Grace Thereof." Instead, it is placed, along with the Methodist Articles of Religion, among "Modern Protestant Creeds," which seems to be a catchall heading for miscellaneous creeds. In Volume I, *A History of the Creeds of Christendom,* Schaff observes that " Continental historians, both Protestant and Catholic, rank the Church of England among the Reformed Churches as distinct from the Lutheran, and her Articles are found in every collection of Reformed Confessions . . . from the *Corpus et syntagma* down to the collections of Niemeyer and Böckel. The Roman Catholic Möhler likewise numbers the Articles among the Reformed (Calvinistic) Confessions.[16] On the other hand, the Articles have no place in any collection of Lutheran symbols." [17] However, Schaff also observes that "the theological interpretation of the Articles by English writers has been mostly conducted in a controversial rather than an historical spirit. . . . Moderate High-Churchmen and Arminians, who dislike Calvinism, represent them as purely Lutheran [Archbishop Laurence and Hardwick]; Anglo-Catholics and Tractarians, who abhor both Lutheranism and Calvinism, endeavor to conform them as much as possible to the contemporary decrees of the Council of Trent [Newman, Pusey, Forbes]; Calvinistic and evangelical Low-Churchmen find in them substantially their own creed." [18] So Schaff makes a detailed comparison of the Articles with the Augsburg (1530) and the Württemberg (1552) Confessions and finds that they are catholic with respect to the doctrines of the Trinity and the incarnation; Augustinian (i.e., Lutheran and Reformed) with respect to the doctrines of free will, sin, and grace; Protestant and Evangelical in regard to the doctrines of Scripture, justification, good works, and the Church; Reformed and moderately Calvinistic in the two doctrines of predestination and the Lord's Supper in which the Lutheran and Reformed Churches differed; Erastian in teaching the closest

---

[16] Johann Adam Möhler, *Symbolik, oder Darstellung der dogmatischen Gegensätze der Katholiken und Protestanten nach ihren öffentlichen Bekenntnis-Schriften* (1832) , p. 22. English translation of the 6th edition, *Symbolism* (1844) , p. 109. E. F. K. Müller also includes the Thirty-nine Articles, along with the Westminster Confession, in his collection of Reformed Confessions.
[17] P. Schaff, *Creeds of Christendom,* p. 622.
[18] *Ibid.*

possible union of church and state. It would, therefore, appear that the Thirty-nine Articles, as well as the Edwardine Articles of 1553, are Reformed in the decisive doctrines. Theologically, they are certainly more Calvinist than Lutheran.[19]

Still another reason cited by Schaff for the inclusion of the Thirty-nine Articles in the collection of Reformed Confessions is the fact that the Puritans accepted the doctrinal articles, and the Westminster Assembly first made them the basis of its Calvinistic Confession. The other side of this coin is that the Westminster Assembly was originally convened to revise the Thirty-nine Articles of the Church of England "to free and vindicate the doctrine of them from all aspersions and false interpretations." The Assembly was called "to effect a more perfect reformation of the Church of England in its liturgy, discipline, and government on the basis of the Word of God and thus to bring it into nearer agreement with the Church of Scotland and the Reformed Churches on the Continent." Moreover, if history — historical effect — is to be the criterion by which a Reformed Confession is determined, the fact is that the Thirty-nine Articles, in spite of their strong Calvinist coloring, did not create a Reformed but an Episcopal Church. The Church of Scotland and the Presbyterian Church in England have never recognized them as one of their doctrinal standards. Unlike Calvin's Geneva Catechism and the Heidelberg Catechism, the Thirty-nine Articles were not recognized by the Church of Scotland and are

---

[19] However, it should be borne in mind that the Edwardine Articles (1553) appeared *before* the major Reformed Confessions appeared on the Continent — the Gallic Confession in 1559; the Belgic in 1561; the Heidelberg Catechism in 1563; the Second Helvetic Confession of Faith in 1566. But Zwingli's and Bullinger's works, Calvin's *Institutes* (1536 ed.), the early Swiss Confessions, Calvin's *Tract on the Lord's Supper* (1541), the Zurich (*Tigurinus*) Consensus (1549), the Geneva Consensus (1552), must have been more or less known in England. Moreover, Cranmer and Ridley rejected the Lutheran doctrine of the real presence and the ubiquity of Christ's humanity as early as December 14, 1548, when a public discussion was held in London on the Eucharist. The doctrinal change was embodied in the revision of the Prayer Book of 1552. Cranmer was in correspondence with Reformed theologians on the Continent such as Peter Martyr, Calvin, Bucer, Bullinger, and also with the mediating Melanchthon. It was characteristic of his ecumenical spirit that he conceived of a plan of inviting these men and others to England to draw up a union creed for all evangelical churches — a plan that proved abortive. See John Strype's *Memorials of Archbishop Cranmer* (2 vols.), Vol. I, p. 584; Charles Hardwick, *History of the Christian Church during the Reformation,* 3d ed. (London, 1873), p. 212. See also the quotation from the letter by Bishop Jewel, the final reviser of the Thirty-nine Articles, to Peter Martyr at Zurich, Feb. 7, 1562, in Schaff, *Creeds of Christendom,* Vol. I, p. 603, concerning agreement with the Reformers.

not found in Dunlop's *Collection of Confessions of Faith.*
For this reason, it does not seem appropriate to include the
Thirty-nine Articles or the Twenty-five Methodist Articles in
a collection of Reformed Confessions. At the same time a Reformed Church would surely see in a Church of England
professing the Thirty-nine Articles a genuine Evangelical
and Protestant Church and which *in this sense* is the one,
holy, catholic Church. Unfortunately, one is never quite sure
whether the Church of England herself wishes her catholicity to be understood in terms of the Thirty-nine Articles!

It may now be asked whether *The Creeds and Platforms
of Congregationalism* [20] should be included in a collection of
Reformed Confessions. The answer to this question is a clear,
strong yes — *if* a collection of Reformed Confessions is to include church orders (polity), books of discipline, and directories for public worship. For the Congregational Churches,
notably in the Cambridge Synod and Platform of 1646 to
1648 and the Savoy Declaration of 1658 (which in turn was
adopted by a Massachusetts Synod at Boston in 1680 with a
few immaterial modifications and by a Synod at Saybrook in
1708 for Connecticut), have consistently affirmed their adherence to the Westminster Confession of Faith and to the
doctrines "generally received in all the reformed Churches
of Christ in Europe." Church polity, then, is the only point of
difference, and even that is relative. For some Presbyterian
Churches have in fact been more congregational than presby-
terial in their church government, as for example, the southern Presbyterian Church of America. On the other hand, Reformed Churches have had General Superintendents and
even bishops, as in the Hungarian Reformed Church. Presby-
terial polity, therefore, is not the distinctive feature of Reformed Churches. Moreover, as we have already observed,
they have been quite congregational in the formation of their
Confessions.[21]

Now in recent times the thesis has been frequently advanced that church orders and polity do belong to the confessional standards of the Reformed Churches. But as Weber
states, it needs to be carefully examined if it is not to become
a fruitless shibboleth. It is true that the Reformed Confes-

---

[20] Edited by Williston Walker, with an introduction by Douglas Horton
(The Pilgrim Press, 1960 edition).

[21] Moreover, with the inclusion of the United Church of Christ in the
World Presbyterian Alliance there is an explicit recognition by the Reformed
Churches that the Congregational Church, as now merged with the Evangeli-
cal and Reformed Church, is one of themselves.

sions contain articles which have to do expressly with polity, as, for example, the assertion that all true pastors enjoy equal power and authority under one head, Jesus Christ, and that "no church shall claim any authority or dominion over any other" (French Conf., XXX; cf. XXXI–XXXIII; Belgic Conf., XXX–XXXII). Article 4 of the Barmen Declaration puts it this way: "The various offices in the Church do not establish a dominion of some over the others; on the contrary, they are for the exercise of a ministry entrusted to and enjoined upon the whole congregation. We reject the false doctrine, as though the Church, apart from this ministry, could or were permitted to give to itself, or allow to be given to it, special leaders vested with ruling powers." Moreover, this view of the government of the Church, which is shared by all Reformed Confessions even when not expressly stated, belongs to the confession of Jesus Christ. As the Barmen Declaration explains in Article 3: "As the Church of pardoned sinners, it has to testify in the midst of a sinful world, with its faith as with its obedience, with its message as with its order, that it is solely his property." When all this is granted, it should be remembered that the detailed and explicit Reformed Church orders were published separately from the Confessions.[22] The Synod of Barmen of May, 1934, issued Declarations Concerning the Legal Status and the Practical Work of the Confessional Synod of the German Evangelical Church, along with the Theological Declaration. It even issued an official commentary on the Theological Declaration by Hans Asmussen. But all these were regarded as quite distinct from and subordinate to the Theological Declaration. It was recognized, however, that statements concerning the polity and program of the Church had to be based upon the Church's Confession. The priority of Confessions, then, justifies their separate publication.

One final question concerning what should go into a collection of Reformed Confessions. Should the early creeds of the Church be included, and if so, what creeds? The Lutheran *Book of Concord* answers this question in the affirmative by explicitly including the texts of the Apostles' Creed, the Nicene Creed, and the so-called Creed of Athanasius. The

---

22 Weber states that with the edition edited by Wilhelm Niesel for the first time the church orders were published in a volume along with the Confessions. This, however, is not correct. Dunlop includes the Books of Discipline in his *Collection of Confessions,* and frequently the Form of Government and the Directory for Worship were published along with the Westminster Confession of Faith and the Larger and Shorter Catechisms.

Chalcedonian Creed is not included.[23] The *Corpus et syntagma* appears to be the only collection of Reformed Confessions in which the creeds were incorporated. The Irish Articles of Religion of 1615 (Art. 7) and the Thirty-nine Articles of the Church of England (Art. VIII) specifically adopt, but do not include, the text of the three ecumenical creeds. Among the Reformed Confessions the Second Helvetic Confession (Chapter XI), the Gallic Confession (Art. V), and the Belgic Confession (Art. IX) expressly approve the three creeds " as agreeing with the written Word of God." The Apostles' Creed, together with the Lord's Prayer and the Ten Commandments, is expounded in the Lutheran, Genevan, Heidelberg, and other standard catechisms.[24]

Although the inclusion of the creeds among the Confessions of the Reformation indicates the continuity and catholicity of the Reformation Churches with the Church of the first centuries, it would seem that there is good reason to separate them on the ground that there is a marked difference between the early creeds and the Confessions which must now be considered.

Oscar Cullmann has shown [25] that the Christian Church makes use of two kinds of confession of faith: 1. " The symbol set up once and for all, and drawn up in the language of the New Testament. This is ascribed to the apostles as an authentic summary of Scripture. 2. The symbol conditioned by circumstances which transcribes the Biblical Gospel into the language and concepts of a certain period. On the basis of the New Testament, this symbol takes up a position over against new problems and heresies unknown in the apostolic age." Cullmann states that the Apostles' Creed is an example of the first type, and the Nicene Creed an example of the second. And of course the Confessions of Faith of the Reformation period definitely belong to the second class. Cullmann's book is concerned with the New Testament period in which confessional formulas were drawn up and which formed the basis for symbols of the first type such as the Apostles' Creed. As early as the second half of the second century unanimity was being reached about the main lines of a confession of faith,

---

[23] However, references to the Chalcedonian Creed are made in the text of the Formula of Concord (the Solid Declaration) and in Luther's Schmalkald Articles.

[24] The Second Helvetic Confession lists the Creeds of Nicaea, Constantinople, Ephesus, Chalcedon, and the so-called Athanasian Creed.

[25] *The Earliest Christian Confessions* (Lutterworth Press, 1949), pp. 10 ff.

and the view spread that the rule of faith was composed by the apostles.[26] It was not until the fifteenth century that the legend that the Apostles' Creed was of apostolic origin was shattered by the humanist, Laurentius Valle.[27] Cullmann states that it is now known that " the apostolic symbol in its present form reaches back no further than the seventh or sixth century, and that its predecessor, the ancient baptismal symbol of Rome, and the kindred symbols of East and West, go back to the second century, but not into the apostolic period." [28] However, the apostolicity of most of the New Testament summaries of Christian faith may be established, and these constituted the basis and pattern for the Apostles' Creed.

The New Testament confessions of faith such as reported in I Cor. 15:3-7; Phil. 2:6-11; I Cor. 11:23 ff. were summaries of facts and deeds concerning Jesus as Lord, and were not doctrinal decisions concerning disputed theological issues. The Apostles' Creed reflects this same character. Their special authority is due not only to their apostolic origin but also to their content. With respect to content they confine themselves to naming the " That " of the divine saving act. Not that they are satisfied to enumerate so-called general or universal truths. On the contrary, they set down God's redemptive acts in history. The creed does not set down the Church's view of Christ but the uninterpreted facts about Christ. In the early confessions of faith the Church established who Jesus Christ is, and what he did. The Apostles' Creed, for instance, is extraordinarily factual, concentrated and unspeculative.[29] However, in the last analysis the authority of the early creeds and confessions is a spiritual authority; that is to say, they bind us and the Church not to themselves or even to the apostles but to Jesus Christ himself. Moreover, it can be shown that these early confessions wanted to say nothing more and nothing less than: Jesus is Lord; Jesus is the Son of God. Because of their summary and factual character the early confessions served admirably as baptismal confessions, in the liturgy of regular worship, in persecution and martyrdom,

---

26 *Ibid.,* p. 13. Cf. Irenaeus, *Adversus haereses* I. x. 1; III. iv. 1 f. Also, J. N. D. Kelly, *Early Christian Creeds,* 2d ed. (London: Longmans, Green & Co., Inc., 1960) .

27 Cullmann, *Earliest Confessions,* p. 16.

28 *Ibid.*

29 Cf. Helmut Gollwitzer, *Die Bedeutung des Bekenntnisses für die Kirche,* in *Hören und Handeln* (Chr. Kaiser Verlag, Munich, 1962) , pp. 158 f.

and as a polemic against various sects that arose.

We turn now to the second class of confessions, those of the Reformation. That which the Reformation Confessions have in common with the early creeds and creedal formulas is that they seek to express what the whole Church, or rather, the one, holy, catholic Church understands as the gospel and why it does so. Both creeds and Confessions are confessions of the Church rather than of individual theologians. The difference between them is that the creeds seek to express *the* confession of the Church in a simple, direct way, whereas the Reformation Confessions of Faith seek to unfold and safeguard the true and right *understanding* of the confession.[30] They seek to explain and clarify the ancient creeds in the face of new problems, heresies, and errors. Thus the Reformation Confessions do not seek to replace the creeds; on the contrary, they wish to say what is old, but say it in a new way. They, too, want to say simply that Jesus is Lord! The purpose of the Reformation Confessions was not to draw up new formulations of the faith, but rather to give a theological exposition of the creeds. Thus we find in many of the Reformation Confessions the early creeds — Apostles', Nicene, Chalcedonian, and so-called Athanasian — explicitly affirmed and sometimes expounded. This was done partly to show the continuity of the Church of the Reformation with that of the first centuries, partly to show that the doctrine of justification by faith was a legitimate explanation and development of the creeds. It is obvious that the creeds enjoy greater ecumenical validity than the Reformation Confessions, not only because they have been actually more widely acknowledged — the Apostles' Creed is recognized by Protestant and Roman Catholic Churches — but because they do restrict themselves to summary statements about God's redemptive deed in Jesus Christ. On the other hand, this cannot mean that those who stand in the tradition of the Reformation Churches can bypass or ignore the Reformation Confessions. Until further notice they are the authentic interpretation of the creeds. Since the Reformation has occurred, one cannot simply go

---

30 *Ibid.*, p. 165. Gollwitzer recognizes a difference between the creeds and Confessions in that the former excluded the Gnostic sects from the Church, whereas the latter made a division within the Church between the true and false or heretical Church. I question whether this distinction is valid. Were not the Gnostics often a party within the Church? No doubt the early formulas and even the Apostles' Creed were used polemically. But was this their purpose when formulated?

back to the Apostles' Creed as if the Reformation had not happened.

It remains to offer some explanation of why certain Confessions and confessional tracts have been *excluded* from the present collection. The same year in which Zwingli issued his Sixty-seven Articles (1523) he published a detailed exposition of these articles. He had been instructed by the City Council of Zurich to compose a letter of instruction in the faith for ministers and pastors. Zwingli entitled it *A Brief Christian Instruction which the Honorable Council of the City of Zurich has sent to the pastors and preachers living in its cities, lands, and wherever its authority extends, so that they may henceforth in unison announce and preach the Gospel.* It possesses semisymbolical character because it was adopted by the Council of Zurich, November 9, 1523, and published on the seventeenth as authoritative instruction in doctrine. It is not included in the present collection, first, because it never acquired ecclesiastical recognition, and second, because of its length. Yet it is found in Müller's and Böckel's collections. In addition to the *Instruction*, Zwingli wrote two expositions of the Christian faith which played a major part in shaping the Reformation in Switzerland, but which never obtained ecclesiastical authority. The first is Zwingli's Confession of Faith to Emperor Charles V of Germany, July 3, 1530. It is Zwingli's personal confession, written on his own authority, and submitted to the judgment of the whole Church on the occasion of the meeting of the Diet of Augsburg shortly after the Lutheran princes had presented theirs (June 25). It was never laid before the Diet. Like the *Instruction*, it is a lengthy document, over twenty pages of fairly small print. It also is to be found in the collections of Niemeyer, Müller, and Böckel. Zwingli's second work is entitled *The Exposition of the Faith to King Francis I of France*, July, 1531. It is to be found in Niemeyer's and Böckel's collections, and a translation with a historical introduction is given in The Library of Christian Classics, Vol. XXIV, edited by G. W. Bromiley.

Of somewhat similar character but of greater importance are two tracts by John Calvin: The Consensus of Zurich (*Consensus Tigurinus*) of 1549 and the Consensus of Geneva Concerning the Eternal Predestination of God of 1552. The first of these is not, strictly speaking, a confession of faith, but an agreement drawn up in an attempt to settle the dispute that had arisen between Zwinglians and Lutherans concerning Christ's presence in the Lord's Supper. Calvin was displeased with both parties, and had counseled moderation. Bullinger had sent Calvin his work on the Sacraments in manuscript in 1549 to secure his opinion of it. Calvin was quite critical, but after correspondence and a personal conference in Zurich the Calvinistic and Zwinglian sections of the Swiss Churches were united in their views of the Supper. The first draft of the *Consensus Tigurinus* of November, 1548, consists of twenty-four brief propositions drawn up by Calvin, with annotations by Bullinger to which Calvin responded in January, 1549. Calvin, in company with William Farel, met with Bullinger in Zurich and they then drew up the Consensus as it now stands with twenty-six articles. It was published at Zurich and Geneva in 1551. Four years after their formulation Calvin sent an exposition of them to the pastors of Zurich, Berne, Basel, Schaffhausen, Coire, the Gaissons, St. Gall, Biel, Mühlhausen, and Neuchâtel. The Consensus was adopted by most of these Churches, and this is what gives it its semiconfessional character. It brought peace and harmony to the Swiss Churches. It was lauded by Melanchthon, but bitterly attacked by Joachim Westphal, of Hamburg, Germany. The attack provoked Calvin's *Second Defence of the Pious and Orthodox Faith Concerning the Sacraments (1556)*. Niemeyer provides a Latin version of the Consensus of Zurich; Böckel, a German translation. An English translation by Henry Beveridge is to be found in Calvin's Tracts and Treatises, Vol. II, reprinted from the 1849 edition of the Calvin Translation Society, Edinburgh, by Wm. B. Eerdmans Publishing Company (1959).

Attacks by Albertus Pighius and Jerome Bolsec upon Calvin's doctrine of predestination were the occasion of the Geneva Consensus which first appeared in 1552 in the name of the ministers of that city. It, too, is not really a confession of faith, but a lengthy polemical defense by Calvin of his doctrine. According to Schaff, opposition to it developed in the civil governments of Berne, Basel, and Zurich. Some of Calvin's old friends withdrew their support. Bullinger counseled moderation, and Melanchthon expressed his dissatisfaction. Yet Calvin's teaching made headway and consolidated predestinarianism as a mark of Reformed Churches. Niemeyer and Böckel provide a Latin and a German version respectively. A new English translation has been made by J. K. S. Reid, *Concerning the Eternal Predestination of God* (London: James Clarke & Company, Ltd., Publishers, 1961).

In addition to the above we have omitted a number of later minor German Confessions which never succeeded in achieving permanence in the German Reformed Churches: The Confession of Elector Frederick III of the Palatinate (1577); the Confession of Anhalt (1581); the Confession of Nassau (1578); the Bremen Consensus (1598); the Hessian Confession adopted at Kassel in 1607 and published in 1608; the Confession of Sigismund (1614); the Leipzig Colloquy (1631); the Bentheim Confession (1613); and the Colloquy of Thorn (1645).[31] To these might be added the Confessions of Bohemia, Poland, and Hungary.[32]

Although this present volume is confined to the principal Reformed Confessions of the sixteenth century, it is readily conceded that any complete collection of Reformed Confessions should include those of the seventeenth century. Chief among these, of course, are the Canons of the Synod of Dort (1619), the Westminster Confession of Faith (1647) and the Savoy Declaration of 1658, and the Helvetic Consensus Formula of 1675. However, we do not believe that the National Covenant (the so-called Second Scottish Confession of Faith) of 1580 (renewed in 1638), and the Solemn League and Covenant of 1648, should be included, as they were more in the nature of politicoreligious agreements to maintain and defend the principles of the Reformation. Nor should the list include the Lambeth (1595) and Irish (1615) Articles which, although strongly Calvinistic and although they paved the way for the Westminster Confession of Faith, are properly to be regarded, like the Edwardine and Elizabethan Articles, as Confessions of the Church of England. On the other hand, no collection of Reformed Confessions would be complete which omitted the Düsseldorf Theses published May 30, 1933, and adopted by the Second Free Reformed Synod in Siegen, March 26–28, 1935; the Declaration Concerning the Right Understanding of the Reformation Confessions of Faith by the Free Reformed Synod in Barmen-Gemarke, January 3–4,

---

[31] Cf. Heinrich Heppe, ed., *Die Bekenntnisschriften der reformierten Kirchen Deutschlands* (Elberfeld, 1860); E. F. K. Müller, *Die Bekenntnisschriften der reformierten Kirche* (Leipzig, 1903); P. Schaff, *Creeds of Christendom*, Vol. I, pp. 554–565.

[32] P. Schaff, *Creeds of Christendom*, Vol. I, pp. 565–592. Also, the collections of Niemeyer and Böckel.

1934; and the Barmen Theological Declaration, May 29–31, 1934.[33] The inclusion of both seventeenth- and twentieth-century confessions would point up the variety of Reformed Confessions, and the freedom of Reformed Churches to confess in different times and places.

While freely admitting the incompleteness of a collection restricted to the sixteenth century, we nevertheless believe there is justification for such a limited compilation. The Reformation Churches were born with the Confessions of the sixteenth century; those of the seventeenth and twentieth centuries are interpretive and explanatory supplements to the original documents. Indeed, it can be argued that in the symbols of the seventeenth century the seeds of a departure from the Reformation may be detected. It is too little known in Presbyterian Churches in the Anglo-Saxon world that the Westminster standards do not belong to the Reformation but are products of Puritanism and post-Reformation scholasticism. They reflect a legalism, moralism, and rationalism that is foreign to the Confessions of a century earlier. They lack the spontaneity, freshness, and joyfulness of the Reformation. If Presbyterian and Reformed Churches today are "to look to the rock from which they were hewn, and to the quarry from which they were digged," they must return to the Confessions of the 16th century. Here they will find the authentic and pristine witness to the content and form of a genuine confession of faith, that is, the original teachings of the Reformed Churches and the Reformed understanding of the nature of a confession.[34] With respect to Reformed doctrines,

[33] The original text of these three Confessions is to be found in *Bekenntnisschriften und Kirchenordnungen der nach Gottes Wort reformierten Kirche*, ed. by Wilhelm Niesel (Munich, 1938). Translations are given in appendixes to my book, *The Church's Confession Under Hitler* (The Westminster Press, 1962).

[34] In an introduction to a collection of the Confessions of Reformed Churches it is not apposite to discuss these two points. For discussions of the theology of Reformed Confessions, the reader may be referred to: P. Schaff, *Creeds of Christendom*, Vol. I, pp. 354–816; Paul Jacobs, *Theologie reformierter Bekenntnisschriften in Grundzügen* (Neukirchener Verlag, 1959); Wilhelm Niesel, *The Gospel and the Churches: A Comparison of Catholicism, Orthodoxy, and Protestantism*, translated by David Lewis (The Westminster Press, 1962). For treatments of the nature of a Confession of Faith, see: Karl Barth, " The Desirability and Possibility of a Universal Reformed Creed " (1925) in *Theology and Church;* " Das Bekenntnis der Reformation u. unser Bekennen," in *Theologische Existenz heute*, No. 29; " Die Möglichkeit einer Bekenntnisunion," in *Evangelische Theologie* (1935); *Church Dogmatics*, I, 2, pp. 620–660; Arthur C. Cochrane, *The Church's Confession Under Hitler*, pp. 181–216; Helmut Gollwitzer, *Die Bedeutung des Bekenntnisses für die Kirche*, and Otto Weber, *Vorerwägungen*, both in *Hören und Handeln*.

the last four Confessions in the present collection are most important: the French, Scottish, Belgic, and Second Helvetic Confessions, composed between 1559 and 1566. They represent the mature yet still fresh teaching of the Reformed Churches. The first eight illustrate the beginnings and the development of Reformed creedal statements. Taken together they comprise the rich heritage of which ministers and laymen in Presbyterian and Reformed Churches in the English-speaking world have hitherto been deprived. May their publication serve not only a present-day reformation of those Churches which are their heirs, but also the current ecumenical dialogue among all Churches — with a view to the confession of the one faith in the one Lord of the one, holy, catholic and apostolic Church!

1

Zwingli's Sixty-seven Articles of 1523

INTRODUCTION

The Ninety-five Theses that Martin Luther nailed to the door of the church in Wittenberg, October 31, 1517, have long been famous the world over. They have been rightly regarded as marking the beginning of the Reformation in Germany. Much less known are the somewhat similar but more comprehensive Sixty-seven Articles or Conclusions which Huldreich Zwingli published in the year 1523, and which initiated the Reformation in Switzerland. Zwingli had prepared the Articles to be debated at a public disputation called by the City Council of Zurich. The cause and purpose of the disputation are self-evident in the invitation:

Since now for a long time much dissension and disagreement have existed among those preaching the Gospel to the common people . . . So this is our command, will and desire, that you preachers, priests, clergymen, all together and each one separately . . . shall appear the 29th day of the month of January, at the early time of the Council, in our city of Zurich, before us in our town hall, and shall announce in German, by the help of true divine Scripture, the matters which you oppose. When we . . . have paid careful attention to the matters, as seems best to us, and after investigations are made with the help of the Holy Scriptures and the truth, we will send each one home with a command either to continue or to desist. After this no one shall continue to preach from the pulpit whatever seems good to him without foundation in the divine Scriptures.[1]

Six hundred people, priests, ministers, and clergy in the territories of Zurich, including foreign representatives, assembled in the Great Council room at the appointed time. The Bishop of Constance was invited, but sent as deputies Chava-

[1] *Selected Works of Huldreich Zwingli*, ed. by Samuel M. Jackson (1901), pp. 43 f. See also his *Huldreich Zwingli* (G. P. Putnam's Sons, 1903), pp. 180 f.

lier James d'Anwyl, grand minister of the episcopal court, and Dr. Johann Faber, the vicar-general, and several doctors of theology. God's Word was to be the ultimate court of appeal, and the German language used in debate. In the middle of the hall was a table on which had been placed Bibles in Hebrew, Greek, and Latin. After Zwingli had presented his Articles, D'Anwyl explained that as deputies of the bishop they were present not to dispute but to secure information about the reasons for the divisions troubling Zurich, and to try to establish peace. He urged that issues be settled by a general Christian assembly of all nations or by a council of bishops and other scholars such as those found at the universities of Paris, Cologne, or Louvain. In any case he had been sent for no other purpose than to listen, and not to dispute. Zwingli had no difficulty in disposing of these efforts to secure a postponement. Every synod is a council, he argued, because Christ said that he is present where two or three are gathered together in his name; that they were not lacking in scholars in Zurich, and that the opinions of the schools could be dispensed with. Moreover, the Bible was to be the only standard. In the debate that ensued concerning the intercession of saints and the Mass, Dr. Faber appealed to the Church fathers, councils, and tradition. But as he could not cite Scripture, the Disputation went round in circles. After dinner another meeting was held at which the Council delivered its decision. It was to the effect that since Zwingli's teaching had not been disproved, the gospel should be preached in all parts of the canton.

Zwingli, not satisfied with a purely political victory, worked on an exposition of his Articles which was finished July 14, 1523. On October 26–28 of the same year, the Second Disputation was held, at which it was decided that images and pictures be removed from churches; that the vernacular be used in church services; and that the Mass, stripped of the traditions of the ages, be celebrated as far as possible in the manner of its first institution. The Third Disputation was held January 19, 1524, with the result that the Reformation was firmly established in Zurich, both in the city and the canton.

Niemeyer gives the original text of the Sixty-seven Articles in the Swiss dialect in which Zwingli wrote them, as well as a Latin translation. On the different editions, see the notices of Niemeyer, *Praefatio*, pp. xvi ff. Schaff has given the original in High German and the Latin text. The English translation offered here has been made from the text in the Swiss dialect. Literature: The records of the First Disputation are to be found in *Zwingli Werke,* edited by Melchior Schuler and Johann Schulthess (Zurich, 1828). They are based upon a detailed report made by a schoolteacher, Erhard Hegenwald, a follower of Zwingli. It was printed in five editions, of which one is in Augsburg, another in Leipzig. A translation of these records is given in *Selected Works of Huldreich Zwingli,* edited by Samuel M. Jackson (1901).

References: A. Bauer, *Die erste Züricher Disputation* (1883); *Realencyklopädie für Protestantische Theologie und Kirche,* Vol. XXI, pp. 785 f.; Walther Köhler, *Huldrych Zwingli* (1943), pp. 92–95; Rudolf Staehlin, *Huldreich Zwingli* (1895), Vol. I, pp. 264–278; Samuel M. Jackson, *Huldreich Zwingli* (G. P. Putnam's Sons, 1903).

Zwingli's Sixty-seven Articles of 1523

The following sixty-seven articles and opinions, I, Huldreich Zwingli, confess that I preached in the venerable city of Zurich on the basis of the Scripture which is called *theopneustos* [i.e., inspired by God], and I offer to debate and defend them; and where I have not now correctly understood the said Scripture, I am ready to be instructed and corrected, but only from the aforesaid Scripture.

I
All who say that the Gospel is nothing without the approbation of the Church err and slander God.

II
The sum of the Gospel is that our Lord Jesus Christ, the true Son of God, has made known to us the will of His heavenly Father, and by his innocence has redeemed us from death and reconciled us unto God.

III
Therefore Christ is the only way to salvation for all who ever lived, do live or ever will live.

IV
He who seeks or points to another door errs — yea, is a murderer of souls and a robber.

V
Therefore all who regard another doctrine as equal to or higher than the Gospel err and do not know what the Gospel is.

VI
For Christ Jesus is the leader and captain whom God has promised and given to the whole human race:

VII
That He [Christ] might be the eternal salvation and the

Head of all believers, who are His body, which, however, is dead and can do nothing without Him.

VIII

From this it follows, first, that all who live in the Head are His members and children of God. And this is the Church or fellowship of the saints, the bride of Christ, *ecclesia catholica.*

IX

Secondly, that, just as the members of a physical body can do nothing without the guidance of the head, so now in the body of Christ no one can do anything without Christ, its Head.

X

Just as that man is demented whose members operate without his head, lacerating, wounding and harming himself, so also are the members of Christ demented when they undertake something without Christ, their Head, tormenting and burdening themselves with foolish ordinances.

XI

Therefore we perceive that the so-called clerical traditions with their pomp, riches, hierarchy, titles and laws are a cause of all nonsense, because they are not in agreement with Christ, the Head.

XII

Thus they continue to rant and rave, not out of concern for the Head (for that is what is being striven for now by the grace of God) but because they are not permitted to rave on and instead are required to listen to the Head alone.

XIII

When we listen to the Head, we acquire a pure and clear knowledge of the will of God, and we are drawn to Him by His Spirit and are conformed to Him.

XIV

Hence all Christians should do their utmost that everywhere only the Gospel of Christ be preached.

XV

For our salvation is based on faith in the Gospel and our damnation on unbelief; for all truth is clear in Him.

XVI

In the Gospel we learn that human doctrines and traditions are of no avail to salvation.

Concerning the Pope

XVII

That Christ is the one, eternal High Priest, from which it follows that those who have pretended to be high priests oppose the honor and authority of Christ — yea, they reject it.

Concerning the Mass

XVIII

That Christ, Who offered Himself up once and for all, is in eternity a perpetual sacrifice in payment of the sins of all believers, from which it follows that the Mass is not a sacrifice but a recollection of the sacrifice and an assurance of the redemption which Christ has manifested to us.

The Intercession of the Saints

XIX

That Christ is the one Mediator between God and us.

XX

That God wants to give us all things in His Name, from which it follows that we need no mediator beyond this life but Christ.

XXI

That when we pray for one another on earth we do so in such wise that we trust that through Christ alone all things are given to us.

Good Works

XXII

That Christ is our righteousness, from which we conclude that our works are good in so far as they are of Christ; in so far as they are our works they are neither righteous nor good.

How Clerical Property Belongs to Christ

XXIII

That Christ condemns the possessions and pomp of this world, from which we conclude that those who heap up riches unto themselves in His name monstrously slander Him, using Him as a cloak to hide their own greed and arrogance.

Concerning the Prohibition of Foods

XXIV

That no Christian is bound to perform works which God has not commanded; he is free to eat all foods at any time. From this we see that dispensations concerning fasting are a Roman fraud.

Concerning Festivals and Pilgrimages

XXV

That the Christian is not bound to times and places; rather they are subject to him. From this we learn that those who bind men to times and places rob Christians of their freedom.

Hoods, Dress, Insignia, etc.

XXVI

That nothing is more displeasing to God than hypocrisy. Hence we learn that everything which simulates holiness in the eyes of men is grievous hypocrisy and infamy. Under this head fall cowls, insignia, tonsures, etc.

Orders and Sects

XXVII

That all Christians are brothers of Christ and brothers one of another and no one on earth should be called father. Thus orders, sects, and fraternities are untenable.

Ministers Marrying

XXVIII

That everything which God permits or does not forbid is lawful. From this we learn that marriage is seemly for all men.

An Incontinent Minister Should Marry

XXIX

That all who are called ministers sin when, having become convinced that God has denied them the gift of continence, they do not safeguard themselves by marrying.

Vows of Chastity

XXX

That those who take a vow of chastity foolishly or childishly undertake too much. From this we learn that those who accept such vows do violence to pious men.

Concerning Excommunication

XXXI

That no single individual may impose a bann of excommunication upon anyone. Only the Church may do it, which is the fellowship of those among whom the one worthy of excommunication dwells, together with the minister, who is their watchman.

XXXII

That only one who has committed a public offense may be excommunicated.

Concerning Ill-gotten Gains

XXXIII

That ill-gotten gain should not be given to temples, cloisters, monks, clerics and nuns, but to the poor, provided it cannot be restored to the rightful owner.

Concerning Rulers

XXXIV

The so-called spiritual power has no basis for its pomp in the teaching of Christ.

Temporal Power Is of God

XXXV

The temporal power, however, does have power and confirmation in the doctrine and work of Christ.

XXXVI

The so-called ecclesiastical estate pretends that the administration of justice rightfully belongs to it. But all this pertains to temporal rulers if they want to be Christians.

XXXVII

Moreover, all Christians, without exception, owe them obedience.

XXXVIII

That is, in so far as they do not require anything contrary to God.

XXXIX

For this reason, all their laws should conform to the divine will so that they protect the oppressed, even when he does not complain.

XL

Only magistrates may lawfully take life, and then only the lives of those who commit a public offense, without provoking God's wrath — unless He commands something else.

XLI

When magistrates offer counsel and help to those for whom they will render an account to God, the latter owe to these magistrates bodily assistance.

XLII

But when they are unfaithful and do not act according to the rule of Christ, they may be deposed in the name of God.

XLIII

In a word, his kingdom is best and is the most stable who governs in the name of God alone; and his kingdom is the worst and the most insecure who governs according to his own will.

Concerning Prayer

XLIV

True worshippers call upon God in spirit and in truth without ostentation before men.

XLV

Hypocrites do their works in order to be seen of men, and they receive their reward in this world.

XLVI

Thus it must follow that chanting and loud clamor which lack true devotion and are done only for the sake of reward, either seek the praise of men or material gain.

Concerning Offenses

XLVII

A man should suffer physical death rather than offend or scandalize a fellow-Christian.

XLVIII

Whoever through stupidity or ignorance wants to take offense without cause should not be permitted to remain in his

weakness or ignorance but should be strengthened in order
that he may not regard as sinful that which is not sinful.

XLIX

I know of no greater offense than to forbid priests to have
wives and then to allow them to hire prostitutes. Away with
this shame!

Concerning the Remission of Sins

L

God alone remits sins, through Jesus Christ, His Son, our only
Lord.

LI

Whoever ascribes the remission of sins to a creature robs God
of His honor and gives it to one who is not God. That is pure
idolatry.

LII

Consequently confession which is made to a priest or to a
neighbor is not for the remission of sins, but for counselling.

LIII

Imposed works of penance stem from human counsel (with
the exception of excommunication). They do not remit sin
and are imposed to warn others.

Christ's Suffering Atones for Sin

LIV

Christ has borne all our pain and misery. Whoever now attributes to works of penance what belongs to Christ alone,
errs and blasphemes God.

Withholding the Remission of Sins

LV

Whoever refuses to remit any sin to a penitent person, would
not be acting in the place of God or of Peter, but of the devil.

LVI

Whoever remits sins solely for the sake of money is the part-
ner of Simon and Balaam and is really a messenger of the
devil.

Concerning Purgatory

LVII

The true Holy Scriptures know nothing of a purgatory after
this life.

LVIII

The judgment of those who have died is known only to God.

LIX

And the less God has let us know about it, the less should we try to know about it.

LX

I do not condemn it when a man, concerned for the dead, calls upon God to show them mercy. But to stipulate the duration of purgatory (seven years for a mortal sin), and to lie for the sake of gain is inhuman and diabolical.

Concerning the Priesthood and Its Consecration

LXI

The divine Scriptures know nothing of an indelible imprint [character] by consecration which the priests have invented in recent times.

LXII

Furthermore the Scriptures do not recognize any priests except those who proclaim God's Word.

LXIII

To such as do [proclaim God's Word] Scripture commands us to show them honor and give support for their bodily needs.

Concerning the Redressing of Abuses

LXIV

Those who recognize their error are not to be made to suffer for it, but are to be allowed to die in peace; afterward their bequests to the Church are to be administered in a Christian manner.

LXV

God will deal with those who do not want to recognize their error. Therefore no violence is to be done to their bodies unless their conduct is so unseemly that it cannot be tolerated.

LXVI

All officials in the Church should forthwith humble themselves, and should exalt the Cross of Christ alone and not the money-chest. Otherwise they will perish; the axe is laid to the root of the tree.

LXVII

If anyone wishes to have a discussion with me about usury, tithes, unbaptized children or confirmation, I declare myself willing to respond.

Here let no one attempt to contend with sophistry or trifles, but let him come having Scripture as judge (Scripture breathes God's Spirit), in order that either the truth be found or, when it is found, as I hope it would be, that it be kept. Amen. May God grant it!

2

The Ten Theses of Berne, 1528

INTRODUCTION

The decisive step for the Reformation in Berne was taken when Berthold Haller was called to succeed Thomas Wyttenbach as canon of the Church of St. Vincent in 1520. Haller was born at Aldingen in 1492, studied at Rothweil and Pforzheim where he made the acquaintance of Melanchthon. After studying theology at the University of Cologne, he taught at Berne from 1513 to 1518. Through a mutual friendship with Myconius, he was introduced to Zwingli and visited with him frequently in 1521. With the Franciscan Sebastian Meyer who since 1511 had taught in Berne as professor of theology, Haller began to gather together an evangelical group. During this period the Small Council of the canton, primarily representative of an older generation, consistently favored the Roman party and opposed any reform. At the same time the Large Council of two hundred tended to sympathize with the Reformers. The numbers of the evangelical party increased rapidly and by the beginning of 1527 they had a majority in both the Small and Large Councils.

On June 5, 1523, the Council adopted the first *Reformations* or *Predigtmandat* for the canton of Berne. This document is a copy of the Basel *Mandat* which forbade the proclamation of Lutheran doctrines. But at the same time the *Mandat* permitted the preaching of Scripture themes (which had been the material concern of the Zurich Disputation). Such an ambiguous decree could only serve the Reformers' cause. Those Roman critics who view this decree as a " lay effort . . . primarily concerned with preserving civil harmony " may well be right.[1] Nonetheless it is an attempt to

---

[1] Cf. Otto Vasella, " Berne, Einführung der Reformation," *Lexikon für Theologie und Kirche,* ed. by Josef Höfer und Karl Rahner, Vol. II (1958), p. 234.

maintain the " old faith " in Berne. As such it was not totally unsuccessful. In the *Volksanfrage* of 1524, which the Roman historians cite as a sign of the Councils' irresponsible act to avoid what was properly their own affair, fourteen of the jurisdictions of the canton favored the retention of the " old faith," only one the " new," while three others decided that the matter should be left in the hands of the Councils. By the promulgation of the *Mandat of the Twelve Cantons,* January 26, 1524, the Councils reasserted that they were committed unconditionally to safeguard the catholic faith.

But the divided sympathy of the two Councils in these matters also permitted the Reformers' activity to proceed apace. In 1525, Haller ceased to celebrate the Mass in the Church of St. Vincent, substituting the preaching of the Scripture. The following year a council was held at Baden (May 21 to June 8) at which the Roman party, led by Dr. Johannes Eck, scored an impressive victory. (Zwingli, fearing for his safety, did not attend.) The Council had the twofold effect of spurring the Reformers on to renewed efforts and of encouraging the " old faith " party to challenge Haller's influence in Berne. The Councils requested that he return to the reading of the Mass. When he refused, the Council withheld his stipend as canon but permitted him to remain as priest of the Church of St. Vincent. Nevertheless, Haller's influence increased, and with the backing of the populace, the Council rejected the so-called Confederation *Glaubensmandat* based on Eck's Seven Theses which had been debated and adopted at Baden. Francis Kolb, who had been banished from the city a decade earlier, was permitted to return as Haller's assistant. The Easter election of 1527 gave the Reformed party control of both councils. A new constitution was drawn up; freedom of preaching was restored by the abolition of the 1523 *Mandat;* and a public disputation of issues between the Reformed and Roman positions was set for January 6, 1528.

The Ten Theses or Conclusions proposed for debate were drawn up by Haller and Kolb. Before they were printed, Haller sent the manuscript to Zwingli, November 19, 1527, and he may have made some editorial changes. A copy of the Theses, with an announcement of the forthcoming disputation and an invitation to participate, was sent to professors in the universities, representatives of neighboring city councils, the Roman Catholic bishops of Constance, Basel, Valais, and Lausanne, and to parish ministers and religious leaders

in the Swiss cantons and the adjoining territories. Efforts
were made to assemble Roman Catholic theologians, and safe
conduct was promised to and from the canton. But few attended, doubtless because they felt that the conference held at
Baden had settled the question and because they knew that
numerically they would be outnumbered. Dr. Eck declined
to come, with the result that the cause of the Roman party
was represented by the Augustinian Konrad Treger, the Do-
minican Alexius Grat, and the priests, Hutter of Appenzell
and Johann Buchstab of Zofingen. The Reformers appeared
from Zurich, Basel, St. Gall, and several South German cities. Bucer and Capito came from Strassburg, Jacob Ausbur-
ger from Mühlhausen, Ambrose Blaarer from Constance,
Sebastian Wagner from Schaffhausen, Oecolampadius from
Basel, and Zwingli from Zurich. Altogether three hundred
and fifty ecclesiastics assembled for the Disputation.

Joachim von Watt, of St. Gall, presided over the Disputation. Debate centered on the published propositions. Each
article was read in turn and alternately introduced by Haller
and Kolb. Haller concluded the twenty-day-long discussions
with a review and an exhortation to the government to take
in hand the Reformation that had now been justified, and
with an admonition to ministers to be faithful shepherds.
Zwingli and others promised to give further accounts of their
doctrines. He observed that although Eck, Faber, and others
had been absent, all their arguments had been presented.
Watt, who presided, handed over the carefully recorded and
collated minutes to the Council. Finally Haller thanked the
assembly in the name of the Council.

The Ten Theses were signed by the cantons and by almost
all ministers in Berne. It resulted in the abolition of the Mass
(which had already ceased in the Cathedral during the Disputation following one of Zwingli's sermons) and in the
orderly removal of pictures and images from the churches.
On February 7, 1528, a Reformation edict imparted to the
Articles the force of law, and declared the powers of the bishops nullified. From the thirteenth on, the congregations were
asked about their acceptance of the Reformation and most of
them declared themselves in favor of it. The Berne Disputation also bore fruit in Biel, Basel, and Schaffhausen. It had its
effect upon the Disputations later held in Geneva (1535) and
Lausanne (1536), and its influence extended even to France,
Holland, Scotland, and England.

Niemeyer gives the German original of the Theses in the Swiss dialect from the Zurich edition of 1528, from which the present translation has been made.

Literature: The original handwritten minutes of the Disputation are still extant in the Berne State Archives in two copies. With only the most necessary abbreviations they were printed in Berne in 1528. Later official editions appeared in 1608 and 1701. See Luthardus Christophus, *Disputationes Bernensis explicatio et defensio* (1660); Samuel Fischer, *Geschichte der Disputation zu Bern* (Berne, 1828); Melch. Kirchhofer, *Berthold Haller, oder die Reformation in Bern* (Zurich, 1828); Carl Pestalozzi, " Berthold Haller," *Leben und ausgewählte Schriften der Väter und Begründer der reformierten Kirche*, ed. by J. W. Baum *et al.*, Vol. IX (Elberfeld, 1861); Oscar Farner, *Huldrych Zwingli*, Vol. 4 (1960), pp. 164 f., 259–291; P. Schaff, *Creeds of Christendom*, Vol. I, pp. 364–366; Vol. III, pp. 208–210; Ernst Blösch, " Berthold Haller," *The New Schaff-Herzog Encyclopedia of Religious Knowledge*, ed. by Samuel M. Jackson, *et al.*, Vol. V (reprinted 1953), p. 126; " Francis Kolb," *ibid.*, Vol. VI, pp. 370 f.; Otto Vasella, " Bern, Einführung der Reformation," *Lexikon für Theologie und Kirche*, ed. by Josef Höfer and Karl Rahner, Vol. II (1958), p. 234.

The Ten Theses of Berne, 1528

I
The holy, Christian Church, whose only Head is Christ, is born of the Word of God, abides in the same, and does not listen to the voice of a stranger.
II
The Church of Christ makes no laws or commandments without God's Word. Hence all human traditions, which are called ecclesiastical commandments, are binding upon us only in so far as they are based on and commanded by God's Word.
III
Christ is our only wisdom, righteousness, redemption, and payment for the sins of the whole world. Hence it is a denial of Christ when we acknowledge another merit for salvation and satisfaction for sin.
IV
It cannot be proved from the Biblical writings that the body and blood of Christ is essentially and corporeally received in the bread of the Eucharist.
V
The mass as now in use, in which Christ is offered up to God the Father for the sins of the living and the dead, is contrary to Scripture, a blasphemy against the most holy sacrifice, passion and death of Christ, and on account of its abuses, an abomination before God.
VI
As Christ alone died for us, so He is to be worshipped as the only Mediator and Advocate between God the Father and us believers. Therefore, to propose the invoking of other mediators and advocates beyond this life is contrary to Scripture.

VII

Scripture knows nothing of a purgatory after this life. Hence all offices for the dead such as vigils, masses, requiems, devotions repeated after the seventh or thirtieth day of each year, lamps, candles and such like are in vain.

VIII

The making of images to be venerated is contrary to the Word of God of the Old and New Testaments. Therefore when the setting up of images involves the danger of veneration, they are to be abolished.

IX

Holy matrimony is not forbidden in Scripture to any class of men, but is granted to all in order to avoid adultery and fornication.

X

Since according to Scripture an open adulterer is to be excommunicated, it follows that because of the scandal involved, fornication and adultery are more pernicious for the clergy than for any other class of men.

May all things be to the honor of God and His holy Word!

3

The Tetrapolitan Confession of 1530

INTRODUCTION

On January 21, 1530, the Emperor Charles I issued a call for a Diet to convene in Augsburg, April 8, for the purpose of an open discussion of various religious questions with a view to achieving a reconciliaton. The Lutherans already had a Confesson of Faith in the Schwabach Articles which had been drawn up in October, 1529, probably by Melanchthon with Luther's advice.[1] In keeping with the emperor's invitation the Elector John of Saxony had his theologians in Wittenberg prepare an account of the beliefs and practices of the churches in his territory. These articles were approved at Torgau, March, 1530. The Schwabach and the Torgau Articles were taken to Augsburg, and the former became the basis of the first part of the Augsburg Confession, the latter the basis of the second part.[2] Melanchthon, using these documents as a basis, worked on a draft of the Augustana, to which revisions and emendations were made up to the eve of the formal presentation to the emperor on June 25, 1530. Luther was not at Augsburg, but Melanchthon sent him a copy which he approved.

Meanwhile, in response to the emperor's invitation to the Diet, Martin Bucer and Wolfgang Capito were at work at Strassburg as early as April 26. The delegates from Strassburg, Johannes Sturm and Matthias Pfarrer, were instructed to avoid the disunion of the Protestant states and a too close questioning of the meaning of particular doctrines. But when they arrived in Augsburg they found that this policy was impracticable, because the circulation of John Eck's 404 articles included the Strassburg delegation in his attack,[3] and because

---

[1] Cf. M. Reu, *The Augsburg Confession* (1930), First Part, pp. 25–30.

[2] *Ibid.*, pp. 48–52.

[3] Cf. Henry E. Jacobs, " The Four Hundred and Four Theses of Dr. John Eck," in Papers of the American Society of Church History, Second Series, Vol. II (1910), pp. 21–81 (includes text of Theses).

a number of north German theologians held themselves entirely aloof. Repeatedly the delegates sent back to Strassburg for Bucer and Capito, but since no invitation or assurance of safe conduct had been given them, the Council feared they would be arrested as outright heretics. Nevertheless, they arrived in Augsburg on June 23 and 26 on their own initiative. However, it became apparent that the princes would not permit those cities to subscribe to the Augsburg Confession which dissented from the article on the doctrine of Christ's corporeal presence in the Lord's Supper. At the same time Bucer arrived in Augsburg, the landgrave Philip of Hesse, in spite of misgivings about the article on the Sacrament, signed the Saxon Articles. Thus Bucer, with the aid of Capito and Caspar Hedio, was constrained to prepare in great haste a confession of his own in the name of the four imperial cities of Strassburg, Constance, Memmingen, and Lindau. It became known as the Tetrapolitan Confession or the Confession of the Four Cities. It is the first Confession of Reformed Churches in Germany. In content it followed as closely as possible the Confession of the princes, and sought to take a mediating position between the teachings of Luther and Zwingli. Accordingly Article XVIII, " Of the Eucharist," declares that Christ " deigns to give his true body and true blood to be truly eaten and drunk for the food and drink of souls, for their nourishment unto life eternal, so that now he may live and abide in them, and they in him, to be raised up by him at the last day to new and immortal life." Indeed, later the adherents of the Tetrapolitan Confession referred to it as being neither Lutheran nor Zwinglian, but in obedience to Christ's command in Scripture. Nevertheless the influence of Zwingli may be seen in the preeminence given to the Scriptural principle, to the centrality of Christ and his grace, to the Sacraments as being not only visible tokens of grace but acts of homage to Christ, and to the denunciation of images and other abuses.

After Melanchthon and his party had presented their Confession, June 25, and Zwingli his *Fidei ratio,* July 8,[4] the four cities handed theirs to the Emperor in German and Latin, July 11. It was not read before the Diet. Instead, the Emperor submitted it to the Catholic theologians Eck, Faber, and Cochlaeus who had composed the Confutation of the Augs-

---

4 See Introduction to the present volume, p. 27.

burg Confession,[5] and now framed one of the Tetrapolitan. This was read before the Diet, but the Strassburg divines were not even given a copy of the Confutation and an opportunity to defend themselves. Eventually they managed to secure a copy secretly, and answered it by a "Vindication and Defense" (as Melanchthon wrote his Apology of the Augsburg Confession during the Diet). The Confession and the Defense were officially published in German and Latin at Strassburg, 1531.

Schaff has rightly observed that the Tetrapolitan Confession may be regarded as "the first attempt at an evangelical union symbol." But in spite of, or perhaps just because of, Bucer's intense efforts to reconcile the differences between the Zwinglians and Lutherans, the Tetrapolitan Confession was soon superseded. The representatives of the four cities later subscribed to the Schmalkald Articles in February, 1531. The Swiss were not satisfied with the compromising language of Article XVIII concerning the Sacrament, with the result that the Tetrapolitan was replaced by the more precise Calvinist confessions. At the Diet of Schweinfurt in 1532 the Strassburg party recognized the Augustana alongside the Tetrapolitan.

The different recensions of the Tetrapolitan Confession are kept in the Strassburg State Archives. The translation printed here is to be found in Henry E. Jacobs, *The Book of Concord* (1883), Vol. II, and was made from the Latin text in Niemeyer's *Collectio confessionum*.

Literature: T. Keim, *Schwäbische Reformations-geschichte* (Tübingen, 1855); F. Dobel, *Memmingen im Reformationszeitalter,* Parts IV–V (Augsburg, 1878); A. Pätzold, *Die Konfutation des Vierstädtebekenntnisses* (Leipzig, 1900); J. Ficker, "Das Konstanzer Bekenntnis" in *Theologische Abhandlungen für H. Holtzmann* (Tübingen and Leipzig, 1902); E. F. K. Müller, "Tetrapolitana, confessio" in *Realencyklopädie für protestantische Theologie und Kirche,* Vol. XIX (1907) and in *The New Schaff-Herzog Encyclopedia of Religious Knowledge,* ed. by Samuel M. Jackson, Vol. XI (1911; reprinted Baker Book House, 1950); P. Schaff, *Creeds of Christendom,* Vol. I, pp. 526 ff.; M. Reu, *The Augsburg Confession* (1930); Hastings Eells, *Martin Bucer* (Yale University Press, 1931); W. Köhler, *Zwingli und Luther,* Vol. II (1953), pp. 193 ff.

---

[5] The text of the Confutation of Augsburg is given in English in Henry E. Jacobs, *The Book of Concord,* Vol. II (1883).

The Tetrapolitan Confession

CONFESSION OF THE FOUR CITIES, STRASBURG, CONSTANCE, MEMMINGEN AND LINDAU. WHEREIN THEY SET FORTH THEIR FAITH TO HIS IMPERIAL MAJESTY IN THE DIET OF AUGSBURG.

EXORDIUM

Thy Worshipful Majesty, Most Powerful and Most Clement Emperor, hath commanded that the orders and estates of the Holy Empire, so far as concerns each and each hopes to act towards tranquillizing the Church, should present to him their opinion, reduced to writing in both languages, Latin and German, concerning religion, as well as concerning the errors and vices which have insinuated themselves in opposition thereto, for discussion and examination, to the end that thereby a mode and way may be found to restore to its place the pure doctrine, all errors being abolished. We desire, as is right, to obey this command, which has not so much originated from a religious design that has in view the profit of the Church as it exhibits and savors of the unparalleled clemency and kindness whereby Thy Worshipful Majesty hath rendered himself so beloved by the entire world. For in these matters we have never sought anything else than that, those things being abrogated which are contrary to the holy Gospels and to Christ's commands, it may be allowed not only us, but also all others who have professed Christ, to follow after his pure doctrine, which alone is vivifying. Wherefore we pray and most humbly beseech Thy Worshipful Majesty to be so disposed to us as to deign to hear and consider what we will present as a reason for the hope that is in us, in order that concerning these matters there may be no doubt that it has been above all our desire to aim only at that whereby we may please, first of all, our Creator and Restorer Christ, and afterward also Thy Worshipful Majesty, and that in obedience to the summons we may show that we have embraced a

doctrine varying somewhat from that in common use, influenced by no other purpose or hope than that, being persuaded as He who has fashioned and refashioned us requires,
we promise ourselves as the result — and this especially because of the eminent praise whereby for a long time already
thou hast been celebrated among us for thy religion, godliness and piety — that His Worshipful Majesty will acknowledge the truth concerning all things which we have received
for some time as Christ's doctrine and as the teaching of a
purer religion, that he will absolutely approve our attempt,
and number us among those who have endeavored to obey
him with the greatest fidelity. For the renowned zeal of Thy
Most Worshipful Majesty for truth and justice and thy
fervent godliness permit us not even to suspect that thou wilt
prejudge us before we have as yet been heard, or wilt not
hear us kindly and attentively, or when thou hast heard us,
and weighed with thy devout deliberation what we present,
God aiding thy spirit, as he has so successfully led Thy Most
Worshipful Majesty in other matters, that thou wilt not immediately perceive that we have followed the very doctrines
of Christ.

CHAPTER I

OF THE SUBJECT–MATTER OF SERMONS

First, therefore, since about ten years ago, by the remarkable goodness of God, the doctrine of Christ began to be
treated with somewhat more certainty and clearness than before everywhere throughout Germany, and hence among us,
just as elsewhere, many doctrines of our religion were publicly controverted, and to a constantly increasing extent,
among the learned, and those especially who held the position of teachers of Christ in the churches; and hence, as was
necessary, while Satan was undoubtedly plying his work, so
that the people were very dangerously divided by conflicting
sermons, considering what St. Paul writes, that " divinely inspired Scripture is profitable for doctrine, that where there
is sin it may be detected and corrected, and every one be instructed in righteousness, that the man of God may be perfect, furnished for every good work," — we also, influenced
and induced to avoid all delay, not only from the fear of
God, but from the certain peril to the state, at length en-

joined our preachers to teach from the pulpit nothing else than is either contained in the Holy Scriptures or hath sure ground therein. For it seemed to us not improper to resort in such a crisis whither of old and always not only the most holy fathers, bishops and princes, but also the children of God everywhere, have always resorted — viz., to the authority of the Holy Scriptures. For, to their praise, St. Luke mentions of some such that they were more noble than those of Thessalonica, since they examined the Gospel of Christ, which they had heard according to the Scriptures, in which Paul most earnestly desired that his scholar Timothy be exercised, and without which no pontiffs have ever required obedience to their decrees, nor fathers credit to their writings, nor princes authority to their laws, and from which only the great council of the Holy Empire assembled at Nuremburg in the year 1523 decreed that holy sermons should be derived. For if St. Paul has taught the truth when he said that by Holy Scripture the man of God is made perfect and furnished for every good work, he can lack nothing of Christian truth or sound doctrine who strives religiously to ask counsel of Scripture.

CHAPTER II

OF THE HOLY TRINITY AND THE MYSTERY OF THE INCARNATE CHRIST

Since, therefore, holy sermons were derived from this source and dangerous contentions ceased, those in whom there was any desire after godliness have obtained a far more certain knowledge of Christ's doctrine and have begun to express it in the life. Just as they have withdrawn from those things which were improperly attached to the doctrines of Christ, so have they been confirmed in those that agree therewith. Among these is what the Church of Christ has hitherto believed concerning the Holy Trinity — viz. that God the Father, the Son and the Holy Ghost is one in substance, and admits no distinction other than of persons. Also that our Saviour Jesus Christ, being true God, became likewise true man, the two natures not being confounded, but so united in the same person that they shall never throughout all ages be sundered. Nor do they vary in these particulars in any respect from what the Church, taught out of the Holy Gospels, be-

lieves concerning our Saviour Jesus Christ, conceived of the
Holy Ghost, then born of the Virgin Mary, and who at length,
after he had performed the office of preaching the Gospel,
having died on the cross and been buried, descended to hell,
and was recalled the third day from the dead into immortal
life; and when by various arguments he had proved this to
witnesses hereunto appointed, was carried up to heaven to
the right hand of his Father, whence we look for him as Judge
of the quick and the dead. Meanwhile, we acknowledge that
he is nevertheless present with his Church, even to the end of
the world; that he renews and sanctifies it and adorns it as
his only beloved bride with all sorts of ornaments of virtues.
In these points, since we vary nothing from the common consent of Christians, we think it sufficient in this manner to
testify our faith.

Chapter III

OF JUSTIFICATION AND FAITH

In regard to those things which were commonly taught concerning the manner in which we become partaker of the redemption made by Christ, and concerning the duties of a
Christian, our preachers differ somewhat from the lately received dogmas. Those points which we have followed we will
endeavor to explain most plainly to Your Most Worshipful
Majesty, and at the same time to indicate in good faith the
Scripture passages that have constrained us thereto. First,
therefore, since for some years we were taught that man's own
works are necessary for his justification, our preachers have
taught that this whole justification is to be ascribed to the
good pleasure of God and the merit of Christ, and to be received by faith alone. Among others, the following passages
of Scripture have moved them thereto: "As many as received
him, to them gave he power to become the sons of God, even
to them that believe on his name: which were born not of
blood, nor of the will of the flesh, but of God" (John 1:12,
13). "Verily, verily, I say unto thee, except a man be born
again, he cannot see the kingdom of God" (John 3:3). "No
man knoweth the Son but the Father; neither knoweth any
man the Father save the Son, and he to whomsoever the Son
will reveal him" (Matt. 11:27). "Blessed art thou, Simon
Bar-Jona; for flesh and blood hath not revealed it unto thee"

[margin handwritten note: The Ground of Justification]

(Matt. 16:17) . " No man can come unto me, unless my Father draw him " (John 6:44) . " By grace are ye saved through faith; and that not of yourselves; it is the gift of God; not of works, lest any man should boast. For we are his workmanship, created in Christ Jesus unto good works, which God hath before ordained that we should walk in them " (Eph. 2:8-10) . For since it is our righteousness and eternal life to know God and Jesus Christ our Saviour, and this is so far from being a work of flesh and blood that it is necessary for this to be born again; neither can we come to the Son, unless the Father draw us; neither know the Father, unless the Son reveal him; and Paul writes so clearly, " not of us, nor of our works," — it is evident enough that our works can help us nothing, so that instead of unrighteous, as we are born, we may become righteous; because as we are by nature the children of wrath, and on this account unrighteous, so we are unable to do anything just or pleasing to God. But the beginning of all our righteousness and salvation must proceed from the mercy of the Lord, who from his own favor and the contemplation of the death of his Son first offers the doctrine of truth and his Gospel, those being sent forth who are to preach it; and, secondly, since " the natural man receiveth not the things of the Spirit of God," as St. Paul says (I Cor. 2:14) , he causes a beam of his light to arise at the same time in the darkness of our heart, so that now we may believe his Gospel preached, being persuaded of the truth thereof by his Spirit from above, and then, relying upon the testimony of this Spirit, may call upon him with filial confidence and say, " Abba, Father," obtaining thereby sure salvation, according to the saying: " Whosoever shall call upon the name of the Lord shall be saved."

CHAPTER IV

OF GOOD WORKS, PROCEEDING OUT OF FAITH THROUGH LOVE

These things we will not have men so to understand, as though we placed salvation and righteousness in slothful thoughts of the mind, or in faith destitute of love, which they call faith without form; seeing that we are sure that no man can be justified or saved except he supremely love and most earnestly imitate God. " For whom he did foreknow, he also did predestinate to be conformed to the image of his Son "; to wit, as in the glory of a blessed life, so in the cultivation of innocence and perfect righteousness; " for we are his workmanship, created unto good works." But no one can love God above all things, and worthily imitate him, but he who indeed knows him and expects all good things from him. Therefore, we cannot be otherwise justified — i.e., become righteous as well as saved (for righteousness is even our salvation) — than by being endued chiefly with faith, whereby, believing the Gospel, and therefore being persuaded that God has adopted us as his children, and that he will ever bestow his paternal kindness upon us, we wholly depend upon his pleasure. This faith St. Augustine in his book, *De Fide et Operibus,* calls " Evangelical " — to wit, that which is efficacious through love. By this only are we regenerated and the image of God is restored in us. By this, although we are born corrupt, our thoughts even from our childhood being altogether prone to evil, we become good and upright. For from this we, being fully satisfied with one God, the perennial fountain of blessings that is copiously effluent, show ourselves to others as gods — i.e., true children of God — by love striving for their advantage so far as we are able. For "he that loveth his brother abideth in the light" and " is born of God," and is wholly given to the new, and at the same time old, commandment concerning mutual love. And this love is the fulfilling of the whole law, as Paul says: " All the law is fulfilled in one word: Thou shalt love thy neighbor as thyself " (Gal. 5:14). For whatever the law of God teaches has this end and requires this one thing, that at length we may be reformed to the perfect image of God, being good in all things, and ready and willing to serve the advantage of men; which we cannot do unless we be furnished with virtues of every kind. For who can purpose and do all things, as the duty of a Christian requires, to the true edifying of the Church and the sound profit of all — i.e., according to God's law and for his glory — except he both think and speak and do everything in order and well, and therefore be very familiarly acquainted with the whole company of virtues?

CHAPTER V

TO WHOM GOOD WORKS ARE TO BE ASCRIBED, AND HOW THEY ARE NECESSARY

But since they who are the children of God are led by the Spirit of God, rather than that they act themselves (Rom. 8:14), and " of him, and through him, and to him, are all things " (Rom. 11:36), whatsoever things we do well and holily are to be ascribed to none other than to this one only Spirit, the Giver of all virtues. However it be, he does not compel us, but leads us, being willing, working in us both to will and to do (Phil. 2:13). Hence Augustine writes wisely that God rewards his own works in us. By this we are so far from rejecting good works that we utterly deny that any one can be saved unless by Christ's Spirit he be brought thus far, that there be in him no lack of good works, for which God has created him. For there are divers members of the same body; therefore each of us has not the same office (I Cor., ch. 12). Inasmuch as it is so necessary for the law to be fulfilled that heaven and earth shall pass away before one iota or the least point thereof be remitted, yet because God alone is good, and has created all things out of nothing, and by his Spirit makes us altogether new, and wholly leads us (for in Christ nothing avails but a new creature), none of these things can be ascribed to human powers; and we must confess that all things are the mere gifts of God, who favors and loves us of his own accord, and not for any merit of ours. From the above it can be sufficiently known what we believe justification to be, by whom it is brought us, and in what way it is received of us, and by what passages of Scripture we are induced to so believe. For although of many we have cited a few, yet by these few any one who is even moderately versed in the Scriptures will be satisfied, and even more than satisfied, that passages of this kind that ascribe nothing but sin and perdition to us, as Hosea says, and all our righteousness and salvation to the Lord, meet readers of the Scriptures everywhere.

CHAPTER VI

OF THE DUTIES OF A CHRISTIAN

Now it cannot be doubted what be the duties of a Christian, and to what actions he should be chiefly devoted;

namely, to all those whereby every one, for his part, may profit his neighbors — first, with respect to life eternal, that they may begin to know, worship and fear God; and then with respect to the present life, that they may want nothing required by bodily necessity. For as the whole law of God, which is a most absolute commandment of all righteousness, is summed up in this one word: " Thou shalt love thy neighbor as thyself " (Rom. 13:9), so in rendering this love it is necessary that all righteousness be comprised and completed. Hence nothing at all is to be reckoned among the duties of a Christian which has not some force to profit our neighbor, and that every such work pertaineth the more to a Christian as more advantage may accrue to his neighbor. Therefore, after ecclesiastical functions we place among the chief duties of a Christian the administration of the government, obedience to magistrates (for these are of importance for the common profit), the care which is devoted to wife, children and family, and the honor which is rendered parents, because without these the life of men cannot subsist; and, lastly, the professions of good arts and all honorable branches of learning, since without the cultivation of these we would necessarily be destitute of the greatest blessings, and those which are peculiar to mankind. Yet in these and all other duties of human life no man must inconsiderately take anything to himself, but conscientiously consider whither God calls him. To conclude, let every man account that his duty, and that duty the more excellent, whereby he may confer the greatest advantage upon men.

CHAPTER VII

OF PRAYERS AND FASTS

We have prayers and fasts, actions nevertheless the most holy and such as are especially proper for Christians, to which our ecclesiastics most diligently exhort their hearers. For true fasting is, as it were, a renouncing of the present life, which is always subject to evil desires, and a meditation upon the future life, that is free from perturbations. Prayer, moreover, is a lifting up of the mind to God, and such conversation with him that no other thing so greatly inflames man with heavenly affections and more mightily conforms the mind to God's will. But however holy and necessary these exercises be to Christians, yet as one's neighbor is not so

much served by them as man is prepared to serve his neighbor with profit, they are not to be preferred to holy doctrine,
godly exhortations and admonitions, and other duties whereby our neighbor at once receives profit. Hence we read of
the Saviour that in the night-time he gave himself to prayer,
but in the day-time to doctrine and healing the sick. For as
love is greater than faith and hope, so we believe that those
things which come nearest — viz. such as bring assured profit
unto men — are to be preferred above all other holy functions. Hence St. Chrysostom wrote that in the whole company of virtues fasting had the last place.

CHAPTER VIII

OF THE COMMANDING OF FASTS

But since no minds, unless they be very ardent and peculiarly influenced by inspiration from above, can either pray
or fast aright and with profit, we believe that it is better, according to the example of the apostles and of the earlier and
purer Church, by holy exhortations to invite men to these
things, rather than to exhort them by precepts, especially
such as bind men under penalty of sin, as the priests that
have been of late, since the order of priests had not a little
degenerated, undertook to do. So we prefer to leave the place,
time and manner both of praying and of fasting to be determined by the Holy Ghost, without whom it is impossible
for any one either to pray or to fast aright, rather than prescribe them by fixed laws, especially such as may not be
broken without some atonement. Yet for the younger and
less perfect our preachers do not disapprove of the appointment of a fixed time and mode for praying and fasting, whereby, as by holy introductions, they may be prepared hereunto,
provided this be done without binding of the conscience. We
were brought to this opinion not only because the nature of
these actions conflicts with all ungrateful compulsion, but
especially by the consideration that neither Christ himself nor
any of his apostles have in any way mentioned such precepts.
This St. Chrysostom also testifies. " Thou seest," says he,
" that an upright life aids more than all other things. Now I
term an upright life not the labor of fasting nor the bed of
hair or ashes, but if thou despisest money no otherwise than
thou shouldst; if thou burn with love; if thou nourish the

hungry with thy bread; if thou overcome thy anger; if thou desire not vain-glory; if thou be not possessed with envy. For these are his instructions. For he does not say that his fast must be imitated, although he could have laid down those forty days, but: ' Learn of me; for I am meek and lowly of heart.' Yea, rather he says, on the contrary: ' Whatsoever is set before you, eat.' "

Moreover, we do not read that any solemn and set fast was appointed the ancient people of God, save that of one day. For the fasts which Scripture testifies were instituted by prophets and kings were evidently not set fasts, but enjoined only for their time, when certain calamities, either impending or already oppressing them, made such demands. Seeing, therefore, Scripture, as St. Paul distinctly affirms, instructs in every good work, but is ignorant of these fasts extorted by precepts, we do not see how it could be lawful for the successors of the apostles to oppress the Church with so great and so dangerous a burden. Truly Irenaeus testifies that in time past the observance of fasts in the churches was diverse and free, as is read in the *Ecclesiastical History,* book viii. chap. 14. In the same book Eusebius mentions that one Apollonius, an ecclesiastical writer, among other arguments used this also to confute the doctrine of the heretic Montanus, that he was the first that made laws for fasts. So unworthy did he deem this of those professing the sound doctrine of Christ. Thereupon Chrysostom says somewhere: "Fasting is good, but let no man be compelled." And in another place he exhorts him that is not able to fast to abstain from dainties, and affirms that this does not differ much from fasting, and that it is a strong weapon to repress the fury of the devil. Moreover, experience itself more than proves that such commandments concerning fasts have been a great hindrance to godliness.

When, therefore, we saw very evidently that the chief men in the Church beyond the authority of Scripture assumed this authority so to enjoin fasts as to bind men's consciences, we allowed consciences to be freed from these snares, but by the Scriptures, and especially Paul's writings, which with singular earnestness remove these rudiments of the world from the necks of Christians. For the saying of Paul ought not to have light weight with us: " Let no man, therefore, judge you in meat, or in drink, or in respect of an holy day, or of the new moon, or of the Sabbath days." And again: " Wherefore if ye be dead with Christ from the rudiments of the world, why,

as though living in the world, are ye subject to ordinances? "
For if St. Paul (than whom no man at any time taught Christ
more certainly) maintains that through Christ we have obtained such liberty in external things that he not only allows
no creature the right to burden those who believe in Christ,
even with those ceremonies and observances which God himself appointed, and wished in their own time to be profitable,
but also denounces as having fallen away from Christ, and
that Christ is of none effect to those who suffer themselves to
be made servant thereto, what verdict do we think should be
passed on those commandments which men have devised of
themselves, not only without any oracle, but also without any
example worthy of being followed, and which, therefore, are
unto most not only beggarly and weak, but also hurtful; not
elements — i.e. rudiments of holy discipline — but impediments of true godliness? How much more unjust will it be
for any one to assume to himself this power over the inheritance of Christ, so as to oppress it with such bondage, and how
far shall it remove us from Christ if we submit ourselves to
these things! For who does not see that the glory of Christ (to
whom we ought wholly to live, as he has wholly redeemed us
to himself and delivered us, and that, too, by his blood) is
more obscured if without his authority we bind our conscience to such laws as are the inventions of men, than to
those which have God as their author, even though they were
once in their own time to be observed? Certainly, it is less
fault to play the Jew than the heathen. But it is the custom
of the heathen to receive laws for the worship of God which
have originated without God's advice, and from man's invention only. Wherefore, if ever elsewhere, the saying of Paul is
in place: " Ye are bought with a price; be not ye the servants
of men."

CHAPTER IX

OF THE CHOICE OF MEATS

For the same cause was remitted also the selection of meats
prescribed for certain days, which St. Paul, writing to Timothy, calls a doctrine of demons. Nor is their answer firmly
grounded who maintain that these expressions were used only
against the Manichaeans, Encratites, Tatianites and Marcionites, who wholly forbad certain kinds of meats and marriage.

The apostle in this place condemned those who command " to abstain from meats which God hath created to be received," etc. Now they also who forbid the taking of certain meats on certain days nevertheless command men to abstain from meats which God created to be taken, and are akin to the doctrines of demons, as is manifest from the reason that the apostle added. For he says God has created everything that is good, and nothing is to be refused that is received with thanksgiving. He excepts no times, although no one favored frugality, temperance, and also choice chastisements of the flesh and lawful fastings, more than he did. Certainly, a Christian must observe frugality, but at all times; and the flesh must sometimes be chastised by diminishing the accustomed diet, but plainness and moderation of meats conduce to this more than does the kind. To conclude: it is meet for Christians now and then to take upon themselves a due fast; but that must not be an abstinence from certain but from all meats; nor from meats only, but from all the dainties whatsoever of this life. For what kind of fast is this, what sort of abstinence, to change only the kind of dainties (as those who are regarded today more devout than others are wont to do) , since St. Chrysostom does not regard it a fast if we continue even entirely without meats until evening, unless, together with abstinence from meats, we are continent also from those things that are hurtful, and bestow much leisure upon the pursuit of spiritual things?

CHAPTER X

THAT BY PRAYERS AND FASTINGS WE MUST NOT LOOK TO MERIT ANYTHING

Moreover, our ecclesiastics have taught that this fault must be amended with respect to prayers and fasts — viz., that men are commonly taught to seek some sort of merit and justification by these their works. For just as we are saved by grace through faith, so also are we justified. And of the works of the law, among which prayers and fastings are reckoned, Paul has written thus: "Christ is become of none effect unto you, whosoever of you are justified by the law; ye are fallen from grace. For we through the Spirit wait for the hope of righteousness by faith." Therefore we must pray, but to the end that we may receive of God, not that we may hereby confer anything upon him. We must fast, that we may the better pray and keep the flesh within duty, not that we may deserve anything for ourselves before God. This end and use alone of prayers and fasts both the Scripture and also the writings and examples of the fathers prescribe. Besides, our circumstances are such that although we could pray and fast with such devoutness, and perform all things that God has enjoined upon us, so that nothing more could be required (which hitherto no mortal has at any time performed), yet we must still confess that we are unprofitable servants. What merit, therefore, can we imagine?

CHAPTER XI

THAT ONE GOD IS TO BE WORSHIPPED THROUGH CHRIST

Another abuse concerning these things has been rejected, by which some think by fastings and prayers they can so oblige the Virgin Mary that bare God, and other saints, as, by their intercession and merits, to be delivered from all evils, both of body and of soul, and to be enriched with every kind of good things. For our preachers teach that the heavenly Father alone is to be invoked through Christ as the only Mediator, and that we are to pray of him all things, as he himself has testified that he will refuse us nothing which we ask only in faith and in the name of Christ. Since, therefore, Paul proclaims this one man Jesus Christ as Mediator between God and men, and no one can love us more or have more influence with the Father, our preachers are accustomed to urge that this one advocate and intercessor with the Father is enough. Yet they teach the duty of honoring the most holy Virgin Mary, the mother of God, and all saints, with the greatest devotion, but that this can be done only when we strive after those things that were especially pleasing to them — viz., innocency and godliness, of which they have afforded us such eminent examples. For since all godly persons love God with all the heart and soul and strength, we can in nothing please them better than together with them, as ardently as possible, both to love and to imitate God. For they do not ascribe their salvation to their own merits, much less ever think of aiding us thereby. For every one of them, when he lived here, said with Paul: " The life which I now live in the flesh I live by the faith of the Son of God, who loved me and gave himself for me. I do not make void the grace of God." Seeing, therefore, that they themselves ascribed all that they had received to the grace of God and the redemption of Jesus Christ, we can gratify them no better than if we also rely upon such assistance.

Chapter XII

OF MONKERY

For the same reason, that all our justification consists in faith in Jesus Christ, whence we derive liberty in all external things, we have permitted the bonds of monkery also among us to be relaxed. For we saw that this liberty of Christians was everywhere earnestly asserted by St. Paul, whereby every Christian, being of himself sure that all righteousness and salvation must be sought for only in Jesus Christ our Lord, and also that he must always use all things of this life as for the advantage of his neighbor, so also for the glory of God, freely permits himself and all that he has to be arbitrated and directed by the Holy Spirit of Christ, the bestower of true adoption and liberty, and also to be appointed and bestowed not only for the profit of his neighbors, but also to the glory of God. In retaining this liberty we show that we are servants of God; in betraying it to men, addicting ourselves to their inventions, we, like renegades, forsake Christ and flee to men. This we do the more wickedly as Christ has purchased us with no common price, as he has redeemed us by his blood from the deadly servitude of Satan. This is the reason why St. Paul, in writing to the Galatians, so greatly detested that they had bound themselves to the ceremonies of the law, although they were divine; yet, as we have shown above, the excuse for this was far better than to submit themselves to the yoke of those ceremonies which men devised of themselves. For he wrote, and of a truth, that those who admit the yoke of these ceremonies despise the grace of God and count the death of Christ as a thing of naught. And hence he says that he fears that he has labored for them in vain, and exhorts them to stand fast in that liberty wherewith Christ hath made them free, and not to be entangled again in the yoke of bondage.

Now, it is manifest that monkery is nothing else than a bondage of human traditions, and of such indeed as Paul has condemned by name in the passages which we have cited. For undoubtedly they who profess monkery consecrate themselves to these inventions of men in the hope of merits. Hence it is that they regard it so heinous an offence to desert these for the liberty of Christ. Therefore as our body as well as our spirit belongs to God (and that in a double respect — viz. of condition and of redemption), it cannot be lawful for Christians to make themselves slaves to this monastic servitude, much less than for temporal servants to change their masters. Besides, it cannot be denied that by such bondage and vows to live after the commandments of men a necessity, as it always used to be formerly, of transgressing God's law is occasioned, since God's law requires that, according to his ability, a Christian should be of service to the magistrate, parents, relatives and all others whom God has made nearest to him and brought to him for assistance, in what place, time or manner soever their profit demands. Then let him embrace that mode of living whereby he may chiefly provide for the affairs of his neighbors. Neither let him choose celibacy, unless it be given him for the kingdom of God — i.e. in order to promote godliness and God's glory to renounce marriage and make himself a eunuch. For the commandment of God, published by Paul, abides, which no vows of men can render void: " To avoid fornication let every man" (he excepts no one) " have his own wife, and let every woman have her own husband." For all do not receive this word concerning adopting a single life for the kingdom of heaven, as Christ himself testifies, than whom no one more exactly knew and more faithfully taught either what is the power of human nature or what is acceptable to the Father. Now, it is well known that by these monastic vows they who assume them are so bound to a certain kind of men that they think it unlawful to be obedient and dutiful any longer to either the magistrate or their parents or any men (the head of the monastery alone excepted), or to relieve them with their substance, and least of all to marry, even when they greatly burn; and hence they necessarily fall into all sorts of disgraceful ways of life.

Since, therefore, it is clear that these monastic vows render a man who is freed from the service of Christ subject not so much to the bondage of men as of Satan, and bring a necessity of transgressing God's law, as is the nature of all human traditions, and therefore conflict manifestly with God's commandments, we very properly believe that they are to be regarded void, as not only the written law, but also the law of nature, commands that a promise be disannulled if its observance hinder good morals, and much more if it hinder religion. Therefore we could not withstand any one who wished to exchange a monastic life — undoubtedly a bondage to Satan — for a Christian life. So also we could not withstand others of the ecclesiastical order who, marrying, embraced a kind of life wherefrom more advantage to their neighbors and greater purity of life could be expected than from that wherein they lived before. To conclude: neither did we undertake to prohibit from the right of marriage those among us who have persevered in the ministry of God, whatever were the vows of chastity that they had assumed. In this we were influenced by the reasons above specified, since St. Paul, the advocate of true chastity, assumes even a bishop to be a married man. For we have justly preferred this one divine law above all human laws — viz.: " To avoid fornication, let every man have his own wife." It is doubtless because this law has been rejected for so long a time that all kinds of lusts, even those that are unmentionable (with all reverence to Your Worshipful Majesty, Most Excellent Emperor), have more than overwhelmed the ecclesiastical order, so that today there is no kind of mortals more abominable than those who bear this name.

CHAPTER XIII

OF THE OFFICE, DIGNITY AND POWER
OF MINISTERS IN THE CHURCH

Concerning the ministry and the dignity of the ecclesiastical order we teach: first, that there is no power in the Church except for edification. Secondly, that we must not think otherwise of any man in this estate than Paul wished himself, Peter, Apollos and others to be esteemed — viz. as ministers of Christ and stewards of the mysteries of God, in whom it is chiefly required that each one be found faithful. These have the keys of the kingdom of heaven, the power to bind and to loose, to remit and to retain sins, yet in such a manner that they be nothing else than ministers of Christ, whose right and prerogative alone this is. For as he is the only one who can renew souls, so he it is alone who by his power opens heaven to men and frees them from sins. Both of these come to us only when it is given us to be renewed in mind and to have our citizenship in heaven. It is the part of ministers to plant and to water, neither of which are efficacious of themselves, for it is God who giveth the increase. For no one is sufficient of himself to think anything as of himself, but his sufficiency is of God, who also hath made whom he wishes ministers of the New Testament, to render men properly convinced concerning Christ truly partakers of him; not to minister the dead letter — i.e., doctrine that sounds forth only externally, without changing the heart — but that which quickens the spirit and renews the heart. Thus they are at length co-workers with God, and truly open heaven and remit sins. Hence it is that in delivering this power to the apostles Christ breathed upon them and said: " Receive ye the Holy Ghost "; and then added: " Whosoever sins ye remit, they are remitted unto them." Therefore, what constitutes fit and properly consecrated ministers of the Church, bishops, teachers and pastors, is that they have been divinely sent (" for how will they preach unless they be sent? ") — i.e., that they have received the power and mind to preach the Gospel and to feed the flock of Christ, and also the Holy Ghost who cooperates — i.e., persuades hearts. Other virtues wherewith men of this order should be furnished St. Paul recounts. Those, therefore, who are sent, anointed, and furnished in this sort have an earnest care for the Lord's flock, and labor faithfully in feeding it; and we acknowledge them in the number of bishops, elders and pastors, and as worthy of double honor, and every Christian ought with the greatest promptness obey their commands. But those who devote themselves to different things put themselves in a different place and are distinguished by a different name. Yet the life of no one should give such offence as that Christians should hesitate to embrace whatever he may declare, either from Moses or the chair of Christ; that is, either from the Law or the Gospel. But Christ's sheep are not to hear the voice of such as introduce strange things. Moreover, they who in secular things have received power as it has been ordained of God have it in such a way that he resists an ordinance of God who is unwilling to obey their direction in matters that do not conflict with God's commands.

Therefore the charge against us by some is a calumny — viz. that our preachers undermine the jurisdiction of ecclesiastics. The temporal jurisdiction which they have has never been interfered with by our preachers. And the spiritual jurisdiction, whereby they ought by the Word of God to free consciences and to faithfully feed them on Christ's Gospel, they have often invoked; so far are they from ever resisting it. But the reason why we did not endure the doctrine of certain ecclesiastics, and, according to our necessity, substituted others in their place, or, as is manifest, have retained those who have been discharged by the episcopal authorities, is that the latter clearly proclaimed the voice of our Shepherd, while the former declared that of strangers. For when the question is concerning the interests of the Gospel and sound doctrine, those who truly believe in Christ must turn themselves entirely to the Bishop of our souls, Jesus Christ, and in no way admit the voice of strangers. In this, injury can be inflicted on no one, since the words of Paul are true: " For all things are yours; whether Paul, or Apollos, or Cephas, or the world, or life, or death, or things present, or things to come; all are yours; and ye are Christ's; and Christ is God's." Certainly, if Peter and Paul, with the entire world, are hitherto ours, and we in no way theirs, but Christ's, and that just as he is his Father's — viz. that in all things that we are we live to him alone, for this end using all things as ours — no one of the ecclesiastics can justly complain of us that we are not sufficiently obedient to them, while it has been manifest that we were following the will of God. These things are taught among us concerning the office, dignity and authority of ministers of the Church, and the passages of Scripture which we have cited and others like them have influenced us to give our faith thereto.

CHAPTER XIV

OF HUMAN TRADITIONS

Furthermore, concerning the traditions of the fathers or such as the bishops and churches at this day ordain, the opinion of our men is as follows: They reckon no traditions among human traditions (such, namely, as are condemned in the Scriptures) except those that conflict with the law of God, such as bind the conscience concerning meat, drink, times and other external things, such as forbid marriage to those to whom it is necessary for an honorable life, and other things of that stamp. For such as agree with the Scripture, and were instituted for good morals and the profit of men, even though

not expressed in Scripture in words, nevertheless, since they
flow from the command of love, which orders all things most
becomingly, are justly regarded divine rather than human.
Of this sort were those of Paul — that women should not pray
in the church bareheaded or men with heads covered; that
they who are to commune should tarry one for the other; that
no one should speak with tongues in the congregation without an interpreter; that the prophets without confusion
should deliver their prophecies to be judged by those who
sit by. Many such the Church even today justly observes, and
according to occasion frames anew, which he who rejects
despises the authority, not of men, but of God, whose tradition whatsoever is profitable. For " whatever truth is said or
written is said and written by His gift who is the truth itself,"
as St. Augustine has devoutly written. But oftentimes there
is disputing about this as to what tradition is profitable, what
not — i.e. what promotes and what retards godliness. But he
who shall seek nothing of his own, and consecrates himself entirely to the public profit, shall easily see what things cor-
respond to God's law and what do not.

Furthermore, since the condition of Christians is such that
they are even helped by injuries, the Christian will refuse to
obey not even unjust laws, provided they make no godless
command, according to the saying of Christ: "Whosoever
shall compel thee to go a mile, go with him twain." Thus,
undoubtedly, the Christian ought to become all things unto
all men, so that he may endeavor both to suffer and to do
everything for the pleasure and profit of men, provided they
be not opposed to God's commands. Hence it is that every one
obeys the civil laws that do not conflict with godliness, the
more readily the more fully he is imbued with the faith of
Christ.

Chapter XV

OF THE CHURCH

We must set forth now what we think concerning the
Church and the sacraments. The Church of Christ, therefore,
which is frequently called the kingdom of heaven, is the fellowship of those who have enlisted under Christ and committed themselves entirely to his faith; with whom, nevertheless, until the end of the world, those are mingled who

feign faith in Christ, but do not truly have it. This the Lord
has taught sufficiently by the parable of the tares; also by the
net cast into the sea, which brought bad fish in with the good;
then, too, by the parable of the king who commanded all to
be invited to the marriage of his son, and afterwards the one
without the wedding-garment to be cast out. Moreover, when
the Church is proclaimed the bride of Christ, for whom he
gave himself that she might be sanctified; also when it is
called the house of God, the pillar and ground of the truth,
Mount Zion, the city of the living God, the heavenly Jerusalem, the Church of the first-born who are written in heaven,
— these encomiums pertain only to those who have truly obtained a place among the children of God because they
firmly believe in Christ. Since in these the Saviour truly
reigns, they are properly called this Church and the communion — i.e. society — of saints, as the term " Church " is
explained in the Apostles' Creed. This the Holy Ghost rules,
from this Christ is never absent, but he sanctifies it to present
it at length to himself blameless, not having spot or wrinkle.
This, finally, he that will not hear is to be regarded a heathen
and a publican.

Although that whereby it is entitled to be called the Church
of Christ — namely, faith in Christ — cannot be seen, yet it
can be seen and plainly known from its fruits. Of these fruits
the chief are a courageous confession of the truth, a true love
tendered to all, and a brave contempt of all things for Christ.
These undoubtedly cannot be absent where the Gospel and
its sacraments are purely administered.

Besides, since it is the Church and kingdom of God, and
for this reason all things must be done in the best order, it
has various offices of ministers. For it is a body compacted of
various members, whereof each has his own work. While they
perform in good faith their ministry, laboring earnestly in
word and doctrine, they truly represent the Church, so that
he who hears them is correctly said to hear the Church.

But with what spirit they should be moved and with what
authority endowed we have declared above and given account
when we explained our faith concerning the ministry of the
Church. For they who teach what conflicts with Christ's commands cannot represent the Church of Christ; nevertheless,
it may occur, and actually does occur frequently, that the
wicked both prophesy in Christ's name and pass judgment in
the Church. But those who propose what differs from Christ's

doctrines, even though they be within the Church, nevertheless, because preoccupied with error, they do not proclaim
the voice of the Shepherd, undoubtedly cannot represent the
Church, the bride of Christ. Therefore they are not to be
heard in his name, since Christ's sheep follow not the voice of
a stranger.

These things our theologians teach of the Church, derived
from the passages cited and similar passages.

CHAPTER XVI

OF THE SACRAMENTS

Furthermore, since the Church lives here in the flesh, even
though not according to the flesh, it has pleased the Lord to
teach, admonish and exhort it also by the outward Word; and
that this might be done the more conveniently he wished his
people to maintain an external society among themselves. For
this reason he has also given to them sacred symbols, which
we call sacraments. Among these, Baptism and the Lord's
Supper are the chief. These we believe were called sacraments by the ancients, not only because they are visible signs
of invisible grace (to use the words of St. Augustine), but also
because in them a profession of faith, as it were, is made.

CHAPTER XVII

OF BAPTISM

Of Baptism, therefore, we confess that which Scripture in
various places declares of it: that by it we are buried into
Christ's death, are united into one body and put on Christ;
that it is the washing of regeneration, that it washes away sins
and saves us. All this we understand as St. Peter has interpreted when he says: "The like figure whereunto even
baptism doth also now save us, not the putting away of the
filth of the flesh, but the answer of a good conscience toward
God." For without faith it is impossible to please God, and we
are saved by grace, not by our works. But since Baptism is
the sacrament of the covenant that God makes with those
who are his, promising to be their God and Protector, as well
as of their seed, and to have them as his people, and finally,
since it is a symbol of renewing through the Spirit, which oc-

curs through Christ, our theologians teach that it is to be given infants also, no less than formerly under Moses they were circumcised. For we are indeed the children of Abraham. Therefore no less to us than to those of old pertains the promise: I will be thy God and the God of thy seed.

CHAPTER XVIII

OF THE EUCHARIST

Concerning this venerable sacrament of the body and blood of Christ, all that the evangelists, Paul and the holy fathers, have left in writing, our men, in the best faith, teach, commend and inculcate. And hence with singular zeal they always publish this goodness of Christ to his people, whereby no less today than at that last Supper, to all those who sincerely have given their names among his disciples and receive this Supper according to his institution, he deigns to give his true body and true blood to be truly eaten and drunk for the food and drink of souls, for their nourishment unto life eternal, so that now he may live and abide in them, and they in him, to be raised up by him at the last day to new and immortal life, according to his words of eternal truth: " Take, eat; this is my body," etc.; " drink ye all of it; for this is my blood," etc. Now, our ecclesiastics with especial diligence withdraw the minds of our people both from all contention and from all superfluous and curious inquiry to that which is alone profitable, and which was alone regarded by Christ our Saviour — namely, that, fed upon him, we may live in and through him a life pleasing to God, holy, and therefore eternal and blessed, and that we who partake of one bread in the Holy Supper may be among ourselves one bread and one body. Hence indeed it occurs that the divine sacraments, the Most Holy Supper of Christ, are administered and received among us very religiously and with singular reverence. From these things, which are truly in this manner, Thy Most Worshipful Majesty, Most Clement Emperor, doth know how falsely our adversaries proclaim that our men change Christ's words and do them violence by human glosses; that nothing save mere bread and mere wine is administered in our Suppers; and thus that among us the Lord's Supper has been despised and rejected. For with the greatest earnestness our men always teach and exhort that every man with simple faith embrace these words of the Lord, rejecting all devices and false glosses of men, and removing all wavering, apply his mind to their true meaning, and finally, with as great devotion as possible, receive these sacraments for the quickening nourishment of their souls and the grateful remembrance of so great a benefit; as is generally done now among us more frequently and devoutly than heretofore. Moreover, our ecclesiastics have always hitherto offered themselves, as they do today also, with all modesty and truth, in order to render an account of their faith and doctrine concerning all that they believe and teach touching this sacrament, as well as other things; and that not only to Thy Worshipful Majesty, but also to every one who demands it.

CHAPTER XIX

THE MASS

Furthermore, since Christ has instituted his Supper in this manner, which afterwards began to be called the mass — to wit, that therein the faithful, being fed with his body and blood unto life eternal, should show forth his death, whereby they are redeemed — our ecclesiastics, by this means giving thanks and commending this salvation to others also, could not do otherwise than condemn, on the one hand, the general neglect of these things, and, on the other, the presumption of the celebrants of masses in offering Christ for the living and the dead, and in making the mass a work whereby almost alone the favor of God and salvation are obtained, without regard to what men either believe or live. Whence that shameful and twice and thrice impious buying and selling of this sacrament crept in, and the result was that today nothing is more a means of gain than the mass. Therefore they rejected private masses, because the Lord commanded this sacrament to his disciples to be used in common. Hence Paul also commands the Corinthians to wait for one another when going to the Holy Supper, and denies that they celebrate the Lord's Supper when each one takes his own supper while they are eating. Moreover, their boast that they offer up Christ as a victim our men condemn, because the Epistle to the Hebrews plainly testifies that as men once die, so Christ was once offered to take away the sins of many, and can no more be offered again than die again; and on this account, as a perfect sacrifice for our sins, he sits for ever at the right hand of God, expecting what remains, until his enemies as a footstool may be placed beneath his feet. " For by one offering he hath perfected for ever them that are sanctified."

But their making of the mass a good work, whereby something is obtained of God, our preachers have taught conflicts with the uniform declaration of Scripture that we are justified and receive God's favor by the Spirit of Christ and through faith, concerning which Scriptural testimonies have been cited above. So, too, our preachers have showed that the not commending in the mass the death of the Lord to the people is contrary to the command of Christ, to receive these sacraments in commemoration of himself, and to that of Paul, that thereby Christ's death is set forth until he come. And since many, without any desire of godliness, commonly celebrate the mass only for the purpose of nourishing the body, our preachers have shown that this is so execrable to God that even though the mass were in itself no hindrance to godliness, yet it should justly and by God's command be abolished. This is clear from Isaiah alone. For our God is spirit and truth, and therefore does not allow himself to be worshipped save in spirit and truth. Moreover, how grievous to the Lord is this indecorous huckstering introduced with reference to these sacraments they have also taught should be conjectured from the fact that Christ so severely and altogether against his accustomed manner, taking to himself external vengeance, cast out of the temple those buying and selling, although they seemed to be doing business only to further sacrifices that were made according to law.

Therefore, since the rite of the mass, as commonly celebrated, conflicts in so many ways with the Scripture of God, just as also it is diverse in many ways from that which the holy fathers observed, it has been very severely condemned among us from the pulpit, and by the Word of God been made so detestable that many have abandoned it of their own accord, and others when it was abrogated by authority of the magistrate. This we have allowed for no other reason than because throughout the whole of Scripture the Spirit of God detests nothing so, and commands nothing so earnestly to be taken away, as a feigned and false worship of himself. Now, no one who is influenced in any way by religion is ignorant what an inevitable necessity is laid upon one who fears God when he is persuaded that God requires anything of him. For any one could easily foresee how many would endure that anything in so holy a rite as the mass should be changed by us; neither were there any who would not have preferred not only not to offend Thy Worshipful Majesty, but even any prince of the lowest rank. But since they did not doubt that by the common rite of the mass God was greatly provoked, and his glory, for which even life ought to be laid down, was obscured, they could not do otherwise than remove it, lest by their connivance they should render themselves liable for diminishing God's glory. Truly, if God is to be loved and worshipped above all, godly men must tolerate nothing less than what he abominates.

That this one cause has constrained us to change certain matters concerning these things we call Him to witness from whom no secret is hid.

CHAPTER XX

OF CONFESSION

Since, indeed, also the confession of sins which arises from godliness can be rendered by no man whom his repentance and true grief of mind do not impel thereto, it cannot be extorted by any precept. Wherefore neither Christ himself nor the apostles would command it. For this cause, therefore, our ecclesiastics exhort men to confess their sins, and therewith show its fruit — viz. that a man should privately seek consolation, advice, doctrine and instruction of one who is a Christian and wise — yet by commandments urge it upon no one, but affirm that such commandments injure godliness. For the institution of confessing sins to a priest has driven innumerable souls into grievous despair, and is subject to so many other faults that it ought long since to have been abrogated; and doubtless would have been abrogated if the presidents of churches in the most recent times had glowed with the same zeal for removing stumbling-blocks as in former times Nestorius, bishop of Constantinople, who abolished secret confession in his church, because a woman of the nobility, who went often to church as though to perform works of penance, was found to have lain frequently with a deacon. Undoubtedly innumerable sins of such kind were committed in many places. Besides, the pontifical laws require that the hearer and judge of confession should be of such character, so holy, learned, wise and merciful, that one could scarcely determine to whom to confess among those who are commonly appointed to hear confessions. Moreover, the Schoolmen also think that it is better to confess sins to a layman than to a priest as cannot be expected to afford edification. The sum of all is, that that confession which sound repentance and true grief of mind for sins does not produce brings more injury than good. Since, therefore, God alone can give repentance and true sorrow for our sins, nothing salutary in this matter can be accomplished by precepts, as experience itself has made too manifest.

CHAPTER XXI

OF THE CHANTS AND PRAYERS
OF ECCLESIASTICS

For the same reason — viz. that there should be no conniving at an offence to God, which might occur under pretext of his service, than which nothing can offend him more — our men have condemned most things in the chants and prayers of ecclesiastics. For it is clearly manifest that these have degenerated from the first institution of the fathers, since no one who has examined the writings of the ancients is ignorant that the custom was current among them to earnestly repeat and also expound a few psalms in connection with a chapter of Scripture; while now many of the psalms are chanted, but almost without thinking, and of the reading of Scripture only the beginnings of the chapters remain, and innumerable things are assumed one after another that serve for superstition rather than for godliness. First, therefore, our ministers have denounced the minglings with holy prayers and chants of not a few things that are contrary to the Scriptures, as they ascribe to some saints what pertains to Christ alone — namely, to free from sins and other evils — and not so much to obtain the favor of God and every kind of blessings by entreaty as to bestow it as a gift. Secondly, that they are increased so infinitely that they cannot be chanted or recited with an attentive mind. Lastly, that these are also made meritorious works, and are wont to be sold for no small price; to say nothing meanwhile of what is contrary to the express command of the Holy Ghost — viz. that all things are said and chanted in such a tongue as the people not only do not understand, but sometimes not even those who obtain their livelihood by these chants and prayers.

CHAPTER XXII

OF STATUES AND IMAGES

Finally, against statues and images our preachers have applied the holy oracles, chiefly because they began to be worshipped and adored openly, and vain expenditure was devoted to them that was due the hungry, thirsty and naked Christ; and lastly, because by their worship and the expenditure they required (both conflicting with God's word) they seek merits with God. Against this religious error they have interposed also the authority of the ancient Church, which undoubtedly abominated the sight of any image, whether painted or graven, in the church, as the deed of Epiphanius, bishop of Salamis in Cyprus, that he reports of himself, abundantly proves. For when he saw on a curtain in a certain church a painting of Christ or some saint (for he writes that he does not exactly remember), he was inflamed with such indignation because he saw an image of a man hanging in the church, contrary to the authority of the Scriptures and to our faith and religion, that he at once tore the curtain and ordered that the corpse of a poor man be wrapped therein. The letter in which this man of God narrates this of himself, writing to John, bishop of Jerusalem, St. Jerome has translated as genuine into the Latin, nor has he uttered a word in the least disapproving this judgment of Epiphanius concerning images. From this it is clearly inferred that neither St. Jerome himself nor the bishop of Jerusalem to whom he wrote thought otherwise concerning images. For the declaration that is commonly made that by statues and images the more rude are taught and instructed will not suffice to prove that they should be carried, especially where they are adored by the populace. God's ancient people were of a ruder class, so that it was needful to instruct them by numerous ceremonies; nevertheless, God did not think that images were of such value to teach and instruct the more rude, since he forbad them among the very chief things. If the answer be made that God forbad such images as were worshipped, it immediately follows that when all have begun to adore them they should be universally removed from the churches, on account of the offence which they occasion. For all things in the

Church should be directed to edification, much less should anything be tolerated which may give occasion for ruin and can contribute no advantage. Besides, as is generally objected concerning teaching, St. Athanasius, refuting the heathen defending their idols by this argument, thus rejects it: " Let them say, I ask, in what way God is known through images? Whether through the matter of which they consist or the form impressed upon the matter? If on account of the matter, what necessity now of form, since God has shone forth in the entire matter already, even before these were formed, since all things bear witness to his glory? Moreover, if the image that is produced is the cause of the divine knowledge, what need now of the picture and other material, for is not God known rather through those very animals whereof images are made? For God's glory would indeed be more clearly seen through animated beings, rational and irrational, than be manifested through the inanimate and motionless. When, therefore, for the purpose of understanding God, you carve or mould images, you make what is in no way worthy of him." Thus far Athanasius. Lactantius has also said much in opposition to this pretext, *Divine Institutions*, book ii. For with him who can be taught with profit, in addition to the word of exhortation, the living and true works of God themselves are of far more service than the vain images that men prepare. Since in so many passages of Scripture God has most fully testified that this is his opinion concerning images, it will not be proper for us men to seek profit from objects the peril of which God has commanded us to shun, especially when we ourselves have learned by experience how greatly they hinder godliness.

Our men also confess that in itself the use of images is free, but, free as it may be, the Christian must consider what is expedient, what edifies, and should use images in such place and manner as not to present a stumbling-block to any. For Paul was prepared to have both meat and wine prohibited him for his entire life if he knew that either in any way injured the welfare of others.

Chapter XXIII

OF MAGISTRATES

We have above set forth that our ecclesiastics have assigned a place among good works of the first rank to the obedience which is rendered magistrates, and that they teach that every one ought the more diligently to adapt himself to the public laws to the degree that he is a more sincere Christian and richer in faith. They accordingly teach that to exercise the office of magistrate is the most sacred function that can be divinely given. Hence it has come to pass that they who exercise public power are called in the Scriptures *gods*. For when they discharge their duty aright and in order the people prosper both in doctrine and in life, because God is wont so to control our affairs that in great part both the welfare and the destruction of subjects depend upon those who are governors. Therefore none exercise the duties of magistrate more worthily than they who of all are the most Christian and holy; whence, beyond all doubt, it happened that bishops and other ecclesiastical men were formerly promoted by most godly emperors and kings to the external government of affairs. In this matter, although they were religious and wise, there was this one fault — viz., that they were not able to render what was needful for the proper administration of both offices, and they had to fail, either in their duty to the churches in ruling them by the Word, or to the state in governing it with authority.

Conclusion

These are the chief points, most invincible and devout Emperor, wherein our men have somewhat receded from the common doctrine of ecclesiastics, being forced thereto by the authority alone of the Scriptures, which is justly to be preferred above all other traditions. These things being set forth as could be done by us in such short time, we wish to offer Thy Sacred Majesty, in order to give an account of our faith to thee, whom next to God we chiefly honor and reverence, and also to show how necessary it is speedily and earnestly to consult of a way and manner whereby a matter of so great importance may be known, weighed and discussed as in the first place respect for God requires, in whose highest interest we must act with fear and trembling; and in the second place, is worthy of Thy Holy Majesty, so greatly renowned for clemency and religion; and finally, the very means to attain the peace at which Thy Majesty aims demands — that certain and firm peace which, when there is dissent concerning faith and religion, cannot be acquired otherwise than when, before all other things, men's minds are plainly instructed concerning the truth.

Moreover, it might perhaps seem needless for us to mention so many things concerning these matters, since the most famous princes, the Elector of Saxony and others, have very fully and thoroughly set forth the matters of present controversy in our holy religion. But because Thy Worshipful Majesty has required that all they who have any interest in this business declare to him their opinion concerning religion, we also thought it our duty to confess to Thy Majesty what is taught among us. Although the subject is so vast and embraces so many things that even what we have declared on both sides is too meagre and brief than to permit the hope of the determination of anything certain in these controversies, and such as may be approved, not of all, but at least of a good part of Christian people, so small in truth is the number of those who subscribe to the truth. Since, therefore, this is a matter of such vast importance, and is so varied and manifold, and cannot be decided profitably unless it be well known and examined by many, we beseech Thy Sacred Majesty, and most humbly request, by God and our Saviour, whose glory undoubtedly thou dost chiefly seek, to cause as speedily as possible a general, free and truly Christian council to be summoned, which hitherto has seemed so necessary both to Thy Sacred Majesty and other princes for pacifying the affairs of the Church, that in almost all the assemblies of the Empire which were held since the beginning of this dissent concerning religion both Thy Sacred Majesty's commissioners and other princes of the Empire publicly testified that by no other way in these matters could that which is profitable be accomplished. Therefore, at the last assembly held at Spires Thy Sacred Majesty gave occasion to hope that the Roman Pontiff would not prevent the speedy summoning of such a council.

But if the opportunity for a general council cannot in time be obtained, yet at least Thy Sacred Majesty might appoint a provincial assembly of the doctors of every degree and estate, whereunto all whom it is expedient to be present may freely and safely resort, every man may be heard, and all things may be weighed and judged by such men, whom it is certain, being endowed with the fear of God, would prefer nothing to his glory. For it is not unknown with what dignity and diligence in times past both emperors and bishops conducted themselves in deciding controversies of faith, which were nevertheless frequently of much less importance than those that are now agitating Germany; so that they thought it worth while to assemble them to examine the same things the second and third time. Now he that shall consider how things are at present cannot doubt but that at this day there is need of greater fidelity, gravity, meekness and skill than ever before, in order that the religion of Christ may be restored to its own place. For if the truth is with us, as we undoubtedly believe, how much time and labor, pray, is requisite that they also may know it without whose consent, or allowance at least, a solid peace cannot be prepared! But if we err, from which we have no doubt that we are far distant, the matter again will require no slothful diligence or short time that so many thousand men be called back again to the way. This diligence and time it will not be so unbecoming for Thy Majesty to bestow, as it is meet for thee to express towards us the mind of Him in whose stead thou dost govern — viz., that of Jesus Christ, the Saviour of us all. Since he came for the purpose of seeking and saving what had perished, there is no reason why Thy Worshipful Majesty, even though thou dost believe without doubt that we have fallen from the truth, should not refuse to leave the ninety-and-nine in the wilderness, and to seek for the hundredth and bring it back into the sheepfold of Christ — i.e. to prefer this business to all other matters, that the meaning of Christ in every one of these things which are at present in controversy may from the Scriptures be clearly and definitely explained to us, though we are but few and of an humble class. We certainly will be teachable, and will lay aside all obstinacy, provided we be permitted to hear the voice of our Shepherd Jesus Christ, and all things be supported by the Scriptures, that teach whatever is good. For if it should so occur that, the care of teaching us being rejected, compendious forms of edicts be sought (which while the matter is in the hands of Thy Worshipful Majesty we in no way fear), it cannot be said into what straits numberless thousands of men would be brought — viz. those who, being persuaded that God is chiefly to be heard, and then that the dogmas that follow are supported upon the undoubted oracles of God, are always appalled by such sayings of the Saviour as: " Fear not them which kill the body "; " He that loseth his life shall find it "; " If any one hate not his father and mother, etc., yea, and his own life also, he cannot be my disciple "; ' Whosoever shall be ashamed of me in this adulterous and sinful generation, of him also shall I be ashamed before my Father and his angels "; and the like.

Moved, indeed, by such thunderbolts, many men would cheerfully suffer every extremity. Many, too, the fear of death would indeed delay, yet only for an opportunity, if they be dealt with in this matter with power before doctrine, with violence before their error is indicated to them. For of what value a sound persuasion concerning religion is, and how it maketh men to take no account of not only of property, but also of life, has been seen sufficiently, and even more than sufficiently, in many during the last ten years, to say nothing of former generations, who have suffered willingly not only exile and proscription, but even bonds, torture and death itself, rather than suffer themselves to be withdrawn from the judgment they had conceived, and which they believed to be true. If now, when there is a disagreement concerning the matters of less importance, few are to be found whom one can bring to unfeigned concord unless persuaded of the law or equity of their conditions, how when the controversy is concerning religion are we to expect true peace and undoubted tranquillity of affairs, such as Thy Worshipful Majesty is seeking to establish, unless on both sides that be agreed upon which God approves and which harmonizes with the Scriptures? For as religion, by right and by the custom of nations, is preferred to all other things, so no controversy of mortals with one another could be more vehement and severe than that which is undertaken for altars and divinities. But since Thy Worshipful Majesty has used such inexpressible clemency towards enemies, and those too, who to be silent of other things, have omitted no kind of hostility, we have justly conceived the hope that thou wilt so moderate things in this matter also that in regard to us thou mayst seem to have sought much more the praise of goodness and kindness, since we have always been most desirous of thy welfare and honor, as we have actually testified and desire sincerely to testify further. For in this cause we have dealt so moderately as to all things that we have sufficiently declared to all good men that it has never been our purpose to hurt any one, or to provide for our advantage at the expense of that of others. Indeed, we have exposed ourselves to dangers and have made great outlays on this account; but we have not even the small-

est gain, with the one exception that, being better instructed
concerning the goodness of God tendered through Christ, we
have begun, by God's grace, to hope better of things to come.
This is justly of such importance to us that we do not think
that we have either done or suffered anything as yet that is
worthy of it, since it is inestimable and should be preferred
to all things that either heaven or earth contains. So far have
we been from longing for the riches of ecclesiastics that when
the husbandmen were in an uproar we defended these resources, in the interests of the ecclesiastics, with the greatest
cost and danger. The Gospel of our Lord Jesus Christ (may
he so love us!) is the only thing that urges us and has induced us to do all those things which we seem to have introduced as innovations.

Let Thy Worshipful Majesty therefore prefer to follow the
examples of the most mighty and truly happy emperors,
Constantine, Jovinian, Theodosius and the like, who by doctrine taught daily with all meekness by most holy and vigilant bishops, and also by councils lawfully assembled, and by
a serious discussion of all things dealt with the erring and
tried all means to bring them back into the way before they
would determine anything against them more severe, than
to follow the example of those who, it is certain, had such
counsellors as were most unlike those ancient and truly holy
fathers, and attained a result in no way corresponding to the
godliness of the latter. Hence let not Thy Worshipful Majesty
be withdrawn to this — viz., that most matters now in controversy were decided long ago, chiefly in the Council of
Constance, especially since it may be seen of innumerable
decrees of former councils that are not less holy than necessary that not the least point is observed by our ecclesiastics,
and that all things among them have so degenerated that every
one furnished with even ordinary sense must exclaim that
there is need of a council for the restoration of religion and
holiness of the ecclesiastical order. But if that which was decreed at Constance is so pleasing to them, how does it happen
that meantime that which was then decreed has in no way
been obtained — viz. that every tenth year a Christian council be held? For in this way much godliness and faith might
either be recovered or preserved.

For who does not confess that as often as a disease breaks
out afresh a remedy must be applied, and that those who
really have the truth think it much both that good men

should teach it and defend it against the wicked where any fruit of this is to be hoped for? Now, when so many thousands are miserably perplexed with the doctrines of our religion, who can deny that there is hope of most plentiful fruit? And such as has justly impelled all whom the Spirit of Christ rules that, forsaking all other things and esteeming no labor or expense too great, they devote themselves with all their powers to this one thing — viz. that Christ's doctrine, the parent of all righteousness and salvation, may be properly considered, may be purged of all errors, and may be offered in its native form to all who love godliness and the true worship of God, whereby a holy and eternally firm peace and the true tranquillity of all things may be restored and confirmed to the sheep of Christ, for whom he has shed his blood, who are now so excessively harassed? As we have said, this peace can be restored and confirmed to them in no other way. For, while in other things they must sometimes yield, in a matter of godliness they must so cling to God's words and rely upon them that if they had a thousand lives they should offer them to be tortured to death, rather than yield a jot or tittle which they are persuaded has been divinely commanded. If, now, only one soul is of more value than the whole world, what should be done for the salvation of so many myriads? Such hope indeed invites us, from the consideration that those who are accused to Thy Worshipful Majesty of error pray nothing else than that they be taught, and have applied themselves entirely to the Holy Scriptures, which are abundantly sufficient to confute every error, as well as from the fact that Christ our Saviour has so clearly promised that where two or three are gathered together in his name he will be in their midst, and will grant them whatever they have agreed upon.

These things, Most Godly Emperor, we here mention for no other reason than to show our obedience to thy wish that we should explain our opinion concerning the reformation of religion. For otherwise we have good hope that Thy Worshipful Majesty hast well considered and sees sufficiently what necessity urges us thereto, what fruit it invites, and finally how worthy a thing this is for Thy Worshipful Majesty, who is so much praised for religion and clemency, that, all the men in highest reputation for learning and godliness being assembled, the effort be made to learn what should be thought of each doctirne just now controverted, and then an explanation be made by suitable ministers of Christ, with all

meekness and fidelity, to those who are believed to be de-
tained in errors. Nevertheless, as it is at the same time to be
feared that there are not those wanting who are endeavoring
to draw Thy Worshipful Majesty otherwise, it has seemed
good to us to reply to them in this sort, as though to Thy
Worshipful Majesty himself; and all other things we have
here set forth and confessed for no other purpose than, on
our part, to maintain the glory of Christ Jesus our God, and
to obey Thy Imperial Majesty, as is right, — we beg thee, according to thy most excellent clemency, for which thou art
renowned, to take and interpret in good part, and to deign
to regard us among those who truly from the heart desire to
show ourselves not less obedient and submissive with the
greatest subjection than our illustrious ancestors, being ready
in this cause, so far as it is lawful, to surrender both property
and our lives. The King of kings, Jesus Christ, grant Thy
Worshipful Majesty in this matter, as well as in others, to do
all things for his glory, and long preserve and happily advance thee in both health and prosperity, to the welfare of
the entire Christian government! AMEN.

4

The First Confession of Basel, 1534

INTRODUCTION

Although the tenets of the Reformation were first preached in Basel by Wolfgang Capito, Caspar Hedio, and Wilhelm Röublin, the man chiefly responsible for establishing the Reformation in that city was the learned and modest John Oecolampadius. Born at Weinsberg in 1482, he was educated at Heilbronn, Bologna, Heidelberg, and Tübingen, and in 1522 assumed permanent residence in Basel as pastor of St. Martin's Church and as a lecturer in theology. The Reformation was formally established February 9, 1529, with the abolition of the Mass, the destruction of images, and the closing of convents. On April 1 the Council ratified a church order which was essentially the work of Oecolampadius and which introduced radical changes in doctrine, worship, and discipline. Oecolampadius died November 24, 1531, a few weeks after his friend Zwingli. In his last address to the Synod of Basel, September 26, he added a brief Confession of Faith and a paraphrase of the Apostles' Creed. It is believed that this was a sort of first draft of the First Confession of Basel which was revised by Oecolampadius' successor, Oswald Myconius, in 1532 and which was issued by the Council with a preface by the burgomaster, Adelberg Meyer, January 21, 1534.

The Confession is a simple statement of the evangelical faith in twelve short articles. It is directed against two fronts: the teachings of Roman Catholicism and the Anabaptists. Although it lacks an article dealing with the doctrine of Holy Scripture, it concludes with the following sentence: " Finally, we desire to submit this our confession to the judgment of the divine Biblical Scriptures. And should we be informed of a better one, we have thereby expressed our readiness to be willing at any time to obey God and His holy Word with great thanksgiving."

A few years after the citizens of Basel had subscribed to the Confession under oath, it was adopted and issued by the city of Mühlhausen; hence it has also been known as the *Confessio Mühlhusana*. Until 1826 it was read each year from the pulpits in Basel on the Wednesday of Holy Week, and until 1872 all ministers were required to subscribe to it.

Six hundred copies of the Confession were printed in the Swiss dialect when it was first promulgated, and two months later two hundred more copies were published. A Latin edition appeared in 1561 and 1581, which was reproduced in the *Corpus et syntagma confessionum fidei* of 1612. A better Latin edition was issued in 1647 and this is to be found in Niemeyer's *Collectio confessionum*. Beck and Böckel give a German translation in their collections. The present English translation has been made from the text in the Swiss dialect in Niemeyer.

Literature: K. R. Hagenbach, *Kritische Geschichte der Entstehung u. der Schicksale der ersten Basler Confession* (Basel, 1827; title ed., 1828) ; J. J. Herzog, *Leben Joh. Oekolampads u. die Reformation der Kirche von Basel*, 2 vols. (Basel, 1843) ; K. R. Hagenbach, *Leben Oekolampads und Myconius* (Elberfeld, 1859) ; Schaff, *Creeds of Christendom*, Vol. III, 4th ed. (1905) ; E. F. K. Müller, *Die Bekenntnisschriften der reformierten Kirche* (Leipzig, 1903) ; E. Staehelin, *Das Buch der Basler Reformation* (1929) ; M. Geiger, *Die Basler Kirche u. Theologie* (1952) .

The First Confession of Basel, 1534

I. CONCERNING GOD

We believe in God the Father, God the Son, God the Holy Spirit, one holy, divine Trinity, three Persons and one single, eternal, almighty God, in essence and substance, and not three gods. We also believe that God has created all things by His eternal Word, that is, by His only-begotten Son, and preserves and strengthens all things by His Spirit, that is, by His power; and therefore, God sustains and governs all things as He created them.[1]

Hence we confess that before He created the world God elected all those upon whom He willed to bestow the inheritance of eternal salvation.[2]

II. CONCERNING MAN

We confess that in the beginning God made man faultless in the likeness of righteousness and holiness. But he willfully fell into sin. Through this fall the whole human race was corrupted and made subject to damnation. Moreover, our nature was enfeebled and became so inclined to sin that, unless it is restored by the Spirit of God, man neither does nor wants to do anything good of himself.[3]

III. GOD'S CARE FOR US

Although man through the fall became subject to damnation and became God's enemy, yet God never ceased to care

---

[1] The universal faith. This is proved by the whole Scriptures of the Old and New Testaments in many passages. Gen. 1:1 ff.; John 1:1-3; I Chron. 29:11-12; Acts 2:23.

[2] Rom. 8:28 ff.; 9:6 ff.; 11:5 ff.; Eph. 1:4 ff.

[3] Gen. 1:26 f.; Eph. 4:24; Gen. 3:6; 5:3; Rom. 5:12, 15 ff.; I Cor. 15:21 f.; Eph. 2:1 ff.; Gen. 6:5; 8:21; John 3:3 ff.; Rom. 3:10 ff., 23; Ps. 142 (143): 2, 10; Eph. 2:1 ff.

for the human race. Witnesses to this are the patriarchs, the promises before and after the flood, the law given by God through Moses, and the holy prophets.[4]

IV. Concerning Christ, True God and True Man

We firmly believe and confess that Christ was given to us by the Father at the appointed time according to the promises of God, and that the eternal, divine Word became flesh, that is, the Son of God, united with human nature in one person, became our brother in order that we might become heirs of God through Him.[5]

Concerning this Jesus Christ, we believe that He was conceived by the Holy Spirit, born of the pure, undefiled Virgin Mary, suffered under Pontius Pilate, was crucified and died for our sins; and thus by offering up Himself He made satisfaction to God for our sins and the sins of all believers and reconciled us to God, our heavenly Father, and by His death has conquered and overcome the world, death and hell. Moreover, we believe that according to the flesh He was buried, descended into hell, on the third day rose from the dead, and when He had sufficiently shown himself, He ascended into heaven with body and soul where He sits at the right hand of God in the glory of God His heavenly Father, whence He will come to judge the living and the dead. Furthermore, as He had promised He sent to His disciples His Holy Spirit, in whom we believe even as we believe in the Father and the Son.[6]

V. Concerning the Church

We believe one holy, Christian Church, the fellowship of the saints, the spiritual assembly of believers which is holy and the one bride of Christ, and in which all are citizens who truly confess that Jesus is the Christ, the Lamb of God who takes away the sin of the world, and who also confirm such faith by works of love.[7]

---

[4] Rom. 5:16 ff.; Gen. 3:15; 21:15; 26:3, 4, 24; 28:13 ff.

[5] Matt. 1:20 ff.; Luke 2:10 ff.; John 1:14; Phil. 2:6-7. We have one Father, namely, God through Christ. Rom. 6:8 f.; Rom. 8:15 ff.; Heb. 2:10 f.

[6] Matt. 1:18 ff.; Luke 1:35; 2:7. All the Evangelists attest it. Matt. 20:28; 26:28; Rom. 5:6 ff.; I Cor. 15:3 f.; I Peter 2:24; Heb. 9:14 f.; 26, 28; 10:10, 12, 14; Rom. 6:10; I Peter 3:18; John 16:11, 33; Phil. 2:9 ff.; Col. 2:14 f.; I Cor. 15:4 ff., 14; Mark 16:19; Luke 24:51; Acts 1:9 ff.; Matt. 26:64; Eph. 1:20 ff.; Col. 3:1; Heb. 1:13; 10:12; 12:2; Acts 2:1 ff.

[7] Matt. 16:18; Eph. 1:22 f.; 5:25 ff.; John 3:29; II Cor. 11:2; Eph. 2:19 f.; Heb. 12:22 f.; John 1:29; Gal. 5:6.

In this Church one and the same sacrament is used, namely, Baptism upon entering the Church, and in due time in later life the Lord's Supper, as a testimony to faith and brotherly love as was promised in Baptism.[8]

This Christian Church endeavors to keep the bonds of peace and love in unity, and therefore it has no fellowship with sects and the rules of religious orders which are determined to distinguish between days, food, clothing, and ecclesiastical pageantry.[9]

VI. Concerning Our Lord's Supper

We confess that the Lord Jesus instituted His holy Supper for the observance of His holy passion with thanksgiving, to proclaim His death, and also to attest Christian love and unity with true faith.[10]

And just as in Baptism, in which the washing away of sins is offered to us by the ministers of the Church but can only be effected by the Father, Son and Holy Spirit, water remains truly water, so also does the bread and wine remain bread and wine in the Lord's Supper, in which the true body and blood of Christ is portrayed and offered to us with the bread and wine of the Lord, together with the words of institution.[11]

We firmly believe, however, that Christ Himself is the food of a believing soul unto eternal life, and that our souls are nourished through true faith in the crucified Christ with the flesh and blood of Christ,[12] and that we, as members of His body of which He is our only Head, live in Him and He in us, so that on the Day of Judgment we may be raised by Him and in Him to eternal joy and blessedness. Therefore we confess this: that Christ is present in His holy Supper for all who truly believe.[13]

---

[8] Matt. 3:11; 28:19; Acts 2:41 f.; 16:15, 33; Col. 2:12; Matt. 26: 26 ff.; 14:22 ff.; Luke 22:19 f.; I Cor. 11:23 ff.

[9] Rom. 12:9 f.; John 15:12, 17; I John 3:11, 14, 16, 23; 4:7 f.; 20 f.

[10] Luke 22:19; I Cor. 11:23 ff.; 10:16 f.

[11] A powerful parable against the enemies of truth. John 6:35 ff. It is indeed a spiritual food and hence it has to be enjoyed by a believing soul.

[12] That is, the souls are satisfied, made strong and robust, contented and at peace, cheerful and a match for anything, just as the body is nourished by bodily food. A man becomes a spiritual member of the spiritual body of Christ. John 11:25 f.; Eph. 1:22 f.; 4:15; 5:23; Col. 1:18 f.

[13] Sacramentally and through the contemplation of faith which raises a man in his thoughts to heaven, but does not draw Christ down in his human nature from the right hand of God.

However, we do not enclose in the bread and wine of the
Lord the natural, true and essential body of Christ who was
born of the pure Virgin Mary, suffered for us and has
ascended into heaven.[14] Consequently we do not adore Christ
in these signs of bread and wine which we commonly call
sacraments of the body and blood of Christ, but in heaven at
the right hand of God the Father, whence He will come to
judge the living and the dead.[15]

VII. Concerning the Use of Excommunication

Because weeds are mixed with the Church of Christ, Christ
has given His Church authority to excommunicate such
weeds when they show themselves by intolerable crimes and
sins against the commandment of the Lord, in order that as
much as possible the Church may keep her appearance un-
spotted. This is the reason we use excommunication in the
Church.[16]

But the Christian Church excommunicates solely for the
sake of the reclamation of offenders, and consequently it
gladly receives them again after they have put away their
scandalous life and have improved.[17]

VIII. Concerning Government

God has charged governments, His servants, with the sword
and with the highest external power for the protection of
the good and for vengeance upon and punishment of evildoers. For this reason, every Christian government with
which we desire to be numbered, should do all in its power
to see that God's Name is hallowed among its subjects, God's
kingdom extended, and His will observed by the assiduous
extirpation of crimes.[18]

IX. Concerning Faith and Works

We confess that there is forgiveness of sins through faith
in Jesus Christ the crucified. Although this faith is continu-

---

14 Acts 1:9 f.; 7:55 f.; Col. 3:1 f.; Heb. 1:3; 10:19 f.
15 Acts 3:21; II Tim. 4:1.
16 Matt. 18:15 ff.; I Cor. 5:3 ff.; II Thess. 3:6, 14; I Tim. 1:19 f.
17 II Cor. 2:6 ff.; I Tim. 1:20.
18 Rom. 13:1 ff.; I Peter 2:13 ff. Pagan governments have always been
charged with this office; how much more should a Christian government be
required to be a true lieutenant of God!

ally exercised, signalized, and thus confirmed by works of love, yet do we not ascribe to works, which are the fruit of faith, the righteousness and satisfaction for our sins. On the contrary, we ascribe it solely to a genuine trust and faith in the shed blood of the Lamb of God. For we freely confess that all things are granted to us in Christ, Who is our righteousness, holiness, redemption, the way, the truth, the wisdom and the life. Therefore the works of believers are not for the satisfaction of their sins, but solely for the purpose of showing in some degree our gratitude to the Lord God for the great kindness He has shown us in Christ.[19]

X. Concerning the Day of Judgment

We believe that there will be a Day of Judgment on which the resurrection of the flesh will take place, when every man will receive from Christ the Judge, according as he has lived in this life: eternal life, if out of true faith and with unfeigned love he has brought works of righteousness which are the fruit of faith; or everlasting fire if he has done either good [20] or evil without faith or with a feigned faith without love.[21]

XI. Concerning Things Commanded and Not Commanded

We confess that just as no one may require things which Christ has not commanded, so in the same way no one may forbid what He has not forbidden. For this reason we hold that the confessional, fasting during Lent, holy days and such things introduced by men are not commanded, and, on the other hand, that the marriage of priests is not forbidden.[22]

Still less may anyone permit what God has forbidden. This is the reason we reject the veneration and invoking of de-

---

[19] Matt. 20:28; Mark 10:45; Luke 7:48, 50; John 3:15 f., 36; 5:24; 6:28 f., 35, 40, 47; Rom. 3:21 ff.; 4; 10:4 ff.; Gal. 2:16 ff.; Rom. 3:27 f.; Eph. 2:8 f., 13 ff.; I Cor. 1:1, 30 f.; Rom. 8:32; Eph. 2:9 f.; John 14:6. Gratitude consists in recompensing blessings received. Now God cannot be recompensed at all since He does not lack anything. Hence we look to His demand, namely, faith and works of love. God demands faith for Himself and love for our fellowman.

[20] " Good " is to be understood as good according to human judgment.

[21] Matt. 24:30; 25:31 ff.; II Tim. 4:1, 8; Rom. 2:5 ff.; II Cor. 5:10; John 5:25 ff.

[22] It is written: " Hear Him! " Matt. 17:5; Luke 9:35; Deut. 18:18 f.; Acts 7:37.

parted saints,[23] the veneration and setting up of images, and such like. Moreover, no one may forbid what God has permitted. For this reason we do not think it is forbidden to enjoy food with thanksgiving.[24]

XII. AGAINST THE ERROR OF THE ANABAPTISTS

We publicly declare that we not only do not accept but reject as an abomination and as blasphemy the alien false doctrines which are among the damnable and wicked opinions uttered by these factious spirits, namely, that children (whom we baptize according to the custom of the apostles and the early Church and because baptism has replaced circumcision) should not be baptized; that in no case may an oath be taken, even though the honor of God and love for one's neighbor require it; [25] and that Christians may not hold political offices; [26] together with all other doctrines which are opposed to the sound, pure teaching of Jesus Christ.

Finally, we desire to submit this our confession to the judgment of the divine Biblical Scriptures. And should we be informed from the same Holy Scriptures of a better one, we have thereby expressed our readiness to be willing at any time to obey God and His holy Word with great thanksgiving.

Enacted at a meeting of our Council, Wednesday, January 21, in the year 1534 after the birth of Christ our only Saviour.

HEINRICH RYHINER

Clerk of the City of Basel

---

23 Concerning them we confess, however, that they are with God, reigning with Christ in eternity, because they have confessed Christ by words and deeds as their Savior, their redemption and righteousness, without any assistance of human merit. Therefore we highly praise them as those who have been pardoned by God and are now heirs of an eternal kingdom, yet all to the honor of God and of Christ.

24 He says: " I am the Lord your God," Lev. 18:2, and in Deut. 10:17 He speaks through Moses: For the Lord your God is God of gods and Lord of lords, the great, the mighty, and the terrible God, etc. Therefore who would want to permit among His creatures what He has forbidden? I Tim. 1:4 ff.

25 An oath may be taken at appropriate times; for God has enjoined it in the Old Testament and Christ has not forbidden it in the New. Christ and also the apostles have themselves taken oaths.

26 Government is only then a true government when it is truly Christian.

5

The First Helvetic Confession of 1536

INTRODUCTION

The First Helvetic Confession of 1536 has also been called
the Second Confession of Basel to distinguish it from the First
Confession of Basel of 1534. Prior to its appearance each city
— Zurich, Berne, and Basel — drew up its own independent
Confession. The movement toward a uniform formula was
precipitated by two factors. Pope Paul III convened a general
council to meet in Mantua in 1537, which turned out later
to be the Council of Trent, and the Strassburg Reformers,
Martin Bucer and Wolfgang Capito, were anxious to bring
about a union between the Lutherans and the Swiss. Accordingly, the magistrates of Zurich, Berne, Basel, Schaffhausen,
St. Gall, Mühlhausen, and Biel sent delegates to a conference
in the Augustinian convent at Basel, January 30, 1536. Bullinger, Grynaeus and Myconius were chosen to draw up the
Confession, and Leo Judae and Megander were added. Although not members of this committee, Bucer and Capito
had considerable influence in the framing of the twenty-eight
articles, especially with the article on the Lord's Supper. The
Confession was first published in Latin and was subscribed
to by all the lay and clerical delegates February 4, 1536. Leo
Judae prepared the German translation, which is considerably fuller, but of equal authority with the Latin. It is divided into twenty-seven articles, having omitted a separate
article on faith. After each magistrate had received a copy,
the delegates met again in Basel on March 27, 1536, without
the theologians present, and in the name of their cities unanimously declared the adoption of the Confession.

Böckel declares that it is uncertain whether a paragraph
which Bullinger and Judae recommended in the interest of
freedom of doctrine and the peace of the Church was ever

really added to the Confession. It is lacking in editions of the Latin text. Nevertheless, it is worth recording here. " By these articles we do not want in any way to prescribe a single rule of faith for all churches. For we acknowledge no other rule of faith than the Holy Scriptures. Therefore whoever concurs in this Confession, even though he has employed a different terminology from that of our Confession, is in agreement with us. For we are to be concerned about the matter itself and the truth and not about words. We therefore grant to anyone the freedom to use the terminology which he believes is most suitable for his church, and we will avail ourselves of the same freedom to defend ourselves against a distortion of the true meaning of this Confession. We have made use of these expressions at the present time in order to convey our conviction." [1]

When the Confession was presented to Luther by Bucer and Capito, Luther expressed his warm approval and promised to do all that he could to further unity and harmony with the Swiss. Luther may have been favorably disposed to the Swiss position at this time because the two Strassburg theologians had not hesitated to sign the so-called " Wittenberg Concord " which Melanchthon had composed, but which proved unacceptable to the Swiss. In any case, Luther's approval of the Swiss churches was short-lived, and to Melanchthon's sorrow, he violently resumed the controversy with the publication of his *Short Confession of the Sacrament* (1544). Thus the First Helvetic Confession failed to achieve the desired union, in spite of the Lutheranizing tendencies, especially in the original Latin text. But it did serve to unite the Reformed Churches in German-speaking Switzerland, and formed the basis upon which the Second Helvetic Confession of 1566 was built.

An original manuscript of the Confession which was doubtless brought back to Zurich from Basel is to be found in the Zurich State Archives. Copies, to which Biblical references were added, are contained in the Zurich Church Archives and the Basel City Library. The present English translation has been made from the German text found in Niemeyer.

Literature: K. R. Hagenbach, *Kritische Geschichte der Entstehung u. der Schicksale der ersten Basler Confession u. der auf sie gegründeten Kirchenlehre* (Basel, 1827) ; C. Pesta-

---

[1] E. G. A. Böckel, *Die Bekenntnisschriften der evangelisch-reformierten Kirche* (Leipzig, 1847) , p. 116.

lozzi, *Heinrich Bullinger* (Elberfeld, 1858) ; E. Blösch, *Geschichte der schweizerisch-reformierten Kirchen* (Bern, 1898–1899) ; P. Schaff, *Creeds of Christendom*, Vol. I, pp. 388 f.; E. F. K. Müller, *Die Bekenntnisschriften der reformierten Kirche* (Leipzig, 1903) and in *The New Schaff-Herzog Encyclopedia of Religious Knowledge*, Vol. V (1909).

The First Helvetic Confession of Faith
of 1536
(THE SECOND BASEL CONFESSION OF FAITH)

A COMMON CONFESSION

OF

THE HOLY, TRUE AND ANCIENT CHRISTIAN FAITH AND OF OUR
FELLOW-CITIZENS AND FELLOW-CHRISTIAN BELIEVERS IN ZÜRICH,
BERN, BASEL, SCHAFHAUSEN, ST. GALLEN, MÜHLHAUSEN AND BIEL,
AND UNTIL FURTHER NOTICE, DRAWN UP, ORDERED, AND DELIV-
ERED AT BASEL. — FEBRUARY 1, 2, 3 AND 4, 1536.

The churches banned together in a confederacy, having accepted
the Gospel of Christ, present a short and common Confession of
Faith to all believing and godly men for their consideration, eval-
uation and judgment.[2]

1. *Concerning Holy Scripture*

The holy, divine, Biblical Scripture, which is the Word of
God inspired by the Holy Spirit and delivered to the world
by the prophets and apostles, is the most ancient, most perfect
and loftiest teaching and alone deals with everything that
serves the true knowledge, love and honor of God, as well
as true piety and the making of a godly, honest and blessed
life.[3]

2. *Concerning the Interpretation of Scripture*

This holy, divine Scripture is to be interpreted in no other
way than out of itself and is to be explained by the rule of
faith and love.[4]

---

[2] I Peter, ch. 3; I John, ch. 4.
[3] Zech. 7:1 ff.; Matt. 22:29 ff.; II Peter 1:19; I Thess. 4:15; II Tim. 3:15 ff.
[4] I John 5:9; Rom. 12:7; I Cor., ch. 13. Thus does Christ put it in Matt.
4:4; 7:10.

3. Concerning the Early Teachers

Where the holy fathers and early teachers, who have explained and expounded the Scripture, have not departed from this rule, we want to recognize and consider them not only as expositors of Scripture, but as elect instruments through whom God has spoken and operated.[5]

4. Concerning Doctrines of Men

We regard all other human doctrines and articles which lead us away from God and true faith as vain and ineffectual, no matter how attractive, fine, esteemed and of long usage they may be, as Saint Matthew himself attests in ch. 15 [6] where he says: " In vain do they worship me, teaching as doctrines the precepts of men." [7]

5. The Purpose of Holy Scripture and That to Which It Finally Points

The entire Biblical Scripture is solely concerned that man understand that God is kind and gracious to him and that He has publicly exhibited and demonstrated this His kindness to the whole human race through Christ His Son. However, it comes to us and is received by faith alone, and is manifested and [8] demonstrated by love for our neighbor.[9]

[handwritten margin note: interesting that every hear the doctrine of Justification comes up.]

6. Concerning God

Concerning God, we hold that there is one only, true, living and almighty God, one in essence, threefold according to the persons, Who has created all things out of nothing by His Word, that is, by His Son, and by His providence justly, truly and wisely rules, governs and preserves all things.[10]

[handwritten margin note: no explicit mention of the Holy Spirit]

---

[5] John 17:11 ff.; Luke 10:1 ff.; Matt. 10:5 ff.; I Thess. 2:4.
[6] V. 9.
[7] Isa. 29:13; Mark 7:6 ff.; I Tim. 4:1 ff.; Titus 1:10 ff.
[8] Böckel observes in his collection, *Die Bekenntnisschriften der evangelisch-reformierten Kirche,* that this sentence is obscure. For, according to the grammatical construction, the kindness of God is the subject of both clauses. In the Latin translation the construction is the same. Mess and Beck in their German translations have made faith the subject of the last clause: " but this must be active through love."
[9] Gen., ch. 3; John, ch. 4; Rom. 8:1 ff.; Eph. 2:4 ff.; I John 4:16 ff.
[10] Deut. 6:4; Matt. 28:19; Gen. 1:1 ff.; Ps. 33:9; Acts 17:24 ff.

7. Concerning Man

Man, the most perfect image of God on earth and among visible creatures the most excellent and eminent, is composed of body and soul. The body is mortal, the soul immortal. This man, whom God made righteous and good,[11] fell into sin through his own guilt, and dragged the whole human race into this fall with him and subjected it to such misery.[12]

8. Concerning Original Sin

This original and inherited sin has so permeated the whole human race and has so ruined and poisoned it that man, who had become a child of wrath and an enemy of God, could not be saved or restored by anyone except God through Christ. Whatever good remained in him is continually enervated through daily faults and imperfections, so that it becomes even more wicked. For the power of sin and imperfection is so strong in us that reason cannot follow what it knows nor can the mind kindle a divine spark and fan it.[13]

9. Concerning Freedom of Choice
Which Is Called Free Will

We ascribe freedom of choice to man because we find in ourselves that we do good and evil knowingly and deliberately. We are able to do evil of ourselves but we can neither embrace nor fulfill the good unless we are illumined, quickened and impelled by the grace of Christ. For God is the one who effects in us the willing and the doing, according to His good pleasure. Our salvation is from God, but from ourselves there is nothing but sin and damnation.[14]

10. How God Has Saved Man
by His Eternal Counsel

Although man through this his guilt and transgression is worthy of eternal damnation and has come under the righteous wrath of God, yet God, the gracious Father, has never ceased to be concerned about him. We can perceive and un-

---

[11] The Latin translation renders this word as " holy."
[12] Gen. 1:26 ff.; 2:7; Rom. 5:12.
[13] Eph. 2:1 ff.; Ps. 51:3 ff.; Rom. 8:3 ff.
[14] John 15:7; 14:15; Phil. 2:15; Acts 17:27 f.; Hos. 13:2, 9.

derstand this sufficiently, clearly and plainly from the first promise and from the whole law by which sin is awakened though not wiped out, and from Christ the Lord who was appointed and given for that purpose.[15]

11. Concerning Christ the Lord, and What We Have Through Him

This Lord Christ, a true Son of God, true God and man, assumed a true human nature, with body and soul, in the time thereto appointed by God from eternity. He has two distinct, unmixed natures in one single, indissoluble Person. The assumption of human nature took place in order that He might quicken us who were dead and make us joint heirs of God. This also is the reason He has become our brother.[16]

From the undefiled Virgin Mary by the cooperation of the Holy Spirit, this Lord Christ, the Son of the living, true God, has assumed flesh, which is holy through its unity with the Godhead, in all things like unto our flesh, yet without sin — since it was to be a pure, unblemished sacrifice, and has delivered it unto death for us as a payment, pardoning and washing away of all sins.[17]

And in order that we might have a perfect hope and trust in our immortal life, He has set His flesh, which He had raised again from death unto life, at the right hand of His almighty Father.[18]

This Lord Christ, Who has overcome and conquered death, sin and the whole power of hell, is our Forerunner, our Leader, and our Head. He is the true High Priest Who sits at God's right hand and always defends and promotes our cause, until He brings us back and restores us to the image in which we were created, and leads us into the fellowship of His divine nature.[19]

We await this Lord Jesus to come at the end of the world as a true, righteous Judge who will pass a true judgment upon flesh which He has raised to judgment. He will lead the godly and believing into heaven, and will condemn and thrust unbelievers with body and soul into eternal damnation.[20]

[15] Eph. 1:4 ff.; Gen. 3:15; Rom. 7:7 ff.
[16] John 1:1 ff.; Gal. 4:4 f.; John 16:15; Heb. 2:4.
[17] Matt. 1:18 ff.; Luke 1:26 ff.; I John 2:1 f.
[18] I Cor., ch. 15; Acts 1:1 ff.
[19] Eph. 1:20 ff.; Rom. 6:23; Eph. 4:8 ff.
[20] Dan. 7:26 ff.; John 5:25 ff.; Matt. 25:31 ff.

As this Lord Jesus is our only Mediator, Advocate, Sacrifice, High Priest, Lord and King, we acknowledge Him alone, and believe with all our hearts that He only is our reconciliation, our redemption, sanctification, payment, wisdom, defense and deliverance. Here we reject everything that represents itself as the means, the sacrifice and the reconciliation of our life and salvation, and we recognize none other than Christ the Lord alone.[21]

12. *The Purpose of Evangelical Doctrine*

Consequently in all evangelical teaching the most sublime and the principal article and the one which should be expressly set forth in every sermon and impressed upon the hearts of men should be that we are preserved and saved solely by the one mercy of God and by the merit of Christ. However, in order that men may understand how necessary Christ is for their salvation and blessedness, the magnitude and gravity of sin should be most clearly and plainly pointed out, depicted and held up before them by means of the law and Christ's death.[22]

13. *How Christ's Grace and Merit Are Communicated to Us and the Fruit That Follows from It*

We do not obtain such sublime and great benefits of God's grace and the true sanctification of God's Spirit through our merits or powers but through faith which is a pure gift of God.

This faith is a sure, firm and solid foundation for and a laying hold of all those things for which one hopes from God, and from which love and subsequently all virtues and the fruits of good works are brought forth.

And although godly believers constantly exercise themselves in such fruits of faith, yet we do not ascribe the piety and the salvation obtained to such works, but only to the grace of God. Although this faith effects innumerable good works, it does not take comfort in them but in the mercy of God. Such a faith is the true and proper service with which a man is pleasing to God.[23]

---

[21] I Tim. 2:5; Heb., ch. 7; Rom. 3:23 ff.; I Cor. 1:30.

[22] I Tim. 1:15; Rom. 3:23 ff. At this point the numbering of the articles varies. The German has 27; the Latin, 28. See Niemeyer, p. 109. But in the *Corpus et syntagma* the Latin also has only 27 articles. We follow the numbering of the German text.

[23] Rom. 3:24; Gal. 2:16; Eph. 2:8; Gal. 5:22; Micah 6:6 ff.

14. Concerning the Church

We hold that from living stones built upon this living rock a holy, universal Church is built and gathered together. It is the fellowship and congregation of all saints which is Christ's bride and spouse which He washes with His blood and finally presents to the Father without blemish or any spot. And although this Church and congregation of Christ is open and known to God's eyes alone, yet it is not only known but also gathered and built up by visible signs, rites and ordinances, which Christ Himself has instituted and appointed by the Word of God as a universal, public and orderly discipline. Without these marks no one is numbered with this Church (speaking generally and without a special permission revealed by God.) [24]

15. Concerning the Ministers of God's Word and the Fruit That Follows from It

Therefore we also believe that the Church's ministers are God's co-workers, as St. Paul calls them, through whom He imparts and offers to those who believe in Him the knowledge of Himself and the forgiveness of sins, converts, strengthens and comforts men, but also threatens and judges them, yet with the understanding that in all things we ascribe all efficacy and power to God the Lord alone, and only the imparting to the minister. For it is certain that this power and efficacy never should or can be attributed to a creature, but God dispenses it to those He chooses according to His free will. [25]

16. Concerning the Authority of the Church

The authority to preach God's Word and to tend the flock of the Lord, which properly speaking is the office of the keys, prescribes one pattern of life for all men whether of high or lowly station. Since it is commanded by God, it is a high and sacred trust which should not be violated. This administrative power should not be conferred upon anyone unless he has first been found and acknowledged to be qualified and fit for the office by divine calling and election and by those who

---

24 I Peter 2:4 ff.; Matt. 16:18; I John 1:7; I Peter 1:3 ff.; Eph. 5:27; John 6:68 f.; II Tim. 2:19; Acts 13:39; Matt. 28:18 ff.; Acts 10:47 f.
25 I Cor. 3:5 ff.; 4:1 ff.; II Cor. 6:4 ff.; John 20:21 ff.; Luke 1:51 ff.

after careful deliberation have been appointed and elected as a committee of the Church for that purpose.[26]

17. Concerning the Election of Ministers of the Church

No one should be charged or entrusted with this office and ministry unless he has first been found and acknowledged by the ministers and elders of the Church, and also by those Christian rulers elected to such office on behalf of the Church, to be well instructed in the Holy Scriptures and in the knowledge of the will of God, blameless in piety and purity of life, and zealous and fervent in promoting the honor and name of Christ with diligence and earnestness. And because this is a true and proper election of God, it is reasonable and right that they should be recognized and accepted by the judgment of the Church and the laying on of hands by the elders.[27]

18. Who the Shepherd and Head of the Church Is

Christ Himself is the only true and proper Head and Shepherd of His Church. He gives to His Church shepherds and teachers who at His command administer the Word and office of the keys in an orderly and regular fashion, as reported above. Consequently we do not acknowledge or accept the head [of the Church] at Rome and those who are bishops in name only.[28]

19. What the Office of Ministers and of the Church Is

The highest and chief thing in this office is that the ministers of the Church preach repentance and sorrow for sins, improvement of life, and forgiveness of sins, and all through Christ. In addition they are to pray unceasingly for the people, to apply themselves earnestly and diligently to Holy Scripture and the Word of God, in reading and devout meditation, and with God's Word as with the sword of the Spirit to pursue the devil with deadly hatred by every means, and to

---

26 Matt. 16:19; John 20:21 ff.; I Thess. 4:1 ff.; Acts 13:2 f.
27 I Tim. 3:2 ff.; 4:12 ff.; Luke 12:8 ff.; Acts 1:15 ff.; Titus 1:5 ff.; Num. 27:28 ff.; Deut. 34:9; Acts 6:2 ff.; 8:14 ff.; 13:2 ff.; I Tim. 1:18; Heb. 6:1 ff.
28 John 10:1 ff.; Eph. 1:3 ff.; 4:1 ff.; 5:25 ff.; Col. 1:18; 2:6 ff.; John 20:28; Zech. 11:15 ff.

crush and weaken his power so that they may defend Christ's stanch citizens and may warn, repel and put away the wicked. And when the wicked in their sacrilege and shameless vices are forever determined to scandalize and destroy the Church, they are to be expelled by the ministers of the Word and the Christian government instituted for that purpose, or they are to be punished and corrected in some other suitable and proper way until they confess their error, change and are restored. But when a citizen of Christ, who has been delinquent and derelict and has been expelled, is converted and earnestly confesses and admits his sin and error (for this is the purpose of the punishment), willingly seeks remedy for his failings, yields to spiritual discipline and gladdens all the pious with his new diligence and zeal in the exercise of piety, he should be accepted again into the Church.[29]

20. Concerning the Power and Efficacy of the Sacraments

The signs, which are called sacraments, are two: Baptism and the Lord's Supper. These sacraments are significant, holy signs of sublime, secret things. However, they are not mere, empty signs, but consist of the sign and substance. For in baptism the water is the sign, but the substance and spiritual thing is rebirth and admission into the people of God. In the Lord's Supper the bread and wine are the signs, but the spiritual substance is the communion of the body and blood of Christ, the salvation acquired on the Cross, and forgiveness of sins. As the signs are bodily received, so these substantial, invisible and spiritual things are received in faith. Moreover, the entire power, efficacy and fruit of the sacraments lies in these spiritual and substantial things.

Consequently we confess that the sacraments are not simply outward signs of Christian fellowship. On the contrary, we confess them to be signs of divine grace by which the ministers of the Church work with the Lord for the purpose and to the end which He Himself promises, offers and efficaciously provides. We confess, however, that all sanctifying and saving power is to be ascribed to God, the Lord, alone, as we said above concerning the servants of the Word.

---

29 Luke 24:25; I Cor. 11:18 f.; Acts 6; I Tim. 4:6 ff.; Eph. 6:13 ff.; II Tim. 4:1 ff.; Ezek. 14:3 ff.; I Cor. 5; II Thess. 3:6; II Cor. 2:24.

21. *Concerning Baptism*

According to the institution of the Lord, baptism is a bath of regeneration which the Lord offers and presents to His elect with a visible sign through the ministry of the Church, as stated and explained above. We baptize our children in this holy bath because it would be unjust if we were to rob of the fellowship of God's people those who have been born of us for a people of God, for which they had been intended by the divine Word and of whom it may be assumed that they have been elected by God.[30]

22. *Concerning the Lord's Supper*

In regard to the Lord's Supper we hold, therefore, that in it the Lord truly offers His body and His blood, that is, Himself, to His own, and enables them to enjoy such fruit that He lives ever more and more in them and they in Him. We do not believe that the body and blood of the Lord is naturally united with the bread and wine or that they are spatially enclosed within them, but that according to the institution of the Lord the bread and wine are highly significant, holy, true signs by which the true communion of His body and blood is administered and offered to believers by the Lord Himself by means of the ministry of the Church — not as perishable food for the belly but the food and nourishment of a spiritual and eternal life. We frequently make use of this sublime and holy food in order that being thereby reminded, we may perceive with the eyes of faith the death and the blood of the crucified Christ, and, with a foretaste of the nature of heaven and with a genuine experience of eternal life, may aspire to our salvation. With this spiritual, quickening, inward food we are delighted and refreshed by its inexpressible sweetness and are overjoyed to find our life in Christ's death. Therefore, we shout for joy in our hearts and all the more break forth into thanksgiving for such a costly and sublime favor He has shown us.[31]

Therefore we are most unjustly blamed for attaching little value to these sublime signs. For these holy signs and sacraments are sacred and venerable things because they have been instituted and used by Christ the High Priest. Thus in the

---

[30] Matt. 28:18 ff.; Mark 16:15 f.; Titus 3:5; Gen. 17:10 ff.; Luke 18:15 ff.
[31] Matt. 26:26 ff.; John 6:48 ff.; 10:23; I Cor. 10:16 f.

way discussed above they present and offer the spiritual things they signify. They bear witness to things that have happened. They portray and remind us of such high and holy things. And by means of a singular resemblance to the things they signify, they shed a great and glorious light upon sacred and divine matters. In addition they are something of an aid and support to faith, and are as much as an oath with which believers obligate and bind themselves to their Head and to the Church. Yet as highly as we prize these sacred and extremely meaningful signs, we ascribe the quickening and sanctifying power always to Him alone Who only is the Life, to Him be the praise forever and ever. Amen.[32]

23. Concerning Sacred Assemblies and Meetings of Believers

We hold that the sacred assemblies and meetings of believers should be conducted in such a way that above all else God's Word be placed before the people at a common place and reserved for that purpose alone; that the mysteries of Scripture be daily expounded and explained by qualified ministers; that the Lord's Supper be observed in order that the faith of believers be exercised continually; and that earnest prayer for the needs of all men be constantly made. Other ceremonies, which are innumerable, such as chalices, priestly gowns for the mass, choir robes, cowls, tonsures, flags, candles, altars, gold and silver, to the extent they serve to hinder and pervert true religion and the proper worship of God, and especially the idols and pictures which are used for worship and are a scandal, and any more such ungodly things — these we want to have banished far from our holy congregations.[33]

24. Concerning Things Which Are Neither Commanded nor Forbidden, but Are Adiaphora and Voluntary

All things that are called, and properly speaking, are adiaphora, may be freely used by devout, believing Christians at all times and in all places, provided he does so judiciously and with love. For a believer is to use all things in such a way

---

[32] Acts 4:12.
[33] Acts 2:41 ff.; I Tim. 2:1 ff.; I Cor. 14:1 ff.; Acts 8:14 ff.; Ex. 20:4; Isa. 40:25; I Cor. 10:7; I Peter 4:3.

that God's honor is promoted and the Church and his neighbor are not offended.[34]

25. Concerning Those Who Divide the Church of Christ by False Doctrines or Separate Themselves from Her and Conspire Against Her

When all those who separate and cut themselves off from the holy fellowship and society of the Church, introduce alien and ungodly doctrines into the Church, or adhere to such doctrines — faults that in our day are chiefly evident in the Anabaptists — do not hear and heed the warning of the Church and Christian instruction, but obstinately want to persist in their contention and error, with consequent injury to and seduction of the Church, they should be punished and suppressed by the supreme power, in order that they may not poison, harm or defile the flock of God with their false doctrine.[35]

26. Concerning the Temporal Government

Since all governmental power is from God, its highest and principal office, if it does not want to be tyrannical, is to protect and promote the true honor of God and the proper service of God by punishing and rooting out all blasphemy, and to exercise all possible diligence to promote and to put into effect what a minister of the Church and a preacher of the Gospel teaches and sets forth from God's Word. However, in order that such true religion — a true service of God and propriety of conduct — may arise and flourish, a government will above all use every effort that the pure Word of God be faithfully proclaimed to the congregation, and no one be prevented from hearing it; that schools be well regulated, the ordinary citizenry well taught, carefully instructed and disciplined; that the ministers of the Church and the poor in the Church be well taken care of, and their necessities properly and adequately be provided for. For this purpose the possessions of the Church should serve.[36]

Furthermore, a government should rule the people accord-

---

[34] Rom. 14:1 ff.; I Cor. 8:1 ff. Whatever does not proceed from faith is sin. Rom. 14:23; I Cor. 10:14 ff.

[35] Isa. 5:20; Acts 3:23.

[36] II Chron. 19:8 ff.; Rom. 13:1 ff.; Ps. 82; Lev. 24:10 ff.; Ex., ch. 18; Dan., chs. 3; 6:10; I Cor. 9:1 ff.; I Tim. 5:17 ff.; Rom. 12:13; I Cor. 16:1 ff.

ing to just, divine laws. It should sit in judgment and administer justice, preserve the public peace and welfare, guard and defend the public interest, and with fairness punish wrong-doers according to the nature of their crimes against life and property. And when a government does this, it serves God its Lord as it ought to do and is obligated to do.

Although we are free in Christ, all of us should obey such supreme authority and be ready to serve with our lives, goods, and possessions. With sincere love and from faith we should show that we are subject to it, performing vows and oaths when its orders and commandments are manifestly not opposed to Him for Whose sake we honor and obey it.[37]

27. Concerning Holy Matrimony

We contend that marriage has been instituted and prescribed by God for all men who are qualified and fit for it and who have not otherwise been called by God to live a chaste life outside marriage. No order or state is so holy and honorable that marriage would be opposed to it and should be forbidden. Since such marriage should be confirmed in the presence of the Church by a public exhortation and vow in keeping with its dignity, the government should also respect it and see to it that a marriage is legally and decently entered into and given legal and honorable recognition, and is not lightly dissolved without serious and legitimate grounds.

Consequently we cannot commend cloisters and the impure and irregular chastity of all supposed clerics and the indolent and useless life they lead which certain people have instituted and arranged out of mistaken zeal. On the contrary, we reject it as an abominable and dreadful thing invented and devised by men in opposition to God's order.[38]

Basel, March 26, 1536.

Approved and unanimously adopted by the delegates from the above-mentioned cities.

---

[37] Ex. 18:13 ff.; Isa. 10:1 ff.; Rom. 13:5 ff.; Matt. 17:24 f.; 22:21; Acts 4:19; 5:29.

[38] Matt. 5:27 ff.; 19:3 ff.; Heb. 13:4; I Cor., ch. 7; I Tim. 3:2; 4:1 ff.

The Lausanne Articles of 1536

INTRODUCTION

The establishment of the Reformed faith in Geneva and French-speaking Switzerland had been a primary objective of the canton of Berne ever since its council had decided, in 1528, to adopt the Reformation. When France seemed about to intervene on behalf of Geneva, Berne renounced its alliance with Savoy on November 29, 1535, and war was declared on January 16. The Bernese army gathered reinforcements from towns such as Neuville, Neuchâtel, Lausanne, and Payerne which felt that the hour of their liberation had struck. Actually there was little fighting and " the greater part of the Pays de Vaud was conquered without striking a blow, and the army of the Duke of Savoy and the Bishop of Geneva was dispersed without a battle." The victory brought deliverance not only to Geneva and Lausanne but to many other Protestant cities in French-speaking Switzerland.

Immediately following the conquest of Lausanne the Roman Mass was abolished and a Reformed order of service introduced. The Council of Berne was determined to instruct the people of its newly acquired territory in evangelical principles and issued an order for a disputation to be held in Lausanne, October 1, 1536. The Ten Articles or Theses were proposed by Guillaume Farel, in a sermon, and thus both the matter and order of discussion were determined in advance. The Articles followed closely the model established earlier at Zurich and Berne. Three hundred and thirty-seven priests, the inmates of thirteen abbeys and convents, of the twenty-five priories, of the two chapters of the canton, were invited to come to Lausanne to refute if they could the theses set forth by Farel. However, only one hundred and seventy-four priests appeared, and of these only four took part. Only ten of the forty religious houses sent representatives, and only one attempted to refute the Reformers. As at Berne in 1528 the Romanists proved no match for their opponents.

The defense of the Articles was conducted chiefly by Farel and Pierre Viret. Farel was born at Gap in 1489 and died at Neuchâtel, September 13, 1565. Upon completing his studies at the University of Paris, he taught for a while in the college of Cardinal le Moine which was connected with the university. Following his conversion to the tenets of the Reformation he preached with greater zeal than discretion in various cities in Switzerland. In October, 1532, he came to Geneva and succeeded in inducing the authorities to adopt the Reformation by edict August 10, 1535. He perceived in John Calvin those theological and administrative gifts which he himself lacked, and in a famous interview prevailed upon Calvin to come to Geneva and join him in the work of reformation. Viret was born at Orbe in 1511 and died at Orthez, France, April 4, 1571. He, too, studied in Paris, and renouncing the Roman Catholic faith, was ordained by Farel in 1531. In 1533 he went to Geneva as Farel's assistant, and thence to Neuchâtel and Lausanne. It was at Lausanne that he was instrumental in introducing the Reformation to French-speaking Switzerland.

Farel preached the opening sermon in the cathedral on October 1 and also the closing sermon on the eighth. The huge cathedral was filled to capacity by the citizens of the city and the surrounding villages for the discussion that began on Monday. According to Lindsay, " in the middle of the church a space was reserved for the disputants. There sat the four secretaries, the two presidents, and five commissioners representing *les Princes Chrétiens Messieurs de Berne,* distinguished by their black doublets and shoulder knots faced with red, and by their broad-brimmed hats ornamented with great bunches of feathers — hats kept stiffly on heads as befitting the representatives of such potent lords." [1]

Calvin attended the Disputation, but as he himself stated, " I held myself absolved from speaking up to now, and would have deliberately abstained until the end, seeing that my word is not very necessary for adding anything to the adequate replies which my brothers Farel and Viret give." However, he was moved to deliver two discourses, first when " the debate concerned the third of the Ten Articles proposed, and

[1] T. M. Lindsay, *A History of the Reformation* (1907), Vol. II, p. 104.

discussion centered on the question of the real presence of the glorified Christ," and the second when the " disputation considers Article 8, and Calvin breaks his silence to attack the dogma of transubstantiation through the person of Pope Gregory VII." [2]

Although the Lausanne Articles do not seem to have been officially adopted, the principles expressed in them were accorded permanent validity by the Reformation Mandate of December 24, 1536.[3] The translation given here is that of J. K. S. Reid in The Library of Christian Classics, Vol. XXII, *Calvin: Theological Treatises,* pp. 35–37.

Literature: A.-L. Herminjard, *Correspondance des réformateurs dans les pays de langue française,* 9 vols., Vol. 4 (Geneva, 1872) ; Ruchat, *Histoire de la réformation de la Suisse,* Vol. 4 (Lausanne, 1836) ; *Corpus Reformatorum* (Brunswick, 1863–1900) ; È. Doumergue, *Jean Calvin — Les hommes et les choses de son temps,* 7 vols. (Lausanne, 1899 ff.) , Vol. II; E. F. K. Müller, *Die Bekenntnisschriften der reformierten Kirche* (Leipzig, 1903) ; T. M. Lindsay, *A History of the Reformation* (1907) ; H. Meylan and R. Deluz, *La Dispute de Lausanne* (1936) ; H. Vuilleumier, *Histoire de l'Église réformée du pays de Vaud* (Lausanne, 1927) , Vol. I.

---

[2] An English translation of Calvin's two discourses is given by J. K. S. Reid in The Library of Christian Classics, Vol. XXII, *Calvin: Theological Treatises* (The Westminster Press, 1954) , pp. 38–46.

[3] Cf. E. F. K. Müller, *Die Bekenntnisschriften der reformierten Kirche* (Leipzig, 1903) , p. XXVII.

The Lausanne Articles

ISSUES TO BE DISCUSSED AT LAUSANNE
IN THE NEW PROVINCE OF BERNE
ON THE FIRST DAY OF OCTOBER 1536

I

Holy Scripture teaches only one way of justification, which is by faith in Jesus Christ once for all offered, and holds as nothing but a destroyer of all the virtue of Christ anyone who makes another satisfaction, oblation, or cleansing for the remission of sins.

II

This Scripture acknowledges Jesus Christ, who is risen from the dead and sits in heaven at the right hand of the Father, as the only chief and true priest, sovereign mediator and true advocate of his Church.

III

Holy Scripture names the Church of God all who believe that they are received by the blood of Jesus Christ alone and who constantly and without vacillation believe and wholly establish and support themselves on the Word, which, having withdrawn from us in corporeal presence, nevertheless by the virtue of his Holy Spirit fills, sustains, governs and vivifies all things.

IV

The said Church contains certain who are known to the eyes of God alone. It possesses always ceremonies ordained by Christ, by which it is seen and known, that is to say Baptism and the Supper of our Lord, which are called sacraments, since they are symbols and signs of secret things, that is to say of divine grace.

V

The said Church acknowledges no ministry except that which preaches the Word of God and administers the sacraments.

VI

Further this Church itself receives no other confession than that which is made to God, no other absolution than that which is given by God for the remission of sins and which alone pardons and remits their sins who to this end confess their fault.

VII

Further this same Church denies all other ways and means of serving God beyond that which is spiritually ordained by the Word of God, which consists in the love of himself and of one's neighbour. Hence it rejects entirely the innumerable mockeries of all ceremonies which pervert religion, such as images and like things.

VIII

Also it acknowledges the civil magistrate ordained by God only as necessary to preserve the peace and tranquillity of the state. To which end, it desires and ordains that all be obedient in so far as nothing contrary to God is commanded.

IX

Next it affirms that marriage, instituted by God for all persons as fit and proper for them, violates the sanctity of no one whatever.

X

Finally as to things that are indifferent, such as foods, drinks and the observation of days, it allows as many as the man of faith can use at all times freely, but not otherwise than wisdom and charity should do.

7

The Geneva Confession of 1536

INTRODUCTION

As has already been noted in the introductory notes to the Lausanne Articles, William Farel had been actively preparing the ground for the Reformation in Geneva since 1532 and had induced the Council of Two Hundred to suspend the celebration of the Mass until further notice by a decree issued August 10, 1535. But " the Genevan Church lacked all organisation, save that the city government favoured Protestantism, supported Protestant preachers, and exercised a kind of ecclesiastical control over Genevan territories. It had no creed, save the determination of the General Assembly to live according to ' the Word of God,' no separate discipline, no existence independent of the will of the civil rulers of the turbulent city." [1] It is proof of Farel's recognition of Calvin's genius and of his own unselfishness that he prevailed upon the younger theologian to come to Geneva in August, 1536.

Calvin's presence was immediately felt, and resulted in the publication of three documents upon which the Reformation was established. These were the Articles concerning church government, a catechism for Christian instruction, and a Confession of Faith for the whole Genevan community. In these Calvin outlined the evangelical principles which were expounded more fully in the 1536 edition of his *Institutes*. The Articles were presented to the Little Council and the Council of Two Hundred on January 16, 1537, and were promptly adopted except for some important reservations.[2]

---

[1] Williston Walker, *John Calvin* (1909), p. 181.

[2] For example, the Lord's Supper was still to be celebrated but four times yearly, although Calvin wished it to be observed at least every Sunday and " because of the weakness of the people," recommended that for the present it be held once a month.

The Articles had proposed a " brief outline of the Christian faith " as a basis of instruction for children. Composed in Latin, it was first published in French at Lausanne, February 17, 1537.[2a] The following year a Latin version was issued in Basel under the title *Catechism or Institute of Christian Religion.* When Calvin returned from Strassburg to Geneva, he adapted and enlarged the work of 1537 and published in French late in 1541 or early in 1542 the Geneva Catechism. In 1545 Calvin published an edition of the catechism in Latin. It was soon translated into other languages and became the basis for a host of catechisms that appeared in the sixteenth and seventeenth centuries. Chief among them is, of course, the Heidelberg Catechism of 1563.

The Articles also provided that a Confession of Faith be drawn up and required of all inhabitants of Geneva. Its title declared it to be " extracted from the Instruction [i.e., Catechism] of which use is made in the Church of the said city," and that " all burghers, inhabitants of Geneva, and subjects of the country, are bound to swear to guard and hold to " it. Scholars are uncertain whether the Confession, together with the Articles, were laid before the authorities on November 10, 1536, by Farel, in compliance with an order issued by the Council as early as May 24, or whether they were presented January 16, 1537.[3] The latter seems more likely. At the request of Farel and Calvin the Little Council voted, on March 13, to " cause the Articles to be observed in full." But the attempt to obtain universal assent to the Confession resulted in widespread opposition. " Dissension over the Confession was aggravated by dissension over the question of ecclesiastical discipline, which the ministers were urging the Council to enforce and to which many of the citizens were by no means disposed to submit." [4] Repeatedly the Council demanded assent and threatened banishment to the recalcitrants. The opposition was strengthened in their stand by criticisms of the Confession by Bernese Commissioners at Geneva. But as a result of a visit to Berne by Calvin and Farel the Bernese

---

2a In the same year Calvin also published *Instruction in Faith,* tr. and ed. by Paul T. Fuhrmann (The Westminster Press, 1949) .

3 On this general subject see Williston Walker, *Calvin,* pp. 184 ff.; A. Rilliet and T. Dufour, *Le catéchisme français de Calvin* (Geneva, 1878) , pp. x–xxxiii; C. A. Cornelius, *Historische Arbeiten* (Leipzig, 1899) , pp. 131–137; É. Doumergue, *Jean Calvin — Les hommes et les choses de son temps,* 7 vols. (Lausanne, 1899 ff.) , Vol. II, pp. 219–227.

4 James Mackinnon, *Calvin and the Reformation* (Russell & Russell, Inc., 1962) , pp. 60 f.

government gave its approval to the Confession, and on January 4, 1538, the leaders in Geneva were induced to swear their adherence. Contrary to the wishes of the Reformers, however, the Council decided that no one should be debarred from partaking of the Lord's Supper who wished to do so.

Doubt has been cast upon the authorship of the Genevan Confession. Beza regards Calvin as the author and in this opinion Collodanus in his *Vie de Calvin* concurs. Recent scholars have attributed it to Farel.[5] Inasmuch as the order and the thought of the Confession is essentially that of the catechism it is highly probable that Calvin was at least involved in compiling and editing it. The Confession was first published in French, April 27, 1537. A year later Calvin issued a Latin text with a detailed foreword in order to give a brief account of his faith for churches in foreign countries. Both the French and Latin editions are found in the *Corpus Reformatorum*. The translation given here is by J. K. S. Reid in The Library of Christian Classics, Vol. XXII, *Calvin: Theological Treatises*, pp. 26–33, and was made from the French.

Literature: A. Rilliet and T. Dufour, *Le catéchisme français de Calvin* (Geneva, 1878) ; C. A. Cornelius, *Historische Arbeiten* (Leipzig, 1899) ; É. Doumergue, *Jean Calvin — Les hommes et les choses de son temps,* 7 vols. (Lausanne, 1899 ff.), Vol. II; Williston Walker, *John Calvin* (1909) ; François Wendel, *Calvin,* tr. by Philip Mairet (Harper & Row, 1950) ; James Mackinnon, *Calvin and the Reformation* (Russell & Russell, Inc., 1962) ; *Corpus Reformatorum* (Brunswick, 1863–1900).

---

[5] É. Doumergue sums up the evidence without coming to any definite conclusion. See *Jean Calvin,* Vol. II, pp. 237–239.

Confession of Faith

WHICH ALL THE CITIZENS AND INHABITANTS OF GENEVA AND THE SUBJECTS OF THE COUNTRY MUST PROMISE TO KEEP AND HOLD

(1536)

1. THE WORD OF GOD

First we affirm that we desire to follow Scripture alone as rule of faith and religion, without mixing with it any other thing which might be devised by the opinion of men apart from the Word of God, and without wishing to accept for our spiritual government any other doctrine than what is conveyed to us by the same Word without addition or diminution, according to the command of our Lord.

2. ONE ONLY GOD

Following, then, the lines laid down in the Holy Scriptures, we acknowledge that there is one only God, whom we are both to worship and serve, and in whom we are to put all our confidence and hope: having this assurance, that in him alone is contained all wisdom, power, justice, goodness and pity. And since he is spirit, he is to be served in spirit and in truth. Therefore we think it an abomination to put our confidence or hope in any created thing, to worship anything else than him, whether angels or any other creatures, and to recognize any other Saviour of our souls than him alone, whether saints or men living upon earth; and likewise to offer the service, which ought to be rendered to him, in external ceremonies or carnal observances, as if he took pleasure in such things, or to make an image to represent his divinity or any other image for adoration.

3. THE LAW OF GOD ALIKE FOR ALL

Because there is one only Lord and Master who has dominion over our consciences, and because his will is the only principle of all justice, we confess all our life ought to be ruled in accordance with the commandments of his holy law in which is contained all perfection of justice, and that we ought to have no other rule of good and just living, nor invent other good works to supplement it than those which are there contained, as follows: Exodus 20: " I am the Lord thy God, who brought thee," and so on.

4. Natural Man

We acknowledge man by nature to be blind, darkened in understanding, and full of corruption and perversity of heart, so that of himself he has no power to be able to comprehend the true knowledge of God as is proper, nor to apply himself to good works. But on the contrary, if he is left by God to what he is by nature, he is only able to live in ignorance and to be abandoned to all iniquity. Hence he has need to be illumined by God, so that he come to the right knowledge of his salvation, and thus to be redirected in his affections and reformed to the obedience of the righteousness of God.

5. Man by Himself Lost

Since man is naturally (as has been said) deprived and destitute in himself of all the light of God, and of all righteousness, we acknowledge that by himself he can only expect the wrath and malediction of God, and hence that he must look outside himself for the means of his salvation.

6. Salvation in Jesus

We confess then that it is Jesus Christ who is given to us by the Father, in order that in him we should recover all of which in ourselves we are deficient. Now all that Jesus Christ has done and suffered for our redemption, we veritably hold without any doubt, as it is contained in the Creed, which is recited in the Church, that is to say: I believe in God the Father Almighty, and so on.

7. Righteousness in Jesus

Therefore we acknowledge the things which are consequently given to us by God in Jesus Christ: first, that being in our own natures enemies of God and subjects of his wrath and judgment, we are reconciled with him and received again in grace through the intercession of Jesus Christ, so that by his righteousness and guiltlessness we have remission of our sins, and by the shedding of his blood we are cleansed and purified from all our stains.

8. REGENERATION IN JESUS

Second, we acknowledge that by his Spirit we are regenerated into a new spiritual nature. That is to say that the evil desires of our flesh are mortified by grace, so that they rule us no longer. On the contrary, our will is rendered conformable to God's will, to follow in his way and to seek what is pleasing to him. Therefore we are by him delivered from the servitude of sin, under whose power we were of ourselves held captive, and by this deliverance we are made capable and able to do good works and not otherwise.

9. REMISSION OF
SINS ALWAYS NECESSARY
FOR THE FAITHFUL

Finally, we acknowledge that this regeneration is so effected in us that, until we slough off this mortal body, there remains always in us much imperfection and infirmity, so that we always remain poor and wretched sinners in the presence of God. And, however much we ought day by day to increase and grow in God's righteousness, there will never be plenitude or perfection while we live here. Thus we always have need of the mercy of God to obtain the remission of our faults and offences. And so we ought always to look for our righteousness in Jesus Christ and not at all in ourselves, and in him be confident and assured, putting no faith in our works.

10. ALL OUR GOOD IN THE GRACE OF GOD

In order that all glory and praise be rendered to God (as is his due), and that we be able to have true peace and rest of conscience, we understand and confess that we receive all benefits from God, as said above, by his clemency and pity, without any consideration of our worthiness or the merit of our works, to which is due no other retribution than eternal confusion. None the less our Saviour in his goodness, having received us into the communion of his son Jesus, regards the works that we have done in faith as pleasing and agreeable; not that they merit it at all, but because, not imputing any of the imperfection that is there, he acknowledges in them nothing but what proceeds from his Spirit.

11. FAITH

We confess that the entrance which we have to the great treasures and riches of the goodness of God that is vouchsafed to us is by faith; inasmuch as, in certain confidence and assurance of heart, we believe in the promises of the Gospel, and receive Jesus Christ as he is offered to us by the Father and described to us by the Word of God.

12. INVOCATION OF GOD ONLY AND INTERCESSION OF CHRIST

As we have declared that we have confidence and hope for salvation and all good only in God through Jesus Christ, so we confess that we ought to invoke him in all necessities in the name of Jesus Christ, who is our Mediator and Advocate with him and has access to him. Likewise we ought to acknowledge that all good things come from him alone, and to give thanks to him for them. On the other hand, we reject the intercession of the saints as a superstition invented by men contrary to Scripture, for the reason that it proceeds from mistrust of the sufficiency of the intercession of Jesus Christ.

13. PRAYER INTELLIGIBLE

Moreover since prayer is nothing but hypocrisy and fantasy unless it proceed from the interior affections of the heart, we believe that all prayers ought to be made with clear understanding. And for this reason, we hold the prayer of our Lord to show fittingly what we ought to ask of him: Our Father which art in heaven, . . . but deliver us from evil. Amen.

14. SACRAMENTS

We believe that the sacraments which our Lord has ordained in his Church are to be regarded as exercises of faith for us, both for fortifying and confirming it in the promises of God and for witnessing before men. Of them there are in the Christian Church only two which are instituted by the authority of our Saviour: Baptism and the Supper of our Lord; for what is held within the realm of the pope concerning seven sacraments, we condemn as fable and lie.

15. BAPTISM

Baptism is an external sign by which our Lord testifies that he desires to receive us for his children, as members of his Son

Jesus. Hence in it there is represented to us the cleansing from sin which we have in the blood of Jesus Christ, the mortification of our flesh which we have by his death that we may live in him by his Spirit. Now since our children belong to such an alliance with our Lord, we are certain that the external sign is rightly applied to them.

16. THE HOLY SUPPER

The Supper of our Lord is a sign by which under bread and wine he represents the true spiritual communion which we have in his body and blood. And we acknowledge that according to his ordinance it ought to be distributed in the company of the faithful, in order that all those who wish to have Jesus for their life be partakers of it. In as much as the mass of the pope was a reprobate and diabolical ordinance subverting the mystery of the Holy Supper, we declare that it is execrable to us, an idolatry condemned by God; for so much is it itself regarded as a sacrifice for the redemption of souls that the bread is in it taken and adored as God. Besides there are other execrable blasphemies and superstitions implied here, and the abuse of the Word of God which is taken in vain without profit or edification.

17. HUMAN TRADITIONS

The ordinances that are necessary for the internal discipline of the Church, and belong solely to the maintenance of peace, honesty and good order in the assembly of Christians, we do not hold to be human traditions at all, in as much as they are comprised under the general command of Paul, where he desires that all be done among them decently and in order. But all laws and regulations made binding on conscience which oblige the faithful to things not commanded by God, or establish another service of God than that which he demands, thus tending to destroy Christian liberty, we condemn as perverse doctrines of Satan, in view of our Lord's declaration that he is honoured in vain by doctrines that are the commandment of men. It is in this estimation that we hold pilgrimages, monasteries, distinctions of foods, prohibition of marriage, confessions and other like things.

18. THE CHURCH

While there is one only Church of Jesus Christ, we always acknowledge that necessity requires companies of the faithful to be distributed in different places. Of these assemblies each one is called Church. But in as much as all companies do not assemble in the name of our Lord, but rather to blaspheme and pollute him by their sacrilegious deeds, we believe that the proper mark by which rightly to discern the Church of Jesus Christ is that his holy gospel be purely and faithfully preached, proclaimed, heard, and kept, that his sacraments be properly administered, even if there be some imperfections and faults, as there always will be among men. On the other hand, where the Gospel is not declared, heard, and received, there we do not acknowledge the form of the Church. Hence the churches governed by the ordinances of the pope are rather synagogues of the devil than Christian churches.

19. Excommunication

Because there are always some who hold God and his Word in contempt, who take account of neither injunction, exhortation nor remonstrance, thus requiring greater chastisement, we hold the discipline of excommunication to be a thing holy and salutary among the faithful, since truly it was instituted by our Lord with good reason. This is in order that the wicked should not by their damnable conduct corrupt the good and dishonour our Lord, and that though proud they may turn to penitence. Therefore we believe that it is expedient according to the ordinance of God that all manifest idolaters, blasphemers, murderers, thieves, lewd persons, false witnesses, seditionmongers, quarrellers, those guilty of defamation or assault, drunkards, dissolute livers, when they have been duly admonished and if they do not make amendment, be separated from the communion of the faithful until their repentance is known.

20. Ministers of the Word

We recognize no other pastors in the Church than faithful pastors of the Word of God, feeding the sheep of Jesus Christ on the one hand with instruction, admonition, consolation, exhortation, deprecation; and on the other resisting all false doctrines and deceptions of the devil, without mixing with the pure doctrine of the Scriptures their dreams or their foolish imaginings. To these we accord no other power or authority but to conduct, rule, and govern the people of God committed to them by the same Word, in which they have power to command, defend, promise, and warn, and without which they neither can nor ought to attempt anything. As we receive the true ministers of the Word of God as messengers and ambassadors of God, it is necessary to listen to them as to him himself, and we hold their ministry to be a commission from God necessary in the Church. On the other hand we hold that all seductive and false prophets, who abandon the purity of the Gospel and deviate to their own inventions, ought not at all to be suffered or maintained, who are not the pastors they pretend, but rather, like ravening wolves, ought to be hunted and ejected from the people of God.

21. MAGISTRATES

We hold the supremacy and dominion of kings and princes as also of other magistrates and officers, to be a holy thing and a good ordinance of God. And since in performing their office they serve God and follow a Christian vocation, whether in defending the afflicted and innocent, or in correcting and punishing the malice of the perverse, we on our part also ought to accord them honour and reverence, to render respect and subservience, to execute their commands, to bear the charges they impose on us, so far as we are able without offence to God. In sum, we ought to regard them as vicars and lieutenants of God, whom one cannot resist without resisting God himself; and their office as a sacred commission from God which has been given them so that they may rule and govern us. Hence we hold that all Christians are bound to pray God for the prosperity of the superiors and lords of the country where they live, to obey the statutes and ordinances which do not contravene the commandments of God, to promote welfare, peace and public good, endeavouring to sustain the honour of those over them and the peace of the people, without contriving or attempting anything to inspire trouble or dissension. On the other hand we declare that all those who conduct themselves unfaithfully towards their superiors, and have not a right concern for the public good of the country where they live, demonstrate thereby their infidelity towards God.

8

The Confession of Faith of the English Congregation at Geneva, 1556

INTRODUCTION

When Mary acceded to the throne of England in July, 1553, the Protestant cause, which had flourished under Edward VI, received a serious setback. The old forms of worship were restored and rigorously enforced. Many professing the evangelical faith were forced to flee to the Continent where they took refuge in various cities, principally Strassburg, Frankfurt, Emden, Zurich, and Geneva. The exiles numbered between eight hundred and a thousand. By 1555 Calvin's authority had been firmly established in Geneva and, as a result of elections held in February of that year, foreigners were admitted to the privilege of citizenship. Thereupon a small band of English sent a request to Calvin that they be permitted to enjoy the privileges granted to exiles from other countries. On June 10 their request was laid before the Council and it ordered that a suitable place should be found where they could worship.[1] John Knox, the great Scottish Reformer, served as their minister on the first occasion for only a few weeks prior to leaving for Scotland in August, 1555. He returned to Geneva on September 13 the following year. During his absence the English congregation had taken root, and on November 14, 1555, had been granted joint use with Italian refugees of the Temple de Notre Dame la Neuve as a place of worship. Two men were chosen pastors, Christopher Goodman and John Knox. (Anthony Gilby took Knox's place during his year of absence.) Thus originated the English congregation at Geneva which formed the link between the Ref-

---

[1] P. Hume Brown, *John Knox* (London, 1895), Vol. I, pp. 189 f.; *Régistre du Conseil*, 1st June 1555.

ormation in French-speaking Switzerland and in Scotland.

During the five years of its existence until its dissolution at the accession of Elizabeth to the throne of England, the membership roll mounted to a total of 186 persons.[2] But the historic importance of this tiny colony was out of all proportions to its slender numbers. Numbering among its members some of the outstanding scholars of the age, it produced a church order which was afterward accepted as the standard of worship in the Church of Scotland and among the Puritans in England until the Westminster Directory appeared in 1644. It also produced a metrical version of part of the psalms which formed the basis of what was subsequently used in England and Scotland. But its greatest accomplishment was the translation, first of the New Testament in 1557, and then of the whole Bible by April, 1560. For three quarters of a century the Genevan Bible was " the household book of the English-speaking nations." [3]

The English congregation in Geneva enjoyed peace and harmony throughout the whole period of its existence. When John Knox returned to the city in 1556 he wrote:

This place . . . is the moist perfyt schoole of Chryst that ever was in the erth since the dayis of the Apostillis. In other places, I confess Chryst to be trewlie preachit, but maneris and religioun so sinceirlie reformat, I have not yit sene in any uther place.[4]

In the historical introduction to the Genevan Confession of 1536 it has been noted already that Calvin published his catechism in that year, along with the Confession and a Discipline for the government of the church. This work was carefully revised and republished in 1545, and translations of it — in whole or in part — appeared in most of the European languages. It served as a model to the Reformed Churches in other countries. Thus it also formed the model for " The

---

[2] William D. Maxwell, *John Knox's Genevan Service Book 1556* (Edinburgh, 1931), p. 7. Hume, *John Knox*, pp. 202 f., states that " those on the church-roll and in the register of inhabitants amounted to 212 persons."

[3] Hume, *John Knox*, pp. 204 f. Cf. B. F. Westcott, *The Bible in the Church* (1901), pp. 285 f.; Ira M. Price, *The Ancestry of Our English Bible: An Account of Manuscripts, Texts, and Versions of the Bible* (1907) ; 3d rev. ed. by William A. Irwin and Allen P. Wikgren (Harper & Brothers, 1956), pp. 262 ff.; F. F. Bruce, *The English Bible: A History of Translations* (Oxford University Press, 1961), pp. 85 ff.; *The Cambridge History of the Bible: The West from the Reformation to the Present Day*, ed. by S. L. Greenslade (London: Cambridge University Press, 1963), pp. 155 ff.

[4] *The Works of John Knox*, ed. by David Laing, 6 vols. (Edinburgh, 1855), Vol. IV, p. 240.

Form of Prayers and Administration of the Sacraments, etc.,"
published by the English congregation at Geneva, February
10, 1556.[5] However, " The Form of Prayers " was substantially
the same as a form of worship which had been prepared
toward the end of January, 1555, by a committee consisting of
Knox, Whittingham, Gilby, Fox, and Cole for the English
congregation at Frankfurt. It was not favorably received in
Frankfurt and does not seem to have been used there. In
Geneva only slight alterations were made to it, and to it were
added a preface, the Confession of Faith which is given here,
a collection of fifty metrical psalms in English, and an English
translation of Calvin's Catechism. Thus since Knox had
doubtless a dominant part in the substance and arrangement
of the service book at Frankfurt, " the familiar title of the
book, ' John Knox's Liturgy,' " as Maxwell remarks, " may
not be so grave a misnomer as it sometimes is supposed." [6]
Knox, however, could hardly have been the author of the
Confession of Faith. It was probably the work of Whittingham. Incidentally, the early editions of " The Form of
Prayers " bore the statement: " And approved by the famous
and godly learned man, John Calvin."

Copies of the original edition of " The Form of Prayers "
(February, 1556) are to be found in the National Library,
Edinburgh, the Bodleian Library, Cambridge University Library, the Town Library at Zurich. It is reproduced in *The
Works of John Knox,* edited by David Laing, Vol. IV, pp.
149–214. A copy of the Confession of Faith is also to be found
in Dunlop's *Collection of Confessions of Faith,* Vol. II (Edinburgh, 1722). The editor states that it is " according to a
copy printed 1600, compared with the Geneva edition, 1558."
There were indeed later editions printed at Geneva in 1558
and 1561, and Maxwell gives an account of these and their
present location in his scholarly work, *John Knox's Genevan
Service Book 1556.* He also gives an account of various editions that were printed in England and Scotland. Moreover,
a full account of all the editions and their principal contents

[5] W. D. Maxwell, *John Knox's Genevan Service Book* (p. 15), declares
that " Laing and M'Crie are wrong in stating that the old style of calendar
was used in Geneva at this time. They may have been moved to suggest this
in order to indicate that the book really appeared in 1557 when Knox was in
Geneva, and not as actually in 1556 during his absence. But however alluring
this view may be, the facts do not sustain it. The new style of dating from
Jan. 1 had been adopted in Geneva at least as early as 1532."

[6] *John Knox's Genevan Service Book,* p. 15.

as used in the Church of Scotland is given in William Cowan, *A Bibliography of the Book of Common Order and Psalm Book of the Church of Scotland, 1556–1644*. After 1564 the Genevan " Form of Prayers " gradually became known as the Book of Common Order, and continued in use until the Westminster Directory superseded it in 1645.

A Latin translation was made of the original English text at the same time for the purpose of submitting it to Calvin for his approval. It is known as the *Ratio et Forma* from its opening words, and seems to have been the only Latin translation made. It is usually attributed to Whittingham. Copies are to be found in the British Museum, the Bodleian Library, the Town Library at Zurich, and in William Cowan's Collection bequeathed in 1929 to the National Library, Edinburgh. Maxwell has reprinted most of the Latin text but not that of the Confession of Faith.

The modern English version of the Confession provided here has been made from the copy in Dunlop's *Collection*. The Apostles' Creed printed in the margins has been omitted, but the Scriptural references have been retained.

Literature: *Livre des Anglois,* a volume kept by the ministers of the English congregation and still preserved in the Hôtel de Ville at Geneva. A transcript of it was printed by J. Southernden Burn (London, 1831). Dunlop, *A Collection of Confessions of Faith,* Vol. II (Edinburgh, 1722) ; David Laing, ed., *The Works of John Knox,* 6 vols. (Edinburgh, 1855), especially Vols. IV and VI; P. Hume Brown, *John Knox* (London, 1895), Vol. I; William Cowan, *A Bibliography of the Book of Common Order and Psalm Book of the Church of Scotland, 1556–1644,* in the papers of the Edinburgh Bibliographical Society, Vol. X (Edinburgh, 1913) ; Charles Martin, *Les Protestants anglais réfugiés à Genève au temps de Calvin, 1555–1560* (Geneva, 1915) ; William D. Maxwell, *John Knox's Genevan Service Book 1556* (Edinburgh, 1931).

The Confession of Faith
Used in the English Congregation at Geneva, 1556

RECEIVED AND APPROVED BY THE CHURCH OF SCOTLAND IN THE
BEGINNING OF THE REFORMATION

I

I believe and confess [7] my Lord God eternal, infinite, immeasurable, incomprehensible and invisible,[8] one in substance [9] and three in persons, Father, Son and Holy Ghost; [10] Who by His almighty power and wisdom [11] has not only created of nothing heaven, earth, and all things therein contained; [12] and man after His own image [13] that in him He might be glorified,[14] but also governs, maintains and preserves the same [15] by His Fatherly providence according to the purpose of His will.[16]

II

I also believe and confess Jesus Christ the only Savior and Messiah,[17] Who being equal with God, made Himself of no reputation, but took on Him the shape of a servant,[18] and became man in all things like unto us, sin excepted,[19] to assure

---

[7] Rom. 10:10.
[8] Gen. 17:1; Ps. 63:1; 30:2; 139:1-16; I Tim. 1:17.
[9] Deut. 6:4; Eph. 4:6.
[10] Gen. 1:26; Matt. 3:16, 17; 28:19; I John 5:7.
[11] Heb. 1:2; Prov. 8:22-30.
[12] Gen. 1:1; Jer. 32:16; Ps. 13:6-7.
[13] Gen. 1:26; Eph. 4:24; Col. 3:10.
[14] Prov. 16:4; John 17:1; I Cor. 6:20.
[15] Matt. 6:26-32; Luke 12:24-30; I Peter 5:7; Phil. 4:6.
[16] Eph. 1:11.
[17] Matt. 1:21; Acts 4:12; I Tim. 1:15.
[18] John, ch. 1; Phil. 2:6-7; I Tim. 3:16; I John 5:20; Rom. 9:5.
[19] Heb. 2:14, 16-17; Phil. 2:7-8; I Peter 2:22; I John 3:5.

us of mercy and forgiveness.[20] For when through our father Adam's transgression we were become children of perdition,[21] there was no means to bring us from that yoke of sin and damnation, but only Jesus Christ our Lord,[22] who giving us by grace that which was His by nature,[23] made us through faith the children of God.[24]

When the fullness of time was come,[25] He was conceived by the power of the Holy Ghost, born of the Virgin Mary, according to the flesh,[26] and preached on earth the Gospel of salvation,[27] till at length, by the tyranny of the priests, He was innocently under Pontius Pilate, then governor, and most slanderously hanged on the Cross between two thieves, as a notorious trespasser,[28] where taking upon him the punishment of our sins, he delivered us from the curse of the law.[29]

And inasmuch as He, being only God, could not feel death, neither being only man, could overcome death, He joined both together, and allowed His humanity to be punished with most cruel death,[30] feeling in Himself the anger and severe judgment of God, even as He had been in the extreme torments of hell, and therefore cried with a loud voice, *My God, my God, why hast Thou forsaken me?* [31]

Thus of His free mercy, without compulsion, he offered up himself as the only sacrifice to purge the sins of all the world,[32] so that all other sacrifices for sins are blasphemous, and derogate from the sufficiency thereof.

Although His death did sufficiently reconcile us to God,[33] yet the Scriptures ordinarily attribute our regeneration to His resurrection.[34] For as by rising again from the grave the third

----

20 Rom. 8:31, etc.; I John 2:1.
21 Gen., ch. 3; Rom. 5:16-18; Eph. 2:3; Gal. 3:10, 13.
22 Acts 4:12; I Peter 2:6; Isa. 28:16; Rom. 9:33.
23 John 1:1-2; Heb. 1:5; Rom. 1:4; Ps. 2:7.
24 Gal. 3:26; Rom. 8:14; John 1:12; Eph. 1:5.
25 Gal. 4:4; Rom. 1:2-3; Acts 2:22.
26 Isa. 7:14; Luke 1:31, 35; Rom. 1:2.
27 Acts 10:36; Heb. 1:2.
28 John 7:32; 11:47, 48, 53; 12:10-11, 42; Matt. 12:14, 27; Luke, ch. 23; Mark, ch. 15; John, chs. 18; 19.
29 Gal. 3:13; Isa. 53:6, 8, 10.
30 Acts 2:24; I Peter 2:24; Isa. 53:4-5, 7, 10.
31 Ps. 22:1; Matt. 27:46.
32 Isa., ch. 53; Heb. 9:12, 14, 25, 26, 28; 10:10, 12, 14; Gal. 1:4; Rom. 4:25; Rom. 5:8-10; I John 1:7.
33 Col. 1:20.
34 Rom. 6:4, 5; I Peter 1:3.

day [35] He conquered death,[36] even so the victory of our faith stands in his resurrection, and therefore without the one we cannot feel the benefit of the other. For as by death sin was taken away, so our righteousness was restored by his resurrection.[37]

And because He would accomplish all things, and take possession for us in His kingdom,[38] He ascended into heaven,[39] to enlarge that same kingdom by the abundant power of his Spirit,[40] by Whom we are most assured of His continual intercession toward God the Father for us.[41] And although He is in heaven according to His corporeal presence [42] where the Father has now set Him on His right hand,[43] committing unto Him the administration of all things in heaven above as well as in the earth beneath,[44] yet He is present with us His members even till the end of the world [45] in preserving and governing us with His effectual power and grace. When all things are fulfilled which God has spoken by the mouth of all his prophets since the world began,[46] He will come in the same visible form in which He ascended,[47] with an unspeakable majesty, power and company, to separate the lambs from the goats, the elect from the reprobate,[48] so that none, whether he be alive then or already dead, shall escape His judgment.

III

Moreover, I believe and confess the Holy Ghost, God equal with the Father and the Son, Who regenerates and sanctifies us, rules and guides us into all truth,[49] persuading us most assuredly in our consciences that we are the children of God, brethren to Jesus Christ, and fellow-heirs with Him of life everlasting.[50]

---

[35] Matt. 28; Acts 10:40; I Cor. 15:4.
[36] Hos. 13:14; I Cor. 15:26, 55-57.
[37] Rom. 4:25.
[38] Eph. 4:10; John 14:2, 3; Heb. 6:20.
[39] Mark 16:19; Luke 24:51; Acts 1:9, 11.
[40] Luke 24:49; John 14:16-17, 26; Acts 1:4; 2:4.
[41] Rom. 8:34; Heb. 7:25; 9:24; I John 2:1.
[42] Acts 3:21.
[43] Col. 3:1; Rom. 8:34; Heb. 1:3; 10:11; 12:2.
[44] Eph. 1:20-22; Phil. 2:9; Col. 2:10.
[45] Matt. 28:20.
[46] Acts 3:21.
[47] Acts 1:11.
[48] Matt. 25:31-46; Phil. 3:20.
[49] Matt. 3:16-17; I John 5:7; I Peter 1:2, 22; I Cor. 6:11, 19; John 16:7-13; Eph. 3:16; II Thess. 2:13.
[50] Rom. 8:13-17; Gal. 4:6-7.

Yet notwithstanding it is not sufficient to believe that God is omnipotent and merciful, that Christ has made satisfaction, or that the Holy Spirit has this power and effect, except we do apply the same benefits to ourselves [51] who are God's elect.[52]

IV

I believe therefore and confess one holy Church [53] which (as members of Jesus Christ the only Head thereof [54]) agree in faith, hope and love,[55] using the gifts of God, whether they be temporal or spiritual, to the profit and furtherance of the same.[56] This Church is not visible to man's eye but only known to God [57] Who of the lost sons of Adam has ordained some as vessels of wrath to damnation,[58] and has chosen others as vessels of His mercy to be saved.[59] In due time He also calls them to integrity of life and godly conversation, to make them a glorious Church for Himself.[60]

But this Church which is visible and seen by the eye [61] has three tokens or marks whereby it may be known. First, the Word of God contained in the Old and New Testament [62] which, since it is above the authority of the same Church [63] and alone is sufficient to instruct us in all things concerning salvation,[64] it is left for all degrees of men to read and understand,[65] for without this Word no Church, council or decree can establish any point concerning salvation.[66]

The second is the holy sacraments, to wit, of baptism and the Lord's Supper which Christ has left unto us as holy signs and seals of God's promises.[67] For as by baptism once received is signified that we (infants as well as others of age and dis-

---

51 Heb. 2:4; Rom. 1:17; 10:9; I John 3:23; John 3:36.
52 John 17:2-3.
53 John 17:2-3.
54 Matt. 16:18; John 10:14-16; Eph. 5:25-27; Rom. 8:28.
55 S. of Sol., ch. 2.
56 Acts 2:41, etc.; 4:32, etc.; Rom. 12:4, etc.; I Cor., ch. 12; Eph. 4:7, 11-12.
57 Rom. 11:33-34; II Tim. 2:19.
58 Rom. 9:21-22.
59 Rom. 9:23; Eph. 1:4-6, 11-12.
60 Rom. 8:30; Eph. 5:26-27.
61 Matt. 18:17; I Cor. 15:9.
62 Matt. 28:19, 20; Rom. 10:14, 17; Luke 16:31; 24:27; Eph. 2:20; John 10:16; II Tim. 3:15-16.
63 II Peter 1:20-21.
64 John 20:31; II Tim. 3:15-17.
65 Deut. 6:6-7; James 1:8; Ps. 78:5; John 5:39.
66 Matt. 15:3, 6, 9; 22:29; Eph. 5:17.
67 Matt. 28:19; 26:26-30; Rom. 4:11.

cretion) being strangers from God by original sin, are received into His family and congregation,[68] with full assurance that although this root of sin lies hidden in us, yet to the elect it shall not be imputed.[69] Similarly the Supper declares that God, as a most provident Father, not only feeds our bodies but also spiritually nourishes our souls with the graces and benefits of Jesus Christ. Scripture calls this the eating of His flesh and drinking of His blood.[70] In the administration of these sacraments we must not follow man's phantasy, but they must be administered as Christ Himself has ordained and by such as by ordinary vocation are thereunto called.[71] Therefore whoever reserves or worships these sacraments, or on the contrary, despises them in time and space, procures damnation for himself.

The third mark of this Church is ecclesiastical discipline which consists of admonition and correction of faults.[72] The final end of discipline is excommunication determined by the consent of the Church if the offender is obstinate.[73]

And besides this ecclesiastical discipline, I acknowledge to the Church a political magistrate who administers justice to every man, defending the good and punishing the evil, to whom we must render honor and obedience in all things [74] which are not contrary to the Word of God.[75]

And as Moses,[76] Hezekiah,[77] Josiah,[78] and other godly rulers purged the Church of God of superstition and idolatry, so the defence of Christ's Church against all idolaters and heretics, as Papists, Anabaptists and such rascals or antichrist pertains to the Christian magistrates, to root out all doctrine of devils and men, such as the mass, purgatory, *Limbus Patrum,* prayers to the saints and for the dead, free will, distinction of meats, apparel and days, vows of single life, presence at a service of idols, human merits and such like [79] which draw us

---

68 Rom. 6:3-5; Gal. 3:27; Col. 2:11-12; Titus 3:5.
69 Rom. 4; Ps. 32:1-2.
70 I Cor. 11:23-29; John 6:48-58.
71 Deut. 12:32; Heb. 5:4; John 1:33; I Cor. 4:1.
72 Matt. 18:15-22; Luke 17:3-4; Lev. 19:17; Ecclus. 19:13-17.
73 I Cor., ch. 5.
74 Rom. 13:1-7; Wisd. of Sol. 6:4; Titus 3:1; I Peter 2:13-14.
75 Acts 4:19; 5:29.
76 Ex., ch. 32.
77 II Kings 18:4; II Chron., chs. 29; 30; 31.
78 II Kings 23:1-25; II Chron., ch. 34.
79 II Tim. 4:2-4; Col. 2:8, 16-23; Matt. 15:1-9; Isa. 29:13; Heb. 9:12, 14, 25, 26, 28; 10:10, 12, 14; Acts 10:15; I John 2:22; Rom. 7:6; Gal. 5:1; Col. 2:8, 16-23; Rom., ch. 14; I Tim. 4:1-8; Matt. 19:10-12; I Cor. 7:2, 9; chs. 8; 10:25; II Cor. 6:16-17; Luke 17:23; Rom. 3:19-29; I Cor. 3:11; Gal. 4:9-10.

from the society of Christ's Church which consists only in the remission of sins purchased by Christ's blood for all those that believe, whether they be Jews or Gentiles,[80] and which lead us to a vain confidence in creatures, and trust in our own imaginations. Although God oftentimes defers in this life their punishment,[81] yet after the general resurrection, when our souls and bodies shall rise again to immortality,[82] they shall be damned to unquenchable fire.[83] And then we who have forsaken all men's wisdom to cleave unto Christ, shall hear the joyful voice, Come ye blessed of my Father, inherit the kingdom prepared for you from the beginning of the world,[84] and thus shall go triumphing with him in body and soul, to remain everlastingly in glory,[85] where we shall see God face to face, and shall no more need one to instruct another; for we shall all know Him, from the highest to the lowest.[86] To whom with the Father and the Holy Ghost, be all praise, honor and glory, now and ever. So be it.

---

[80] Isa. 33:24; Matt. 18:18; John 20:23; II Cor. 5:18; Rom. 1:16; 10:11-12; Eph. 2:11.
[81] II Peter, ch. 2; Jude; Rom. 9:22.
[82] Acts 24:15; I Cor. 15:12; Phil. 3:11, 21; I Thess. 4:13.
[83] II Thess. 1:7-9; 2:12; Isa. 30:27; John 3:36; 5:28-29; Matt. 25:30, 41, **46.**
[84] Matt. 25:21, 23, 34, 46.
[85] I Thess. 4:16, 17; 5:9, 10; John 5:29; Isa. 26:19.
[86] I Cor. 13:12; I John 3:2; Jer. 31:34; Heb. 8:11.

9

The French Confession of Faith, 1559

INTRODUCTION

The seeds of the Reformation in France were sown by Jacques Le Fèvre d'Étaples (1455–1537), a professor at the Sorbonne who in 1530 translated the Bible from the Vulgate, and taught, even before Luther and Zwingli, the doctrine of justification by faith and the supreme authority of the Bible, and by his friends and pupils: Briçonnet, bishop of Meaux; Melchior Wolmar, professor of Greek in Bourges and teacher of Calvin; Louis de Berquin (1489–1529), who was burned at the stake; Clément Marot (1495–1544), the poet who translated the psalms into verse; Peter Robert Olivetan (d. 1538), a relative of Calvin's who published a translation of the Bible in French at Neuchâtel in 1535. Even more effective were Guillaume Farel, Peter Viret, Calvin and Beza who were driven into French Switzerland. Farel, by his writings and itinerant preaching, was especially effective in spreading the gospel among the common people.

From the outset the Protestants in France were sorely persecuted. But the fire of persecution only served to increase their numbers, and it has been estimated that by 1555 there were four hundred thousand Reformed Protestants in the country. The earliest Confession arose out of the persecutions that broke out in Paris during September, 1557, when thirty-five members of the Church in that city were arrested. Seven were immediately condemned and executed. The Reformed Christians wrote letters to their brethren in Switzerland, urging them to intercede with the King of France. Calvin's efforts in this direction were unavailing. However, they did send to Calvin a brief statement of faith drawn up in eighteen articles and addressed to the King. Calvin had been repeatedly requested to draw up a Confession of Faith which would serve the needs of the Reformed Christians in France. According to Jacques Pannier, the historian of the French Confession,[1] Calvin was on principle opposed to the idea of a Confession written by a single hand. Hence the draft Confession was probably the joint work of Calvin, Beza, and Viret. It consisted of thirty-five articles in which portions of the 1557 Confession were incorporated verbatim.

When during 1558 and 1559 the persecutions temporarily abated, the Church in Paris was emboldened to summon a general assembly or synod of the Churches in France with a view to establishing a Church constitution based upon a common Confession of Faith.[2] On May 23, 1559, twenty delegates representing seventy-two churches met secretly in a private house in Paris. François de Morel was elected moderator. After four days of deliberation the delegates adopted the Genevan draft with a few alterations. Antoine de la Roche Chandieu, a pupil of Calvin's, has been credited with making the final revision, but this claim has been questioned by scholars.

The Genevan draft had thirty-five articles. The French Synod recast the first two and expanded them into six, with the result that the Confession now has forty articles. The alteration of the first article was fraught with fateful consequences. Under the influence of the rediscovery of Stoicism in the so-called humanism that was contemporaneous with the Reformation, natural theology here first gained an entry into Reformed Confessions. Article II reads in part: " God reveals himself to men; firstly, in his works, in their creation, as well as in their preservation and control. Secondly, and more clearly, in his Word." B. A. Gerrish offers the following translation of the original first Genevan Article.

Since the foundation of believing is through the Word of God, as Paul says (Rom. 10:17), we believe that the Living God has revealed Himself in His law, and through His prophets, and finally in the Gospel; that He has there provided such witness to His will as is expedient for the salvation of men. Hence we hold to the Books of the Holy Scripture, of the Old and New Testament, as the sum of the sole infallible truth which has proceeded from God; against which it is not permissible to contradict. Also [likewise], since the perfect rule of all wisdom is contained

---

[1] Cited by B. A. Gerrish, *The Faith of Christendom: A Source Book of Creeds and Confessions* (The World Publishing Company, 1963) , p. 128.

[2] Here and in most collections only the Confession of Faith is reproduced. But the text of the constitution or " ecclesiastical discipline " is also given in *Bekenntnisschriften und Kirchenordnungen,* ed. W. Niesel (Munich, 1938) .

therein, we believe that it is not permissible to add to it or subtract from it in any respect, but that it is necessary to comply with it in every detail (en tout et par tout). [Echoed in part by the 1559 Address.] Rather, because this doctrine receives its authority neither from men nor from angels (Gal. 1:8), but from God alone, we also believe (more especially as it is something surpassing all human judgment to discern that it is God who speaks) that He alone gives the certainty of that doctrine to His elect and seals it in their hearts by His Spirit.[3]

Having gained admission in the French Confession, the virus of natural theology quickly spread to the Belgic Confession of 1561 (Articles II–III), and thence to the Westminster Confession of Faith of 1643. Not until the Barmen Theological Declaration of 1934 was natural theology categorically rejected in its first article, and the original witness of the Reformed Confessions of the 16th century reaffirmed.

The following year (1560) the French Confession was presented to King Francis II with a preface that is an eloquent plea for justice from a persecuted Church. Although the preface was not part of the original Confession, it is included here because it illustrates how the French Church understood the Confession of Faith for which it was suffering. " We can declare this before God and men, that we suffer for no other reason than for maintaining our Lord Jesus Christ to be our only Saviour and Redeemer, and his doctrine to be the only doctrine of life and salvation." At the Seventh National Synod held at La Rochelle in 1571 the Confession was confirmed by all the Churches of France. It was approved and signed by representatives of three national Churches — Admiral Coligny for the French Church, Theodore Beza for the Church of Geneva, and by Jeanne d'Albret, Queen of Navarre (mother of Henry IV, future king of France). For this reason the Confession is also known as " the Confession of La Rochelle." It is also referred to as the Gallican Confession. In a Declaration of Faith the Reformed Church of France in 1936 expressly reaffirmed the Confession of La Rochelle.[4] In Germany it was recognized by synods in Wesel (1568) and Emden (1571). The Confession, together with the Discipline, influenced the faith and polity of Reformed Churches in Holland, England, and Scotland.

---

[3] *The Faith of Christendom,* p. 130. Cf. K. Barth, *Church Dogmatics,* II, 1, p. 127.

[4] A translation of the text of this Declaration is given by Paul T. Fuhrmann, *An Introduction to the Great Creeds of the Church* (The Westminster Press, 1960), pp. 101 ff.

According to Schaff and Müller, three copies of the original text were written on parchment in French — one for La Rochelle, one for Geneva, one for Béarn. The French original, with the old spelling, is printed in Beza's *Histoire ecclésiastique des églises réformées au royaume de France,* in Niemeyer's *Collectio confessionum* (pp. 313–326), and by Heinrich Heppe, in the *Zeitschrift für die historische Theologie* (Gotha, 1875), pp. 524 ff., from the manuscript copy in the Geneva State Archives. Heppe's version is reproduced by Müller in his collection with slight simplifications of the punctuation. The text is also printed in the *Corpus Reformatorum (Calvini Opera,* Vol. IX) with the citations from the 1557 Confession in italics and the variations from the Geneva draft in footnotes.[5] The earliest German translation appeared at Heidelberg in 1562 and Böckel offers a version in modern German in his collection. A Latin translation is to be found in the *Corpus et syntagma* and in Niemeyer (pp. 329–339). Schaff provides the authoritative text, in modern spelling, from the edition published by the *Société des Livres religieux,* at Toulouse, 1864, as well as an English translation prepared by Miss Emily O. Butler. It is this latter which has been used in the present collection.[6]

Literature: E. F. K. Müller, *Die Bekenntnisschriften der reformierten Kirche* (Leipzig, 1903); P. Schaff, *Creeds of Christendom,* Vol. I, pp. 490–498; G. Bonet, " Maury," *The New Schaff-Herzog Encyclopedia of Religious Knowledge,* Vol. IV (1950), pp. 423 f.; *Guillaume Farel, 1489–1565, Biographie nouvelle écrite d'après les documents originaux par un groupe d'historiens, professeurs et pasteurs de Suisse, de France et d'Italie* (Neuchâtel and Paris, 1930); P. Imbart de la Tour, *Les Origines de la Réforme,* Vol. IV (Paris, 1935); Jacques Pannier, *Les origines de la confession de foi et la discipline des églises réformées de France* (Paris, 1936); Roger Mehl, *Explication de la confession de foi de la Rochelle,* Collection " *Les Bergers et les Mages* " (Paris, n.d.); Wilhelm Niesel, ed., *Bekenntnisschriften und Kirchenordnungen* (Munich, 1938); Paul Jacobs, *Theologie reformierter Bekenntnisschriften in Grundzügen* (Neukirchener Verlag, 1959).

---

[5] See B. A. Gerrish, *The Faith of Christendom,* p. 128.

[6] Professor Gerrish has used the same translation in his *The Faith of Christendom* and has drawn attention in his notes to some " unaccountable departures from the French version." (See pp. 347 ff.)

The French Confession of Faith. A.D. *1559*

THE FRENCH SUBJECTS WHO WISH TO LIVE IN THE PURITY OF THE
GOSPEL OF OUR LORD JESUS CHRIST

TO THE KING

Sire, we thank God that hitherto having had no access to
your Majesty to make known the rigor of the persecutions
that we have suffered, and suffer daily, for wishing to live in
the purity of the Gospel and in peace with our own consciences, he now permits us to see that you wish to know the
worthiness of our cause, as is shown by the last Edict given at
Amboise in the month of March of this present year, 1559,
which it has pleased your Majesty to cause to be published.
This emboldens us to speak, which we have been prevented
from doing hitherto through the injustice and violence of
some of your officers, incited rather by hatred of us than by
love of your service. And to the end, Sire, that we may fully
inform your Majesty of what concerns this cause, we humbly
beseech that you will see and hear our Confession of Faith,
which we present to you, hoping that it will prove a sufficient answer to the blame and opprobrium unjustly laid upon
us by those who have always made a point of condemning us
without having any knowledge of our cause. In the which,
Sire, we can affirm that there is nothing contrary to the Word
of God, or to the homage which we owe to you.

For the articles of our faith, which are all declared at some
length in our Confession, all come to this: that since God has
sufficiently declared his will to us through his Prophets and
Apostles, and even by the mouth of his Son, our Lord Jesus
Christ, we owe such respect and reverence to the Word of
God as shall prevent us from adding to it any thing of our
own, but shall make us conform entirely to the rules it prescribes. And inasmuch as the Roman Church, forsaking the
use and customs of the primitive Church, has introduced new

commandments and a new form of worship of God, we esteem it but reasonable to prefer the commandments of God, who is himself truth, to the commandments of men, who by their nature are inclined to deceit and vanity. And whatever our enemies may say against us, we can declare this before God and men, that we suffer for no other reason than for maintaining our Lord Jesus Christ to be our only Saviour and Redeemer, and his doctrine to be the only doctrine of life and salvation.

And this is the only reason, Sire, why the executioners' hands have been stained so often with the blood of your poor subjects, who, sparing not their lives to maintain this same Confession of Faith, have shown to all that they were moved by some other spirit than that of men, who naturally care more for their own peace and comfort than for the honor and glory of God.

And therefore, Sire, in accordance with your promises of goodness and mercy toward your poor subjects, we humbly beseech your Majesty graciously to examine the cause for which, being threatened at all times with death or exile, we thus lose the power of rendering the humble service that we owe you. May it please your Majesty, then, instead of the fire and sword which have been used hitherto, to have our Confession of Faith decided by the Word of God: giving permission and security for this. And we hope that you yourself will be the judge of our innocence, knowing that there is in us no rebellion or heresy whatsoever, but that our only endeavor is to live in peace of conscience, serving God according to his commandments, and honoring your Majesty by all obedience and submission.

And because we have great need, by the preaching of the Word of God, to be kept in our duty to him, as well as to yourself, we humbly beg, Sire, that we may sometimes be permitted to gather together, to be exhorted to the fear of God by his Word, as well as to be confirmed by the administration of the Sacraments which the Lord Jesus Christ instituted in his Church. And if it should please your Majesty to give us a place where any one may see what passes in our assemblies, we shall thereby be absolved from the charge of the enormous crimes with which these same assemblies have been defamed. For nothing will be seen but what is decent and well-ordered, and nothing will be heard but the praise of God, exhortations to his service, and prayers for the preservation of your Majesty and of your kingdom. And if it do not please you to grant us this favor, at least let it be permitted us to follow the established order in private among ourselves.

We beseech you most humbly, Sire, to believe that in listening to this supplication which is now presented to you, you listen to the cries and groans of an infinite number of your poor subjects, who implore of your mercy that you extinguish the fires which the cruelty of your judges has lighted in your kingdom. And that we may thus be permitted, in serving your Majesty, to serve him who has raised you to your power and dignity.

And if it should not please you, Sire, to listen to our voice, may it please you to listen to that of the Son of God, who, having given you power over our property, our bodies, and even our lives, demands that the control and dominion of our souls and consciences, which he purchased with his own blood, be reserved to him.

We beseech him, Sire, that he may lead you always by his Spirit, increasing with your age, your greatness and power, giving you victory over all your enemies, and establishing forever, in all equity and justice, the throne of your Majesty: before whom, may it please him that we find grace, and some fruit of this our present supplication, so that having exchanged our pains and afflictions for some peace and liberty, we may also change our tears and lamentations into a perpetual thanksgiving to God, and to your Majesty for having done that which is most agreeable to him, most worthy of your goodness and mercy, and most necessary for the preservation of your most humble and obedient subjects and servants.

Confession of Faith

MADE IN ONE ACCORD BY THE FRENCH PEOPLE, WHO DESIRE TO LIVE ACCORDING TO THE PURITY OF THE GOSPEL OF OUR LORD JESUS CHRIST. A.D. 1559

ART. I

We believe and confess that there is but one God, who is one sole and simple essence,[7] spiritual,[8] eternal,[9] invisible,[10] immutable,[11] infinite,[12] incomprehensible,[13] ineffable, omnipotent; who is all-wise,[14] all-good,[15] all-just, and all-merciful.[16]

ART. II

As such this God reveals himself to men;[17] firstly, in his works, in their creation, as well as in their preservation and control. Secondly, and more clearly, in his Word,[18] which was in the beginning revealed through oracles,[19] and which was afterward committed to writing [20] in the books which we call the Holy Scriptures.[21]

ART. III

These Holy Scriptures are comprised in the canonical books of the Old and New Testaments, as follows: the five books of Moses, namely: GENESIS, EXODUS, LEVITICUS, NUMBERS, DEUTERONOMY; then JOSHUA, JUDGES, RUTH, the first and second books of SAMUEL, the first and second books of the KINGS, the first and second books of the CHRONICLES,

---

[7] Deut. 4:35, 39; I Cor. 8:4, 6.
[8] Gen. 1:3; John 4:24; II Cor. 3:17.
[9] Ex. 3:15-16, 18.
[10] Rom. 1:20; I Tim. 1:47.
[11] Mal. 3:6.
[12] Rom. 11:33; Acts 7:48.
[13] Jer. 10:7, 10; Luke 1:37.
[14] Rom. 16:27.
[15] Matt. 19:17.
[16] Jer. 12:1.
[17] Ex. 34:6-7.
[18] Rom. 1:20.
[19] Heb. 1:4.
[20] Gen. 15:1.
[21] Ex. 24:3-4; Rom. 1:2.

otherwise called Paralipomenon, the first book of EZRA; then NEHEMIAH, the book of ESTHER, JOB, the PSALMS of DAVID, the PROVERBS or Maxims of Solomon; the book of ECCLESIASTES, called the Preacher, the SONG OF SOLOMON; then the book of ISAIAH, JEREMIAH, LAMENTATIONS of Jeremiah, EZEKIEL, DANIEL, HOSEA, JOEL, AMOS, OBADIAH, JONAH, MICAH, NAHUM, HABAKKUK, ZEPHANIAH, HAGGAI, ZECHARIAH, MALACHI; then the Holy Gospel according to St. MATTHEW, according to St. MARK, according to St. LUKE, and according to St. JOHN; then the second book of St. LUKE, otherwise called the ACTS of the Apostles; then the Epistles of St. PAUL: one to the ROMANS, two to the CORINTHIANS, one to the GALATIANS, one to the EPHESIANS, one to the PHILIPPIANS, one to the COLOSSIANS, two to the THESSALONIANS, two to TIMOTHY, one to TITUS, one to PHILEMON; then the Epistle to the HEBREWS, the Epistle of St. JAMES, the first and second Epistles of St. PETER, the first, second, and third Epistles of St. JOHN, the Epistle of St. JUDE; and then the APOCALYPSE, or Revelation of St. JOHN.

ART. IV

We know these books to be canonical, and the sure rule of our faith,[22] not so much by the common accord and consent of the Church, as by the testimony and inward illumination of the Holy Spirit, which enables us to distinguish them from other ecclesiastical books upon which, however useful, we can not found any articles of faith.

ART. V

We believe that the Word contained in these books has proceeded from God,[23] and receives its authority [24] from him alone, and not from men. And inasmuch as it is the rule of all truth,[25] containing all that is necessary for the service of God and for our salvation, it is not lawful for men, nor even for angels, to add to it, to take away from it, or to change it.[26] Whence it follows that no authority, whether of antiquity, or custom, or numbers, or human wisdom, or judgments, or

22 Ps. 19:9; 12:7.
23 II Tim. 3:15-16; II Peter 1:21.
24 John 3:31, 34; I Tim. 1:15.
25 John 15:11; Acts 20:27.
26 Deut. 12:32; 4:1; Gal. 1:8; Rev. 22:18-19.

proclamations, or edicts, or decrees, or councils, or visions, or miracles, should be opposed to these Holy Scriptures,[27] but, on the contrary, all things should be examined, regulated, and reformed according to them.[28] And therefore we confess the three creeds, to wit: the Apostles', the Nicene, and the Athanasian, because they are in accordance with the Word of God.

Art. VI

These Holy Scriptures teach us that in this one sole and simple divine essence, whom we have confessed, there are three persons: the Father, the Son, and the Holy Spirit.[29] The Father, first cause, principle, and origin of all things. The Son, his Word and eternal wisdom. The Holy Spirit, his virtue, power, and efficacy. The Son begotten from eternity by the Father. The Holy Spirit proceeding eternally from them both; the three persons not confused, but distinct, and yet not separate, but of the same essence, equal in eternity and power. And in this we confess that which hath been established by the ancient councils, and we detest all sects and heresies which were rejected by the holy doctors, such as St. Hilary, St. Athanasius, St. Ambrose, and St. Cyril.

Art. VII

We believe that God, in three co-working persons, by his power, wisdom, and incomprehensible goodness, created all things, not only the heavens and the earth and all that in them is, but also invisible [30] spirits, some of whom have fallen away and gone into perdition,[31] while others have continued in obedience.[32] That the first, being corrupted by evil, are enemies of all good, consequently of the whole Church.[33] The second, having been preserved by the grace of God, are ministers to glorify God's name, and to promote the salvation of his elect.[34]

---

[27] Matt. 15:9; Acts 5:28-29.
[28] I Cor. 11:1-2, 23.
[29] Deut. 4:12; Matt. 28:19; II Cor. 13:14; I John 5:7[?]; John 1:1, 17, 32.
[30] Gen. 1:1; John 1:3; Jude, ch. 6; Col. 1:16; Heb. 1:2.
[31] II Peter 2:4.
[32] Ps. 103:20-21.
[33] John 8:44.
[34] Heb. 1:7, 14.

Art. VIII

We believe that he not only created all things, but that he governs and directs them,[35] disposing and ordaining by his sovereign will all that happens in the world;[36] not that he is the author of evil, or that the guilt of it can be imputed [37] to him, as his will is the sovereign and infallible rule of all right and justice;[38] but he hath wonderful means of so making use of devils and sinners that he can turn to good the evil which they do, and of which they are guilty.[39] And thus, confessing that the providence of God orders all things, we humbly bow before the secrets which are hidden to us, without questioning what is above our understanding; but rather making use of what is revealed to us in Holy Scripture for our peace and safety,[40] inasmuch as God, who has all things in subjection to him, watches over us with a Father's care, so that not a hair of our heads shall fall without his will.[41] And yet he restrains the devils and all our enemies, so that they can not harm us without his leave.[42]

Art. IX

We believe that man was created pure and perfect in the image of God, and that by his own guilt he fell from the grace which he received,[43] and is thus alienated from God, the fountain of justice and of all good, so that his nature is totally corrupt. And being blinded in mind, and depraved in heart, he has lost all integrity, and there is no good in him.[44] And although he can still discern good and evil,[45] we say, notwithstanding, that the light he has becomes darkness when he seeks for God, so that he can in nowise approach him by his intelligence and reason.[46] And although he has a will that incites him to do this or that, yet it is altogether captive to

---

[35] Ps. 104.
[36] Prov. 16:4; Matt. 10:29; Rom. 9:11; Acts 17:24, 26, 28.
[37] I John 2:16; Hosea 13:9; I John 3:8.
[38] Ps. 5:5; 119; Job 1:22.
[39] Acts 2:23-24, 27.
[40] Rom. 9:19-20; 11:33.
[41] Matt. 10:30; Luke 21:18.
[42] Job 1:12; Gen. 3:15.
[43] Gen. 1:26; Eccl. 7:10; Rom. 5:12; Eph. 2:2-3.
[44] Gen. 6:5; 8:21.
[45] Rom. 1:21; 2:18-20.
[46] I Cor. 2:14.

sin, so that he has no other liberty to do right than that which God gives him.[47]

ART. X

We believe that all the posterity of Adam is in bondage to original sin, which is an hereditary evil, and not an imitation merely, as was declared by the Pelagians, whom we detest in their errors. And we consider that it is not necessary to inquire how sin was conveyed from one man to another, for what God had given Adam was not for him alone, but for all his posterity; and thus in his person we have been deprived of all good things, and have fallen with him into a state of sin and misery.[48]

ART. XI

We believe, also, that this evil is truly sin, sufficient for the condemnation of the whole human race, even of little children in the mother's womb, and that God considers it as such; [49] even after baptism it is still of the nature of sin, but the condemnation of it is abolished for the children of God, out of his mere free grace and love.[50] And further, that it is a perversity always producing fruits of malice and of rebellion,[51] so that the most holy men, although they resist it, are still stained with many weaknesses and imperfections while they are in this life.[52]

ART. XII

We believe that from this corruption and general condemnation in which all men are plunged, God, according to his eternal and immutable counsel, calleth those whom he hath chosen by his goodness and mercy alone in our Lord Jesus Christ, without consideration of their works,[53] to display in them the riches of his mercy; [54] leaving the rest in this same corruption and condemnation to show in them his justice. For the ones are no better than the others, until God discerns

47 John 1:4-5, 7; 8:36; Rom. 8:6-7.
48 Gen. 8:21; Rom. 5:12; Job 14:4.
49 Ps. 51:7; Rom. 3:9-13; 5:12.
50 Rom., ch. 7.
51 Rom. 7:5.
52 Rom. 7:18-19; II Cor. 12:7.
53 Rom. 3:2; 9:23; II Tim. 2:20; Titus 3:5, 7; Eph. 1:4; II Tim. 1:9.
54 Ex. 9:16; Rom. 9:22.

them according to his immutable purpose which he has determined in Jesus Christ before the creation of the world. Neither can any man gain such a reward by his own virtue, as by nature we can not have a single good feeling, affection, or thought, except God has first put it into our hearts.[55]

Art. XIII

We believe that all that is necessary for our salvation was offered and communicated to us in Jesus Christ. He is given to us for our salvation, and " is made unto us wisdom, and righteousness, and sanctification, and redemption ": so that if we refuse him, we renounce the mercy of the Father, in which alone we can find a refuge.[56]

Art. XIV

We believe that Jesus Christ, being the wisdom of God and his eternal Son, has put on our flesh, so as to be God and man in one person; [57] man, like unto us, capable of suffering in body and soul, yet free from all stain of sin.[58] And as to his humanity, he was the true seed of Abraham and of David,[59] although he was conceived by the secret power of the Holy Spirit.[60] In this we detest all the heresies that have of old troubled the Church, and especially the diabolical conceits of Servetus, which attribute a fantastical divinity to the Lord Jesus, calling him the idea and pattern of all things, and the personal or figurative Son of God, and, finally, attribute to him a body of three uncreated elements, thus confusing and destroying the two natures.

Art. XV

We believe that in one person, that is, Jesus Christ, the two natures are actually and inseparably joined and united, and yet each remains in its proper character: so that in this union the divine nature, retaining its attributes,[61] remained uncreated, infinite, and all-pervading; and the human nature re-

---

55 Jer. 10:23; Eph. 1:4-5.
56 I Cor. 1:30; Eph. 1:6-7; Col. 1:13-14; Titus 2:14.
57 John 1:14; Phil. 2:6.
58 Heb. 2:17; II Cor. 5:21.
59 Acts 13:23; Rom. 1:3; 8:3; 9:5; Phil. 2:7; Heb. 2:14, 16; ch. 5.
60 Matt. 1:18; Luke 1:35.
61 Matt., ch. 1; Luke, ch. 1; John 1:14; I Tim. 2:5; 3:16; Heb. 5:8.

Contra Lutheranism

mained finite, having its form, measure, and attributes; [62] and although Jesus Christ, in rising from the dead, bestowed immortality upon his body, yet he did not take from it the truth of its nature, and we so consider him in his divinity that we do not despoil him of his humanity.

Art. XVI

We believe that God, in sending his Son, intended to show his love and inestimable goodness towards us, giving him up to die to accomplish all righteousness, and raising him from the dead to secure for us the heavenly life.[63]

Art. XVII

We believe that by the perfect sacrifice that the Lord Jesus offered on the cross,[64] we are reconciled to God, and justified before him; for we can not be acceptable to him, nor become partakers of the grace of adoption, except as he pardons [all] our sins, and blots them out.[65] Thus we declare that through Jesus Christ we are cleansed and made perfect; by his death we are fully justified, and through him only can we be delivered from our iniquities and transgressions.[66]

grounds

Art. XVIII

We believe that all our justification rests upon the remission of our sins, in which also is our only blessedness, as saith the Psalmist [67] (Ps. 32:2). We therefore reject all other means of justification before God,[68] and without claiming any virtue or merit, we rest simply in the obedience of Jesus Christ, which is imputed to us as much to blot out all our sins as to make us find grace and favor in the sight of God. And, in fact, we believe that in falling away from this foundation, however slightly, we could not find rest elsewhere, but should always be troubled. Forasmuch as we are never at peace with God till we resolve to be loved in Jesus Christ, for of ourselves we are worthy of hatred.

Positive side to Justification: "find grace and favor in the sight of God"

Negative side Justification "to blot out all our sins"

Complete surrender to God "we resolve to be loved in Jesus Christ"

---

62 Luke 24:38-39; Rom. 1:4; Phil. 2:6-11.
63 John 3:16; 15:13.
64 II Cor. 5:19; Heb. 5:7-9.
65 I Peter 2:24-25.
66 Heb. 9:14; Eph. 5:26; I Peter 1:18-19.
67 Ps. 32:2; John 17:23; Rom. 4:7-8; 8:1-3; II Cor. 5:19-20.
68 I Tim. 2:5; I John 2:1; Rom. 5:19; Acts 4:12.

ART. XIX

We believe that by this means we have the liberty and privilege of calling upon God, in full confidence that he will show himself a Father to us.[69] For we should have no access to the Father except through this Mediator. And to be heard in his name, we must hold our life from him as from our chief.

ART. XX

means

We believe that we are made partakers of this justification by faith alone, as it is written: " He suffered for our salvation, that whosoever believeth on him should not perish." [70] And this is done inasmuch as we appropriate to our use the promises of life which are given to us through him, and feel their effect when we accept them, being assured that we are established by the Word of God and shall not be deceived.[71] Thus our justification through faith depends upon the free promises by which God declares and testifies his love to us.[72]

ART. XXI

We believe that we are enlightened in faith by the secret power of the Holy Spirit, that it is a gratuitous and special gift which God grants to whom he will, so that the elect have no cause to glory, but are bound to be doubly thankful that they have been preferred to others.[73] We believe also that faith is not given to the elect only to introduce them into the right way, but also to make them continue in it to the end.[74] For as it is God who hath begun the work, he will also perfect it.[75]

Faith is a sovereign act of Grace

Perseverance of the elect

ART. XXII

We believe that by this faith we are regenerated in newness of life, being by nature subject to sin.[76] Now we receive by faith grace to live holily and in the fear of God, in accepting the promise which is given to us by the Gospel, namely: that

The Grace of God given to us to "live holily is his Holy Spirit.

---

[69] Rom. 5:12; 8:15; Gal. 4:4-7; Eph. 2:13-15.
[70] Rom., ch. 3; Gal., chs. 2; 3:24; John 3:15.
[71] Matt. 17:20; John 3:16-17; 10:4.
[72] Rom. 1:17; 3:24-25, 27, 30; 4:1-3; Gal. 2:20-21.
[73] Eph. 2:8; I Thess. 1:5; I Cor. 2:12; II Peter 1:3-4.
[74] I Cor. 1:8-9.
[75] Phil. 2:13; 1:6.
[76] Rom. 6:1-2; 7:1-2; Col. 1:13; 3:10; I Peter 1:3.

God will give us his Holy Spirit. This faith not only doth not hinder us from holy living, or turn us from the love of righteousness, but of necessity begetteth in us all good works.[77] Moreover, although God worketh in us for our salvation, and reneweth our hearts, determining us to that which is good,[78] yet we confess that the good works which we do proceed from his Spirit, and can not be accounted to us for justification, neither do they entitle us to the adoption of sons, for we should always be doubting and restless in our hearts, if we did not rest upon the atonement by which Jesus Christ hath acquitted us.[79]

Art. XXIII

We believe that the ordinances of the law came to an end at the advent of Jesus Christ; [80] but, although the ceremonies are no more in use, yet their substance and truth remain in the person of him in whom they are fulfilled.[81] And, moreover, we must seek aid from the law and the prophets for the ruling of our lives, as well as for our confirmation in the promises of the gospel.

Art. XXIV

We believe, as Jesus Christ is our only advocate,[82] and as he commands us to ask of the Father [83] in his name, and as it is not lawful for us to pray except in accordance with the model God hath taught us by his Word,[84] that all imaginations of men concerning the intercession of dead saints are an abuse and a device of Satan to lead men from the right way of worship.[85] We reject, also, all other means by which men hope to redeem themselves before God, as derogating from the sacrifice and passion of Jesus Christ.

Finally, we consider purgatory as an illusion proceeding from the same shop, from which have also sprung monastic vows, pilgrimages, the prohibition of marriage, and of eating meat, the ceremonial observance of days, auricular confes-

---

[77] James, ch. 2; Gal. 5:6; I John 2:3-4; 5:18.
[78] Deut. 30:6; John 3:5.
[79] Luke 17:10; Ps. 16:2; Rom., ch. 3; Titus 3:5; Rom., ch. 4.
[80] Rom. 10:4; Gal., chs. 3; 4; Col. 2:17.
[81] II Tim. 3:16; II Peter 1:19; 3:2.
[82] I Tim. 2:5; Acts 4:12; I John 2:1-2.
[83] John 16:23-24.
[84] Matt. 6:9; Luke 11:1.
[85] Acts 10:25-26; 14:14; Rev. 19:10.

sion, indulgences, and all such things by which they hope to merit forgiveness and salvation.[86] These things we reject, not only for the false idea of merit which is attached to them, but also because they are human inventions imposing a yoke upon the conscience.

Art. XXV

Now as we enjoy Christ only through the gospel,[87] we believe that the order of the Church, established by his authority, ought to be sacred and inviolable, and that, therefore, the Church can not exist without pastors for instruction,[88] whom we should respect and reverently listen to, when they are properly called and exercise their office faithfully.[89] Not that God is bound to such aid and subordinate means, but because it pleaseth him to govern us by such restraints. In this we detest all visionaries who would like, so far as lies in their power, to destroy the ministry and preaching of the Word and sacraments.

Art. XXVI

We believe that no one ought to seclude himself and be contented to be alone; but that all jointly should keep and maintain the union of the Church, and submit to the public teaching, and to the yoke of Jesus Christ,[90] wherever God shall have established a true order of the Church, even if the magistrates and their edicts are contrary to it. For if they do not take part in it, or if they separate themselves from it, they do contrary to the Word of God.[91]

Art. XXVII

Nevertheless we believe that it is important to discern with care and prudence which is the true Church, for this title has been much abused.[92] We say, then, according to the Word of God, that it is the company of the faithful who agree to follow his Word, and the pure religion which it teaches; who

[86] Matt. 15:11; Acts 10:14-15; Rom. 4:1-4; Gal. 4:9-10; Col. 2:18-23; I Tim. 4:2-5.
[87] Rom. 1:16-17; 10:3.
[88] Matt. 18:20; Eph. 1:22-23.
[89] Matt. 10:40; John 13:20; Rom. 10:15.
[90] Ps. 5:8; 22:23; 42:5; Eph. 4:11; Heb. 2:12.
[91] Acts 4:19-20; Heb. 10:25.
[92] Jer. 7:4, 8, 11-12; Matt. 3:9; 7:22; 24:5.

advance in it all their lives, growing and becoming more confirmed in the fear of God according as they feel the want of growing and pressing onward.[93] Even although they strive continually, they can have no hope save in the remission of their sins.[94] Nevertheless we do not deny that among the faithful there may be hypocrites and reprobates, but their wickedness can not destroy the title of the Church.[95]

Art. XXVIII

In this belief we declare that, properly speaking, there can be no Church where the Word of God is not received, nor profession made of subjection to it, nor use of the sacraments. Therefore we condemn the papal assemblies, as the pure Word of God [96] is banished from them, their sacraments are corrupted, or falsified, or destroyed, and all superstitions and idolatries are in them. We hold, then, that all who take part in these acts, and commune in that Church, separate and cut themselves off from the body of Christ.[97] Nevertheless, as some trace of the Church is left in the papacy, and the virtue and substance of baptism remain, and as the efficacy of baptism does not depend upon the person who administers it, we confess that those baptized in it do not need a second baptism.[98] But, on account of its corruptions, we can not present children to be baptized in it without incurring pollution.

Art. XXIX

As to the true Church, we believe that it should be governed according to the order established by our Lord Jesus Christ.[99] That there should be pastors, overseers, and deacons, so that true doctrine may have its course, that errors may be corrected and suppressed, and the poor and all who are in affliction may be helped in their necessities; and that assemblies may be held in the name of God, so that great and small may be edified.

---

93 Eph. 2:20; 4:11-12; I Tim. 3:15; Deut. 31:12.
94 Rom. 3:3.
95 Matt. 13:30; I Tim. 1:18-20.
96 Matt. 10:14-15; John 10:1; I Cor. 3:12-13.
97 II Cor. 6:14-16; I Cor. 6:15.
98 Matt. 3:11; 28:19; Mark 1:8; Acts 1:5; 11:15-17; 19:4-6.
99 Acts 6:3-5; Eph. 4:11-13; I Tim., ch. 3; Titus, chs. 1; 2; Matt. 18:17.

Art. XXX

We believe that all true pastors, wherever they may be, have the same authority and equal power under one head, one only sovereign and universal bishop, Jesus Christ; [100] and that consequently no Church shall claim any authority or dominion over any other.

Art. XXXI

We believe that no person should undertake to govern the Church upon his own authority, but that this should be derived from election, as far as it is possible, and as God will permit.[101] And we make this exception especially, because sometimes, and even in our own days, when the state of the Church has been interrupted, it has been necessary for God to raise men in an extraordinary manner to restore the Church which was in ruin and desolation. But, notwithstanding, we believe that this rule must always be binding: that all pastors, overseers, and deacons should have evidence of being called to their office.[102]

Art. XXXII

We believe, also, that it is desirable and useful that those elected to be superintendents devise among themselves what means should be adopted for the government of the whole body,[103] and yet that they should never depart from that which was ordained by our Lord Jesus Christ.[104] Which does not prevent there being some special ordinances in each place, as convenience may require.

Art. XXXIII

However, we reject all human inventions, and all laws which men may introduce under the pretense of serving God, by which they wish to bind consciences; [105] and we receive only that which conduces to concord and holds all in

100 Matt. 20:26-27; 18:2-4; I Cor. 3:1-6; Eph. 1:22; Col. 1:18-19.
101 Matt. 28:18-19; Mark 16:15; John 15:16; Acts 1:21-26; 6:1-2; Rom. 10:15; Titus 1:5-7.
102 Gal. 1:15; I Tim. 3:7-10, 15.
103 Acts 15:2, 6, 7, 25, 28; Rom. 12:6-8; I Cor. 14:12; II Cor. 12:7-8.
104 I Peter, ch. 5; I Cor. 14:40.
105 Rom. 15:17-18; I Cor. 3:11; Col. 2:6-8; Gal. 5:1.

obedience, from the greatest to the least. In this we must follow that which the Lord Jesus Christ declared as to excommunication,[106] which we approve and confess to be necessary with all its antecedents and consequences.

Art. XXXIV

We believe that the sacraments are added to the Word for more ample confirmation, that they may be to us pledges and seals of the grace of God, and by this means aid and comfort our faith, because of the infirmity which is in us,[107] and that they are outward signs through which God operates by his Spirit, so that he may not signify any thing to us in vain.[108] Yet we hold that their substance and truth is in Jesus Christ,[109] and that of themselves they are only smoke and shadow.

Art. XXXV

We confess only two sacraments common to the whole Church, of which the first, baptism, is given as a pledge of our adoption; for by it we are grafted into the body of Christ, so as to be washed and cleansed by his blood, and then renewed in purity of life by his Holy Spirit.[110] We hold, also, that although we are baptized only once, yet the gain that it symbolizes to us reaches over our whole lives and to our death, so that we have a lasting witness that Jesus Christ will always be our justification and sanctification.[111] Nevertheless, although it is a sacrament of faith and penitence, yet as God receives little children into the Church with their fathers, we say, upon the authority of Jesus Christ, that the children of believing parents should be baptized.[112]

Art. XXXVI

We confess that the Lord's Supper, which is the second sacrament, is a witness of the union which we have with

---

106 Matt. 18:17; I Cor. 5:5; I Tim. 1:9-10.
107 I Cor., chs. 10; 11:23-34; Ex. 12:13; Matt. 26:26-27; Rom. 4:11; Acts 22:16.
108 Gal. 3:27; Eph. 5:26.
109 John 6:50-57; 3:12.
110 Rom. 6:3; Titus 3:5-6; Acts 22:16.
111 Matt. 3:11-12; Mark 16:16; Rom. 6:1-4.
112 Matt. 19:14; I Cor. 7:14.

Christ,[113] inasmuch as he not only died and rose again for us once, but also feeds and nourishes us truly with his flesh and blood, so that we may be one in him, and that our life may be in common.[114] Although he be in heaven until he come to judge all the earth,[115] still we believe that by the secret and incomprehensible power of his Spirit he feeds and strengthens us with the substance of his body and of his blood.[116] We hold that this is done spiritually, not because we put imagination and fancy in the place of fact and truth, but because the greatness of this mystery exceeds the measure of our senses and the laws of nature. In short, because it is heavenly, it can only be apprehended by faith.

Art. XXXVII

We believe, as has been said, that in the Lord's Supper, as well as in baptism, God gives us really and in fact that which he there sets forth to us; and that consequently with these signs is given the true possession and enjoyment of that which they present to us. And thus all who bring a pure faith, like a vessel, to the sacred table of Christ, receive truly that of which it is a sign; for the body and the blood of Jesus Christ give food and drink to the soul, no less than bread and wine nourish the body.[117]

Art. XXXVIII

Thus we hold that water, being a feeble element, still testifies to us in truth the inward cleansing of our souls in the blood of Jesus Christ by the efficacy of his Spirit,[118] and that the bread and wine given to us in the sacrament serve to our spiritual nourishment, inasmuch as they show, as to our sight, that the body of Christ is our meat, and his blood our drink.[119] And we reject the Enthusiasts and Sacramentarians who will not receive such signs and marks, although our Saviour said: " This is my body, and this cup is my blood." [120]

---

113 I Cor. 10:16-17; 11:24.
114 John 6:56-57; 17:11, 22.
115 Mark 16:19; Acts 3:21.
116 I Cor. 10:16; John, ch. 6.
117 I Cor., ch. 11; John, ch. 6.
118 Rom. 6:3.
119 John, ch. 6; I Cor., ch. 11.
120 Matt. 26:26; I Cor., ch. 11.

ART. XXXIX

We believe that God wishes to have the world governed by laws and magistrates,[121] so that some restraint may be put upon its disordered appetites. And as he has established kingdoms, republics, and all sorts of principalities, either hereditary or otherwise, and all that belongs to a just government, and wishes to be considered as their Author, so he has put the sword into the hands of magistrates to suppress crimes against the first as well as against the second table of the Commandments of God. We must, therefore, on his account, not only submit to them as superiors, but honor and hold them in all reverence as his lieutenants and officers,[122] whom he has commissioned to exercise a legitimate and holy authority.

ART. XL

We hold, then, that we must obey their laws and statutes,[123] pay customs, taxes, and other dues, and bear the yoke of subjection with a good and free will, even if they are unbelievers, provided that the sovereign empire of God remain intact.[124] Therefore we detest all those who would like to reject authority, to establish community and confusion of property, and overthrow the order of justice.

---

[121] Ex. 18:20-21; Matt. 17:24-27; Rom., ch. 13.
[122] I Peter 2:13-14; I Tim. 2:2.
[123] Matt. 17:24.
[124] Acts 4:17-20; 18:9.

10

The Scottish Confession of Faith, 1560

INTRODUCTION

According to A. Taylor Innes, " the Creed of Scotland and the Church of Scotland emerge into history so nearly at the same moment that it is difficult to say which has the precedence even in order of time. It is at least equally difficult to say which is first in respect of authority." [1] Legally, the Reformed Church of Scotland was not established by Act of Parliament until 1567, seven years after the Scottish Confession of Faith was adopted and the first General Assembly was held. But it owes its inception to the action of a number of Protestant nobles and gentlemen who on December 3, 1557, in Edinburgh entered into a covenant to maintain, nourish, and defend to the death " the whole congregation of Christ, and every member thereof." The leaders became known as the " Lords of the Congregation." For a few years the Liturgy of Edward VI and the Confession of Faith of the English Congregation at Geneva, 1556, appear to have been used, but " there is no record of any formal approval of a doctrinal standard before 1560." [2]

The protracted and wearisome struggles that had to be waged before the Reformation could be carried out in Scotland ended with the peace that was proclaimed in Edinburgh on July 8, 1560, between the Queen Regent, Mary of Guise, and her French allies on the one hand, and the Protestant nobles and the English on the other. The treaty provided that Parliament should meet on August 1 in Edinburgh. But before Parliament convened a public service of thanksgiving was held at the Great Kirk of Edinburgh, at which a sermon was preached and prayers of thanksgiving were offered for

---

[1] *The Law of Creeds in Scotland* (Edinburgh, 1902), p. 4.
[2] P. Schaff, *Creeds of Christendom*, Vol. I, p. 681.

God's " merciful deliverance from the tyranny of the French."
The attendance at the Parliament was the largest in Scottish
history. Many lords who had not attended since the reign of
James I were present. While Parliament was in session John
Knox preached a series of sermons on The Book of Haggai
concerning the rebuilding of the Temple. Under the impact
of these sermons Knox and his associates drew up a petition
which was submitted to Parliament. The petition called for
the abolition by Act of Parliament of " such doctrine and
idolatry " as the doctrine of transubstantiation, the adoration
of Christ's body under the form of bread, the merits of works
and justification thereby, together with the doctrine of Papal Indulgences, purgatory, pilgrimage, and praying to departed saints; the authority of the Pope; and for the reformation of the life and manners of the clergy, and the devotion
of Church revenues to the support of true ministers of the
Word of God, the promotion of learning, and the relief of
the poor. After this petition was read in the audience of the
whole assembly, a commission was appointed " to draw, in
plain and several heads, the sum of that doctrine which they
would maintain, and would desire that present parliament to
establish as wholesome, true, and only necessary to be believed, and to be received within the realm." The commission was composed of six men with a common Christian name
— John Winram, John Spottiswood, John Douglas, John
Row, John Willock, and John Knox. Within four days the
Scottish Confession of Faith was completed. It has been assumed that Knox was the chief author because he had been
consulted about the Edwardine Articles of Religion, prepared the Confession of Faith of the English congregation in
Geneva, and must have been familiar with the Swiss Confessions. We give Knox's own account of the adoption of the
Confession in his *History of the Reformation in Scotland:* [3]

Our Confession was publicly read, first in audience of the Lords
of Articles, and after in audience of the whole Parliament; where
were present, not only such as professed Christ Jesus, but also a
great number of the adversaries of our religion, such as the forenamed Bishops, and some others of the Temporal Estate, who
were commanded in God's name to object, if they could, any
thing against that doctrine. Some of our Ministers were present,
standing upon their feet, ready to have answered, in case any
would have defended the Papistry, and impugned our affirma-

[3] Edited by William Croft Dickinson, 2 vols. (London: Thomas Nelson &
Sons, 1949) , Vol. I, pp. 338 f.

tives: but while that no objection was made, there was a day appointed to voting in that and other heads. Our Confession was read, every article by itself, over again, as they were written in order, and the votes of every man were required accordingly. Of the Temporal Estate, only voted in the contrary the Earl of Atholl, the Lords Somerville and Borthwick; and yet for their dissenting they produced no better reason, but, " We will believe as our fathers believed." [4] The Bishops (papistical, we mean) spake nothing. The rest of the whole three Estates by their public votes affirmed the doctrine; and many, the rather, because that the Bishops would nor durst say nothing in the contrary.

After the Confession had been adopted August 24, 1560, two Acts of Parliament were passed abolishing the Mass and the jurisdiction of the Pope. With these Acts, Sir James Sandelandis was dispatched to Queen Mary, in Paris, to secure royal approval which she not unnaturally withheld. Knox commented: " But that we little regarded, or yet do regard; for all that we did was rather to show our debtful obedience than to beg of them any strength to our Religion which from God has full power, and needeth not the suffrage of man." [5] Thus it was not until 1567 that the Scottish Confession was constitutionally ratified by the first Parliament of James VI and " authorized as a doctrine grounded upon the infallible Word of God." In 1572 subscription was first required of all ministers. It remained the official doctrinal statement of the Church of Scotland until superseded (though not abrogated) by the adoption of the Westminster Confession in 1647 in the interests of uniformity. However, it should be observed that in Scotland there was no unwillingness to approve and to use other evangelical documents, as was in fact done with the Second Helvetic Confession (1566) and the Heidelberg Catechism.

The first printings of the Scottish Confession in the original Scottish dialect were made by John Scott (Edinburgh, 1561), Robert Lekprewik (Edinburgh, 1561), and Robert Hall (London, 1561). Another text is to be found in the Acts of Parliament of 1567, printed in 1568. The original text may also be found in Dunlop, *A Collection of Confessions of Faith*, etc. (1719–1722) ; in D. Laing's edition of *The Works*

---

[4] Knox's account (which is followed by Spottiswoode, *History*, i, 327) here differs considerably from that given by Randolph who, writing to Cecil on August 19, says " Of the temporall lords, Cassillis and Caithness said ' Nae! ' The rest, with common consent and as glad will as ever I heard men speak, allowed it " (Calendar of Scottish Papers, i, No. 886). Somerville, it should be noted, had subscribed the Band of April, 1560.

[5] Knox, *History of the Reformation*, p. 342.

of John Knox (1845) , Vol. II, pp. 93 ff. (cf. the slightly mod-
ernized version in John Knox's *History of the Reformation
in Scotland,* ed. by William Croft Dickinson, Vol. II, pp. 257–
272) ; in D. Calderwood, *History of the Kirk of Scotland*
(1842) , Vol. II, pp. 16 ff.; and in Edward Irving, *Confessions
of Faith . . . of the Church of Scotland before 1647* (1831) .
In *The Writings of John Knox* (Philadelphia, 1842) , it is
given in modern English. The footnotes in Laing's edition explain textual variants. An official Latin translation was made
by Patrick Adamson and printed in Andreapolis (St. Andrew's) in 1572. The publisher of the *Corpus et syntagma*
(Geneva, 1612 and 1654) did not know about this translation and made his own from the English text of the Acts of
Parliament published in 1568. This translation is reproduced
in Niemeyer's *Collectio confessionum,* pp. 340 ff. Both the
original text in the Scottish dialect and Adamson's Latin
translation, as contained in Dunlop's *Collection,* are reproduced in P. Schaff, *Creeds of Christendom* (1877) , Vol. III,
and in E. F. K. Müller, *Die Bekenntnisschriften der reformierten Kirche* (Leipzig, 1903) .

Three more recent editions of the Scottish Confession are:
Scots Confession 1560 . . . with introduction by G. D. Henderson (Edinburgh, 1937) ; the critical edition by Theodor
Hesse in *Bekenntnisschriften und Kirchenordnungen,* ed. by
Wilhelm Niesel (Munich, 1938) ; and *The Scots Confession,
1560,* edited with an introduction by G. D. Henderson, together with a rendering into modern English by James Bulloch (Edinburgh: The Saint Andrew Press, 1960) . We have
used Dr. Bulloch's version in the present volume. It is based
upon the text found in Dunlop. However, for scholarly purposes the Hesse edition is quite superior. It is based upon a
photostat of a copy of the text printed by John Scott that is
preserved in the London British Museum. It gives all the variants in the English texts and in the Latin translations.

Literature: Thos. McCrie, *Life of John Knox* (1845) ;
P. Schaff, *Creeds of Christendom* (1877) , Vol. I; A. Taylor
Innes, *The Law of Creeds in Scotland* (Edinburgh, 1902) ;
A. R. MacEwen, *A History of the Church of Scotland* (Lon-
don, 1918) , Vol. II; Karl Barth, *The Knowledge of God and
the Service of God* (London, 1938) ; Geddes MacGregor, *The
Thundering Scot: A Portrait of John Knox* (The Westmin-
ster Press, 1957) ; Gordon Donaldson, *The Scottish Reforma-
tion* (Cambridge University Press, 1960) ; James S. McEwen,
The Faith of John Knox (John Knox Press, 1961) .

THE

Confession

OF THE

FAITH AND DOCTRINE

BELIEVED AND PROFESSED BY THE

Protestants of Scotland

Exhibited to the Estates of Scotland in Parliament in August 1560 and Approved by Their Public Vote as Doctrine Founded Upon the Infallible Word of God, and Afterwards Established and Publicly Confirmed by Various Acts of Parliament and of Lawful
GENERAL ASSEMBLIES.

St. Matthew 24 v 14

And this glad tidings of the Kingdom shall be preached through the whole world for a witness to all nations; and then shall the end come.

THE PREFACE

The Estates of Scotland, with the inhabitants of Scotland who profess the holy Evangel of Jesus Christ, to their fellow country-men and to all other nations who confess the Lord Jesus with them, wish grace, mercy, and peace from God the Father of our Lord Jesus Christ, with the Spirit of righteous judgment, for salvation.

Long have we thirsted, dear brethren, to have made known to the world the doctrine which we profess and for which we have suffered abuse and danger; but such has been the rage of Satan against us, and against the eternal truth of Christ now recently reborn among us, that until this day we have had neither time nor opportunity to set forth our faith, as gladly we would have done. For how we have been afflicted until now the greater part of Europe, we suppose, knows well.

But since by the infinite goodness of our God (who never suffers His afflicted to be utterly confounded) we have received unexpected rest and liberty, we could not do other than set forth this brief and plain Confession of that doctrine which is set before us, and which we believe and confess; partly to satisfy our brethren whose hearts, we suspect, have been and are grieved by the slanders against us; and partly to silence impudent blasphemers who boldly condemn that which they have not heard and do not understand.

We do not suppose that such malice can be cured merely by our Confession, for we know that the sweet savour of the Gospel is, and shall be, death to the sons of perdition; but we are considering chiefly our own weaker brethren, to whom we would communicate our deepest thoughts, lest they be troubled or carried away by the different rumours which Satan spreads against us to defeat our godly enterprise, protesting that if any man will note in our Confession any chapter or sentence contrary to God's Holy Word, that it would please him of his gentleness and for Christian charity's sake to inform us of it in writing; and we, upon our honour, do promise him that by God's grace we shall give him satisfaction from the mouth of God, that is, from Holy Scripture, or else we shall alter whatever he can prove to be wrong. For we call on God to record that from our hearts we abhor all heretical sects and all teachers of false doctrine, and that with all humility we embrace the purity of Christ's Gospel, which is the one food of our souls and therefore so precious to us that we are determined to suffer the greatest of worldly dangers, rather than let our souls be defrauded of it. For we are completely convinced that whoever denies Christ Jesus, or is ashamed of Him in the presence of men, shall be denied before the Father and before His holy angels. Therefore by the aid of the mighty Spirit of our Lord Jesus Christ we firmly intend to endure to the end in the confession of our faith, as in the following chapters.

The Scots Confession, 1560

Chapter I

GOD

We confess and acknowledge one God alone, to whom alone we must cleave, whom alone we must serve, whom only we must worship, and in whom alone we put our trust. Who is eternal, infinite, immeasurable, incomprehensible, omnipotent, invisible; one in substance and yet distinct in three persons, the Father, the Son, and the Holy Ghost. By whom we confess and believe all things in heaven and earth, visible and invisible, to have been created, to be retained in their being, and to be ruled and guided by His inscrutable providence for such end as His eternal wisdom, goodness, and justice have appointed, and to the manifestation of His own glory.

Chapter II

THE CREATION OF MAN

We confess and acknowledge that our God has created man, i.e., our first father, Adam, after His own image and likeness, to whom He gave wisdom, lordship, justice, free will, and self-consciousness, so that in the whole nature of man no imperfection could be found. From this dignity and perfection man and woman both fell; the woman being deceived by the serpent and man obeying the voice of the woman, both conspiring against the sovereign majesty of God, who in clear words had previously threatened death if they presumed to eat of the forbidden tree.

CHAPTER III

ORIGINAL SIN

By this transgression, generally known as original sin, the image of God was utterly defaced in man, and he and his children became by nature hostile to God, slaves to Satan, and servants to sin. And thus everlasting death has had, and shall have, power and dominion over all who have not been, are not, or shall not be reborn from above. This rebirth is wrought by the power of the Holy Ghost creating in the hearts of God's chosen ones an assured faith in the promise of God revealed to us in His word; by this faith we grasp Christ Jesus with the graces and blessings promised in Him.

CHAPTER IV

THE REVELATION OF THE PROMISE

We constantly believe that God, after the fearful and horrible departure of man from His obedience, did seek Adam again, call upon him, rebuke and convict him of his sin, and in the end made unto him a most joyful promise, that " the seed of the woman should bruise the head of the serpent," that is, that he should destroy the works of the devil. This promise was repeated and made clearer from time to time; it was embraced with joy, and most constantly received by all the faithful from Adam to Noah, from Noah to Abraham, from Abraham to David, and so onwards to the incarnation of Christ Jesus; all (we mean the believing fathers under the law) did see the joyful day of Christ Jesus, and did rejoice.

CHAPTER V

THE CONTINUANCE, INCREASE, AND PRESERVATION OF THE KIRK

We most surely believe that God preserved, instructed, multiplied, honoured, adorned, and called from death to life His Kirk in all ages since Adam until the coming of Christ Jesus in the flesh. For He called Abraham from his father's country, instructed him, and multiplied his seed; He marvellously preserved him, and more marvellously delivered his seed from the bondage and tyranny of Pharaoh; to them He gave His laws, constitutions, and ceremonies; to them He gave the land of Canaan; after He had given them judges, and afterwards Saul, He gave David to be king, to whom He gave promise that of the fruit of his loins should one sit forever upon his royal throne. To this same people from time to time He sent prophets, to recall them to the right way of their God, from which sometimes they strayed by idolatry. And although, because of their stubborn contempt for righteousness He was compelled to give them into the hands of their enemies, as had previously been threatened by the mouth of Moses, so that the holy city was destroyed, the temple burned with fire, and the whole land desolate for seventy years, yet in mercy He restored them again to Jerusalem, where the city and temple were rebuilt, and they endured against all temptations and assaults of Satan till the Messiah came according to the promise.

CHAPTER VI

THE INCARNATION OF CHRIST JESUS

When the fulness of time came God sent His Son, His eternal Wisdom, the substance of His own glory, into this world, who took the nature of humanity from the substance of a woman, a virgin, by means of the Holy Ghost. And so was born the " just seed of David," the " Angel of the great counsel of God," the very Messiah promised, whom we confess and acknowledge to be Emmanuel, true God and true man, two perfect natures united and joined in one person. So by our Confession we condemn the damnable and pestilent heresies of Arius, Marcion, Eutyches, Nestorius, and such others as did either deny the eternity of His Godhead, or the truth of His humanity, or confounded them, or else divided them.

CHAPTER VII

WHY THE MEDIATOR HAD TO BE
TRUE GOD AND TRUE MAN

We acknowledge and confess that this wonderful union between the Godhead and the humanity in Christ Jesus did arise from the eternal and immutable decree of God from which all our salvation springs and depends.

CHAPTER VIII

ELECTION

That same eternal God and Father, who by grace alone chose us in His Son Christ Jesus before the foundation of the world was laid, appointed Him to be our head, our brother, our pastor, and the great bishop of our souls. But since the opposition between the justice of God and our sins was such that no flesh by itself could or might have attained unto God, it behoved the Son of God to descend unto us and take Himself a body of our body, flesh of our flesh, and bone of our bone, and so become the Mediator between God and man, giving power to as many as believe in Him to be the sons of God; as He Himself says, " I ascend to My Father and to your Father, to My God and to your God." By this most holy brotherhood whatever we have lost in Adam is restored to us again. Therefore we are not afraid to call God our Father, not so much because He has created us, which we have in common with the reprobate, as because He has given unto us His only Son to be our brother, and given us grace to acknowledge and embrace Him as our only Mediator. Further, it behoved the Messiah and Redeemer to be true God and true man, because He was able to undergo the punishment of our transgressions and to present Himself in the presence of His Father's Judgment, as in our stead, to suffer for our transgression and disobedience, and by death to overcome him that was the author of death. But because the Godhead alone could not suffer death, and neither could manhood overcome death, He joined both together in one person, that the weakness of one should suffer and be subject to death — which we had deserved — and the infinite and invincible power of the other, that is, of the Godhead, should triumph, and purchase for us life, liberty, and perpetual victory. So we confess, and most undoubtedly believe.

CHAPTER IX

CHRIST'S DEATH, PASSION, AND BURIAL

That our Lord Jesus offered Himself a voluntary sacrifice unto His Father for us, that He suffered contradiction of sinners, that He was wounded and plagued for our transgressions, that He, the clean innocent Lamb of God, was condemned in the presence of an earthly judge, that we should be absolved before the judgment seat of our God; that He suffered not only the cruel death of the cross, which was accursed by the sentence of God; but also that He suffered for a season the wrath of His Father which sinners had deserved. But yet we avow that He remained the only, well beloved, and blessed Son of His Father even in the midst of His anguish and torment which He suffered in body and soul to make full atonement for the sins of His people. From this we confess and avow that there remains no other sacrifice for sin; if any affirm so, we do not hesitate to say that they are blasphemers against Christ's death and the everlasting atonement thereby purchased for us.

CHAPTER X

THE RESURRECTION

We undoubtedly believe, since it was impossible that the sorrows of death should retain in bondage the Author of life, that our Lord Jesus crucified, dead, and buried, who descended into hell, did rise again for our justification, and the destruction of him who was the author of death, and brought life again to us who were subject to death and its bondage. We know that His resurrection was confirmed by the testimony of His enemies, and by the resurrection of the dead, whose sepulchres did open, and they did rise and appear to many within the city of Jerusalem. It was also confirmed by the testimony of His angels, and by the senses and judgment of His apostles and of others, who had conversation, and did eat and drink with Him after His resurrection.

CHAPTER XI

THE ASCENSION

We do not doubt but that the selfsame body which was born of the virgin, was crucified, dead, and buried, and which did rise again, did ascend into the heavens, for the accomplishment of all things, where in our name and for our comfort He has received all power in heaven and earth, where He sits at the right hand of the Father, having received His kingdom, the only advocate and mediator for us. Which glory, honour, and prerogative, He alone amongst the brethren shall possess till all His enemies are made His footstool, as we undoubtedly believe they shall be in the Last Judgment. We believe that the same Lord Jesus shall visibly return for this Last Judgment as He was seen to ascend. And then, we firmly believe, the time of refreshing and restitution of all things shall come, so that those who from the beginning have suffered violence, injury, and wrong, for righteousness' sake, shall inherit that blessed immortality promised them from the beginning. But, on the other hand, the stubborn, disobedient, cruel persecutors, filthy persons, idolators, and all sorts of the unbelieving, shall be cast into the dungeon of utter darkness, where their worm shall not die, nor their fire be quenched. The remembrance of that day, and of the Judgment to be executed in it, is not only a bridle by which our carnal lusts are restrained but also such inestimable comfort that neither the threatening of worldly princes, nor the fear of present danger or of temporal death, may move us to renounce and forsake that blessed society which we, the members, have with our Head and only Mediator, Christ Jesus: whom we confess and avow to be the promised Messiah, the only Head of His Kirk, our just Lawgiver, our only High Priest, Advocate, and Mediator. To which honours and offices, if man or angel presume to intrude themselves, we utterly detest and abhor them, as blasphemous to our sovereign and supreme Governor, Christ Jesus.

CHAPTER XII

FAITH IN THE HOLY GHOST

Our faith and its assurance do not proceed from flesh and blood, that is to say, from natural powers within us, but are the inspiration of the Holy Ghost; whom we confess to be God, equal with the Father and with His Son, who sanctifies us, and brings us into all truth by His own working, without whom we should remain forever enemies to God and ignorant of His Son, Christ Jesus. For by nature we are so dead, blind, and perverse, that neither can we feel when we are pricked, see the light when it shines, nor assent to the will of God when it is revealed, unless the Spirit of the Lord Jesus quicken that which is dead, remove the darkness from our minds, and bow our stubborn hearts to the obedience of His blessed will. And so, as we confess that God the Father created us when we were not, as His Son our Lord Jesus redeemed us when we were enemies to Him, so also do we confess that the Holy Ghost does sanctify and regenerate us, without respect to any merit proceeding from us, be it before or be it after our regeneration. To put this even more plainly; as we willingly disclaim any honour and glory for our own creation and redemption, so do we willingly also for our regeneration and sanctification; for by ourselves we are not capable of thinking one good thought, but He who has begun the work in us alone continues us in it, to the praise and glory of His undeserved grace.

CHAPTER XIII

THE CAUSE OF GOOD WORKS

The cause of good works, we confess, is not our free will, but the Spirit of the Lord Jesus, who dwells in our hearts by true faith, brings forth such works as God has prepared for us to walk in. For we most boldly affirm that it is blasphemy to say that Christ abides in the hearts of those in whom is no spirit of sanctification. Therefore we do not hesitate to affirm that murderers, oppressors, cruel persecutors, adulterers, filthy persons, idolators, drunkards, thieves, and all workers of iniquity, have neither true faith nor anything of the Spirit of the Lord Jesus, so long as they obstinately continue in wickedness. For as soon as the Spirit of the Lord Jesus, whom God's chosen children receive by true faith, takes possession of the heart of any man, so soon does He regenerate and renew him, so that he begins to hate what before he loved, and to love what he hated before. Thence comes that continual battle which is between the flesh and the Spirit in God's children, while the flesh and the natural man, being corrupt, lust for things pleasant and delightful to themselves, are envious in adversity and proud in prosperity, and every moment prone and ready to offend the majesty of God. But the Spirit of God, who bears witness to our spirit that we are the sons of God, makes us resist filthy pleasures and groan in God's presence for deliverance from this bondage of corruption, and finally to triumph over sin so that it does not reign in our mortal bodies. Other men do not share this conflict since they do not have God's Spirit, but they readily follow and obey sin and feel no regrets, since they act as the devil and their corrupt nature urge. But the sons of God fight against sin; sob and mourn when they find themselves tempted to do evil; and, if they fall, rise again with earnest and unfeigned repentance. They do these things, not by their own power, but by the power of the Lord Jesus, apart from whom they can do nothing.

CHAPTER XIV

THE WORKS WHICH ARE COUNTED GOOD BEFORE GOD

We confess and acknowledge that God has given to man His holy law, in which not only all such works as displease and offend His godly majesty are forbidden, but also those which please Him and which He has promised to reward are commanded. These works are of two kinds. The one is done *Matt. 22* to the honour of God, the other to the profit of our neighbour, and both have the revealed will of God as their assurance. To have one God, to worship and honour Him, to call upon Him in all our troubles, to reverence His holy Name, to hear His Word and to believe it, and to share in His holy sacraments, belong to the first kind. To honour father, mother, princes, rulers, and superior powers; to love them, to support them, to obey their orders if they are not contrary to the commands of God, to save the lives of the innocent, to repress tyranny, to defend the oppressed, to keep our bodies clean and holy, to live in soberness and temperance, to deal justly with all men in word and deed, and, finally, to repress any desire to harm our neighbour, are the good works of the second kind, and these are most pleasing and acceptable to God as He has commanded them Himself. Acts to the contrary are sins, which always displease Him and provoke Him to anger, such as, not to call upon Him alone when we have need, not to hear His Word with reverence, but to condemn and despise it, to have or worship idols, to maintain and defend idolatry, lightly to esteem the reverend name of God, to profane, abuse, or condemn the sacraments of Christ Jesus, to disobey or resist any whom God has placed in authority, so long as they do not exceed the bounds of their office, to murder, or to consent thereto, to bear hatred, or to let innocent blood be shed if we can prevent it. In conclusion, we confess and affirm that the breach of any other commandment of the first or second kind is sin, by which God's anger and displeasure are kindled against the proud, unthankful world. So that we affirm good works to be those alone which are done in faith and at the command of God who, in His law, has set forth the things that please Him. We affirm that evil works are not only those expressly done against God's command, but also, in religious matters and the worship of God, those things which have no other warrant than the invention and opinion of man. From the beginning God has rejected such, as we learn from the words of the prophet Isaiah and of our master, Christ Jesus, "In vain do they worship Me, teaching the doctrines and commandments of men."

CHAPTER XV

THE PERFECTION OF THE LAW AND THE IMPERFECTION OF MAN

We confess and acknowledge that the law of God is most just, equal, holy, and perfect, commanding those things which, when perfectly done, can give life and bring man to eternal felicity; but our nature is so corrupt, weak, and imperfect, that we are never able perfectly to fulfil the works of the law. Even after we are reborn, if we say that we have no sin, we deceive ourselves and the truth of God is not in us. It is therefore essential for us to lay hold on Christ Jesus, in His righteousness and His atonement, since He is the end and consummation of the Law and since it is by Him that we are set at liberty so that the curse of God may not fall upon us, even though we do not fulfil the Law in all points. For as God the Father beholds us in the body of His Son Christ Jesus, He accepts our imperfect obedience as if it were perfect, and covers our works, which are defiled with many stains, with the righteousness of His Son. We do not mean that we are so set at liberty that we owe no obedience to the Law — for we have already acknowledged its place — but we affirm that no man on earth, with the sole exception of Christ Jesus, has given, gives, or shall give in action that obedience to the Law which the Law requires. When we have done all things we must fall down and unfeignedly confess that we are unprofitable servants. Therefore, whoever boasts of the merits of his own works or puts his trust in works of supererogation, boasts of what does not exist, and puts his trust in damnable idolatry.

CHAPTER XVI

THE KIRK

As we believe in one God, Father, Son, and Holy Ghost, so we firmly believe that from the beginning there has been, now is, and to the end of the world shall be, one Kirk, that is to say, one company and multitude of men chosen by God, who rightly worship and embrace Him by true faith in Christ Jesus, who is the only Head of the Kirk, even as it is the body and spouse of Christ Jesus. This Kirk is Catholic, that is, universal, because it contains the chosen of all ages, of all realms, nations, and tongues, be they of the Jews or be they of the Gentiles, who have communion and society with God the Father, and with His Son, Christ Jesus, through the sanctification of His Holy Spirit. It is therefore called the communion, not of profane persons, but of saints, who, as citizens of the heavenly Jerusalem, have the fruit of inestimable benefits, one God, one Lord Jesus, one faith, and one baptism. Out of this Kirk there is neither life nor eternal felicity. Therefore we utterly abhor the blasphemy of those who hold that men who live according to equity and justice shall be saved, no matter what religion they profess. For since there is neither life nor salvation without Christ Jesus; so shall none have part therein but those whom the Father has given unto His Son Christ Jesus, and those who in time come to Him, avow His doctrine, and believe in Him. (We include the children with the believing parents.) This Kirk is invisible, known only to God, who alone knows whom He has chosen, and includes both the chosen who are departed, the Kirk triumphant, those who yet live and fight against sin and Satan, and those who shall live hereafter.

CHAPTER XVII

THE IMMORTALITY OF SOULS

The chosen departed are in peace, and rest from their labours; not that they sleep and are lost in oblivion as some

fanatics hold, for they are delivered from all fear and torment, and all the temptations to which we and all God's
chosen are subject in this life, and because of which we are
called the Kirk Militant. On the other hand, the reprobate
and unfaithful departed have anguish, torment, and pain
which cannot be expressed. Neither the one nor the other is
in such sleep that they feel no joy or torment, as is testified
by Christ's parable in St. Luke XVI, His words to the thief,
and the words of the souls crying under the altar, " O Lord,
Thou that art righteous and just, how long shalt Thou not
revenge our blood upon those that dwell in the earth? "

CHAPTER XVIII

THE NOTES BY WHICH THE TRUE KIRK SHALL BE DETERMINED FROM THE FALSE AND WHO SHALL BE JUDGE OF DOCTRINE

Since Satan has laboured from the beginning to adorn his
pestilent synagogue with the title of the Kirk of God, and has
incited cruel murderers to persecute, trouble, and molest the
true Kirk and its members, as Cain did to Abel, Ishmael to
Isaac, Esau to Jacob, and the whole priesthood of the Jews to
Christ Jesus Himself and His apostles after Him. So it is essential that the true Kirk be distinguished from the filthy
synagogues by clear and perfect notes lest we, being deceived,
receive and embrace, to our own condemnation, the one for
the other. The notes, signs, and assured tokens whereby the
spotless bride of Christ is known from the horrible harlot,
the false Kirk, we state, are neither antiquity, usurped title,
lineal succession, appointed place, nor the numbers of men
approving an error. For Cain was before Abel and Seth in
age and title; Jerusalem had precedence above all other parts
of the earth, for in it were priests lineally descended from
Aaron, and greater numbers followed the scribes, pharisees,
and priests, than unfeignedly believed and followed Christ
Jesus and His doctrine . . . and yet no man of judgment, we
suppose, will hold that any of the forenamed were the Kirk
of God. The notes of the true Kirk, therefore, we believe,
(1) confess, and avow to be: first, the true preaching of the Word
of God, in which God has revealed Himself to us, as the writings of the prophets and apostles declare; secondly, the right
(2) administration of the sacraments of Christ Jesus, with which
must be associated the Word and promise of God to seal and

confirm them in our hearts; and lastly, ecclesiastical discipline (3) uprightly ministered, as God's Word prescribes, whereby vice is repressed and virtue nourished. Then wherever these notes are seen and continue for any time, be the number complete or not, there, beyond any doubt, is the true Kirk of Christ, who, according to His promise, is in its midst. This is not that universal Kirk of which we have spoken before, but particular Kirks, such as were in Corinth, Galatia, Ephesus, and other places where the ministry was planted by Paul and which he himself called Kirks of God. Such Kirks, we the inhabitants of the realm of Scotland confessing Christ Jesus, do claim to have in our cities, towns, and reformed districts because of the doctrine taught in our Kirks, contained in the written Word of God, that is, the Old and New Testaments, in those books which were originally reckoned canonical. We affirm that in these all things necessary to be believed for the salvation of man are sufficiently expressed. The interpretation of Scripture, we confess, does not belong to any private or public person, nor yet to any Kirk for pre-eminence or precedence, personal or local, which it has above others, but pertains to the Spirit of God by whom the Scriptures were written. When controversy arises about the right understanding of any passage or sentence of Scripture, or for the reformation of any abuse within the Kirk of God, we ought not so much to ask what men have said or done before us, as what the Holy Ghost uniformly speaks within the body of the Scriptures and what Christ Jesus Himself did and commanded. For it is agreed by all that the Spirit of God, who is the Spirit of unity, cannot contradict Himself. So if the interpretation or opinion of any theologian, Kirk, or council, is contrary to the plain Word of God written in any other passage of the Scripture, it is most certain that this is not the true understanding and meaning of the Holy Ghost, although councils, realms, and nations have approved and received it. We dare not receive or admit any interpretation which is contrary to any principal point of our faith, or to any other plain text of Scripture, or to the rule of love.

Chapter XIX

THE AUTHORITY OF THE SCRIPTURES

As we believe and confess the Scriptures of God sufficient to instruct and make perfect the man of God, so do we affirm and avow their authority to be from God, and not to depend on men or angels. We affirm, therefore, that those who say the Scriptures have no other authority save that which they have received from the Kirk are blasphemous against God and injurious to the true Kirk, which always hears and obeys the voice of her own Spouse and Pastor, but takes not upon her to be mistress over the same.

CHAPTER XX

GENERAL COUNCILS, THEIR POWER, AUTHORITY, AND THE CAUSE OF THEIR SUMMONING

As we do not rashly condemn what good men, assembled together in General Councils lawfully gathered, have set before us; so we do not receive uncritically whatever has been declared to men under the name of the General Councils, for it is plain that, being human, some of them have manifestly erred, and that in matters of great weight and importance. So far then as the Council confirms its decrees by the plain Word of God, so far do we reverence and embrace them. But if men, under the name of a Council, pretend to forge for us new articles of faith, or to make decisions contrary to the Word of God, then we must utterly deny them as the doctrine of devils, drawing our souls from the voice of the one God to follow the doctrines and teachings of men. The reason why the General Councils met was not to make any permanent law which God had not made before, nor yet to form new articles for our belief, nor to give the Word of God authority; much less to make that to be His Word, or even the true interpretation of it, which was not expressed previously by His holy will in His Word; but the reason for Councils, at least of those that deserve that name, was partly to refute heresies, and to give public confession of their faith to the generations following, which they did by the authority of God's written Word, and not by any opinion or prerogative that they could not err by reason of their numbers. This, we judge, was the primary reason for General Councils. The second was that good policy and order should be constituted and observed in the Kirk where, as in the house of God, it becomes all things to be done decently and in order. Not that we think any policy or order of ceremonies can be appointed for all ages, times, and places; for as ceremonies which men have devised are but temporal, so they may, and ought to be, changed, when they foster superstition rather than edify the Kirk.

CHAPTER XXI

THE SACRAMENTS

As the fathers under the Law, besides the reality of the sacrifices, had two chief sacraments, that is, circumcision and the passover, and those who rejected these were not reckoned among God's people; so do we acknowledge and confess that now in the time of the Gospel we have two chief sacraments, which alone were instituted by the Lord Jesus and commanded to be used by all who will be counted members of His body, that is, Baptism and the Supper or Table of the Lord Jesus, also called the Communion of His Body and Blood. These sacraments, both of the Old Testament and of the New, were instituted by God not only to make a visible distinction between His people and those who were without the Covenant, but also to exercise the faith of His children and, by participation of these sacraments, to seal in their hearts the assurance of His promise, and of that most blessed conjunction, union, and society, which the chosen have with their Head, Christ Jesus. And so we utterly condemn the vanity of those who affirm the sacraments to be nothing else than naked and bare signs. No, we assuredly believe that by Baptism we are engrafted into Christ Jesus, to be made partakers of His righteousness, by which our sins are covered and remitted, and also that in the Supper rightly used, Christ Jesus is so joined with us that He becomes the very nourishment and food of our souls. Not that we imagine any transubstantiation of bread into Christ's body, and of wine into His natural blood, as the Romanists have perniciously taught and wrongly believed; but this union and conjunction which we have with the body and blood of Christ Jesus in the right use of the sacraments is wrought by means of the Holy Ghost, who by true faith carries us above all things that are visible, carnal, and earthly, and makes us feed upon the body and blood of Christ Jesus, once broken and shed for us but now in heaven, and appearing for us in the presence of His Father. Notwithstanding the distance between His glorified body in heaven and mortal men on earth, yet we must assuredly believe that the bread which we break is the communion of Christ's body and the cup which we bless the communion of His blood. Thus we confess and believe without doubt that the faithful, in the right use of the Lord's Table, do so eat the body and drink the blood of the Lord Jesus that He remains in them and they in Him; they are so made flesh of His flesh and bone of His bone that as the eternal Godhood has given to the flesh of Christ Jesus, which by nature was corruptible and mortal, life and immortality, so the eating and drinking of the flesh and blood of Christ Jesus does the like for us. We grant that this is neither given to us merely at the time nor by the power and virtue of the sacrament alone, but we affirm that the faithful, in the right use of the Lord's Table, have such union with Christ Jesus as the natural man cannot apprehend. Further we affirm that although the faithful, hindered by negligence and human weakness, do not profit as much as they ought in the actual moment of the Supper, yet afterwards it shall bring forth fruit, being living seed sown in good ground; for the Holy Spirit, who can never be separated from the right institution of the Lord Jesus, will not deprive the faithful of the fruit of that mystical action. Yet all this, we say again, comes of that true faith which apprehends Christ Jesus, who alone makes the sacrament effective in us. Therefore, if anyone slanders us by saying that we affirm or believe the sacraments to be symbols and nothing more, they are libellous and speak against the plain facts. On the other hand we readily admit that we make a distinction between Christ Jesus in His eternal substance and the elements of the sacramental signs. So we neither worship the elements, in place of that which they signify, nor yet do we despise them or undervalue them, but we use them with great reverence, examining ourselves diligently before we participate, since we are assured by the mouth of the apostle that " whosoever shall eat this bread, and drink this cup of the Lord, unworthily, shall be guilty of the body and blood of the Lord."

CHAPTER XXII

THE RIGHT ADMINISTRATION
OF THE SACRAMENTS

Two things are necessary for the right administration of the sacraments. The first is that they should be ministered by lawful ministers, and we declare that these are men appointed to preach the Word, unto whom God has given the power to preach the Gospel, and who are lawfully called by some Kirk. The second is that they should be ministered in the elements and manner which God has appointed. Otherwise they cease to be the sacraments of Christ Jesus. This is why we abandon the teaching of the Roman Church and withdraw from its sacraments; firstly, because their ministers are not true ministers of Christ Jesus (indeed they even allow women, whom the Holy Ghost will not permit to preach in the congregation, to baptize) and, secondly, because they have so adulterated both the sacraments with their own additions that no part of Christ's original act remains in its original simplicity. The addition of oil, salt, spittle, and such like in baptism, are merely human additions. To adore or venerate the sacrament, to carry it through streets and towns in procession, or to reserve it in a special case, is not the proper use of Christ's sacrament but an abuse of it. Christ Jesus said, " Take ye, eat ye," and " Do this in remembrance of Me." By these words and commands He sanctified bread and wine to be the sacrament of His holy body and blood, so that the one should be eaten and that all should drink of the other, and not that they should be reserved for worship or honoured as God, as the Romanists do. Further, in withdrawing one part of the sacrament — the blessed cup — from the people, they have committed sacrilege. Moreover, if the sacraments *must be understood* are to be rightly used it is essential that the end and purpose of their institution should be understood, not only by the minister but by the recipients. For if the recipient does not understand what is being done, the sacrament is not being rightly used, as is seen in the case of the Old Testament sacrifices. Similarly, if the teacher teaches false doctrine which *must be united to God's promise* is hateful to God, even though the sacraments are His own ordinance, they are not rightly used, since wicked men have used them for another end than what God commanded. We affirm that this has been done to the sacraments in the Roman Church, for there the whole action of the Lord Jesus is adulterated in form, purpose, and meaning. What Christ Jesus did, and commanded to be done, is evident from the Gospels and from St. Paul; what the priest does at the altar we do not need to tell. The end and purpose of Christ's institution, for which it should be used, is set forth in the words, " Do this in remembrance of Me," and " For as often as ye eat this bread and drink this cup ye do show " — that is, extol, preach, magnify, and praise — " the Lord's death, till He come." But let the words of the mass, and their own doctors and teachings witness, what is the purpose and meaning of the mass; it is that, as mediators between Christ and His Kirk, they should offer to God the Father a sacrifice in propitiation for the sins of the living and of the dead. This doctrine is blasphemous to Christ Jesus and would deprive His unique sacrifice, once offered on the cross for the cleansing of all who are to be sanctified, of its sufficiency; so we detest and renounce it.

CHAPTER XXIII

TO WHOM SACRAMENTS APPERTAIN

We hold that baptism applies as much to the children of the faithful as to those who are of age and discretion, and so we condemn the error of the Anabaptists, who deny that children should be baptized before they have faith and understanding. But we hold that the Supper of the Lord is only for those who are of the household of faith and can try and examine themselves both in their faith and their duty to their neighbours. Those who eat and drink at that holy table without faith, or without peace and goodwill to their brethren, eat unworthily. This is the reason why ministers in our Kirk make public and individual examination of those who are to be admitted to the table of the Lord Jesus.

CHAPTER XXIV

THE CIVIL MAGISTRATE

We confess and acknowledge that empires, kingdoms, dominions, and cities are appointed and ordained by God; the powers and authorities in them, emperors in empires, kings in their realms, dukes and princes in their dominions, and magistrates in cities, are ordained by God's holy ordinance for the manifestation of His own glory and for the good and well being of all men. We hold that any men who conspire to rebel or to overturn the civil powers, as duly established, are not merely enemies to humanity but rebels against God's will. Further, we confess and acknowledge that such persons as are set in authority are to be loved, honoured, feared, and held in the highest respect, because they are the lieutenants of God, and in their councils God Himself doth sit and judge. They are the judges and princes to whom God has given the sword for the praise and defence of good men and the punishment of all open evil doers. Moreover, we state that the preservation and purification of religion is particularly the duty of kings, princes, rulers, and magistrates. They are not only appointed for civil government but also to maintain true religion and to suppress all idolatry and superstition. This may be seen in David, Jehosaphat, Hezekiah, Josiah, and others highly commended for their zeal in that cause.

Therefore we confess and avow that those who resist the supreme powers, so long as they are acting in their own spheres, are resisting God's ordinance and cannot be held guiltless. We further state that so long as princes and rulers vigilantly fulfil their office, anyone who denies them aid, counsel, or service, denies it to God, who by His lieutenant craves it of them.

Chapter XXV

THE GIFTS FREELY GIVEN TO THE KIRK

Although the Word of God truly preached, the Sacraments rightly ministered, and discipline executed according to the Word of God, are certain and infallible signs of the true Kirk, we do not mean that every individual person in that company is a chosen member of Christ Jesus. We acknowledge and confess that many weeds and tares are sown among the corn and grow in great abundance in its midst, and that the reprobate may be found in the fellowship of the chosen and may take an outward part with them in the benefits of the Word and sacraments. But since they only confess God for a time with their mouths and not with their hearts, they lapse, and do not continue to the end. Therefore they do not share the fruits of Christ's death, resurrection, and ascension. But such as unfeignedly believe with the heart and boldly confess the Lord Jesus with their mouths shall certainly receive His gifts. Firstly, in this life, they shall receive remission of sins and that by faith in Christ's blood alone; for though sin shall remain and continually abide in our mortal bodies, yet it shall not be counted against us, but be pardoned, and covered with Christ's righteousness. Secondly, in the general judgment, there shall be given to every man and woman resurrection of the flesh. The seas shall give up her dead, and the earth those who are buried within her. Yea, the Eternal, our God, shall stretch out His hand on the dust, and the dead shall arise incorruptible, and in the very substance of the selfsame flesh which very man now bears, to receive according to their works, glory or punishment. Such as now delight in vanity, cruelty, filthiness, superstition, or idolatry, shall be condemned to the fire unquenchable, in which those who now serve the devil in all abominations shall be tormented forever, both in body and in spirit. But such as continue in welldoing to the end, boldly confessing the Lord Jesus, shall receive glory, honour, and immortality, we constantly believe, to reign forever in life everlasting with Christ Jesus, to whose glorified body all His chosen shall be made like, when He shall appear again in judgment and shall render up the Kingdom to God His Father, who then shall be and ever shall remain, all in all things, God blessed forever. To whom, with the Son and the Holy Ghost, be all honour and glory, now and ever. Amen.

Arise, O Lord, and let Thine enemies be confounded; let them flee from Thy presence that hate Thy godly Name. Give Thy servants strength to speak Thy Word with boldness, and let all nations cleave to the true knowledge of Thee. Amen.

These acts and articles were read in the face of the Parliament and ratified by the Three Estates, at Edinburgh the 17 day of August the year of God, 1560 years.

11

The Belgic Confession of Faith, 1561

INTRODUCTION

The principles of the Reformation spread rapidly from Germany and France into the Low Countries, and the converts were subjected to the fiercest persecution. It has been said that the number of the martyrs of the Reformed Church of the Netherlands " exceeds that of any other Protestant Church during the sixteenth century, and perhaps that of the whole primitive Church under the Roman empire." As in France, the Confessions of Faith in Jesus Christ were born in the fire of persecution. During early years of oppression many fled to England where under Edward VI they found asylum. A congregation of these refugees was formed in London, and in 1551 it submitted to the king a *Compendium doctrinae* composed by Martin Micron as a testimony of their faith. A translation into Dutch was made by J. v. Utenhove and was widely used as a Confession in evangelical congregations in the Netherlands until the adoption of the Belgic Confession.

The author of the Belgic Confession was Guido de Brès (Guy de Bray). He was born at Mons in 1523, educated in the Roman Church and converted to the evangelical faith through reading the Bible. He was executed as a rebel against the crown May 31, 1567. In 1548 he was driven from his homeland and joined the exiles in London. After four years he returned and preached at Ryssel and Tournay. In the vain hope of convincing the authorities that he and his followers were not seditious or fanatical, de Brès composed a Confession of Faith of thirty-seven articles in 1559. It followed closely in order and content the French Confession of the same year. In its composition, de Brès was assisted by Adrian Saravia, professor of theology at Leiden, H. Modetus, chaplain to William of Orange, and Godfrey van Wingen. According to Leonard Verduin,[1] Saravia took the Confession to Geneva in 1559 for approval, and, for reasons that were never made public, this was denied. As a result of pressures exerted by van Wingen and in spite of Saravia's objections, it was printed in Rouen in 1561. As the Reformed Churches in the Low Countries were still " under the Cross," the authorities endeavored to have all copies destroyed. The Regent, Margaret of Parma, confiscated two hundred copies at one time. Verduin states that for a long time it was thought that not a single copy had survived. However, late in the nineteenth century a copy was found by Jonkheer Trip van Zoutlandt. This text was reproduced by J. J. Van Toorenenbergen in his *Eene Bladzijde in de Geschiedenis der Nederlandsche Geloofsbelijdensis*. Also about 1561 another printing of the original was made by a Pastor Frossard of Lille in his *Eglise soubs la Croix pendant la domination Espagvol*. It was translated into Dutch and printed in Emden in 1562. (The first German translation was published by J. Mayer in Heidelberg in 1566). A copy of the original in French was presented to Philip II in 1562, together with an address that breathes the spirit of martyrdom. It denies the charges of sedition and fanaticism, affirms loyalty to the government in all lawful things, but insists that rather than deny Christ before men they would " offer our backs to be beaten, our tongues to be cut out, our mouths to be bridled, and our whole bodies to be burned, because we know that whoever will follow Christ must take up his Cross and deny himself." [2] The Confession, however, did not succeed in placating the bigoted king.

In 1566 the fortunes of Reformed Christians in the Low Countries began to change. The nobles who were anxious to gain independence from Spain joined forces with the Reformed consistories which wished to throw off the yoke of the Papacy. An alliance of the nobles was formed, and a synod of the churches was convened in Antwerp for the purpose of revising the Confession. In the work of revision the leading role was played by Francis Junius, a pupil of Calvin's and

---

[1] *Twentieth Century Encyclopedia of Religious Knowledge,* ed. by Lefferts A. Loetscher (Baker Book House, 1955), Vol. I, pp. 121 ff. Cf. L. A. van Langeraad, " Bray, Guy de " in *Realencyklopädie für protestantische Theologie und Kirche* (Leipzig, 1897), Vol. III, pp. 364–367.
[2] A German translation of the address is given in full in E. G. A. Böckel, *Die Bekenntnisschriften der evangelisch-reformierten Kirche* (Leipzig, 1847), pp. 480–484.

later a professor at Leiden. The principal change was in Article 36 which deals with relations between the civil magistrate and the Kingdom of Christ. Thus as Paul Jacobs has observed, the Belgic Confession is " of truly fundamental importance for the history of the founding of the Netherland State, because the formation of this state was a history of faith. The faith that was basic to this Confession enabled the nobles to form an alliance, and the Reformed Christians from Antwerp to Wesel to unite." [3]

The revised Confession was again submitted to Geneva for approval and this time it was granted. However, the revision did not enjoy unanimous approval in the Low Countries, and it was not until about 1580 that it acquired undisputed acceptance. In 1568 it was adopted by the Synod of Wesel and in 1571 by the Synod of Emden. At the provincial Synod of Dort in 1574 all ministers and schoolteachers were directed to sign. At the Great Synod of Dort the French, Latin, and Dutch texts were carefully revised, and the Confession, along with the Heidelberg Catechism and the Canons, was adopted, and since April 29, 1619, has been the doctrinal standard of the Dutch Reformed Churches in Holland, Belgium, and America.

In Philip Schaff's *Creeds of Christendom,* Vol. III, is to be found the French text as revised at Dort and reprinted in 1850 at Brussels by the *Société évangélique Belge* under the title *La Confession de foi des églises réformées Walonnes et Flamandes.* The English text in Schaff, made from the Latin, is the one authorized by the Reformed (Dutch) Church in America, and is the text employed here. A Latin translation, probably made by Beza, appeared in the *Harmonia confessionum* (Geneva, 1581), and in the first edition of the *Corpus et syntagma* (Geneva, 1612); another by Festus Hommius (Leiden, 1618). This was revised by the Synod of Dort and reprinted (as revised) in the second edition of the *Corpus et syntagma* (1654), and (in its original form) with various readings in Niemeyer's *Collectio confessionum.* There are several Dutch and German versions, and a Greek version made by Jac. Revius in 1635.

Literature: L. A. van Langeraad, " Bray, Guy de," *Realencyklopädie für protestantische Theologie und Kirche* (Leipzig, 1897), Vol. III, pp. 364–367; E. G. A. Böckel, *Die*

---

[3] *Theologie reformierter Bekenntnisschriften in Grundzügen* (Neukirchener Verlag, 1959), p. 48.

Bekenntnisschriften der evangelisch-reformierten Kirche (Leipzig, 1903) ; P. Schaff, *Creeds of Christendom,* 6th ed. (Harper & Brothers, 1931), Vol. I, pp. 502–507; *Reformed Standards of Unity,* with an introduction by Leroy Nixon (1952) ; Leonard Verduin, " Belgic Confession " and " Guido de Brès," *Twentieth Century Encyclopedia of Religious Knowledge,* ed. by Lefferts A. Loetscher (Baker Book House, 1955), Vol. I, pp. 121 f. and pp. 178–180; Paul Jacobs, *Theologie reformierter Bekenntnisschriften in Grundzügen* (Neukirchener Verlag, 1959).

The Belgic Confession A.D. 1561
Revised 1619

THE CONFESSION OF FAITH
OF THE
REFORMED CHURCH

Revised in the National Synod, held at
Dordrecht, in the Years 1618 and 1619

ART. I

There Is One Only God

We all believe with the heart, and confess with the mouth,
that there is one only simple [4] and spiritual [5] Being, which
we call God; and that he is eternal,[6] incomprehensible,[7] invisible,[8] immutable,[9] infinite,[10] almighty, perfectly wise,[11] just,[12]
good, [13] and the overflowing fountain [14] of all good.[15]—*Add since the French*

ART. II

By What Means God Is Made Known Unto Us

We know him by two means: first, by the creation, preservation, and government of the universe; [16] which is before

---

[4] Eph. 4:6; Deut. 6:4; I Tim. 2:5; I Cor. 8:6.
[5] John 4:24.
[6] Isa. 40:28.
[7] Rom. 11:33.
[8] Rom. 1:20.
[9] Mal. 3:6.
[10] Isa. 44:6.
[11] I Tim. 1:17.
[12] Jer. 12:1.
[13] Matt. 19:17.
[14] James 1:17; I Chron. 29:10-12.
[15] English *Harm. of Conf.*: "A most plentiful well-spring of all good
things."
[16] Ps. 19:2; Eph. 4:6.

our eyes as a most elegant book, wherein all creatures, great and small, are as so many characters leading us to contemplate *the invisible things of God,* namely, *his eternal power and Godhead,* as the Apostle Paul saith (Rom. 1:20). All which things are sufficient to convince men, and leave them without excuse.

Secondly, he makes himself more clearly and fully known to us by his holy and divine Word; [17] that is to say, as far as is necessary for us to know in this life, to his glory and our salvation.

ART. III

Of the Written Word of God

We confess that this Word of God was not sent nor delivered by the will of man, but that *holy men of God spake as they were moved by the Holy Ghost,* as the Apostle Peter saith.[18] And that afterwards God, from a special care which he has for us and our salvation, commanded his servants, the Prophets [19] and Apostles,[20] to commit his revealed Word to writing; and he himself wrote with his own finger the two tables of the law.[21] Therefore we call such writings holy and divine Scriptures.

ART. IV

Canonical Books of the Holy Scriptures

We believe that the Holy Scriptures are contained in two books, namely, the Old and New Testaments, which are canonical, against which nothing can be alleged. These are thus named in the Church of God.

The books of the Old Testament are: the five books of Moses, viz., Genesis, Exodus, Leviticus, Numbers, Deuteronomy; the book of Joshua, Judges, Ruth, two books of Samuel, and two of the Kings, two books of the Chronicles, commonly called Paralipomenon, the first of Ezra, Nehemiah, Esther; Job, the Psalms of David, the three books of Solomon, namely, the Proverbs, Ecclesiastes, and the Song of Songs; the four great Prophets: Isaiah, Jeremiah, Ezekiel, and Daniel; and the twelve lesser Prophets, viz., Hosea, Joel, Amos,

---

[17] Ps. 19:8; I Cor. 12:6.
[18] II Peter 1:21.
[19] Ex. 24:4; Ps. 102:19; Hab. 2:2.

[20] II Tim. 3:16; Apoc. 1:11.
[21] Ex. 31:18.

Obadiah, Jonah, Micah, Nahum, Habakkuk, Zephaniah, Haggai, Zechariah, and Malachi.

Those of the New Testament are: the four Evangelists, viz., Matthew, Mark, Luke, and John; the Acts of the Apostles; the fourteen Epistles of the Apostle Paul, viz., one to the Romans, two to the Corinthians, one to the Galatians, one to the Ephesians, one to the Philippians, one to the Colossians, two to the Thessalonians, two to Timothy, one to Titus, one to Philemon, and one to the Hebrews; the seven Epistles of the other Apostles, viz., one of James, two of Peter, three of John, one of Jude; and the Revelation of the Apostle John.

ART. V

Whence Do the Holy Scriptures Derive Their Dignity and Authority

We receive all these books, and these only, as holy and canonical, for the regulation, foundation, and confirmation of our faith; believing, without any doubt, all things contained in them, not so much because the Church receives and approves them as such, but more especially because the Holy Ghost witnesseth in our hearts that they are from God, whereof they carry the evidence in themselves. For the very blind are able to perceive that the things foretold in them are fulfilling.

ART. VI

The Difference Between the Canonical and Apocryphal Books

We distinguish these sacred books from the apocryphal, viz., the third and fourth book of Esdras, the books of Tobias, Judith, Wisdom, Jesus Syrach, Baruch, the appendix to the book of Esther, the Song of the Three Children in the Furnace, the History of Susannah, of Bel and the Dragon, the Prayer of Manasses, and the two books of Maccabees. All which the Church may read and take instruction from, so far as they agree with the canonical books; but they are far from having such power and efficacy as that we may from their testimony confirm any point of faith or of the Christian religion; much less to detract from the authority of the other sacred books.

ART. VII

*The Sufficiency of the Holy Scriptures to Be the Only
Rule of Faith*

<u>We believe that these Holy Scriptures fully contain the
will of God, and that whatsoever man ought to believe unto
salvation, is sufficiently taught therein.</u>[22] For since the whole
manner of worship which God requires of us is written in
them at large, it is unlawful for any one, though an Apostle,
to teach otherwise [23] than we are now taught in the Holy
Scriptures: *nay, though it were an angel from heaven,* as the
Apostle Paul saith.[24] For since it is forbidden *to add unto or
take away any thing from the Word of God,*[25] it doth thereby
evidently appear that the doctrine thereof is most perfect and
complete in all respects. Neither may we compare any
writings of men, though ever so holy, with those divine Scriptures; [26] nor ought we to compare custom, or the great multitude, or antiquity, or succession of times or persons, or councils, decrees, or statutes, with the truth of God,[27] for the truth
is above all: for all men are of themselves liars,[28] and more
vain than vanity itself. <u>Therefore we reject with all our hearts
whatsoever doth not agree with this infallible rule,</u>[29] which
the Apostles have taught us, saying, Try the spirits whether
they are of God; [30] likewise, *If there come any unto you, and
bring not this doctrine, receive him not into your house.*[31]

ART. VIII

*God Is One in Essence, yet Distinguished
in Three Persons*

According to this truth and this Word of God, we believe
in one only God, who is one single essence, [32] in which are

---

22 Rom. 15:4; John 4:25; II Tim. 3:15-17; I Peter 1:1; Prov. 30:5; Gal.
30:15; Apoc. 22:18; John 15:15; Acts 2:27.
23 I Peter 4:11; I Cor. 15:2-3; II Tim. 3:14; I Tim. 1:3; II John, ch. 10.
24 Gal. 1:8-9; I Cor. 15:2; Acts 26:22; Rom. 15:4; I Peter 4:11; II Tim. 3:14.
25 Deut. 12:32; Prov. 30:6; Apoc. 22:18; John 4:25.
26 Matt. 15:3; 17:5; Mark 7:7; Isa. 1:12; I Cor. 2:4.
27 Isa. 1:12; Rom. 3:4; II Tim. 4:3-4.
28 Ps. 62:10.
29 Gal. 6:16; I Cor. 3:11; II Thess. 2:2.
30 I John 4:1.
31 II John, ch. 10.
32 Isa. 43:10.

three persons,[33] really, truly, and eternally distinct, according
to their incommunicable properties; namely, the Father, and
the Son, and the Holy Ghost.[34] The Father is the cause, origin,
and beginning of all things, visible and invisible; [35] the Son
is the Word,[36] Wisdom, and Image of the Father; [37] the Holy
Ghost is the eternal Power and Might,[38] proceeding from the
Father and the Son.[39] Nevertheless God is not by this distinction divided into three, since the Holy Scriptures teach
us that the Father, and the Son, and the Holy Ghost have
each his personality, distinguished by their properties; but
in such wise that these three persons are but one only God.
Hence, then, it is evident that the Father is not the Son, nor
the Son the Father, and likewise the Holy Ghost is neither
the Father nor the Son. Nevertheless these persons thus distinguished are not divided nor intermixed; for the Father
hath not assumed the flesh, nor hath the Holy Ghost, but the
Son only. The Father hath never been without his Son,[40] or
without his Holy Ghost. For they are all three co-eternal and
co-essential. There is neither first nor last; for they are all
three one, in truth, in power, in goodness, and in mercy.

ART. IX

*The Proof of the Foregoing Article of the Trinity of Persons
in One God*

All this we know, as well from the testimonies of Holy
Writ as from their operations, and chiefly by those we feel in
ourselves. The testimonies of the Holy Scriptures, that teach
us to believe this Holy Trinity, are written in many places
of the Old Testament, which are not so necessary to enumerate as to choose them out with discretion and judgment. In
Genesis 1:26, 27, God saith: *Let us make man in our image,
after our likeness,* etc. *So God created man in his own image,*[41]
male and female created he them. And Gen. 3:22: *Behold,
the man has become as one of us.*[42] From this saying, *Let us*

33 I John 5:7; Heb. 1:3.
34 Matt. 28:19.
35 I Cor. 8:6; Col. 1:16.
36 John 1:1-2; Rev. 19:13; Prov. 8:12.
37 Prov. 8:12, 22, etc.
38 Col. 1:15; Heb. 1:3.
39 Matt. 12:28; John 15:26; Gal. 4:6.
40 Phil. 2:6-7; Gal. 4:4; John 1:14.
41 Gen. 1:26-27.
42 Gen. 3:22.

make man in our image, it appears that there are more persons than one in the Godhead; and when he saith *God created,* this signifies the unity. It is true he doth not say how many persons there are, but that which appears to us somewhat obscure in the Old Testament is very plain in the New.

For when our Lord was baptized in Jordan,[43] the voice of the Father was heard, saying, *This is my beloved Son:* the Son was seen in the water; and the Holy Ghost appeared in the shape of a dove. This form is also instituted by Christ in the baptism of all believers. *Baptize all nations, in the name of the Father and of the Son, and of the Holy Ghost.*[44] In the Gospel of Luke the angel Gabriel thus addressed Mary, the mother of our Lord: *The Holy Ghost shall come upon thee, and the power of the Highest shall overshadow thee, therefore also that holy thing which shall be born of thee shall be called the Son of God.*[45] Likewise, *The grace of our Lord Jesus Christ, and the love of God, and the communion of the Holy Ghost be with you.*[46] And *There are three that bear record in heaven, the Father, the Word, and the Holy Ghost, and these three are one.*[47] In all which places we are fully taught that there are three persons in one only divine essence. And although this doctrine far surpasses all human understanding, nevertheless we now believe it by means of the Word of God, but expect hereafter to enjoy the perfect knowledge and benefit thereof in heaven.[48]

Moreover we must observe the particular offices and operations of these three persons towards us. The Father is called our Creator by his power; [49] the Son is our Saviour and Redeemer by his blood; [50] the Holy Ghost is our Sanctifier by his dwelling in our hearts.[51]

This doctrine of the Holy Trinity hath always been defended and maintained by the true Church, since the times of the Apostles to this very day, against the Jews, Mohammedans, and some false Christians and heretics, as Marcion, Manes, Praxeas, Sabellius, Samosatenus, Arius, and such like, who have been justly condemned by the orthodox fathers.

Therefore, in this point, we do willingly receive the three

---

43 Matt. 3:16-17.
44 Matt. 28:19.
45 Luke 1:35.
46 II Cor. 13:13.
47 I John 5:7 [?].
48 Ps. 45:8; Isa. 61:1.
49 Eccl. 12:3; Mal. 2:10; I Peter 1:2.
50 I Peter 1:2; I John 1:7; 4:14.
51 I Cor. 6:11; I Peter 1:2; Gal. 4:6; Titus 3:5; Rom. 8:9; John 14:16.

creeds, namely, that of the Apostles, of Nice, and of Athanasius; likewise that which, conformable thereunto, is agreed upon by the ancient fathers.

Art. X

Jesus Christ Is True and Eternal God

We believe that Jesus Christ, according to his divine nature, is the only begotten Son of God,[52] begotten from eternity,[53] not made nor created (for then he would be a creature), but co-essential and co-eternal [54] with the Father,[55] *the express image of his person, and the brightness of his glory,*[56] equal unto him in all things.[57] Who is the Son of God, not only from the time that he assumed our nature, but from all eternity,[58] as these testimonies, when compared together, teach us. Moses saith that *God created the world;* [59] and John saith that *all things were made by that Word, which he calleth God;* [60] and the Apostle saith that *God made the worlds by his Son;* [61] likewise, that *God created all things by Jesus Christ.*[62] Therefore it must needs follow that he — who is called God, the Word, the Son, and Jesus Christ — did exist at that time when all things were created by him.[63] Therefore the Prophet Micah saith: *His goings forth have been from of old, from everlasting.*[64] And the Apostle: *He hath neither beginning of days nor end of life.*[65] He therefore is that true, eternal, and almighty God, whom we invoke, worship, and serve.

Art. XI

The Holy Ghost Is True and Eternal God

We believe and confess also that the Holy Ghost from eternity proceeds from the Father [66] and Son; [67] and therefore

---

[52] John 1:18, 49.
[53] John 1:14; Col. 1:15.
[54] John 1:2; 17:5; Rev. 1:8.
[55] John 10:30; Phil. 2:6.
[56] Heb. 1:3.
[57] Phil. 2:6.
[58] John 8:23, 58; 9:35-37; Acts 8:37; Rom. 9:5.
[59] Gen. 1:1.
[60] John 1:3.
[61] Heb. 1:2.
[62] Col. 1:16.
[63] Col. 1:16.
[64] Micah 5:2.
[65] Heb. 7:3.
[66] Ps. 33:6, 17; John 14:16.
[67] Gal. 4:6; Rom. 8:9; John 15:26.

is neither made, created, nor begotten, but only proceedeth
from both; who in order is the third person of the Holy
Trinity; of one and the same essence, majesty, and glory with
the Father and the Son; and therefore is the true and eternal
God, as the Holy Scripture teaches us.[68]

Art. XII

Of the Creation

We believe that the Father, by the Word — that is, by his
Son [69] — created of nothing the heaven, the earth, and all
creatures, as it seemed good unto him, giving unto every creature its being, shape, form, and several offices to serve its Creator; that he doth also still uphold and govern them by his
eternal providence and infinite [70] power for the service of
mankind, to the end that man [71] may serve his God.[72] He also
created the angels good,[73] to be his messengers [74] and to serve
his elect: [75] some of whom are fallen from that excellency, in
which God created them, into everlasting perdition; [76] and the
others have, by the grace of God, remained steadfast, and
continued in their primitive state.[77] The devils and evil
spirits are so depraved that they are enemies of God and every
good thing to the utmost of their power,[78] as murderers watch-
ing to ruin the Church and every member thereof, and by
their wicked stratagems to destroy all; [79] and are therefore, by
their own wickedness, adjudged to eternal damnation, daily
expecting their horrible torments.[80] Therefore we reject and
abhor the error of the Sadducees, who deny the existence of
spirits and angels; [81] and also that of the Manichees, who assert that the devils have their origin of themselves, and that

---

[68] Gen. 1:2; Isa. 48:16; 61:1; Acts 5:3-4; 28:25; I Cor. 3:16; 6:19; Ps. 139:7.
[69] Gen. 1:1; Isa. 40:26; Heb. 3:4; Apoc. 4:11; I Cor. 8:6; John 1:3; Col. 1:16.
[70] Heb. 1:3; Ps. 104:10, etc.; Acts 17:25.
[71] I Tim. 4:3-4; Gen. 1:29-30; 9:2-3; Ps. 104:14-15.
[72] I Cor. 3:22; 7:20; Matt. 4:10.
[73] Col. 1:16.
[74] Ps. 103:20; 34:8; 143:2.
[75] Heb. 1:14; Ps. 34:8.
[76] John 8:44; II Peter 2:4; Luke 8:31; Jude 6.
[77] Matt. 25:31.
[78] I Peter 5:8; Job 1:7.
[79] Gen. 3:1; Matt. 13:25; II Cor. 2:11; 11:3, 14.
[80] Matt. 25:41; Luke 8:30-31.
[81] Acts 23:8.

they are wicked of their own nature, without having been corrupted.

Art. XIII

Of Divine Providence

We believe that the same God, after he had created all things, did not forsake them, or give them up to fortune or chance, but that he rules and governs them, according to his holy will,[82] so that nothing happens in this world without his appointment; [83] nevertheless, God neither is the author of, nor can be charged with, the sins which are committed. For his power and goodness are so great and incomprehensible, that he orders and executes his work in the most excellent and just manner even when the devil and wicked men act unjustly.[84] And as to what he doth surpassing human understanding we will not curiously inquire into it further than our capacity will admit of; but with the greatest humility and reverence adore the righteous judgments of God which are hid from us,[85] contenting ourselves that we are disciples of Christ, to learn only those things which he has revealed to us in his Word without transgressing these limits.

This doctrine affords us unspeakable consolation, since we are taught thereby that nothing can befall us by chance, but by the direction of our most gracious and heavenly Father, who watches over us with a paternal care, keeping all creatures so under his power [86] that not a hair of our head (for they are all numbered), nor a sparrow, can fall to the ground, without the will of our Father,[87] in whom we do entirely trust; being persuaded that he so restrains the devil and all our enemies that, without his will and permission, they can not hurt us.

And therefore we reject that damnable error of the Epicureans, who say that God regards nothing, but leaves all things to chance.

---

[82] John 5:17; Heb. 1:3; Prov. 16:4; Ps. 104:9, etc.; Ps. 139:2, etc.
[83] James 4:15; Job 1:21; I Kings 22:20; Acts 4:28; I Sam. 2:25; Ps. 115:3; 45:7; Amos 3:6; Deut. 19:5; Prov. 21:1; Ps. 105:25; Isa. 10:5-7; II Thess. 2:11; Ezek. 14:9; Rom. 1:29; Gen. 45:8; 50:20; II Sam. 16:10; Gen. 27:20; Ps. 75:7-8; Isa. 45:7; Prov. 16:4; Lam. 3:37-38; I Kings 22:34, 38; Ex. 21:13.
[84] Matt. 8:31-32; John 3:8.
[85] Rom. 11:33-34.
[86] Matt. 8:31; Job 1:12; 2:6.
[87] Matt. 10:29-30.

Art. XIV

Of the Creation and Fall of Man, and His Incapacity to Perform What Is Truly Good

We believe that God created man out of the dust of the earth, and made and formed him after his own image and likeness,[88] good, righteous, and holy, capable in all things to will agreeably to the will of God.[89] But being in honor, he understood it not, neither knew his excellency,[90] but willfully subjected himself to sin, and consequently to death and the curse, giving ear to the words of the devil.[91] For the commandment of life, which he had received,[92] he transgressed; and by sin separated himself from God, who was his true life,[93] having corrupted his whole nature,[94] whereby he made himself liable to corporal and spiritual death.[95] And being thus become wicked, perverse, and corrupt in all his ways, he hath lost all his excellent gifts which he had received from God,[96] and only retained a few remains thereof,[97] which, however, are sufficient to leave man without excuse;[98] for all the light which is in us is changed into darkness,[99] as the Scriptures teach us, saying: *The light shineth in darkness, and the darkness comprehendeth it not:*[100] where St. John calleth men darkness.

Therefore we reject all that is taught repugnant to this concerning the free will of man, since man is but a slave to sin;[101] and has nothing of himself unless it is given him from heaven.[102] For who may presume to boast that he of himself can do any good, since Christ saith, *No man can come to me, except the Father which hath sent me draw him?*[103] Who will glory in his own will, who understands that to be *carnally*

---

[88] Gen. 1:26; Eccl. 7:29; Eph. 4:24.
[89] Gen. 1:31; Eph. 4:24.
[90] Ps. 49:21; Isa. 59:2.
[91] Gen. 3:6, 17.
[92] Gen. 1:3, 7.
[93] Isa. 59:2.
[94] Eph. 4:18.
[95] Rom. 5:12; Gen. 2:17; 3:19.
[96] Rom. 3:10, etc.
[97] Acts 14:16-17; 17:27.
[98] Rom. 1:20-21; Acts 17:27.
[99] Eph. 5:8; Matt. 6:23.
[100] John 1:5.
[101] Isa. 26:12; Ps. 94:11; John 8:34; Rom. 6:17; 7:5, 17.
[102] John 3:27; Isa. 26:12.
[103] John 3:27; 6:44, 65.

minded is enmity against God? [104] Who can speak of his
knowledge, since *the natural man receiveth not the things of
the Spirit of God?* [105] In short, who dare suggest any thought,
since he knows that *we are not sufficient of ourselves to think
any thing as of ourselves, but that our sufficiency is of God?* [106]
And therefore what the Apostle saith ought justly to be held
sure and firm, that *God worketh in us both to will and to do
of his good pleasure.* [107] For there is no will nor understanding,
conformable to the divine will and understanding, but what
Christ hath wrought in man: which he teaches us when he
saith, *Without me ye can do nothing.* [108]

ART. XV

Of Original Sin

We believe that, through the disobedience of Adam, original sin is extended to all mankind; [109] which is a corruption of
the whole nature, and an hereditary disease, wherewith infants themselves are infected even in their mother's womb,[110]
and which produceth in man all sorts of sin, being in him as
a root thereof; [111] and therefore is so vile and abominable in
the sight of God that it is sufficient to condemn all mankind.[112] Nor is it by any means abolished or done away by
baptism; since sin always issues forth from this woful source,
as water from a fountain: notwithstanding it is not imputed
to the children of God unto condemnation, but by his grace
and mercy is forgiven them. Not that they should rest securely
in sin, but that a sense of this corruption should make believers often to sigh, desiring to be delivered from this body
of death.[113] Wherefore we reject the error of the Pelagians,
who assert that sin proceeds only from imitation.

ART. XVI

Of Eternal Election

We believe that all the posterity of Adam, being thus fallen
into perdition and ruin by the sin of our first parents, God

[104] Rom. 8:7.
[105] I Cor. 2:14; Ps. 94:11.
[106] II Cor. 3:5.
[107] Phil. 2:13.
[108] John 15:5.
[109] Rom. 5:12-13; Ps. 51:7; Rom. 3:10; Gen. 6:3; John 3:6; Job 14:4.
[110] Isa. 48:8; Rom. 5:14.
[111] Gal. 5:19; Rom. 7:8, 10, 13, 17-18, 20, 23.
[112] Eph. 2:3, 5.
[113] Rom. 7:18, 24.

then did manifest himself such as he is; that is to say, MERCI-
FUL AND JUST: [114] MERCIFUL, since he delivers and preserves
from this perdition all whom he, in his eternal and unchangeable council, of mere goodness hath elected in Christ Jesus our
Lord, without any respect to their works: [115] JUST, in leaving
others in the fall and perdition wherein they have involved
themselves.[116]

ART. XVII

Of the Recovery of Fallen Man

We believe that our most gracious God, in his admirable
wisdom and goodness, seeing that man had thus thrown himself into temporal and spiritual death, and made himself
wholly miserable, was pleased to seek and comfort him when
he trembling fled from his presence,[117] promising him that he
would give his Son, who should *be made of a woman, to
bruise the head of the serpent,* and would make him happy.[118]

ART. XVIII

Of the Incarnation of Jesus Christ

We confess, therefore, that God did fulfill the promise
which he made to the fathers by the mouth of his holy prophets when he sent into the world,[119] at the time appointed by
him, his own only-begotten and eternal Son, *who took upon
him the form of a servant, and became like unto men,*[120] really
assuming the true human nature, with all its infirmities, sin
excepted,[121] being conceived in the womb of the blessed Virgin Mary, by the power of the Holy Ghost, without the means
of man; [122] and did not only assume human nature as to the
body, but also a true human soul,[123] that he might be a real

114 Rom. 9:18, 22-23; 3:12.
115 Rom. 9:15-16; 11:32; Eph. 2:8-10; Ps. 100:3; I John 4:10; Deut. 32:8;
I Sam. 12:22; Ps. 65:5; Mal. 1:2; II Tim. 1:9; Rom. 8:29; 9:11, 21; 11:5-6;
Eph. 1:4; Titus 3:4-5; Acts 2:47; 13:48; II Tim. 2:19-20; I Peter 1:2; John
6:27; 15:16; 17:9.
116 Rom. 9:17-18; II Tim. 2:20.
117 Gen. 3:8-9, 19; Isa. 65:1-2.
118 Heb. 2:14; Gen. 22:18; Isa. 7:14; John 7:42; II Tim. 2:8; Heb. 7:14; Gen.
3:15; Gal. 4:4.
119 Isa. 11:1; Luke 1:55; Gen. 26:4; II Sam. 7:12; Ps. 132:11; Acts 13:23.
120 I Tim. 2:5; 3:16; Phil. 2:7.
121 Heb. 2:14-15; 4:15.
122 Luke 1:31, 34-35.
123 Matt. 26:38; John 12:27.

man. For since the soul was lost as well as the body, it was necessary that he should take both upon him, to save both. Therefore we confess (in opposition to the heresy of the Anabaptists, who deny that Christ assumed human flesh of his mother) that Christ is become *a partaker of the flesh and blood of the children;* [124] that he is a *fruit of the loins of David* after the flesh; [125] *made of the seed of David according to the flesh;* [126] a *fruit of the womb* of the Virgin Mary; [127] *made of a woman;* [128] a *branch* of David; [129] a shoot of *the root of Jesse;* [130] *sprung from the tribe of Judah;* [131] *descended from the Jews according to the flesh:* [132] *of the seed of Abraham,* [133] since he took upon him the seed of Abraham, and became like unto his brethren in all things, sin excepted; [134] so that in truth he is our IMMANUEL, that is to say, *God with us.* [135]

ART. XIX

Of the Union and Distinction of the Two Natures in the Person of Christ

We believe that by this conception the person of the Son is inseparably united and connected with the human nature; so that there are not two Sons of God, nor two persons, but two natures united in one single person; yet each nature retains its own distinct properties. As then the divine nature hath always remained uncreated, without beginning of days or end of life, [136] filling heaven and earth, so also hath the human nature not lost its properties, but remained a creature, having beginning of days, being a finite nature, and retaining all the properties of a real body. [137] And though he hath by his resurrection given immortality to the same, nevertheless

---

124 Heb. 2:14.
125 Acts 2:30.
126 Ps. 132:11; Rom. 1:3.
127 Luke 1:42.
128 Gal. 4:4.
129 Jer. 33:15.
130 Isa. 11:1.
131 Heb. 7:14.
132 Rom. 9:5.
133 Gen. 22:18; II Sam. 7:12; Matt. 1:1; Gal. 3:16.
134 Heb. 2:15-17.
135 Isa. 7:14; Matt. 1:23.
136 Heb. 7:3.
137 I Cor. 15:13, 21; Phil. 3:21; Matt. 26:11; Acts 1:2, 11; 3:21; Luke 24:39; John 20:25, 27.

he hath not changed the reality of his human nature; forasmuch as our salvation and resurrection also depend on the reality of his body. But these two natures are so closely united in one person, that they were not separated even by his death. Therefore that which he, when dying, commended into the hands of his Father, was a real human spirit, departing from his body.[138] But in the mean time the divine nature always remained united with the human, even when he lay in the grave; and the Godhead did not cease to be in him, any more than it did when he was an infant, though it did not so clearly manifest itself for a while.

Wherefore we confess that he is VERY GOD and VERY MAN: very God by his power to conquer death, and very man that he might die for us according to the infirmity of his flesh.

ART. XX

God Hath Manifested His Justice and Mercy in Christ

We believe that God, who is perfectly merciful and also perfectly just, sent his Son to assume that nature in which the disobedience was committed, to make satisfaction in the same, and to bear the punishment of sin by his most bitter passion and death.[139] God therefore manifested his justice against his Son when he laid our iniquities upon him,[140] and poured forth his mercy and goodness on us, who were guilty and worthy of damnation, out of mere and perfect love, giving his Son unto death for us, and raising him for our justification,[141] that through him we might obtain immortality and life eternal.

ART. XXI

Of the Satisfaction of Christ, Our Only High-Priest, for Us

We believe that Jesus Christ is ordained with an oath to be an everlasting High-Priest, after the order of Melchisedec: [142] who hath presented himself in our behalf before his Father, to appease his wrath by his full satisfaction,[143] by offering himself on the tree of the cross, and pouring out his

[138] Luke 23:46; Matt. 27:50.
[139] Heb. 2:14; Rom. 8:3, 32-33.
[140] Isa. 53:6; John 1:29; I John 4:9.
[141] Rom. 4:25.
[142] Ps. 110:4; Heb. 5:10.
[143] Col. 1:14; Rom. 5:8-9; Col. 2:14; Heb. 2:17; 9:14; Rom. 3:24; 8:2; John 15:3; Acts 2:24; 13:28; John 3:16; I Tim. 2:6.

precious blood to purge away our sins; as the prophets had foretold. For it is written, *He was wounded for our transgressions, he was bruised for our iniquities:* [144] *the chastisement of our peace was upon him, and with his stripes we are healed; he was brought as a lamb to the slaughter, and numbered with the transgressors;* and condemned by Pontius Pilate as a malefactor, though he had first declared him innocent. [145] Therefore, *he restored* [146] *that which he took not away,* and *suffered the just for the unjust,* [147] as well in his body as in his soul, feeling the terrible punishment which our sins had merited; insomuch *that his sweat became like unto drops of blood falling on the ground.* [148] He called out, *My God, my God, why hast thou forsaken me?* [149] And hath suffered all this for the remission of our sins. Wherefore we justly say with the Apostle Paul, *that we know nothing but Jesus Christ, and him crucified;* [150] *we count all things but loss and dung for the excellency of the knowledge of Christ Jesus our Lord:* [151] in whose wounds we find all manner of consolation. Neither is it necessary to seek or invent any other means of being reconciled to God, than this only sacrifice, once offered, by which believers are made perfect forever. [152] This is also the reason why he was called by the angel of God, JESUS, that is to say, SAVIOUR, because he should save his people from their sins. [153]

ART. XXII

Of Our Justification Through Faith in Jesus Christ

We believe that, to attain the true knowledge of this great mystery, the Holy Ghost kindleth in our hearts an upright faith, which embraces Jesus Christ with all his merits, appropriates him, [154] and seeks nothing more besides him. [155] For it must needs follow, either that all things which are requisite to our salvation are not in Jesus Christ, or if all things are

144 Isa. 53:5, 7, 12.
145 Luke 23:22, 24; Acts 13:28; Ps. 22:16; John 18:38; Ps. 69:5; I Peter 3:18.
146 Ps. 69:5.
147 I Peter 3:18.
148 Luke 22:44.
149 Ps. 22:2; Matt. 27:46.
150 I Cor. 2:2.
151 Phil. 3:8.
152 Heb. 9:25-26; 10:14.
153 Matt. 1:21; Acts 4:12.
154 Eph. 3:16-17; Ps. 51:13; Eph. 1:17-18; I Cor. 2:12.
155 I Cor. 2:2; Acts 4:12; Gal. 2:21; Jer. 23:6; I Cor. 1:30; Jer. 31:10.

in him, that then those who possess Jesus Christ through faith have complete salvation in Him.[156] Therefore, for any to assert that Christ is not sufficient, but that something more is required besides him, would be too gross a blasphemy; for hence it would follow that Christ was but half a Saviour. Therefore we justly say with Paul, *that we are justified by faith alone,* or *by faith without works.*[157] However, to speak more clearly, we do not mean that faith itself justifies us, for it is only an instrument with which we embrace Christ our Righteousness. But Jesus Christ, imputing to us all his merits, and so many holy works, which he hath done for us and in our stead, is our Righteousness.[158] And faith is an instrument that keeps us in communion with him in all his benefits, which, when they become ours, are more than sufficient to acquit us of our sins.

Art. XXIII

Our Justification Consists in the Forgiveness of Sin and the Imputation of Christ's Righteousness

We believe that our salvation consists in the remission of our sins for Jesus Christ's sake, and that therein our righteousness before God is implied; as David and Paul teach us, declaring this to be the happiness of man, that God imputes righteousness to him without works.[159] And the same Apostle saith, *that we are justified freely by his grace, through the redemption which is in Jesus Christ.*[160] And therefore we always hold fast this foundation, ascribing all the glory to God,[161] humbling ourselves before him, and acknowledging ourselves to be such as we really are, without presuming to trust in any thing in ourselves, or in any merit of ours,[162] relying and resting upon the obedience of Christ crucified alone,[163] which becomes ours when we believe in him.[164] This is sufficient to cover all our iniquities, and to give us confidence in approaching to God; [165] freeing the conscience of

156 Matt. 1:21; Rom. 3:27; 8:1, 33.
157 Rom. 3:27; Gal. 2:6; I Peter 1:4-5; Rom. 10:4.
158 Jer. 23:6; I Cor. 1:30; II Tim. 1:2; Luke 1:77; Rom. 3:24-25; 4:5; Ps. 32:1-2; Phil. 3:9; Titus 3:5; II Tim. 1:9.
159 Luke 1:77; Col. 1:14; Ps. 32:1-2; Rom. 4:6-7.
160 Rom. 3:23-24; Acts 4:12.
161 Ps. 115:1; I Cor. 4:7; Rom. 4:2.
162 I Cor., 4:7; Rom. 4:2; I Cor. 1:29, 31.
163 Rom. 5:19.
164 Heb. 11:6-7; Eph. 2:8; II Cor. 5:19; I Tim. 2:6.
165 Rom. 5:1; Eph. 3:12; I John 2:1.

fear, terror, and dread, without following the example of our first father, Adam, who, trembling, attempted to cover himself with fig-leaves.[166] And, verily, if we should appear before God, relying on ourselves or on any other creature, though ever so little, we should, alas! be consumed.[167] And therefore every one must pray with David: *O Lord, enter not into judgment with thy servant: for in thy sight shall no man living be justified.*[168]

ART. XXIV

Of Man's Sanctification and Good Works

We believe that this true faith, being wrought in man by the hearing of the Word of God and the operation of the Holy Ghost,[169] doth regenerate and make him a new man, causing him to live a new life,[170] and freeing him from the bondage of sin.[171] Therefore it is so far from being true, that this justifying faith makes men remiss in a pious and holy life,[172] that on the contrary without it they would never do any thing out of love to God, but only out of self-love or fear of damnation. Therefore it is impossible that this holy faith can be unfruitful in man: for we do not speak of a vain faith,[173] but of such a faith as is called in Scripture *a faith that worketh by love*,[174] which excites man to the practice of those works which God has commanded in his Word. Which works, as they proceed from the good root of faith, are good and acceptable in the sight of God, forasmuch as they are all sanctified by his grace: howbeit they are of no account towards our justification.[175] For it is by faith in Christ that we are justified, even before we do good works,[176] otherwise they could not be good works any more than the fruit of a tree can be good before the tree itself is good.[177]

Therefore we do good works, but not to merit by them (for what can we merit?) — nay, we are beholden to God for the

166 Gen. 3:7.
167 Isa. 33:14; Deut. 27:26; James 2:10.
168 Ps. 130:3; Matt. 18:23-26; Ps. 143:2; Luke 16:15.
169 I Peter 1:23; Rom. 10:17; John 5:24.
170 I Thess. 1:5; Rom. 8:15; John 6:29; Col. 2:12; Phil. 1:1, 29; Eph. 2:8.
171 Acts 15:9; Rom. 6:4, 22; Titus 2:12; John 8:36.
172 Titus 2:12.
173 Titus 3:8; John 15:5; Heb. 11:6; I Tim. 1:5.
174 I Tim. 1:5; Gal. 5:6; Titus 3:8.
175 II Tim. 1:9; Rom. 9:32; Titus 3:5.
176 Rom. 4:4; Gen. 4:4.
177 Heb. 11:6; Rom. 14:23; Gen. 4:4; Matt. 7:17.

good works we do, and not he to us, *since it is he that worketh in us both to will and to do* [178] *of his good pleasure.*[179] Let us therefore attend to what is written: *When ye shall have done all those things which are commanded you, say we are unprofitable servants: we have done that which was our duty to do.*[180]

In the mean time we do not deny that God rewards good works, but it is through his grace that he crowns his gifts.[181] Moreover, though we do good works, we do not found our salvation upon them; [182] for we can do no work but what is polluted by our flesh, and also punishable; [183] and although we could perform such works, still the remembrance of one sin is sufficient to make God reject them. Thus, then, we should always be in doubt, tossed to and fro without any certainty, and our poor consciences would be continually vexed if they relied not on the merits of the suffering and death of our Saviour.[184]

ART. XXV

Of the Abolishing of the Ceremonial Law

We believe that the ceremonies and figures of the law ceased at the coming of Christ,[185] and that all the shadows are accomplished; so that the use of them must be abolished among Christians: [186] yet the truth and substance of them remain with us in Jesus Christ, in whom they have their completion. In the mean time we still use the testimonies taken out of the law and the prophets, to confirm us in the doctrine of the gospel,[187] and to regulate our life in all honesty to the glory of God, according to his will.

ART. XXVI

Of Christ's Intercession

We believe that we have no access unto God save alone through the only Mediator and Advocate, Jesus Christ the

---

[178] I Cor. 4:7; Isa. 26:12; Gal. 3:5; I Thess. 2:13.
[179] Phil. 2:13.
[180] Luke 17:10.
[181] Matt. 10:42; 25:34-35; Rev. 3:12, 21; Rom. 2:6; Apoc. 2:11; II John 8; Rom. 11:6.
[182] Eph. 2:9-10.
[183] Isa. 64:6.
[184] Isa. 28:16; Rom. 10:11; Hab. 2:4.
[185] Rom. 10:4.
[186] Gal. 5:2-4; 3:1; 4:10-11; Col. 2:16-17.
[187] II Peter 1:19.

righteous,[188] who therefore became man, having united in one person the divine and human natures, that we men might have access to the divine Majesty, which access would otherwise be barred against us. But this Mediator, whom the Father hath appointed between him and us, ought in nowise to affright us by his majesty, or cause us to seek another according to our fancy.[189] For there is no creature, either in heaven or on earth, who loveth us more than Jesus Christ; [190] *who, though he was in the form of God, yet made himself of no reputation, and took upon him the form of a man and of a servant for us,*[191] *and was made like unto his brethren in all things.* If, then, we should seek for another mediator, who would be well affected towards us, whom could we find who loved us more than he who laid down his life for us, even when we were his enemies? [192] And if we seek for one who hath power and majesty, who is there that hath so much of both as *he who sits at the right hand of his Father,* and who hath *all power in heaven and on earth?* [193] And who will sooner be heard than the own well-beloved Son of God?

Therefore it was only through diffidence that this practice of dishonoring instead of honoring the saints was introduced, doing that which they never have done nor required, but have, on the contrary, steadfastly rejected, according to their bounden duty, as appears by their writings.[194] Neither must we plead here our unworthiness; for the meaning is not that we should offer our prayers to God on account of our own worthiness, but only on account of the excellence and worthiness of our Lord Jesus Christ,[195] whose righteousness is become ours by faith.

Therefore the Apostle, to remove this foolish fear or, rather, distrust from us, justly saith that *Jesus Christ was made like unto his brethren in all things, that he might be a merciful and faithful high-priest, to make reconciliation for the sins of the people. For in that he himself hath suffered, being tempted, he is able to succor them that are tempted.*[196] And further to encourage us, he adds: *Seeing, then, that we have a great high-priest that is passed into the heavens, Jesus*

---

188 I Tim. 2:5; I John 2:1; Rom. 8:33.
189 Hos. 13:9; Jer 2:13, 33.
190 John 10:11; I John 4:10; Rom. 5:8; Eph. 3:19; John 15:13.
191 Phil. 2:7.
192 Rom. 5:8.
193 Mark 16:19; Col. 3:1; Rom. 8:33; Matt. 11:27; 28:18.
194 Acts 10:26; 14:15.
195 Dan. 9:17-18; John 16:23; Eph. 3:12; Acts 4:12; I Cor. 1:31; Eph. 2:18.
196 Heb. 2:17-18.

*the Son of God, let us hold fast our profession. For we have
not a high-priest which can not be touched with the feeling
of our infirmities; but was in all points tempted like as we
are, yet without sin. Let us therefore come boldly unto the
throne of grace, that we may obtain mercy, and find grace to
help in time of need.*[197] The same Apostle saith: *Having boldness to enter into the holiest by the blood of Jesus, let us
draw near with a true heart in full assurance of faith,* etc.
Likewise, *Christ hath an unchangeable priesthood,*[198] *wherefore he is able also to save them to the uttermost that come
unto God by him, seeing he ever liveth to make intercession
for them.*[199] What more can be required? since Christ himself
saith: *I am the way, and the truth, and the life; no man com-
eth unto the Father but by me.*[200] To what purpose should we
then seek another advocate,[201] since it hath pleased God to
give us his own Son as our Advocate? [202] Let us not forsake
him to take another, or rather to seek after another, without
ever being able to find him; for God well knew, when he gave
him to us, that we were sinners.

Therefore, according to the command of Christ, we call
upon the heavenly Father through Jesus Christ, our only
Mediator, as we are taught in the Lord's Prayer; [203] being assured that whatever we ask of the Father in his name will be
granted us.[204]

Art. XXVII

Of the Catholic Christian Church

We believe and profess one catholic or universal Church,[205]
which is a holy congregation and assembly of true Christian believers, expecting all their salvation in Jesus Christ,
being washed by his blood, sanctified and sealed by the Holy
Ghost.

This Church hath been from the beginning of the world,
and will be to the end thereof; [206] which is evident from this,

---

197 Heb. 4:14-16.
198 Heb. 10:19, 22.
199 Heb. 7:24-25.
200 John 14:6.
201 Ps. 44:21.
202 I Tim. 2:5; I John 2:1; Rom. 8:33.
203 Luke 11:2.
204 John 4:17; 16:23; 14:13.
205 Isa. 2:2; Ps. 46:5; 102:14; Jer. 31:36.
206 Matt. 28:20; II Sam. 7:16.

that Christ is an eternal king, which, without subjects, he can not be.[207] And this holy Church is preserved or supported by God against the rage of the whole world; [208] though she sometimes (for a while) appear very small, and, in the eyes of men, to be reduced to nothing: [209] as during the perilous reign of Ahab, when nevertheless *the Lord reserved unto him seven thousand men, who had not bowed their knees to Baal.*[210]

Furthermore, this holy Church is not confined, bound, or limited to a certain place or to certain persons, but is spread and dispersed over the whole world; and yet is joined and united with heart and will,[211] by the power of faith, in one and the same spirit.[212]

Art. XXVIII

Every One Is Bound to Join Himself to the True Church

We believe, since this holy congregation is an assemblage of those who are saved, and out of it there is no salvation,[213] that no person [214] of whatsoever state or condition he may be, ought to withdraw himself, to live in a separate state from it; but that all men are in duty bound to join and unite themselves with it; maintaining the unity of the Church; [215] submitting themselves to the doctrine and discipline thereof; bowing ther necks under the yoke of Jesus Christ; [216] and as mutual members of the same body,[217] serving to the edification of the brethren, according to the talents God has given them. And that this may be better observed, it is the duty of all believers, according to the Word of God, to separate themselves from those who do not belong to the Church,[218] and to join themselves to this congregation, wheresoever God hath established it,[219] even though the magistrates and edicts of

---

207 Luke 1:32-33; Ps. 89:37-38; 110:2-4.
208 Matt. 16:18; John 16:33; Gen. 22:17; II Tim. 2:19.
209 Luke 12:32; Isa. 1:9; Rev. 12:6, 14; Luke 17:21; Matt. 16:18.
210 Rom. 12:4; 11:2, 4; I Kings 19:18; Isa. 1:9; Rom. 9:29.
211 Acts 4:32.
212 Eph. 4:3-4.
213 I Peter 3:20; Joel 2:32.
214 Acts 2:40; Isa. 52:11.
215 Ps. 22:23; Eph. 4:3, 12; Heb. 2:12.
216 Ps. 2:10-12; Matt. 11:29.
217 Eph. 4:12, 16; I Cor. 12:12, etc.
218 Acts 2:40; Isa. 52:11; II Cor. 6:17; Rev. 18:4.
219 Matt. 12:30; 24:28; Isa. 49:22; Rev. 17:14.

princes be against it; yea, though they should suffer death or bodily punishment.[220]

Therefore all those who separate themselves from the same, or do not join themselves to it, act contrary to the ordinance of God.

ART. XXIX

Of the Marks of the True Church, and Wherein She Differs from the False Church

We believe that we ought diligently and circumspectly to discern from the Word of God which is the true Church, since all sects which are in the world assume to themselves the name of the Church.

But we speak here not of the company of hypocrites, who are mixed in the Church with the good, yet are not of the Church, though externally in it; but we say that the body and communion of the true Church must be distinguished from all sects who call themselves the Church.[221]

The marks by which the true Church is known are these: If the pure doctrine of the gospel is preached therein; [222] if she maintains the pure administration of the sacraments as instituted by Christ; [223] if church discipline is exercised in punishing of sin;[224] in short, if all things are managed according to the pure Word of God, all things contrary thereto rejected,[225] and Jesus Christ acknowledged as the only Head of the Church.[226] Hereby the true Church may certainly be known, from which no man has a right to separate himself. With respect to those who are members of the Church, they may be known by the marks of Christians, namely, by faith; [227] and when they have received Jesus Christ the only Saviour,[228] they avoid sin, follow after righteousness,[229] love the true God and their neighbor, neither turn aside to the right or left, and crucify the flesh with the works thereof.[230] But this is not

---

220 Dan. 3:17-18; 6:8-10; Apoc. 14:14; Acts 4:17, 19; 17:7; 18:13.
221 Matt. 13:22; II Tim. 2:18-20; Rom. 9:6.
222 John 10:27; Eph. 2:20; Acts 17:11-12; Col. 1:23; John 8:47.
223 Matt. 28:19; Luke 22:19, etc.; I Cor. 11:23, etc.
224 Matt. 18:15-18; II Thess. 3:14-15.
225 Matt. 28:2; Gal. 1:6-8.
226 Eph. 1:22-23; John 10:4-5, 14.
227 Eph. 1:13; John 17:20.
228 I John 4:2.
229 I John 3:8-10.
230 Rom. 6:2; Gal. 5:24.

to be understood as if there did not remain in them great infirmities; but they fight against them through the Spirit all
the days of their life,[231] continually taking their refuge in
the blood, death, passion, and obedience of our Lord Jesus
Christ, *in whom they have remission of sins through faith in
him.*[232]

As for the false Church, she ascribes more power and authority to herself and her ordinances than to the Word of
God,[233] and will not submit herself to the yoke of Christ.[234]
Neither does she administer the Sacraments, as appointed by
Christ in his Word, but adds to and takes from them as she
thinks proper; she relieth more upon men than upon Christ;
and persecutes those who live holily according to the Word
of God,[235] and rebuke her for her errors, covetousness, and
idolatry.[236] These two Churches are easily known and distinguished from each other.

Art. XXX

Concerning the Government of, and Offices in, the Church

We believe that this true Church must be governed by the
spiritual policy which our Lord has taught us in his Word —
namely, that there must be Ministers or Pastors to preach the
Word of God, and to administer the Sacraments; [237] also
elders and deacons, who, together with the pastors, form the
council of the Church;[238] that by these means the true religion
may be preserved, and the true doctrine every where propagated, likewise transgressors punished and restrained by spiritual means; also that the poor and distressed may be relieved
and comforted, according to their necessities.[239] By these
means every thing will be carried on in the Church with good
order and decency, when faithful men are chosen, according
to the rule prescribed by St. Paul to Timothy.[240]

---

[231] Rom. 7:6, 17, etc.; Gal. 5:17.
[232] Col. 1:14.
[233] Col. 2:18-19.
[234] Ps. 2:3.
[235] Rev. 12:4; John 16:2.
[236] Rev. 17:3-4, 6.
[237] Eph. 4:11; I Cor. 4:1-2; II Cor. 5:20; John 20:23; Acts 26:17-18; Luke 10:16.
[238] Acts 6:3; 14:23.
[239] Matt. 18:17; I Cor. 5:4-5.
[240] I Tim. 3:1, etc.; Titus 1:5, etc.

Art. XXXI

Of the Ministers, Elders, and Deacons

We believe that the Ministers of God's Word,[241] and the Elders and Deacons,[242] ought to be chosen to their respective offices by a lawful election of the Church, with calling upon the name of the Lord, and in that order which the Word of God teacheth. Therefore every one must take heed not to intrude himself by indecent means, but is bound to wait till it shall please God to call him; [243] that he may have testimony of his calling, and be certain and assured that it is of the Lord.

As for the Ministers of God's Word, they have equally the same power and authority wheresoever they are, as they are all Ministers of Christ,[244] the only universal Bishop, and the only Head of the Church.[245]

Moreover, that this holy ordinance of God may not be violated or slighted, we say that every one ought to esteem the Ministers of God's Word and the Elders of the Church very highly for their work's sake, and be at peace with them without murmuring, strife, or contention, as much as possible.[246]

Art. XXXII

Of the Order and Discipline of the Church

In the mean time we believe, though it is useful and beneficial, that those who are rulers of the Church institute and establish certain ordinances among themselves for maintaining the body of the Church; yet they ought studiously to take care that they do not depart from those things which Christ, our only master, hath instituted.[247] And, therefore, we reject all human inventions, and all laws which man would introduce into the worship of God, thereby to bind and compel the conscience in any manner whatever.[248]

Therefore we admit only of that which tends to nourish and preserve concord and unity, and to keep all men in obedience to God. For this purpose excommunication or church

---

241 I Tim. 5:22.
242 Acts 6:3.
243 Jer. 23:21; Heb. 5:4; Acts 1:23; 13:2.
244 I Cor. 4:1; 3:9; II Cor. 5:20; Acts 26:16-17.
245 I Peter 2:25; 5:4; Isa. 61:1; Eph., ch. 1.
246 I Thess. 5:12-13; I Tim. 5:17; Heb. 13:17.
247 Col. 2:6-7.
248 I Cor. 7:23; Matt. 15:9; Isa. 29:13; Gal. 5:1; Rom. 16:17-18.

discipline is requisite, with the several circumstances belonging to it, according to the Word of God.[249]

Art. XXXIII

Of the Sacraments

We believe that our gracious God, on account of our weakness and infirmities, hath ordained the Sacraments for us, thereby to seal unto us his promises,[250] and to be pledges of the good will and grace of God towards us, and also to nourish and strengthen our faith, which he hath joined to the word of the gospel, the better to present to our senses, both that which he signifies to us by his Word, and that which he works inwardly in our hearts, thereby assuring and confirming in us the salvation which he imparts to us. For they are visible signs and seals of an inward and invisible thing, by means whereof God worketh in us by the power of the Holy Ghost. Therefore the signs are not in vain or insignificant, so as to deceive us. For Jesus Christ is the true object presented by them, without whom they would be of no moment.[251]

Moreover, we are satisfied with the number of Sacraments which Christ our Lord hath instituted, which are two only, namely, the Sacrament of Baptism, and the Holy Supper of our Lord Jesus Christ.[252]

Art. XXXIV

Of Holy Baptism

We believe and confess that Jesus Christ, who is the end of the law,[253] hath made an end, by the shedding of his blood, of all other sheddings of blood which men could or would make as a propitiation or satisfaction for sin; and that he, having abolished circumcision, which was done with blood, hath instituted the Sacrament of Baptism [254] instead thereof, by which we are received into the Church of God, and separated from all other people and strange religions, that we may wholly belong to him whose ensign and banner we bear, and which serves as a testimony unto us that he will forever

[249] Matt. 18:17; I Cor. 5:5; I Tim. 1:20.
[250] Rom. 4:11; Gen. 9:13; 17:11.
[251] Col. 2:11, 17; I Cor. 5:7.
[252] Matt. 26:36; 28:19.
[253] Rom. 10:4.
[254] Col. 2:11; I Peter 3:21; I Cor. 10:2,

be our gracious God and Father. Therefore he has commanded all those who are his to be baptized with pure water, *in the name of the Father, and of the Son, and of the Holy Ghost:* [255] thereby signifying to us, that as water washeth away the filth of the body, when poured upon it, and is seen on the body of the baptized, when sprinkled upon him, so doth the blood of Christ, by the power of the Holy Ghost, internally sprinkle the soul, cleanse it from its sins, and regenerate us from children of wrath unto children of God.[256] Not that this is effected by the external water, but by the sprinkling of the precious blood of the Son of God; [257] who is our Red Sea, through which we must pass to escape the tyranny of Pharaoh, that is, the devil, and to enter into the spiritual land of Canaan. Therefore, the Ministers, on their part, administer the Sacrament, and that which is visible,[258] but our Lord giveth that which is signified by the Sacrament, namely, the gifts and invisible grace; washing, cleansing, and purging our souls of all filth and unrighteousness; [259] renewing our hearts and filling them with all comfort; giving unto us a true assurance of his fatherly goodness; putting on us the new man, and putting off the old man with all his deeds.[260]

Therefore, we believe that every man who is earnestly studious of obtaining life eternal ought to be but once baptized with this only Baptism, without ever repeating the same: [261] since we can not be born twice. Neither doth this Baptism only avail us at the time when the water is poured upon us and received by us, but also through the whole course of our life.[262] Therefore we detest the error of the Anabaptists, who are not content with the one only baptism they have once received, and moreover condemn the baptism of the infants of believers, who, we believe, ought to be baptized and sealed with the sign of the covenant,[263] as the children in Israel formerly were circumcised upon the same promises which are made unto our children.[264] And, indeed, Christ shed his blood no less for the washing of the children of the faithful

---

255 Matt. 28:19.
256 I Cor. 6:11; Titus 3:5; Heb. 9:14; I John 1:7; Apoc. 1:6.
257 John 19:34.
258 Matt. 3:11; I Cor. 3:5, 7; Rom. 6:3.
259 Eph. 5:26; Acts 22:16; I Peter 3:21.
260 Gal. 3:27; I Cor. 12:13; Eph. 4:22-24.
261 Mark 16:16; Matt. 28:19; Eph. 4:5; Heb. 6:2.
262 Acts 2:38; 8:16.
263 Matt. 19:14; I Cor. 7:14.
264 Gen. 17:11-12.

than for adult persons; [265] and, therefore, they ought to receive the sign and sacrament of that which Christ hath done for them; as the Lord commanded in the law, that they should be made partakers of the sacrament of Christ's suffering and death shortly after they were born, by offering for them a lamb, which was a sacrament of Jesus Christ.[266] Moreover, what Circumcision was to the Jews, that Baptism is to our children. And for this reason Paul calls Baptism the *Circumcision of Christ.*[267]

Art. XXXV

Of the Holy Supper of Our Lord Jesus Christ

We believe and confess that our Saviour Jesus Christ did ordain and institute the Sacrament of the Holy Supper,[268] to nourish and support those whom he hath already regenerated and incorporated into his family, which is his Church. Now those who are regenerated have in them a twofold life,[269] the one bodily and temporal, which they have from the first birth, and is common to all men; the other spiritual and heavenly, which is given them in their second birth,[270] which is effected by the word of the gospel,[271] in the communion of the body of Christ; and this life is not common, but is peculiar to God's elect.[272] In like manner God hath given us, for the support of the bodily and earthly life, earthly and common bread, which is subservient thereto, and is common to all men, even as life itself. But for the support of the spiritual and heavenly life which believers have, he hath sent a living bread, which descended from heaven, namely, Jesus Christ,[273] who nourishes and strengthens the spiritual life of believers, when they eat him, that is to say, when they apply and receive him by faith, in the Spirit.[274] Christ, that he might represent unto us this spiritual and heavenly bread, hath instituted an earthly and visible bread as a Sacrament of his body, and wine as a Sacrament of his blood,[275] to testify by them unto us,

265 Col. 2:11-12.
266 John 1:29; Lev. 12:6.
267 Col. 2:11.
268 Matt. 26:26; Mark 14:22; Luke 22:19; I Cor. 11:23-25.
269 John 3:6.
270 John 3:5.
271 John 5:23, 25.
272 I John 5:12; John 10:28.
273 John 6:32-33, 51.
274 John 6:63.
275 Mark 6:26.

that, as certainly as we receive and hold this Sacrament in
our hands, and eat and drink the same with our mouths, by
which our life is afterwards nourished, we also do as certainly
receive by faith (which is the hand and mouth of our soul)
the true body and blood of Christ our only Saviour in our
souls, for the support of our spiritual life.[276]

Now, as it is certain and beyond all doubt that Jesus Christ
hath not enjoined to us the use of his Sacraments in vain, so
he works in us all that he represents to us by these holy signs,
though the manner surpasses our understanding, and can not
be comprehended by us, as the operations of the Holy Ghost
are hidden and incomprehensible. In the mean time we err
not when we say that what is eaten and drunk by us is the
proper and natural body and the proper blood of Christ.[277]
But the manner of our partaking of the same is not by the
mouth, but by the Spirit through faith. Thus, then, though
Christ always sits at the right hand of his Father in the heavens,[278] yet doth he not, therefore, cease to make us partakers
of himself by faith. This feast is a spiritual table, at which
Christ communicates himself with all his benefits to us, and
gives us there to enjoy both himself and the merits of his sufferings and death,[279] nourishing, strengthening, and comforting our poor comfortless souls, by the eating of his flesh,
quickening and refreshing them by the drinking of his
blood.[280]

Further, though the Sacraments are connected with the
thing signified, nevertheless both are not received by all men:
the ungodly indeed receives the Sacrament to his condemnation,[281] but he doth not receive the truth of the Sacrament.
As Judas and Simon the sorcerer both, indeed, received the
Sacrament, but not Christ, who was signified by it, of whom
believers only are made partakers. Lastly, we receive this holy
Sacrament in the assembly of the people of God, with humility and reverence,[282] keeping up among us a holy remembrance of the death of Christ our Saviour, with thanksgiving,
making there confession of our faith and of the Christian
religion. Therefore no one ought to come to this table with-

---

[276] I Cor. 10:16-17; Eph. 3:17; John 6:35.
[277] John 6:55-56; I Cor. 10:16.
[278] Acts 3:21; Mark 16:19; Matt. 26:11.
[279] Matt. 26:26, etc.; Luke 22:19-20; I Cor. 10:2-4.
[280] Isa. 55:2; Rom. 8:22-23.
[281] I Cor. 11:29; II Cor. 6:14-15; I Cor. 2:14.
[282] Acts 2:42; 20:7.

out previously rightly examined himself; lest by eating of this bread and drinking of this cup he eat and drink judgment to himself.[283] In a word, we are excited by the use of this holy Sacrament to a fervent love towards God and our neighbor.

Therefore, we reject all mixtures and damnable inventions, which men have added unto and blended with the Sacraments, as profanations of them, and affirm that we ought to rest satisfied with the ordinance which Christ and his Apostles have taught us, and that we must speak of them in the same manner as they have spoken.

Art. XXXVI

Of Magistrates

We believe that our gracious God, because of the depravity of mankind, hath appointed kings, princes, and magistrates,[284] willing that the world should be governed by certain laws and policies; to the end that the dissoluteness of men might be restrained, and all things carried on among them with good order and decency. For this purpose he hath invested the magistracy with the sword, *for the punishment of evil doers, and for the praise of them that do well.* And their office is, not only to have regard unto and watch for the welfare of the civil state, but also that they protect the sacred ministry, and thus may remove and prevent all idolatry and false worship; that the kingdom of antichrist may be thus destroyed, and the kingdom of Christ promoted.[285] They must, therefore, countenance the preaching of the word of the gospel every where, that God may be honored and worshiped by every one, as he commands in his Word.[286]

Moreover, it is the bounden duty of every one, of what state, quality, or condition soever he may be, to subject himself to the magistrates; [287] to pay tribute,[288] to show due honor and respect to them, and to obey them in all things which are not repugnant to the Word of God; [289] to supplicate for them

---

283 I Cor. 11:27-28.
284 Ex. 18:20, etc.; Rom. 13:1; Prov. 8:15; Jer. 21:12; 22:2-3; Ps. 82:1, 6; 101:2, etc.; Deut. 1:15-16; 16:18; 17:15; Dan. 2:21, 37; 5:18.
285 Isa. 49:23, 25; I Kings 15:12; II Kings 23:2-4, etc.
286 [This section, like the corresponding sections in other Reformed Confessions, is framed on the theory of a union of church and state, and is applicable to Free Churches only so far as they may justly claim from the civil government legal protection in all their rights — Ed.]
287 Titus 3:1; Rom. 13:1.
288 Mark 12:17; Matt. 17:24.
289 Acts 4:17-19; 5:29; Hosea 5:11.

in their prayers, that God may rule and guide them in all their ways, and that we may lead a quiet and peaceable life in all godliness and honesty.[290]

Wherefore we detest the error of the Anabaptists and other seditious people, and in general all those who reject the higher powers and magistrates, and would subvert justice,[291] introduce a community of goods, and confound that decency and good order which God hath established among men.[292]

ART. XXXVII

Of the Last Judgment

Finally, we believe, according to the Word of God, when the time appointed by the Lord (which is unknown to all creatures) [293] is come, and the number of the elect complete, that our Lord Jesus Christ will come from heaven, corporally and visibly, as he ascended with great glory and majesty,[294] to declare himself Judge of the quick and the dead,[295] burning this old world with fire and flame to cleanse it.[296] And then all men will personally appear before this great Judge, both men and women and children, that have been from the beginning of the world to the end thereof,[297] being summoned by the voice of the archangel, and by the sound of the trumpet of God.[298] For all the dead shall be raised out of the earth, and their souls joined and united with their proper bodies in which they formerly lived.[299] As for those who shall then be living, they shall not die as the others, but be changed in the twinkling of an eye, and from corruptible become incorruptible.[300]

Then the books (that is to say, the consciences) shall be opened, and the dead judged according to what they shall have done in this world, whether it be good or evil.[301] Nay, all

---

[290] Jer. 29:7; I Tim. 2:1-2.
[291] II Peter 2:10.
[292] Jude 8, 10.
[293] Matt. 24:36; 25:13; I Thess. 5:1-2; Rev. 6:11; Acts 1:7; II Peter 3:10.
[294] Acts 1:11.
[295] II Thess. 1:7-8; Acts 17:31; Matt. 24:30; 25:31; Jude 15; I Peter 4:5; II Tim. 4:1.
[296] II Peter 3:7, 10; II Thess. 1:8.
[297] Rev. 20:12-13; Acts 17:31; Heb. 6:2; 9:27; II Cor. 5:10; Rom. 14:10.
[298] I Cor. 15:42; Rev. 20:12-13; I Thess. 4:16.
[299] John 5:28-29; 6:54; Dan. 12:2; Job 19:26-27.
[300] I Cor. 15:51-53.
[301] Rev. 20:12-13; I Cor. 4:5; Rom. 14:11-12; Job 34:11; John 5:24; Dan. 12:2; Ps. 62:13; Matt. 11:22; 23:33; John 5:29; Rom. 2:5-6; II Cor. 5:10; Heb. 6:2; 9:27.

men shall give an account of every idle word they have spoken, which the world only counts amusement and jest; [302] and then the secrets and hypocrisy of men shall be disclosed and laid open before all.[303]

And, therefore, the consideration of this judgment is justly terrible and dreadful to the wicked and ungodly,[304] but most desirable and comfortable to the righteous and the elect; because then their full deliverance shall be perfected, and there they shall receive the fruits of their labor and trouble which they have borne.[305] Their innocence shall be known to all, and they shall see the terrible vengeance which God shall execute on the wicked,[306] who most cruelly persecuted, oppressed, and tormented them in this world; [307] and who shall be convicted by the testimony of their own consciences,[308] and, being immortal,[309] shall be tormented in that everlasting fire which is prepared for the devil and his angels.[310]

But on the contrary, the faithful and elect shall be crowned with glory and honor; [311] and the Son of God will confess their names before God his Father, and his elect angels; [312] all tears shall be wiped from their eyes; [313] and their cause, which is now condemned by many judges and magistrates as heretical and impious, will then be known to be the cause of the Son of God.[314] And, for a gracious reward, the Lord will cause them to possess such a glory as never entered into the heart of man to conceive.[315]

Therefore we expect that great day with a most ardent desire, to the end that we may fully enjoy the promises of God in Christ Jesus our Lord.[316] Amen.

Even so, come Lord Jesus. Rev. 22:20.[317]

---

302 Rom. 2:5; Jude 15; Matt. 12:36.
303 I Cor. 4:5; Rom. 2:1-2, 16; Matt. 7:1-2.
304 Rev. 6:15-16; Heb. 10:27.
305 Luke 21:28; I John 3:2; 4:17; Rev. 14:7; II Thess. 1:5, 7; Luke 14:14.
306 Dan. 7:26.
307 Matt. 25:46; II Thess. 1:6-8; Mal. 4:3.
308 Rom. 2:15.
309 Rev. 21:8; II Peter 2:9.
310 Mal. 4:1; Matt. 25:41.
311 Matt. 25:34; 13:43.
312 Matt. 10:32.
313 Isa. 25:8; Rev. 21:4.
314 Isa. 66:5.
315 Isa. 64:4; I Cor. 2:9.
316 Heb. 10:36-38.
317 [From the Latin edition, which closes — " *Apocal.* xxii.20: *Etiam veni Domine Jesu.*"]

12

The Second Helvetic Confession, 1566

INTRODUCTION

The Second Helvetic Confession was composed by the Reformer Heinrich Bullinger (1504–1575) in 1561, forty years after he had succeeded Zwingli as head of the Zurich Church. The bulky twenty-five-thousand-word Latin document followed the outlines of the First Helvetic Confession of which Bullinger was a participating author. It is noteworthy that this Confession was not commissioned by any Church and was the work of a single hand, yet it became the most widely received among Reformed Confessions. In 1581 a largely Genevan committee under the influence of Beza used the Second Helvetic Confession to supply the organizing structure of the " Salnar " *Harmonia confessionum*. Since the *Harmonia* was meant to display the consensus among various Reformed Confessions, this choice is a witness to early recognition of its comprehensiveness and structural excellence.

Bullinger, whose steady hand was felt in all Reformation lands through the incredibly large correspondence he carried on with countless Church leaders, might be said to belong personally to three generations of the Reformation. He was converted in Cologne in 1522 where, as a highly gifted and precocious student, he read Luther and the Church fathers, then went on to become an associate of Oecolampadius and Zwingli in his native Switzerland. He was called to be head of the Zurich Church even before Calvin was converted to the evangelical cause. Through his middle years he ranked easily with his friend Calvin as a leader of the maturing Reformation, not only by the eminence of his position in the strong Zurich Church, but through his voluminous Biblical, theological, historical, and ecclesiastical writings. Subsequently he outlived Calvin by eleven years and was looked to as senior leader of the Reformed Churches by such third-generation figures as Beza, Olevianus, and Ursinus. The Second Helvetic Confession is evidence of the degree to which Bullinger embodied the Reformation in his own life and thought.

Some problems about the date of writing the Confession have been resolved by recent research. It will suffice to say here that our document is certainly the *brevis expositio* mentioned by Bullinger in his *Diary* as written in 1561 and discussed with Vermigli before the latter's death in 1562. During the subsequent plague epidemic it was attached to Bullinger's will as his testament to the magistrates of the city. Finally, it was forwarded to Frederick III, elector of the Palatinate, in response to the request of his chancellor for a statement to offset aggressive Lutheran criticism of the Reformed point of view. Immediately thereafter it earned the designation " Helvetic " (from the Latin name for Switzerland) when it was adopted with quite minor emendations by the Swiss cantons, except Basel, and published simultaneously in Latin and Bullinger's own German translation both in Heidelberg and Zurich in March of 1566. The Confession was translated into French (by Beza, 1566), English, Dutch, Italian, Romansh, Hungarian, Polish, Turkish, and Arabic. Official recognition was given by the Reformed Churches of France, Scotland, Hungary, Poland, the Netherlands, and Canton Basel (1642). Swiss pastors were generally bound to the Confession by an ordination oath, but this practice waned under the anticonfessional influence of Enlightenment theology, and the document was formally set aside in all Switzerland by the mid nineteenth century. It remains the official statement in most of the Reformed Churches of Eastern Europe and the Hungarian Reformed Church in America.

A Preface to the Confession by Josias Simmler, Bullinger's son-in-law, stresses the ancient Catholic orthodoxy of its contents, its harmony with the Churches of France, Germany, and England, and the continuing freedom of Churches to express themselves variously in " Formulations of doctrine, in rites, and ceremonies " subject to correction by the teaching of Scripture. Between the Preface and text of the Confession were printed two documents from the ancient Church: a portion from the Code of Justinian and the Creed of Pope Damasus I taken from the writings of Jerome.

The Confession divides roughly into two parts of equal length, theology proper (Chs. I–XVI) and the Church and

Sacraments (Chs. XVII–XXX). The former part begins with Scripture and its interpretation (Chs. I–II), then develops classical theological themes from the doctrine of God through Christology with much reference to the early Church and a marked Reformation emphasis on providence, election, and the problems of man and free will (Chs. III–XI). The Confession pivots, as it were, on the doctrine of Christ (Ch. XI) from which it turns to soteriology. Here is a splendid interweaving of the themes law and gospel, repentance, justification, faith, and good works throughout the entire section (Chs. XII–XVI). Remarkable in the latter half of the Confession is the treatment not only of the Church, minstry, and Sacraments, but such pastoral concerns as catechizing the young, visiting the sick, funerals, church property, marriage, and family life. The concluding chapter on the state (Ch. XXX) favors a measure of state responsibility for religion that is notably out of harmony with the position of contemporary Reformed Churches.

In general, the emphasis of this theological *expositio* upon the actual historical concerns of church life (e.g., preaching in Ch. I, the assurance of election, Ch. X), and the avoidance of speculative doctrines (a theory of Biblical inspiration or divine decree) show this Confession belonging to the mature Reformation, but remaining unmarked by the scholastic confessionalism that was already emerging and was to dominate the following century. In addition, the deep Biblical and church historical grounding of the whole, and the interweaving of patristic and Reformation interests, exhibits incomparably the catholic consciousness both of Bullinger's own theology and that of the Reformed Church generally. It is quite correct to call the Confession " a truly classic presentation of Reformed theology " (Herrenbrück), " the quintessence of the entire development of the Reformed faith " (Hildebrandt), and " on some accounts, . . . the most authoritative symbol of the Reformed Church " (Charles Hodge).

The original manuscripts of the Confession are accessible in the State Archives of Zurich. It should be noted that the marginal rubrics are in the original and are emphatically part of the text, although they have been generally omitted in English translations (e.g., Schaff) following the practice of the *Harmonia,* which substituted its own analytical device. The following is a new English translation by the editor of this collection from the Latin text in Wilhelm Niesel's *Bekenntnisschriften und Kirchenordnungen.*

Literature: Wilhelm Niesel, ed., *Bekenntnisschriften und Kirchenordnungen* (Second Helvetic Confession, tr. by Walter Herrenbrück) (Munich, 1938) ; Walter Hildebrandt and Rudolf Zimmermann, *Das Zweite helvetische Bekenntnis,* and *Bedeutung und Geschichte des zweiten helvetischen Bekenntnisses* (Zurich, 1938) ; P. Schaff, *Creeds of Christendom,* Vols. I, III (n.b., English translation of Second Helvetic Confession in appendix to Vol. III of later editions only) , 6th edition (1931) ; Ernst Koch, *Die Theologie der Confessio Helvetica Posterior* (Leipzig dissertation on microfilm, 1960) ; Paul Jacobs, *Theologie reformierter Bekenntnisschriften in Grundzügen* (Neukirchener Verlag, 1959) .

A Simple Confession and Exposition
of the Orthodox Faith

THE SECOND HELVETIC CONFESSION OF 1566

Chapter I. OF THE HOLY SCRIPTURE BEING THE TRUE
WORD OF GOD

Canonical Scripture. We believe and confess the canonical Scriptures of the holy prophets and apostles of both Testaments to be the true Word of God, and to have sufficient authority of themselves, not of men. For God himself spoke to the fathers, prophets, apostles, and still speaks to us through the Holy Scriptures.

And in this Holy Scripture, the universal Church of Christ has the most complete exposition of all that pertains to a saving faith, and also to the framing of a life acceptable to God; and in this respect it is expressly commanded by God that nothing be either added to or taken from the same.

Scripture Teaches Fully All Godliness. We judge, therefore, that from these Scriptures are to be derived true wisdom and godliness, the reformation and government of churches; as also instruction in all duties of piety; and, to be short, the confirmation of doctrines, and the rejection of all errors, moreover, all exhortations according to that word of the apostle, " All Scripture is inspired by God and profitable for teaching, for reproof," etc. (II Tim. 3:16-17). Again, " I am writing these instructions to you," says the apostle to Timothy, " so that you may know how one ought to behave in the household of God," etc. (I Tim. 3:14-15). *Scripture Is the Word of God.* Again, the selfsame apostle to the Thessalonians: " When," says he, " you received the Word of God which you heard from us, you accepted it, not as the word of men but as what it really is, the Word of God," etc. (I Thess. 2:13.) For the Lord himself has said in the Gospel, " It is not you who speak, but the Spirit of my Father speaking through you "; therefore " he who hears you hears me, and he who rejects me rejects him who sent me " (Matt. 10:20; Luke 10:16; John 13:20).

The Preaching of the Word of God Is the Word of God. Wherefore when this Word of God is now preached in the church by preachers lawfully called, we believe that the very Word of God is proclaimed, and received by the faithful; and that neither any other Word of God is to be invented nor is to be expected from heaven: and that now the Word itself which is preached is to be regarded, not the minister that preaches; for even if he be evil and a sinner, nevertheless the Word of God remains still true and good.

Neither do we think that therefore the outward preaching is to be thought as fruitless because the instruction in true religion depends on the inward illumination of the Spirit, or because it is written " And no longer shall each man teach his neighbor . . . , for they shall all know me " (Jer. 31:34), and " Neither he who plants nor he who waters is anything, but only God who gives the growth " (I Cor. 3:7). For although " no one can come to Christ unless he be drawn by the Father " (John 6:44), and unless the Holy Spirit inwardly illumines him, yet we know that it is surely the will of God that his Word should be preached outwardly also. God could indeed, by his Holy Spirit, or by the ministry of an angel, without the ministry of St. Peter, have taught Cornelius in the Acts; but, nevertheless, he refers him to Peter, of whom the angel speaking says, " He shall tell you what you ought to do."

Inward Illumination Does Not Eliminate External Preaching. For he that illuminates inwardly by giving men the Holy Spirit, the same one, by way of commandment, said unto his disciples, " Go into all the world, and preach the Gospel to the whole creation " (Mark 16:15). And so in Philippi, Paul preached the Word outwardly to Lydia, a seller of purple goods; but the Lord inwardly opened the woman's heart (Acts 16:14). And the same Paul, after a beautiful development of his thought, in Rom. 10:17 at length comes to the conclusion, " So faith comes from hearing, and hearing from the Word of God by the preaching of Christ."

At the same time we recognize that God can illuminate whom and when he will, even without the external ministry, for that is in his power; but we speak of the usual way of instructing men, delivered unto us from God, both by commandment and examples.

Heresies. We therefore detest all the heresies of Artemon, the Manichaeans, the Valentinians, of Cerdon, and the Marcionites, who denied that the Scriptures proceeded from the Holy Spirit; or did not accept some parts of them, or interpolated and corrupted them.

Apocrypha. And yet we do not conceal the fact that certain books of the Old Testament were by the ancient authors called *Apocryphal,* and by others *Ecclesiastical;* inasmuch as some would have them read in the churches, but not advanced as an authority from which the faith is to be established. As Augstine also, in his *De Civitate Dei,* book 18, ch. 38, remarks that " in the books of the Kings, the names and books of certain prophets are cited "; but he adds that " they are not in the canon "; and that " those books which we have suffice unto godliness."

Chapter II. OF INTERPRETING THE HOLY SCRIPTURES; AND OF FATHERS, COUNCILS, AND TRADITIONS

The True Interpretation of Scripture. The apostle Peter has said that the Holy Scriptures are not of private interpretation (II Peter 1:20), and thus we do not allow all possible interpretations. Nor consequently do we acknowledge as the true or genuine interpretation of the Scriptures what is called the conception of the Roman Church, that is, what the defenders of the Roman Church plainly maintain should be thrust upon all for acceptance. But we hold that interpretation of the Scripture to be orthodox and genuine which is gleaned from the Scriptures themselves (from the nature of the language in which they were written, likewise according to the circumstances in which they were set down, and expounded in the light of like and unlike passages and of many and clearer passages) and which agree with the rule of faith and love, and contributes much to the glory of God and man's salvation.

Interpretations of the Holy Fathers. Wherefore we do not despise the interpretations of the holy Greek and Latin fathers, nor reject their disputations and treatises concerning sacred matters as far as they agree with the Scriptures; but we modestly dissent from them when they are found to set down things differing from, or altogether contrary to, the Scriptures. Neither do we think that we do them any wrong in this matter; seeing that they all, with one consent, will not have their writings equated with the canonical Scriptures, but command us to prove how far they agree or disagree with them, and to accept what is in agreement and to reject what is in disagreement.

Councils. And in the same order also we place the decrees and canons of councils.

Wherefore we do not permit ourselves, in controversies about religion or matters of faith, to urge our case with only the opinions of the fathers or decrees of councils; much less by received customs, or by the large number of those who share the same opinion, or by the prescription of a long time. *Who Is the Judge?* Therefore, we do not admit any other judge than God himself, who proclaims by the Holy Scriptures what is true, what is false, what is to be followed, or what to be avoided. So we do assent to the judgments of spiritual men which are drawn from the Word of God. Certainly Jeremiah and other prophets vehemently condemned the assemblies of priests which were set up against the law of God; and diligently admonished us that we should not listen to the fathers, or tread in their path who, walking in their own inventions, swerved from the law of God.

Traditions of Men. Likewise we reject human traditions, even if they be adorned with high-sounding titles, as though they were divine and apostolical, delivered to the Church by the living voice of the apostles, and, as it were, through the hands of apostolical men to succeeding bishops which, when compared with the Scriptures, disagree with them; and by their disagreement show that they are not apostolic at all. For as the apostles did not contradict themselves in doctrine, so the apostolic men did not set forth things contrary to the apostles. On the contrary, it would be wicked to assert that the apostles by a living voice delivered anything contrary to their writings. Paul affirms expressly that he taught the same things in all churches (I Cor. 4:17). And, again, " For we write you nothing but what you can read and understand " (II Cor. 1:13). Also, in another place, he testifies that he and his disciples — that is, apostolic men — walked in the same way, and jointly by the same Spirit did all things (II Cor. 12:18). Moreover, the Jews in former times had the traditions of their elders; but these traditions were severely rejected by the Lord, indicating that the keeping of them hinders God's law, and that God is worshipped in vain by such traditions (Matt. 15:1 ff.; Mark 7:1 ff.) .

Chapter III. OF GOD, HIS UNITY AND TRINITY

God Is One. We believe and teach that God is one in essence or nature, subsisting in himself, all sufficient in himself, invisible, incorporeal, immense, eternal, Creator of all things both visible and invisible, the greatest good, living, quickening and preserving all things, omnipotent and supremely wise, kind and merciful, just and true. Truly we detest many gods because it is expressly written: " The Lord your God is one Lord " (Deut. 6:4). " I am the Lord your God. You shall have no other gods before me " (Ex. 20:2-3). " I am the Lord, and there is no other god besides me. Am I not the Lord, and there is no other God beside me? A righteous God and a Savior; there is none besides me " (Isa. 45:5, 21). " The Lord, the Lord, a God merciful and gracious, slow to anger, and abounding in steadfast love and faithfulness " (Ex. 34:6).

God Is Three. Notwithstanding we believe and teach that the same immense, one and indivisible God is in person inseparably and without confusion distinguished as Father, Son and Holy Spirit so, as the Father has begotten the Son from eternity, the Son is begotten by an ineffable generation, and the Holy Spirit truly proceeds from them both, and the same from eternity and is to be worshipped with both. Thus there are not three gods, but three persons, consubstantial, coeternal, and coequal; distinct with respect to hypostases, and with respect to order, the one preceding the other yet without any inequality. For according to the nature or essence they are so joined together that they are one God, and the divine nature is common to the Father, Son and Holy Spirit.

For Scripture has delivered to us a manifest distinction of persons, the angel saying, among other things, to the Blessed Virgin, " The Holy Spirit will come upon you, and the power of the Most High will overshadow you; therefore the child to be born will be called holy, the Son of God " (Luke 1:35). And also in the baptism of Christ a voice is heard from heaven concerning Christ, saying, " This is my beloved Son " (Matt. 3:17). The Holy Spirit also appeared in the form of a dove. (John 1:32.) And when the Lord himself commanded the apostles to baptize, he commanded them to baptize " in the name of the Father, and the Son, and the Holy Spirit " (Matt. 28:19). Elsewhere in the Gospel he said: " The Father will send the Holy Spirit in my name " (John 14:26), and again he said: " When the Counselor comes, whom I shall

send to you from the Father, even the Spirit of truth, who
proceeds from the Father, he will bear witness to me," etc.
(John 15:26). In short, we receive the Apostles' Creed because it delivers to us the true faith.

Heresies. Therefore we condemn the Jews and Mohammedans, and all those who blaspheme that sacred and adorable
Trinity. We also condemn all heresies and heretics who teach
that the Son and Holy Spirit are God in name only, and also
that there is something created and subservient, or subordinate to another in the Trinity, and that there is something
unequal in it, a greater or a less, something corporeal or corporeally conceived, something different with respect to character or will, something mixed or solitary, as if the Son and
Holy Spirit were the affections and properties of one God the
Father, as the Monarchians, Novatians, Praxeas, Patripassians,
Sabellius, Paul of Samosata, Aëtius, Macedonius, Anthropo-
morphites, Arius, and such like, have thought.

Chapter IV. Of Idols or Images of God, Christ and the Saints

Images of God. Since God as Spirit is in essence invisible
and immense, he cannot really be expressed by any art or
image. For this reason we have no fear pronouncing with
Scripture that images of God are mere lies. Therefore we reject not only the idols of the Gentiles, but also the images of
Christians. *Images of Christ.* Although Christ assumed human nature, yet he did not on that account assume it in order
to provide a model for carvers and painters. He denied that
he had come " to abolish the law and the prophets " (Matt.
5:17). But images are forbidden by the law and the prophets
(Deut. 4:15; Isa. 44:9). He denied that his bodily presence
would be profitable for the Church, and promised that he
would be near us by his Spirit forever (John 16:7). Who,
therefore, would believe that a shadow or likeness of his body
would contribute any benefit to the pious? (II Cor. 5:5).
Since he abides in us by his Spirit, we are therefore the temple of God (I Cor. 3:16). But " what agreement has the temple of God with idols? " (II Cor. 6:16). *Images of Saints.* And
since the blessed spirits and saints in heaven, while they lived
here on earth, rejected all worship of themselves (Acts
3:12 f.; 14:11 ff.; Rev. 14:7; 22:9) and condemned images,
shall anyone find it likely that the heavenly saints and angels
are pleased with their own images before which men kneel,

uncover their heads, and bestow other honors?

But in fact in order to instruct men in religion and to remind them of divine things and of their salvation, the Lord commanded the preaching of the Gospel (Mark 16:15) — not to paint and to teach the laity by means of pictures. Moreover, he instituted sacraments, but nowhere did he set up images. *The Scriptures of the Laity.* Furthermore, wherever we turn our eyes, we see the living and true creatures of God which, if they be observed, as is proper, make a much more vivid impression on the beholders than all the images or vain, motionless, feeble and dead pictures made by men, of which the prophet truly said: " They have eyes, but do not see " (Ps. 115:5).

Lactantius. Therefore we approved the judgment of Lactantius, an ancient writer, who says: " Undoubtedly no religion exists where there is an image." *Epiphanius and Jerome.* We also assert that the blessed bishop Epiphanius did right when, finding on the doors of a church a veil on which was painted a picture supposedly of Christ or some saint, he ripped it down and took it away, because to see a picture of a man hanging in the Church of Christ was contrary to the authority of Scripture. Wherefore he charged that from henceforth no such veils, which were contrary to our religion, should be hung in the Church of Christ, and that rather such questionable things, unworthy of the Church of Christ and the faithful people, should be removed. Moreover, we approve of this opinion of St. Augustine concerning true religion: " Let not the worship of the works of men be a religion for us. For the artists themselves who make such things are better; yet we ought not to worship them " (*De Vera Religione,* cap. 55).

Chapter V. OF THE ADORATION, WORSHIP AND INVOCATION OF GOD THROUGH THE ONLY MEDIATOR JESUS CHRIST

God Alone Is to Be Adored and Worshipped. We teach that the true God alone is to be adored and worshipped. This honor we impart to none other, according to the commandment of the Lord, " You shall worship the Lord your God and him only shall you serve " (Matt. 4:10). Indeed, all the prophets severely inveighed against the people of Israel whenever they adored and worshipped strange gods, and not the only true God. But we teach that God is to be adored and worshipped as he himself has taught us to worship, namely,

" in spirit and in truth " (John 4:23 f.) , not with any super-stition, but with sincerity, according to his Word; lest at any time he should say to us: " Who has required these things from your hands? " (Isa. 1:12; Jer. 6:20) . For Paul also says: " God is not served by human hands, as though he needed anything," etc. (Acts 17:25) .

God Alone Is to Be Invoked Through the Mediation of Christ Alone. In all crises and trials of our life we call upon him alone, and that by the mediation of our only mediator and intercessor, Jesus Christ. For we have been explicitly commanded: " Call upon me in the day of trouble; I will deliver you, and you shall glorify me " (Ps. 1:15) . Moreover, we have a most generous promise from the Lord Who said: " If you ask anything of the Father, he will give it to you " (John 16:23) , and: " Come to me, all who labor and are heavy laden, and I will give you rest " (Matt. 11:28) . And since it is written: " How are men to call upon him in whom they have not believed? " (Rom. 10:14) , and since we do believe in God alone, we assuredly call upon him alone, and we do so through Christ. For as the apostle says, " There is one God and there is one mediator between God and men, the man Christ Jesus " (I Tim. 2:5) , and, " If any one does sin, we have an advocate with the Father, Jesus Christ the righteous," etc. (I John 2:1) .

The Saints Are Not to Be Adored, Worshipped or In-voked. For this reason we do not adore, worship, or pray to the saints in heaven, or to other gods, and we do not acknowl-edge them as our intercessors or mediators before the Father in heaven. For God and Christ the Mediator are sufficient for us; neither do we give to others the honor that is due to God alone and to his Son, because he has expressly said: " My glory I give to no other " (Isa. 42:8) , and because Peter has said: " There is no other name under heaven given among men by which we must be saved," except the name of Christ (Acts 4:12) . In him, those who give their assent by faith do not seek anything outside Christ.

The Due Honor to Be Rendered to the Saints. At the same time we do not despise the saints or think basely of them. For we acknowledge them to be living members of Christ and friends of God who have gloriously overcome the flesh and the world. Hence we love them as brothers, and also honor them; yet not with any kind of worship but by an honorable opinion of them and just praises of them. We also imitate them. For with ardent longings and supplications we earnestly desire to be imitators of their faith and virtues, to share eternal salvation with them, to dwell eternally with them in the presence of God, and to rejoice with them in Christ. And in this respect we approve of the opinion of St. Augustine in *De Vera Religione:* " Let not our religion be the cult of men who have died. For if they have lived holy lives, they are not to be thought of as seeking such honors; on the contrary, they want us to worship him by whose illumination they rejoice that we are fellow-servants of his merits. They are therefore to be honored by way of imitation, but not to be adored in a religious manner," etc.

Relics of the Saints. Much less do we believe that the relics of the saints are to be adored and reverenced. Those ancient saints seemed to have sufficiently honored their dead when they decently committed their remains to the earth after the spirit had ascended on high. And they thought that the most noble relics of their ancestors were their virtues, their doctrine, and their faith. Moreover, as they commend these " relics " when praising the dead, so they strive to copy them during their life on earth.

Swearing by God's Name Alone. These ancient men did not swear except by the name of the only God, Yahweh, as prescribed by the divine law. Therefore, as it is forbidden to swear by the names of strange gods (Ex. 23:13; Deut. 10:20), so we do not perform oaths to the saints that are demanded of us. We therefore reject in all these matters a doctrine that ascribes much too much to the saints in heaven.

Chapter VI. OF THE PROVIDENCE OF GOD

All Things Are Governed by the Providence of God. We believe that all things in heaven and on earth, and in all creatures, are preserved and governed by the providence of this wise, eternal and almighty God. For David testifies and says: " The Lord is high above all nations, and his glory above the heavens! Who is like the Lord our God, who is seated on high, who looks far down upon the heavens and the earth? " (Ps. 113:4 ff.). Again: " Thou searchest out . . . all my ways. Even before a word is on my tongue, lo, O Lord, Thou knowest it altogether " (Ps. 139:3 f.). Paul also testifies and declares: " In him we live and move and have our being " (Acts 17:28), and " from him and through him and to him are all things " (Rom. 11:36). Therefore Augustine most truly and according to Scripture declared in his book *De Agone Christi,* cap. 8, "The Lord said, 'Are not two sparrows sold for a penny? And not one of them will fall to the ground without your Father's will'" (Matt. 10:29). By speaking thus, he wanted to show that what men regard as of least value is governed by God's omnipotence. For he who is the truth says that the birds of the air are fed by him and the lilies of the field are clothed by him; he also says that the hairs of our head are numbered. (Matt. 6:26 ff.)

The Epicureans. We therefore condemn the Epicureans who deny the providence of God, and all those who blasphemously say that God is busy with the heavens and neither sees nor cares about us and our affairs. David, the royal prophet, also condemned this when he said: "O Lord, how long shall the wicked exult? They say, 'The Lord does not see; the God of Jacob does not perceive.' Understand, O dullest of the people! Fools, when will you be wise? He who planted the ear, does he not hear? He who formed the eye, does he not see?" (Ps. 94:3, 7–9).

Means Not to Be Despised. Nevertheless, we do not spurn as useless the means by which divine providence works, but we teach that we are to adapt ourselves to them in so far as they are recommended to us in the Word of God. Wherefore we disapprove of the rash statements of those who say that if all things are managed by the providence of God, then our efforts and endeavors are in vain. It will be sufficient if we leave everything to the governance of divine providence, and we will not have to worry about anything or do anything. For although Paul understood that he sailed under the providence of God who had said to him: "You must bear witness also at Rome" (Acts 23:11), and in addition had given him the promise, "There will be no loss of life among you . . . and not a hair is to perish from the head of any of you" (Acts 27:22, 34), yet when the sailors were nevertheless thinking about abandoning ship the same Paul said to the centurion and the soldiers: "Unless these men stay in the ship, you cannot be saved" (Acts 27:31). For God, who has appointed to everything its end, has ordained the beginning and the means by which it reaches its goal. The heathen ascribe things to blind fortune and uncertain chance. But St. James does not want us to say: "Today or tomorrow we will go into such and such a town and trade," but adds: "Instead you ought to say, 'If the Lord wills, we shall live and we shall do

[handwritten marginal note: There is no such thing as Chance.]

this or that ' " (James 4:13, 15). And Augustine says: " Everything which to vain men seems to happen in nature by accident, occurs only by his Word, because it happens only at his command " (*Enarrationes in Psalmos* 148). Thus it seemed to happen by mere chance when Saul, while seeking his father's asses, unexpectedly fell in with the prophet Samuel. But previously the Lord had said to the prophet: " Tomorrow I will send to you a man from the land of Benjamin " (I Sam. 9:16).

Chapter VII. OF THE CREATION OF ALL THINGS: OF ANGELS, THE DEVIL, AND MAN

God Created All Things. This good and almighty God created all things, both visible and invisible, by his co-eternal Word, and preserves them by his co-eternal Spirit, as David testified when he said: " By the word of the Lord the heavens were made, and all their host by the breath of his mouth " (Ps. 33:6). And, as Scripture says, everything that God had made was very good, and was made for the profit and use of man. Now we assert that all those things proceed from one beginning. *Manichaeans and Marcionites.* Therefore, we condemn the Manichaeans and Marcionites who impiously imagined two substances and natures, one good, the other evil; also two beginnings and two gods contrary to each other, a good and an evil one.

Of Angels and the Devil. Among all creatures, angels and men are most excellent. Concerning angels, Holy Scripture declares: " Who makest the winds thy messengers, fire and flame thy ministers " (Ps. 104:4). Also it says: " Are they not all ministering spirits sent forth to serve, for the sake of those who are to obtain salvation? " (Heb. 1:14). Concerning the devil, the Lord Jesus himself testifies: " He was a murderer from the beginning, and has nothing to do with the truth, because there is no truth in him. When he lies, he speaks according to his own nature, for he is a liar and the father of lies " (John 8:44). Consequently we teach that some angels persisted in obedience and were appointed for faithful service to God and men, but others fell of their own free will and were cast into destruction, becoming enemies of all good and of the faithful, etc.

Of Man. Now concerning man, Scripture says that in the beginning he was made good according to the image and likeness of God; [1] that God placed him in Paradise and made all

---

[1] *Ad imaginem et simulitudinem Dei.*

things subject to him (Gen., ch. 2). This is what David magnificently sets forth in Psalm 8. Moreover, God gave him a wife and blessed them. We also affirm that man consists of two different substances in one person: an immortal soul which, when separated from the body, neither sleeps nor dies, and a mortal body which will nevertheless be raised up from the dead at the last judgment, in order that then the whole man, either in life or in death, abide forever.

The sects. We condemn all who ridicule or by subtle arguments cast doubt upon the immortality of souls, or who say that the soul sleeps or is a part of God. In short, we condemn all opinions of all men, however many, that depart from what has been delivered unto us by the Holy Scriptures in the apostolic Church of Christ concerning creation, angels, and demons, and man.

Chapter VIII. OF MAN'S FALL, SIN AND THE CAUSE OF SIN

The Fall of Man. In the beginning, man was made according to the image of God, in righteousness and true holiness, good and upright. But when at the instigation of the serpent and by his own fault he abandoned goodness and righteousness, he became subject to sin, death and various calamities. And what he became by the fall, that is, subject to sin, death and various calamities, so are all those who have descended from him.

Sin. By sin we understand that innate corruption of man which has been derived or propagated in us all from our first parents, by which we, immersed in perverse desires and averse to all good, are inclined to all evil. Full of all wickedness, distrust, contempt and hatred of God, we are unable to do or even to think anything good of ourselves. Moreover, even as we grow older, so by wicked thoughts, words and deeds committed against God's law, we bring forth corrupt fruit worthy of an evil tree (Matt. 12:33 ff.). For this reason by our own deserts, being subject to the wrath of God, we are liable to just punishment, so that all of us would have been cast away by God if Christ, the Deliverer, had not brought us back.

Death. By death we understand not only bodily death, which all of us must once suffer on account of sins, but also eternal punishment due to our sins and corruption. For the apostle says: " We were dead through trespasses and sins . . . and were by nature children of wrath, like the rest of mankind. But God, who is rich in mercy . . . even when we were dead through our trespasses, made us alive together with Christ " (Eph. 2:1 ff.) . Also: " As sin came into the world through one man and death through sin, and so death spread to all men because all men sinned " (Rom. 5:12) .

Original Sin. We therefore acknowledge that there is original sin in all men. *Actual Sins.* We acknowledge that all other sins which arise from it are called and truly are sins, no matter by what name they may be called, whether mortal, venial or that which is said to be the sin against the Holy Spirit which is never forgiven (Mark 3:29; I John 5:16) . We also confess that sins are not equal; although they arise from the same fountain of corruption and unbelief, some are more serious than others. As the Lord said, it will be more tolerable for Sodom than for the city that rejects the word of the Gospel (Matt. 10:14 f.; 11:20 ff.) .

The Sects. We therefore condemn all who have taught contrary to this, especially Pelagius and all Pelagians, together with the Jovinians who, with the Stoics, regard all sins as equal. In this whole matter we agree with St. Augustine who derived and defended his view from Holy Scriptures. Moreover, we condemn Florinus and Blastus, against whom Irenaeus wrote, and all who make God the author of sin.

God Is Not the Author of Sin, and How Far He Is Said to Harden. It is expressly written: " Thou art not a God who delights in wickedness. Thou hatest all evildoers. Thou destroyest those who speak lies " (Ps. 5:4 ff.) . And again: " When the devil lies, he speaks according to his own nature, for he is a liar and the father of lies " (John 8:44) . Moreover, there is enough sinfulness and corruption in us that it is not necessary for God to infuse into us a new or still greater perversity. When, therefore, it is said in Scripture that God hardens, blinds and delivers up to a reprobate mind, it is to be understood that God does it by a just judgment as a just Judge and Avenger. Finally, as often as God in Scripture is said or seems to do something evil, it is not thereby said that man does not do evil, but that God permits it and does not prevent it, according to his just judgment, who could prevent it if he wished, or because he turns man's evil into good, as he did in the case of the sin of Joseph's brethren, or because he governs sins lest they break out and rage more than is appropriate. St. Augustine writes in his *Enchiridion:* " What happens contrary to his will occurs, in a wonderful and ineffable way, not apart from his will. For it would not happen if he did not allow it. And yet he does not allow it unwillingly but willingly. But he who is good would not permit evil to be done, unless, being omnipotent, he could bring good out of evil." Thus wrote Augustine.

Curious Questions. Other questions, such as whether God willed Adam to fall, or incited him to fall, or why he did not prevent the fall, and similar questions, we reckon among curious questions (unless perchance the wickedness of heretics or of other churlish men compels us also to explain them out of the Word of God, as the godly teachers of the Church have frequently done), knowing that the Lord forbade man to eat of the forbidden fruit and punished his transgression. We also know that what things are done are not evil with respect to the providence, will, and power of God, but in respect of Satan and our will opposing the will of God.

Chapter IX. OF FREE WILL, AND THUS OF HUMAN POWERS

In this matter, which has always produced many conflicts in the Church, we teach that a threefold condition or state of man is to be considered. *What Man Was Before the Fall.* There is the state in which man was in the beginning before the fall, namely, upright and free, so that he could both continue in goodness and decline to evil. However, he declined to evil, and has involved himself and the whole human race in sin and death, as has been said already. *What Man Was After the Fall.* Then we are to consider what man was after the fall. To be sure, his reason was not taken from him, nor was he deprived of will, and he was not entirely changed into a stone or a tree. But they were so altered and weakened that they no longer can do what they could before the fall. For the understanding is darkened, and the will which was free has become an enslaved will. Now it serves sin, not unwillingly but willingly. And indeed, it is called a will, not an unwill (ing) .[2]

Man Does Evil by His Own Free Will. Therefore, in regard to evil or sin, man is not forced by God or by the devil but does evil by his own free will, and in this respect he has a most free will. But when we frequently see that the worst crimes and designs of men are prevented by God from reaching their purpose, this does not take away man's freedom in doing evil, but God by his own power prevents what man freely planned otherwise. Thus Joseph's brothers freely determined to get rid of him, but they were unable to do it because something else seemed good to the counsel of God.

---

[2] *Etenim voluntas, non noluntas dicitur.*

Man Is Not Capable of Good Per Se. In regard to goodness
and virtue man's reason does not judge rightly of itself concerning divine things. For the evangelical and apostolic
Scripture requires regeneration of whoever among us wishes
to be saved. Hence our first birth from Adam contributes
nothing to our salvation. Paul says: "The unspiritual man
does not receive the gifts of the Spirit of God," etc. (I Cor.
2:14). And in another place he denies that we of ourselves
are capable of thinking anything good (II Cor. 3:5). Now
it is known that the mind or intellect is the guide of the will,
and when the guide is blind, it is obvious how far the
will reaches. Wherefore, man not yet regenerate has no free
will for good, no strength to perform what is good. The Lord
says in the Gospel: "Truly, truly, I say to you, everyone who
commits sin is a slave to sin." (John 8:34.) And the apostle
Paul says: "The mind that is set on the flesh is hostile to
God; it does not submit to God's law, indeed it cannot."
(Rom. 8:7.) Yet in regard to earthly things, fallen man is not
entirely lacking in understanding.

Understanding of the Arts. For God in his mercy has permitted the powers of the intellect to remain, though differing greatly from what was in man before the fall. God commands us to cultivate our natural talents, and meanwhile adds
both gifts and success. And it is obvious that we make no
progress in all the arts without God's blessing. In any case,
Scripture refers all the arts to God; and, indeed, the heathen
trace the origin of the arts to the gods who invented them.

*Of What Kind Are the Powers of the Regenerate, and in
What Way Their Wills Are Free.* Finally, we must see whether
the regenerate have free wills, and to what extent. In regeneration the understanding is illumined by the Holy Spirit
in order that it may understand both the mysteries and the
will of God. And the will itself is not only changed by the
Spirit, but it is also equipped with faculties so that it wills
and is able to do the good of its own accord. (Rom. 8:1 ff.)
Unless we grant this, we will deny Christian liberty and introduce a legal bondage. But the prophet has God saying: " I
will put my law within them, and I will write it upon their
hearts " (Jer. 31:33; Ezek. 36:26 f.). The Lord also says in
the Gospel: " If the Son makes you free, you will be free indeed " (John 8:36). Paul also writes to the Philippians: " It
has been granted to you that for the sake of Christ you should
not only believe in him but also suffer for his sake " (Phil.

1:29). Again: " I am sure that he who began a good work in you will bring it to completion at the day of Jesus Christ " (v. 6). Also: " God is at work in you, both to will and to work for his good pleasure " (ch. 2:13).

The Regenerate Work Not Only Passively but Actively. However, in this connection we teach that there are two things to be observed: First, that the regenerate, in choosing and doing good, work not only passively but actively. For they are moved by God that they may do themselves what they do. For Augustine rightly adduces the saying that " God is said to be our helper. But no one can be helped unless he does something." The Manichaeans robbed man of all activity and made him like a stone or a block of wood.

The Free Will Is Weak in the Regenerate. Secondly, in the regenerate a weakness remains. For since sin dwells in us, and in the regenerate the flesh struggles against the Spirit till the end of our lives, they do not easily accomplish in all things what they had planned. These things are confirmed by the apostle in Rom., ch. 7, and Gal., ch. 5. Therefore that free will is weak in us on acount of the remnants of the old Adam and of innate human corruption remaining in us until the end of our lives. Meanwhile, since the powers of the flesh and the remnants of the old man are not so efficacious that they wholly extinguish the work of the Spirit, for that reason the faithful are said to be free, yet so that they acknowledge their infirmity and do not glory at all in their free will. For believers ought always to keep in mind what St. Augustine so many times inculcated according to the apostle: " What have you that you did not receive? If then you received it, why do you boast as if it were not a gift? " To this he adds that what we have planned does not immediately come to pass. For the issue of things lies in the hand of God. This is the reason Paul prayed to the Lord to prosper his journey (Rom. 1:10). And this also is the reason the free will is weak.

In External Things There Is Liberty. Moreover, no one denies that in external things both the regenerate and the unregenerate enjoy free will. For man has in common with other living creatures (to which he is not inferior) this nature to will some things and not to will others. Thus he is able to speak or to keep silent, to go out of his house or to remain at home, etc. However, even here God's power is always to be observed, for it was the cause that Balaam could not go as far as he wanted (Num., ch. 24), and Zacharias upon returning from the temple could not speak as he wanted (Luke, ch. 1).

Heresies. In this matter we condemn the Manichaeans who deny that the beginning of evil was for man [created] good, from his free will. We also condemn the Pelagians who assert that an evil man has sufficient free will to do the good that is commanded. Both are refuted by Holy Scripture which says to the former, " God made man upright " and to the latter, " If the Son makes you free, you will be free indeed " (John 8:36).

Chapter X. Of the Predestination of God and the Election of the Saints

God Has Elected Us Out of Grace. From eternity God has freely, and of his mere grace, without any respect to men, predestinated or elected the saints whom he wills to save in Christ, according to the saying of the apostle, " God chose us in him before the foundation of the world " (Eph. 1:4). And again: " Who saved us and called us with a holy calling, not in virtue of our works but in virtue of his own purpose and the grace which he gave us in Christ Jesus ages ago, and now has manifested through the appearing of our Saviour Christ Jesus " (II Tim. 1:9 f.).

We Are Elected or Predestinated in Christ. Therefore, although not on account of any merit of ours, God has elected us, not directly, but in Christ, and on account of Christ, in order that those who are now ingrafted into Christ by faith might also be elected. But those who were outside Christ were rejected, according to the word of the apostle, " Examine yourselves, to see whether you are holding to your faith. Test yourselves. Do you not realize that Jesus Christ is in you? — unless indeed you fail to meet the test! " (II Cor. 13:5).

We Are Elected for a Definite Purpose. Finally, the saints are chosen in Christ by God for a definite purpose, which the apostle himself explains when he says, " He chose us in him for adoption that we should be holy and blameless before him in love. He destined us for adoption to be his sons through Jesus Christ that they should be to the praise of the glory of his grace " (Eph. 1:4 ff.).

We Are to Have a Good Hope for All. And although God knows who are his, and here and there mention is made of the small number of elect, yet we must hope well of all, and not rashly judge any man to be a reprobate. For Paul says to the Philippians, " I thank my God for you all " (now he speaks of the whole Church in Philippi), " because of your fellowship in the Gospel, being persuaded that he who began a good work in you will bring it to completion at the day of Jesus Christ. It is also right that I have this opinion of you all " (Phil. 1:3 ff.).

Whether Few Are Elect. And when the Lord was asked whether there were few that should be saved, he does not answer and tell them that few or many should be saved or damned, but rather he exhorts every man to " strive to enter by the narrow door " (Luke 13:24) : as if he should say, It is not for you curiously to inquire about these matters, but rather to endeavor that you may enter into heaven by the straight way.

What in This Matter Is to Be Condemned. Therefore we do not approve of the impious speeches of some who say, " Few are chosen, and since I do not know whether I am among the number of the few, I will enjoy myself." Others say, " If I am predestinated and elected by God, nothing can hinder me from salvation, which is already certainly appointed for me, no matter what I do. But if I am in the number of the reprobate, no faith or repentance will help me, since the decree of God cannot be changed. Therefore all doctrines and admonitions are useless." Now the saying of the apostle contradicts these men: " The Lord's servant must be ready to teach, instructing those who oppose him, so that if God should grant that they repent to know the truth, they may recover from the snare of the devil, after being held captive by him to do his will " (II Tim. 2:23 ff.).

Admonitions Are Not in Vain Because Salvation Proceeds from Election. Augustine also shows that both the grace of free election and predestination, and also salutary admonitions and doctrines, are to be preached (*Lib. de Dono Perseverantiae,* cap. 14 ff.).

Whether We Are Elected. We therefore find fault with those who outside of Christ ask whether they are elected.[3] And what has God decreed concerning them before all eternity? For the preaching of the Gospel is to be heard, and it is to be believed; and it is to be held as beyond doubt that if you believe and are in Christ, you are elected. For the Father has revealed unto us in Christ the eternal purpose of his

[3] The edition of 1568 reads: " whether they are elected from eternity? "

predestination, as I have just now shown from the apostle in II Tim. 1:9-10. This is therefore above all to be taught and considered, what great love of the Father toward us is revealed to us in Christ. We must hear what the Lord himself daily preaches to us in the Gospel, how he calls and says: " Come to me all who labor and are heavy-laden, and I will give you rest " (Matt. 11:28). " God so loved the world, that he gave his only Son, that whoever believes in him should not perish, but have eternal life." (John 3:16.) Also, " It is not the will of my Father that one of these little ones should perish." (Matt. 18:14.)

Let Christ, therefore be the looking glass, in whom we may contemplate our predestination. We shall have a sufficiently clear and sure testimony that we are inscribed in the Book of Life if we have fellowship with Christ, and he is ours and we are his in true faith.

Temptation in Regard to Predestination. In the temptation in regard to predestination, than which there is scarcely any other more dangerous, we are confronted by the fact that God's promises apply to all the faithful, for he says: " Ask, and everyone who seeks, shall receive " (Luke 11:9 f.). This finally we pray, with the whole Church of God, " Our Father who art in heaven " (Matt. 6:9), both because by baptism we are ingrafted into the body of Christ, and we are often fed in his Church with his flesh and blood unto life eternal. Thereby, being strengthened, we are commanded to work out our salvation with fear and trembling, according to the precept of Paul.

Chapter XI. OF JESUS CHRIST, TRUE GOD AND MAN, THE ONLY SAVIOR OF THE WORLD

Christ Is True God. We further believe and teach that the Son of God, our Lord Jesus Christ, was predestinated or fore-ordained from eternity by the Father to be the Savior of the world. And we believe that he was born, not only when he assumed flesh of the Virgin Mary, and not only before the foundation of the world was laid, but by the Father before all eternity in an inexpressible manner. For Isaiah said: " Who can tell his generation? " (Ch. 53:8.) And Micah says: " His origin is from of old, from ancient days " (Micah 5:2.) And John said in the Gospel: " In the beginning was the Word, and the Word was with God, and the Word was God," etc. (Ch. 1:1.) Therefore, with respect to his divinity the

Son is coequal and consubstantial with the Father; true God (Phil. 2:11), not only in name or by adoption or by any merit, but in substance and nature, as the apostle John has often said: " This is the true God and eternal life " (I John 5:20). Paul also says: " He appointed the Son the heir of all things, through whom also he created the world. He reflects the glory of God and bears the very stamp of his nature, upholding all things by his word of power " (Heb. 1:2 f.). For in the Gospel the Lord himself said: " Father, glorify Thou me in Thy own presence with the glory which I had with Thee before the world was made " (John 17:5). And in another place in the Gospel it is written: " The Jews sought all the more to kill him because he . . . called God his Father, making himself equal with God " (John 5:18).

The Sects. We therefore abhor the impious doctrine of Arius and the Arians against the Son of God, and especially the blasphemies of the Spaniard, Michael Servetus, and all his followers, which Satan through them has, as it were, dragged up out of hell and has most audaciously and impiously spread abroad in the world.

Christ Is True Man, Having Real Flesh. We also believe and teach that the eternal Son of the eternal God was made the Son of man, from the seed of Abraham and David, not from the coitus of a man, as the Ebionites said, but was most chastely conceived by the Holy Spirit and born of the ever virgin Mary, as the evangelical history carefully explains to us (Matt., ch. 1). And Paul says: " He took not on him the nature of angels, but of the seed of Abraham." Also the apostle John says that whoever does not believe that Jesus Christ has come in the flesh, is not of God. Therefore, the flesh of Christ was neither imaginary nor brought from heaven, as Valentinus and Marcion wrongly imagined.

A Rational Soul in Christ. Moreover, our Lord Jesus Christ did not have a soul bereft of sense and reason, as Apollinaris thought, nor flesh without a soul, as Eunomius taught, but a soul with its reason, and flesh with its senses, by which in the time of his passion he sustained real bodily pain, as he himself testified when he said: " My soul is very sorrowful, even to death " (Matt. 26:38). And, " Now is my soul troubled " (John 12:27).

Two Natures in Christ. We therefore acknowledge two natures or substances, the divine and the human, in one and the same Jesus Christ our Lord (Heb., ch. 2). And we say that these are bound and united with one another in such a way that they are not absorbed, or confused, or mixed, but are united or joined together in one person — the properties of the natures being unimpaired and permanent.

Not Two but One Christ. Thus we worship not two but one Christ the Lord. We repeat: one true God and man. With respect to his divine nature he is consubstantial with the Father, and with respect to the human nature he is consubstantial with us men, and like us in all things, sin excepted (Heb. 4:15).

The Sects. And indeed we detest the dogma of the Nestorians who make two of the one Christ and dissolve the unity of the Person. Likewise we thoroughly execrate the madness of Eutyches and of the Monothelites or Monophysites who destroy the property of the human nature.

The Divine Nature of Christ Is Not Passible, and the Human Nature Is Not Everywhere. Therefore, we do not in any way teach that the divine nature in Christ has suffered or that Christ according to his human nature is still in this world and thus is everywhere. For neither do we think or teach that the body of Christ ceased to be a true body after his glorification, or was deified, and deified in such a way that it laid aside its properties as regards body and soul, and changed entirely into a divine nature and began to be merely one substance.

The Sects. Hence we by no means approve of or accept the strained, confused and obscure subtleties of Schwenkfeldt and of similar sophists with their self-contradictory arguments; neither are we Schwenkfeldians.

Our Lord Truly Suffered. We believe, moreover, that our Lord Jesus Christ truly suffered and died for us in the flesh, as Peter says (I Peter 4:1). We abhor the most impious madness of the Jacobites and all the Turks who execrate the suffering of the Lord. At the same time we do not deny that the Lord of glory was crucified for us, according to Paul's words (I Cor. 2:8).

Impartation of Properties. We piously and reverently accept and use the impartation of properties which is derived from Scripture and which has been used by all antiquity in explaining and reconciling apparently contradictory passages.

Christ Is Truly Risen from the Dead. We believe and teach that the same Jesus Christ our Lord, in his true flesh in which he was crucified and died, rose again from the dead, and that not another flesh was raised other than the one buried, or that a spirit was taken up instead of the flesh, but that he retained his true body. Therefore, while his disciples thought they saw the spirit of the Lord, he showed them his hands and feet which were marked by the prints of the nails and wounds, and added: " See my hands and my feet, that it is I myself; handle me, and see, for a spirit has not flesh and bones as you see that I have " (Luke 24:39) .

Christ Is Truly Ascended Into Heaven. We believe that our Lord Jesus Christ, in his same flesh, ascended above all visible heavens into the highest heaven, that is, the dwelling-place of God and the blessed ones, at the right hand of God the Father. Although it signifies an equal participation in glory and majesty, it is also taken to be a certain place about which the Lord, speaking in the Gospel, says: " I go to prepare a place for you " (John 14:2) . The apostle Peter also says: " Heaven must receive Christ until the time of restoring all things " (Acts 3:21). And from heaven the same Christ will return in judgment, when wickedness will then be at its greatest in the world and when the Antichrist, having corrupted true religion, will fill up all things with superstition and impiety and will cruelly lay waste the Church with bloodshed and flames (Dan., ch. 11) . But Christ will come again to claim his own, and by his coming to destroy the Antichrist, and to judge the living and the dead (Acts 17:31) . For the dead will rise again (I Thess. 4:14 ff.) , and those who on that day (which is unknown to all creatures [Mark 13:32]) will be alive will be changed " in the twinkling of an eye," and all the faithful will be caught up to meet Christ in the air, so that then they may enter with him into the blessed dwelling-places to live forever (I Cor. 15:51 f.) . But the unbelievers and ungodly will descend with the devils into hell to burn forever and never to be redeemed from torments (Matt. 25:46) .

The Sects. We therefore condemn all who deny a real resurrection of the flesh (II Tim. 2:18) , or who with John of Jerusalem, against whom Jerome wrote, do not have a correct view of the glorification of bodies. We also condemn those who thought that the devil and all the ungodly would at some time be saved, and that there would be an end to punishments. For the Lord has plainly declared: " Their fire is not quenched, and their worm does not die " (Mark 9:44) . We further condemn Jewish dreams that there will be a golden age on earth before the Day of Judgment, and that the pious, having subdued all their godless enemies, will possess all the kingdoms of the earth. For evangelical truth in Matt., chs. 24 and 25, and Luke, ch. 18, and apostolic teaching in II Thess., ch. 2, and II Tim., chs. 3 and 4, present something quite different.

The Fruit of Christ's Death and Ressurrection. Further by his passion and death and everything which he did and endured for our sake by his coming in the flesh, our Lord reconciled all the faithful to the heavenly Father, made expiation for sins, disarmed death, overcame damnation and hell, and by his resurrection from the dead brought again and restored life and immortality. For he is our righteousness, life and resurrection, in a word, the fulness and perfection of all the faithful, salvation and all sufficiency. For the apostle says: " In him all the fulness of God was pleased to dwell," and, " You have come to fulness of life in him." (Col., chs. 1 and 2.)

Jesus Christ Is the Only Savior of the World, and the True Awaited Messiah. For we teach and believe that this Jesus Christ our Lord is the unique and eternal Savior of the human race, and thus of the whole world, in whom by faith are saved all who before the law, under the law, and under the Gospel were saved, and however many will be saved at the end of the world. For the Lord himself says in the Gospel: " He who does not enter the sheepfold by the door but climbs in by another way, that man is a thief and a robber. . . . I am the door of the sheep " (John 10:1 and 7). And also in another place in the same Gospel he says: " Abraham saw my day and was glad " (ch. 8:56). The apostle Peter also says: " There is salvation in no one else, for there is no other name under heaven given among men by which we must be saved." We therefore believe that we will be saved through the grace of our Lord Jesus Christ, as our fathers were. (Acts 4:12; 10:43; 15:11.) For Paul also says: " All our fathers ate the same spiritual food, and all drank the same spiritual drink. For they drank from the spiritual Rock which followed them, and the Rock was Christ " (I Cor. 10:3 f.). And thus we read that John says: " Christ was the Lamb which was slain from the foundation of the world " (Rev. 13:8), and John the Baptist testified that Christ is that " Lamb of God, who takes away the sin of the world " (John 1:29). Wherefore, we quite openly profess and preach that Jesus Christ is the sole Redeemer and Savior of the world, the King and High Priest, the true and awaited Messiah, that holy and blessed one whom all the types of the law and predictions of the prophets prefigured and promised; and that God appointed him beforehand and sent him to us, so that we are not now to look for any other. Now there only remains for all of us to give all glory to Christ, believe in him, rest in him alone, despising and rejecting all other aids in life. For however many seek salvation in any other than in Christ alone, have fallen from the grace of God and have rendered Christ null and void for themselves (Gal. 5:4).

The Creeds of Four Councils Received. And, to say many things with a few words, with a sincere heart we believe, and freely confess with open mouth, whatever things are defined from the Holy Scriptures concerning the mystery of the incarnation of our Lord Jesus Christ, and are summed up in the Creeds and decrees of the first four most excellent synods convened at Nicaea, Constantinople, Ephesus and Chalcedon — together with the Creed of blessed Athanasius,[4] and all similar symbols; and we condemn everything contrary to these.

The Sects. And in this way we retain the Christian, orthodox and catholic faith whole and unimpaired; knowing that nothing is contained in the aforesaid symbols which is not agreeable to the Word of God, and does not altogether make for a sincere exposition of the faith.

Chapter XII. OF THE LAW OF GOD

The Will of God Is Explained for Us in the Law of God. We teach that the will of God is explained for us in the law of God, what he wills or does not will us to do, what is good and just, or what is evil and unjust. Therefore, we confess that the law is good and holy.

The Law of Nature. And this law was at one time written in the hearts of men by the finger of God (Rom. 2:15), and is called the law of nature (*the law of Moses is in two Tables*), and at another it was inscribed by his finger on the two Tables of Moses, and eloquently expounded in the books of Moses (Ex. 20:1 ff.; Deut. 5:6 ff.). For the sake of clarity we distinguish the moral law which is contained in the Decalogue or two Tables and expounded in the books of Moses,

---

4 The so-called Athanasian Creed was not written by Athanasius but dates from the ninth century. It is also called the " Quicunque " from the opening word of the Latin text.

the ceremonial law which determines the ceremonies and worship of God, and the judicial law which is concerned with political and domestic matters.

The Law Is Complete and Perfect. We believe that the whole will of God and all necessary precepts for every sphere of life are taught in this law. For otherwise the Lord would not have forbidden us to add or to take away anything from this law; neither would he have commanded us to walk in a straight path before this law, and not to turn aside from it by turning to the right or to the left (Deut. 4:2; 12:32).

Why the Law Was Given. We teach that this law was not given to men that they might be justified by keeping it, but that rather from what it teaches we may know (our) weakness, sin and condemnation, and, despairing of our strength, might be converted to Christ in faith. For the apostle openly declares: " The law brings wrath," and, " Through the law comes knowledge of sin " (Rom. 4:15; 3:20), and, " If a law had been given which could justify or make alive, then righteousness would indeed be by the law. But the Scripture (that is, the law) has concluded all under sin, that the promise which was of the faith of Jesus might be given to those who believe. . . . Therefore, the law was our schoolmaster unto Christ, that we might be justified by faith " (Gal. 3:21 ff.).

The Flesh Does Not Fulfil the Law. For no flesh could or can satisfy the law of God and fulfil it, because of the weakness in our flesh which adheres and remains in us until our last breath. For the apostle says again: " God has done what the law, weakened by the flesh, could not do: sending his own Son in the likeness of sinful flesh and for sin " (Rom. 8:3). Therefore, Christ is the perfecting of the law and our fulfilment of it (Rom. 10:4), who, in order to take away the curse of the law, was made a curse for us (Gal. 3:13). Thus he imparts to us through faith his fulfilment of the law, and his righteousness and obedience are imputed to us.

How Far the Law Is Abrogated. The law of God is therefore abrogated to the extent that it no longer condemns us, nor works wrath in us. For we are under grace and not under the law. Moreover, Christ has fulfilled all the figures of the law. Hence, with the coming of the body, the shadows ceased, so that in Christ we now have the truth and all fulness. But yet we do not on that account contemptuously reject the law. For we remember the words of the Lord when he said: " I have not come to abolish the law and the prophets but to fulfil them " (Matt. 5:17). We know that in the law is delivered to us the patterns of virtues and vices. We know that the written law when explained by the Gospel is useful to the Church, and that therefore its reading is not to be banished from the Church. For although Moses' face was covered with a veil, yet the apostle says that the veil has been taken away and abolished by Christ. *The Sects.* We condemn everything that heretics old and new have taught against the law.

Chapter XIII. OF THE GOSPEL OF JESUS CHRIST, OF THE PROMISES, AND OF THE SPIRIT AND LETTER

The Ancients Had Evangelical Promises. The Gospel is, indeed, opposed to the law. For the law works wrath and announces a curse, whereas the Gospel preaches grace and blessing. John says: " For the law was given through Moses; grace and truth came through Jesus Christ." (John 1:17.) Yet notwithstanding it is most certain that those who were before the law and under the law, were not altogether destitute of the Gospel. For they had extraordinary evangelical promises such as these are: " The seed of the woman shall bruise the serpent's head " (Gen. 3:15). " In thy seed shall all the nations of the earth be blessed " (Gen. 22:18). " The scepter shall not depart from Judah . . . until he comes " (Gen. 49:10). " The Lord will raise up a prophet from among his own brethren " (Deut. 18:15; Acts. 3:22), etc.

The Promises Twofold. And we acknowledge that two kinds of promises were revealed to the fathers, as also to us. For some were of present or earthly things, such as the promises of the Land of Canaan and of victories, and as the promise today still of daily bread. Others were then and are still now of heavenly and eternal things, namely, divine grace, remission of sins, and eternal life through faith in Jesus Christ.

The Fathers Also Had Not Only Carnal but Spiritual Promises. Moreover, the ancients had not only external and earthly but also spiritual and heavenly promises in Christ. Peter says: " The prophets who prophesied of the grace that was to be yours searched and inquired about this salvation." (I Peter 1:10.) Wherefore the apostle Paul also said: " The Gospel of God was promised beforehand through his prophets in the holy scriptures " (Rom. 1:2). Thereby it is clear that the ancients were not entirely destitute of the whole Gospel.

What Is the Gospel Properly Speaking? And although our fathers had the Gospel in this way in the writings of the prophets by which they attained salvation in Christ through faith, yet the Gospel is properly called glad and joyous news, in which, first by John the Baptist, then by Christ the Lord himself, and afterwards by the apostles and their successors, is preached to us in the world that God has now performed what he promised from the beginning of the world, and has sent, nay more, has given us his only Son and in him reconciliation with the Father, the remission of sins, all fulness and everlasting life. Therefore, the history delineated by the four Evangelists and explaining how these things were done or fulfilled by Christ, what things Christ taught and did, and that those who believe in him have all fulness, is rightly called the Gospel. The preaching and writings of the apostles, in which the apostles explain for us how the Son was given to us by the Father, and in him everything that has to do with life and salvation, is also rightly called evangelical doctrine, so that not even today, if sincerely preached, does it lose its illustrious title.

Of the Spirit and the Letter. That same preaching of the Gospel is also called by the apostle " the spirit " and " the ministry of the spirit " because by faith it becomes effectual and living in the ears, nay more, in the hearts of believers through the illumination of the Holy Spirit (II Cor. 3:6). For the letter, which is opposed to the Spirit, signifies everything external, but especially the doctrine of the law which, without the Spirit and faith, works wrath and provokes sin in the minds of those who do not have a living faith. For this reason the apostle calls it " the ministry of death." In this connection the saying of the apostle is pertinent: " The letter kills, but the Spirit gives life." And false apostles preached a corrupted Gospel, having combined it with the law, as if Christ could not save without the law.

The Sects. Such were the Ebionites said to be, who were descended from Ebion the heretic, and the Nazarites who were formerly called Mineans. All these we condemn, while preaching the pure Gospel and teaching that believers are justified by the Spirit [5] alone, and not by the law. A more detailed exposition of this matter will follow presently under the heading of justification.

The Teaching of the Gospel Is Not New, but Most Ancient Doctrine. And although the teaching of the Gospel, compared with the teaching of the Pharisees concerning the law, seemed

---

[5] The original manuscript has " Christ " instead of " Spirit."

to be a new doctrine when first preached by Christ (which Jeremiah also prophesied concerning the New Testament), yet actually it not only was and still is an old doctrine (even if today it is called new by the Papists when compared with the teaching now received among them), but is the most ancient of all in the world. For God predestinated from eternity to save the world through Christ, and he has disclosed to the world through the Gospel this his predestination and eternal counsel (II Tim. 2:9 f.). Hence it is evident that the religion and teaching of the Gospel among all who ever were, are and will be, is the most ancient of all. Wherefore we assert that all who say that the religion and teaching of the Gospel is a faith which has recently arisen, being scarcely thirty years old, err disgracefully and speak shamefully of the eternal counsel of God. To them applies the saying of Isaiah the prophet: " Woe to those who call evil good and good evil, who put darkness for light and light for darkness, who put bitter for sweet and sweet for bitter! " (Isa. 5:20).

Ch. XIV. OF REPENTANCE AND THE CONVERSION OF MAN

The doctrine of repentance is joined with the Gospel. For so has the Lord said in the Gospel: " Repentance and forgiveness of sins should be preached in my name to all nations " (Luke 24:47). *What Is Repentance?* By repentance we understand (1) the recovery of a right mind in sinful man awakened by the Word of the Gospel and the Holy Spirit, and received by true faith, by which the sinner immediately acknowledges his innate corruption and all his sins accused by the Word of God; and (2) grieves for them from his heart, and not only bewails and frankly confesses them before God with a feeling of shame, but also (3) with indignation abominates them; and (4) now zealously considers the amendment of his ways and constantly strives for innocence and virtue in which conscientiously to exercise himself all the rest of his life.

True Repentance Is Conversion to God. And this is true repentance, namely, a sincere turning to God and all good, and earnest turning away from the devil and all evil. *1. Repentance is a gift of God.* Now we expressly say that this repentance is a sheer gift of God and not a work of our strength. For the apostle commands a faithful minister diligently to instruct those who oppose the truth, if " God may perhaps grant that they will repent and come to know the truth " (II

Tim. 2:25) . *2. Laments sins committed.* Now that sinful
woman who washed the feet of the Lord with her tears, and
Peter who wept bitterly and bewailed his denial of the Lord
(Luke 7:38; 22:62) show clearly how the mind of a penitent
man ought to be seriously lamenting the sins he has committed. *3. Confesses sins to God.* Moreover, the prodigal son
and the publican in the Gospel, when compared with the
Pharisee, present us with the most suitable pattern of how our
sins are to be confessed to God. The former said: " ' Father,
I have sinned against heaven and before you; I am no longer
worthy to be called your son; treat me as one of your hired
servants.' " (Luke 15:8 ff.) And the latter, not daring to
raise his eyes to heaven, beat his breast, saying, " God be
merciful to me a sinner " (ch. 18:13) . And we do not doubt
that they were accepted by God into grace. For the apostle
John says: " If we confess our sins, he is faithful and just, and
will forgive our sins and cleanse us from all unrighteousness.
If we say we have not sinned, we make him a liar, and his
word is not in us " (I John 1:9 f.) .

Sacerdotal Confession and Absolution. But we believe that
this sincere confession which is made to God alone, either privately between God and the sinner, or publicly in the Church
where the general confession of sins is said, is sufficient, and
that in order to obtain forgiveness of sins it is not necessary
for anyone to confess his sins to a priest, murmuring them in
his ears, that in turn he might receive absolution from the
priest with his laying on of hands, because there is neither a
commandment nor an example of this in Holy Scriptures.
David testifies and says: " I acknowledged my sin to thee, and
did not hide my iniquity; I said, ' I will confess my transgressions to the Lord '; then thou didst forgive the guilt of my
sin " (Ps. 32:5) . And the Lord who taught us to pray and at
the same time to confess our sins said: " Pray then like this:
Our Father, who art in heaven, . . . forgive us our debts, as
we also forgive our debtors " (Matt. 6:12) . Therefore it is
necessary that we confess our sins to God our Father, and be
reconciled with our neighbor if we have offended him. Concerning this kind of confession, the Apostle James says: " Confess your sins to one another " (James 5:16) . If, however,
anyone is overwhelmed by the burden of his sins and by perplexing temptations, and will seek counsel, instruction and
comfort privately, either from a minister of the Church, or
from any other brother who is instructed in God's law, we

do not disapprove; just as we also fully approve of that general and public confession of sins which is usually said in Church and in meetings for worship, as we noted above, inasmuch as it is agreeable to Scripture.

Of the Keys of the Kingdom of Heaven. Concerning the keys of the Kingdom of Heaven which the Lord gave to the apostles, many babble many astonishing things, and out of them forge swords, spears, scepters and crowns, and complete power over the greatest kingdoms, indeed, over souls and bodies. Judging simply according to the Word of the Lord, we say that all properly called ministers possess and exercise the keys or the use of them when they proclaim the Gospel; that is, when they teach, exhort, comfort, rebuke, and keep in discipline the people committed to their trust.

Keys of the Kingdom

Opening and Shutting (the Kingdom). For in this way they open the Kingdom of Heaven to the obedient and shut it to the disobedient. The Lord promised these keys to the apostles in Matt., ch. 16, and gave them in John, ch. 20, Mark, ch. 16, and Luke, ch. 24, when he sent out his disciples and commanded them to preach the Gospel in all the world, and to remit sins.

The Ministry of Reconciliation. In the letter to the Corinthians the apostle says that the Lord gave the ministry of reconciliation to his ministers (II Cor. 5:18 ff.). And what this is he then explains, saying that it is the preaching or teaching of reconciliation. And explaining his words still more clearly he adds that Christ's ministers discharge the office of an ambassador in Christ's name, as if God himself through ministers exhorted the people to be reconciled to God, doubtless by faithful obedience. Therefore, they exercise the keys when they persuade [men] to believe and repent. Thus they reconcile men to God.

Ministers Remit Sins. Thus they remit sins. Thus they open the Kingdom of Heaven, and bring believers into it: very different from those of whom the Lord said in the Gospel, " Woe to you lawyers! for you have taken away the key of knowledge; you did not enter yourselves, and you hindered those who were entering."

How Ministers Absolve. Ministers, therefore, rightly and effectually absolve when they preach the Gospel of Christ and thereby the remission of sins, which is promised to each one who believes, just as each one is baptized, and when they testify that it pertains to each one peculiarly. Neither do we think that this absolution becomes more effectual by being murmured in the ear of someone or by being murmured singly over someone's head. We are nevertheless of the opinion that the remission of sins in the blood of Christ is to be diligently proclaimed, and that each one is to be admonished that the forgiveness of sins pertains to him.

Diligence in the Renewal of Life. But the examples in the Gospel teach us how vigilant and diligent the penitent ought to be in striving for newness of life and in mortifying the old man and quickening the new. For the Lord said to the man he healed of palsy: " See, you are well! Sin no more, that nothing worse befall you " (John 5:14). Likewise to the adulteress whom he set free he said: " Go, and sin no more " (ch. 8:11). To be sure, by these words he did not mean that any man, as long as he lived in the flesh, could not sin; he simply recommends diligence and a careful devotion, so that we should strive by all means, and beseech God in prayers lest we fall back into sins from which, as it were, we have been resurrected, and lest we be overcome by the flesh, the world and the devil. Zacchaeus the publican, whom the Lord had received back into favor, exclaims in the Gospel: " Behold, Lord, the half of my goods I give to the poor; and if I have defrauded any one of anything, I restore it fourfold " (Luke 19:8). Therefore, in the same way we preach that restitution and compassion, and even almsgiving, are necessary for those who truly repent, and we exhort all men everywhere in the words of the apostle: " Let not sin therefore reign in your mortal bodies, to make you obey their passions. Do not yield your members to sin as instruments of wickedness, but yield yourselves to God as men who have been brought from death to life, and your members to God as instruments of righteousness " (Rom. 6:12 f.).

Errors. Wherefore we condemn all impious utterances of some who wrongly use the preaching of the Gospel and say that it is easy to return to God. Christ has atoned for all sins. Forgiveness of sins is easy. Therefore, what harm is there in sinning? Nor need we be greatly concerned about repentance, etc. Notwithstanding we always teach that an access to God is open to all sinners, and that he forgives all sinners of all sins except the one sin against the Holy Spirit (Mark 3:29).

The Sects. Wherefore we condemn both old and new Novatians and Catharists.

Papal Indulgences. We especially condemn the lucrative

doctrine of the Pope concerning penance, and against his simony and his simoniacal indulgences we avail ourselves of Peter's judgment concerning Simon: " Your silver perish with you, because you thought you could obtain the gift of God with money! You have neither part nor lot in this matter, for your heart is not right before God " (Acts 8:20 f.).

Satisfactions. We also disapprove of those who think that by their own satisfactions they make amends for sins committed. For we teach that Christ alone by his death or passion is the satisfaction, propitiation or expiation of all sins (Isa., ch. 53; I Cor. 1:30). Yet as we have already said, we do not cease to urge the mortification of the flesh. We add, however, that this mortification is not to be proudly obtruded upon God as a satisfaction for sins, but is to be performed humbly, in keeping with the nature of the children of God, as a new obedience out of gratitude for the deliverance and full satisfaction obtained by the death and satisfaction of the Son of God.

Chapter XV. OF THE TRUE JUSTIFICATION OF THE FAITHFUL

What Is Justification? According to the apostle in his treatment of justification, to justify means to remit sins, to absolve from guilt and punishment, to receive into favor, and to pronounce a man just. For in his epistle to the Romans the apostle says: " It is God who justifies; who is to condemn? " (Rom. 8:33). To justify and to condemn are opposed. And in The Acts of the Apostles the apostle states: " Through Christ forgiveness of sins is proclaimed to you, and by him everyone that believes is freed from everything from which you could not be freed by the law of Moses " (Acts 13:38 f.). For in the Law and also in the Prophets we read: " If there is a dispute between men, and they come into court . . . the judges decide between them, acquitting the innocent and condemning the guilty " (Deut. 25:1). And in Isa., ch. 5: " Woe to those . . . who acquit the guilty for a bribe."

We Are Justified on Account of Christ. Now it is most certain that all of us are by nature sinners and godless, and before God's judgment-seat are convicted of godlessness and are guilty of death, but that, solely by the grace of Christ and not from any merit of ours or consideration for us, we are justified, that is, absolved from sin and death by God the Judge. For what is clearer than what Paul said: " Since all have sinned and fall short of the glory of God, they are justified by

his grace as a gift, through the redemption which is in Christ
Jesus " (Rom. 3:23 f.) .

Imputed Righteousness. For Christ took upon himself and
bore the sins of the world, and satisfied divine justice. Therefore, solely on account of Christ's sufferings and resurrection
God is propitious with respect to our sins and does not impute them to us, but imputes Christ's righteousness to us as
our own (II Cor. 5:19 ff.; Rom. 4:25), so that now we are
not only cleansed and purged from sins or are holy, but also,
granted the righteousness of Christ, and so absolved from sin,
death and condemnation, are at last righteous and heirs of
eternal life. Properly speaking, therefore, God alone justifies
us, and justifies only on account of Christ, not imputing sins
to us but imputing his righteousness to us.

We Are Justified by Faith Alone. But because we receive
this justification, not through any works, but through faith
in the mercy of God and in Christ, we therefore teach and
believe with the apostle that sinful man is justified by faith
alone in Christ, not by the law or any works. For the apostle
says: " We hold that a man is justified by faith apart from
works of law " (Rom. 3:28). Also: " If Abraham was justified
by works, he has something to boast about, but not before
God. For what does the scripture say? Abraham believed God,
and it was reckoned to him as righteousness. . . . And to one
who does not work but believes in him who justifies the ungodly, his faith is reckoned as righteousness " (Rom. 4:2 ff.;
Gen. 15:6). And again: " By grace you have been saved
through faith; and this is not your own doing, it is the gift of
God — not because of works, lest any man should boast,"
etc. (Eph. 2:8 f.). Therefore, because faith receives Christ
our righteousness and attributes everything to the grace of
God in Christ, on that account justification is attributed to
faith, chiefly because of Christ and not therefore because it is
our work. For it is the gift of God.

We Receive Christ by Faith. Moreover, the Lord abundantly shows that we receive Christ by faith in John, ch. 6,
where he puts eating for believing, and believing for eating.
For as we receive food by eating, so we participate in Christ
by believing. *Justification Is Not Attributed Partly to Christ
or to Faith, Partly to Us.* Therefore, we do not share in the
benefit of justification partly because of the grace of God or
Christ, and partly because of ourselves, our love, works or
merit, but we attribute it wholly to the grace of God in Christ

through faith. For our love and our works could not please God if performed by unrighteous men. Therefore, it is necessary for us to be righteous before we may love and do good works. We are made truly righteous, as we have said, by faith in Christ purely by the grace of God, who does not impute to us our sins, but the righteousness of Christ, or rather, he imputes faith in Christ to us for righteousness. Moreover, the apostle very clearly derives love from faith when he says: "The aim of our command is love that issues from a pure heart, a good conscience, and a sincere faith" (I Tim. 1:5).

James Compared with Paul. Wherefore, in this matter we are not speaking of a fictitious, empty, lazy and dead faith, but of a living, quickening faith. It is and is called a living faith because it apprehends Christ who is life and makes alive, and shows that it is alive by living works. And so James does not contradict anything in this doctrine of ours. For he speaks of an empty, dead faith of which some boasted but who did not have Christ living in them by faith (James 2:14 ff.). James said that works justify, yet without contradicting the apostle (otherwise he would have to be rejected) but showing that Abraham proved his living and justifying faith by works. This all the pious do, but they trust in Christ alone and not in their own works. For again the apostle said: "It is no longer I who live, but Christ who lives in me; and the life I now live in the flesh I live by faith in the Son of God,[6] who loved me and gave himself for me. I do not reject the grace of God; for if justification were through the law, then Christ died to no purpose," etc. (Gal. 2:20 f.).

Chapter XVI. OF FAITH AND GOOD WORKS, AND OF THEIR REWARD, AND OF MAN'S MERIT

What Is Faith? Christian faith is not an opinion or human conviction, but a most firm trust and a clear and steadfast assent of the mind, and then a most certain apprehension of the truth of God presented in the Scriptures and in the Apostles' Creed, and thus also of God himself, the greatest good, and especially of God's promise and of Christ who is the fulfilment of all promises.

Faith Is the Gift of God. But this faith is a pure gift of God which God alone of his grace gives to his elect according to his measure when, to whom and to the degree he wills. And he does this by the Holy Spirit by means of the preaching of

---

[6] The Latin reads: "by the faith of the Son of God."

the Gospel and steadfast prayer. *The Increase of Faith.* This faith also has its increase, and unless it were given by God, the apostles would not have said: " Lord, increase our faith " (Luke 17:5) . And all these things which up to this point we have said concerning faith, the apostles have taught before us. For Paul said: " For faith is the ὑποστασις or sure subsistence, of things hoped for, and the ἔλεγχος, that is, the clear and certain apprehension " (Heb. 11:1) . And again he says that all the promises of God are Yes through Christ and through Christ are Amen (II Cor. 1:20) . And to the Philippians he said that it has been given to them to believe in Christ (Phil. 1:29) . Again, God assigned to each the measure of faith (Rom. 12:3) . Again: " Not all have faith " and, " Not all obey the Gospel " (II Thess. 3:2; Rom. 10:16) . But Luke also bears witness, saying: " As many as were ordained to life believed " (Acts 13:48) . Wherefore Paul also calls faith " the faith of God's elect " (Titus 1:1) , and again: " Faith comes from hearing, and hearing comes by the Word of God " (Rom. 10:17) . Elsewhere he often commands men to pray for faith.

Faith Efficacious and Active. The same apostle calls faith efficacious and active through love (Gal. 5:6) . It also quiets the conscience and opens a free access to God, so that we may draw near to him with confidence and may obtain from him what is useful and necessary. The same [faith] keeps us in the service we owe to God and our neighbor, strengthens our patience in adversity, fashions and makes a true confession, and in a word, brings forth good fruit of all kinds, and good works.

Concerning Good Works. For we teach that truly good works grow out of a living faith by the Holy Spirit and are done by the faithful according to the will or rule of God's Word. Now the apostle Peter says: " Make every effort to supplement your faith with virtue, and virtue with knowledge, and knowledge with self-control," etc. (II Peter 1:5 ff.) But we have said above that the law of God, which is his will, prescribes for us the pattern of good works. And the apostle says: " This is the will of God, your sanctification, that you abstain from immorality . . . that no man transgress, and wrong his brother in business." (I Thess. 4:3 ff.)

Works of Human Choice. And indeed works and worship which we choose arbitrarily are not pleasing to God. These Paul calls ἐθλεοθρησκειας (Col. 2:23 — " self-devised worship "). Of such the Lord says in the Gospel: " In vain do they worship me, teaching as doctrines the precepts of men " (Matt. 15:9). Therefore, we disapprove of such works, and approve and urge those that are of God's will and commission.

The End of Good Works. These same works ought not to be done in order that we may earn eternal life by them, for, as the apostle says, eternal life is the gift of God. Nor are they to be done for ostentation which the Lord rejects in Matt., ch. 6, nor for gain which he also rejects in Matt., ch. 23, but for the glory of God, to adorn our calling, to show gratitude to God, and for the profit of the neighbor. For our Lord says again in the Gospel: " Let your light so shine before men, that they may see your good works and give glory to your Father who is in heaven " (Matt. 5:16). And the apostle Paul says: " Lead a life worthy of the calling to which you have been called." (Eph. 4:1.) Also: " And whatever you do, in word or deed, do everything in the name of the Lord Jesus, giving thanks to God and to the Father through him ' (Col. 3:17), and, " Let each of you look not to his own interests, but to the interests of others " (Phil. 2:4), and, " Let our people learn to apply themselves to good deeds, so as to help cases of urgent need, and not to be unfruitful " (Titus 3:14).

Good Works Not Rejected. Therefore, although we teach with the apostle that a man is justified by grace through faith in Christ and not through any good works, yet we do not think that good works are of little value and condemn them. We know that man was not created or regenerated through faith in order to be idle, but rather that without ceasing he should do those things which are good and useful. For in the Gospel the Lord says that a good tree brings forth good fruit (Matt. 12:33), and that he who abides in me bears much fruit (John 15:5). The apostle says: " For we are his workmanship, created in Christ Jesus for good works, which God prepared beforehand, that we should walk in them " (Eph. 2:10), and again: " Who gave himself for us to redeem us from all iniquity and to purify for himself a people of his own who are zealous for good deeds " (Titus 2:14). We therefore condemn all who despise good works and who babble that they are useless and that we do not need to pay attention to them.

We Are Not Saved by Good Works. Nevertheless, as was said above, we do not think that we are saved by good works, and that they are so necessary for salvation that no one was ever saved without them. For we are saved by grace and the favor of Christ alone. Works necessarily proceed from faith. And salvation is improperly attributed to them, but is most properly ascribed to grace. The apostle's sentence is well known: " If it is by grace, then it no longer of works; otherwise grace would no longer be grace. But if it is of works, then it is no longer grace, because otherwise work is no longer work " (Rom. 11:6).

Good Works Please God. Now the works which we do by faith are pleasing to God and are approved by him. Because of faith in Christ, those who do good works which, moreover, are done from God's grace through the Holy Spirit, are pleasing to God. For St. Peter said: " In every nation any one who fears God and does what is right is acceptable to him." (Acts 10:35.) And Paul said: " We have not ceased to pray for you . . . that you may walk worthily of the Lord, fully pleasing to him, bearing fruit in every good work." (Col. 1:9 f.)

We Teach True, Not False and Philosophical Virtues. And so we diligently teach true, not false and philosophical virtues, truly good works, and the genuine service of a Christian. And as much as we can we diligently and zealously press them upon all men, while censuring the sloth and hypocrisy of all those who praise and profess the Gospel with their lips and dishonor it by their disgraceful lives. In this matter we place before them God's terrible threats and then his rich promises and generous rewards — exhorting, consoling and rebuking.

God Gives a Reward for Good Works. For we teach that God gives a rich reward to those who do good works, according to that saying of the prophet: " Keep your voice from weeping, . . . for your work shall be rewarded " (Jer. 31:16; Isa., ch. 4). The Lord also said in the Gospel: " Rejoice and be glad, for your reward is great in heaven " (Matt. 5:12), and, " Whoever gives to one of these my little ones a cup of cold water, truly, I say to you, he shall not lose his reward " (ch. 10:42). However, we do not ascribe this reward, which the Lord gives, to the merit of the man who receives it, but to the goodness, generosity and truthfulness of God who promises and gives it, and who, although he owes nothing to anyone, nevertheless promises that he will give a reward to his faithful worshippers; meanwhile he also gives them that they may honor him. Moreover, in the works even of the saints there is much that is unworthy of God and very much that is imperfect. But because God receives into favor and embraces those who do works for Christ's sake, he grants to them the promised reward. For in other respects our righteousnesses are compared to a filthy wrap (Isa. 64:6). And the Lord says in the Gospel: " When you have done all that is commanded you, say, ' We are unworthy servants; we have only done what was our duty.' " (Luke 17:10.)

There Are No Merits of Men. Therefore, although we teach that God rewards our good deeds, yet at the same time we teach, with Augustine, that God does not crown in us our merits but his gifts. Accordingly we say that whatever reward we receive is also grace, and is more grace than reward, because the good we do, we do more through God than through ourselves, and because Paul says: " What have you that you did not receive? If then you received it, why do you boast as if you had not received it? " (I Cor. 4:7). And this is what the blessed martyr Cyprian concluded from this verse: We are not to glory in anything in us, since nothing is our own. We therefore condemn those who defend the merits of men in such a way that they invalidate the grace of God.

Chapter XVII. OF THE CATHOLIC AND HOLY CHURCH OF GOD, AND OF THE ONE ONLY HEAD OF THE CHURCH

The Church Has Always Existed and It Will Always Exist. But because God from the beginning would have men to be saved, and to come to the knowledge of the truth (I Tim. 2:4), it is altogether necessary that there always should have been, and should be now, and to the end of the world, a Church.

What Is the Church? The Church is an assembly of the faithful called or gathered out of the world; a communion, I say, of all saints, namely, of those who truly know and rightly worship and serve the true God in Christ the Savior, by the Word and Holy Spirit, and who by faith are partakers of all benefits which are freely offered through Christ. *Citizens of One Commonwealth.* They are all citizens of the one city, living under the same Lord, under the same laws, and in the same fellowship of all good things. For the apostle calls them " fellow citizens with the saints and members of the household of God " (Eph. 2:19), calling the faithful on earth saints (I Cor. 4:1), who are sanctified by the blood of the Son of God. The article of the Creed, " I believe in the holy catholic Church, the communion of saints," is to be understood wholly as concerning these saints.

Only One Church for All Times. And since there is always but one God, and there is one mediator between God and men, Jesus the Messiah, and one Shepherd of the whole flock, one Head of this body, and, to conclude, one Spirit, one salvation, one faith, one Testament or covenant, it necessarily follows that there is only one Church. *The Catholic Church.* We, therefore, call this Church catholic because it is universal, scattered through all parts of the world, and extended unto all times, and is not limited to any times or places. Therefore, we condemn the Donatists who confined the Church to I know not what corners of Africa. Nor do we approve of the Roman clergy who have recently passed off only the Roman Church as catholic.

Parts or Forms of the Church. The Church is divided into different parts or forms; not because it is divided or rent asunder in itself, but rather because it is distinguished by the diversity of the numbers that are in it. *Militant and Triumphant.* For the one is called the Church Militant, the other the Church Triumphant. The former still wages war on earth, and fights against the flesh, the world, and the prince of this world, the devil; against sin and death. But the latter, having been now discharged, triumphs in heaven immediately after having overcome all those things and rejoices before the Lord. Notwithstanding both have fellowship and union one with another.

The Particular Church. Moreover, the Church Militant upon the earth has always had many particular churches. Yet all these are to be referred to the unity of the catholic Church. This [Militant] Church was set up differently before the Law among the patriarchs; otherwise under Moses by the Law; and differently by Christ through the Gospel.

The Two Peoples. Generally two peoples are usually counted, namely, the Israelites and Gentiles, or those who have been gathered from among Jews and Gentiles into the Church. There are also two Testaments, the Old and the New. *The Same Church for the Old and the New People.* Yet from all these people there was and is one fellowship, one salvation in the one Messiah; in whom, as members of one body under one Head, all united together in the same faith, partaking also of the same spiritual food and drink. Yet here we acknowledge a diversity of times, and a diversity in the signs of the promised and delivered Christ; and that now the ceremonies being abolished, the light shines unto us more clearly, and blessings are given to us more abundantly, and a fuller liberty.

The Church the Temple of the Living God. This holy Church of God is called the temple of the living God, built of living and spiritual stones and founded upon a firm rock, upon a foundation which no other can lay, and therefore it is called " the pillar and bulwark of the truth " (I Tim. 3:15). *The Church Does Not Err.* It does not err as long as it rests upon the rock Christ, and upon the foundation of the prophets and apostles. And it is no wonder if it errs, as often as it deserts him who alone is the truth. *The Church as Bride and Virgin.* This Church is also called a virgin and the Bride of Christ, and even the only Beloved. For the apostle says: " I betrothed you to Christ to present you as a pure bride to Christ." (II Cor. 11:2.) *The Church as a Flock of Sheep.* The Church is called a flock of sheep under the one shepherd, Christ, according to Ezek., ch. 34, and John, ch. 10. *The Church as the Body.* It is also called the body of Christ because the faithful are living members of Christ under Christ the Head.

Christ the Sole Head of the Church. It is the head which has the preeminence in the body, and from it the whole body receives life; by its spirit the body is governed in all things; from it, also, the body receives increase, that it may grow up. Also, there is one head of the body, and it is suited to the body. Therefore the Church cannot have any other head besides Christ. For as the Church is a spiritual body, so it must also have a spiritual head in harmony with itself. Neither can it be governed by any other spirit than by the Spirit of Christ. Wherefore Paul says: " He is the head of the body, the church; he is the beginning, the firstborn from the dead, that in everything he might be preeminent " (Col. 1:18). And in another place: " Christ is the head of the church, his body, and is himself its Savior " (Eph. 5:23). And again: he is " the head over all things for the church, which is his body, the fulness of him who fills all in all " (Eph. 1:22 f.). Also: " We are to grow up in every way into him who is the head, into Christ, from whom the whole body, joined and knit together, makes bodily growth " (Eph. 4:15 f.). And therefore we do not approve of the doctrine of the Roman clergy, who make their Pope at Rome the universal shepherd and supreme head of the Church Militant here on earth, and so the very vicar of Jesus Christ, who has (as they say) all fulness of power and sovereign authority in the Church. *Christ the Only Pastor of the Church.* For we teach that Christ the Lord is, and remains the only universal pastor, and highest Pontiff before God the Father; and that in the Church he himself performs all the duties of a bishop or pastor, even to the world's end; [*Vicar*] and therefore does not need a substitute for one who is absent. For Christ is present with his Church, and is its life-giving Head. *No Primacy in the Church.* He has strictly forbidden his apostles and their successors to have any primacy and dominion in the Church. Who does not see, therefore, that whoever contradicts and opposes this plain truth is rather to be counted among the number of those of whom Christ's apostles prophesied: Peter in II Peter, ch. 2, and Paul in Acts 20:2; II Cor. 11:2; II Thess., ch. 2, and also in other places?

No Disorder in the Church. However, by doing away with a Roman head we do not bring any confusion or disorder into the Church, since we teach that the government of the Church which the apostles handed down is sufficient to keep the Church in proper order. In the beginning when the Church was without any such Roman head as is now said to keep it in order, the Church was not disordered or in confusion. The Roman head does indeed preserve his tyranny and the corruption that has been brought into the Church, and meanwhile he hinders, resists, and with all the strength he can muster cuts off the proper reformation of the Church.

Dissensions and Strife in the Church. We are reproached because there have been manifold dissensions and strife in our churches since they separated themselves from the Church of Rome, and therefore cannot be true churches. As though there were never in the Church of Rome any sects, nor contentions and quarrels concerning religion, and indeed, carried on not so much in the schools as from pulpits in the midst of the people. We know, to be sure, that the apostle said: " God is not a God of confusion but of peace " (I Cor. 14:33), and, " While there is jealousy and strife among you, are you not of the flesh? " Yet we cannot deny that God was in the apostolic Church and that it was a true Church, even though there were wranglings and dissensions in it. The apostle Paul reprehended Peter, an apostle (Gal. 2:11 ff.), and Barnabas dissented from Paul. Great contention arose in the Church of Antioch between them that preached the one Christ, as Luke records in The Acts of the Apostles, ch. 15.

And there have at all times been great contentions in the Church, and the most excellent teachers of the Church have differed among themselves about important matters without meanwhile the Church ceasing to be the Church because of these contentions. For thus it pleases God to use the dissensions that arise in the Church to the glory of his name, to illustrate the truth, and in order that those who are in the right might be manifest (I Cor. 11:19).

Of the Notes or Signs of the True Church. Moreover, as we acknowledge no other head of the Church than Christ, so we do not acknowledge every church to be the true Church which vaunts herself to be such; but we teach that the true Church is that in which the signs or marks of the true Church are to be found, especially the lawful and sincere preaching of the Word of God as it was delivered to us in the books of the prophets and the apostles, which all lead us unto Christ, who said in the Gospel: " My sheep hear my voice, and I know them, and they follow me; and I give unto them eternal life. A stranger they do not follow, but they flee from him, for they do not know the voice of strangers " (John 10:5, 27, 28).

And those who are such in the Church have one faith and one spirit; and therefore they worship but one God, and him alone they worship in spirit and in truth, loving him alone with all their hearts and with all their strength, praying unto him alone through Jesus Christ, the only Mediator and Intercessor; and they do not seek righteousness and life outside Christ and faith in him. Because they acknowledge Christ the only head and foundation of the Church, and, resting on him, daily renew themselves by repentance, and patiently bear the cross laid upon them. Moreover, joined together with all the members of Christ by an unfeigned love, they show that they are Christ's disciples by persevering in the bond of peace and holy unity. At the same time they participate in the sacraments instituted by Christ, and delivered unto us by his apostles, using them in no other way than as they received them from the Lord. That saying of the apostle Paul is well known to all: " I received from the Lord what I also delivered to you " (I Cor. 11:23 ff.). Accordingly, we condemn all such churches as strangers from the true Church of Christ, which are not such as we have heard they ought to be, no matter how much they brag of a succession of bishops, of unity, and of antiquity. Moreover, we have a charge from the apostles of Christ " to shun the worship of idols " (I Cor. 10:14; I John 5:21), and " to come out of Babylon," and to have no fellowship with her, unless we want to be partakers with her of all God's plagues (Rev. 18:4; II Cor. 6:17).

Outside the Church of God There Is No Salvation. But we esteem fellowship with the true Church of Christ so highly that we deny that those can live before God who do not stand in fellowship with the true Church of God, but separate themselves from it. For as there was no salvation outside Noah's ark when the world perished in the flood; so we believe that there is no certain salvation outside Christ, who offers himself to be enjoyed by the elect in the Church; and hence we teach that those who wish to live ought not to be separated from the true Church of Christ.

The Church Is Not Bound to Its Signs. Nevertheless, by the signs [of the true Church] mentioned above, we do not so narrowly restrict the Church as to teach that all those are outside the Church who either do not participate in the sacraments, at least not willingly and through contempt, but rather, being forced by necessity, unwillingly abstain from them or are deprived of them; or in whom faith sometimes fails, though it is not entirely extinguished and does not wholly cease; or in whom imperfections and errors due to weakness are found. For we know that God had some friends in the world outside the commonwealth of Israel. We know what befell the people of God in the captivity of Babylon, where they were deprived of their sacrifices for seventy years. We know what happened to St. Peter, who denied his Master, and what is wont to happen daily to God's elect and faithful people who go astray and are weak. We know, moreover, what kind of churches the churches in Galatia and Corinth were in the apostles' time, in which the apostle found fault with many serious offenses; yet he calls them holy churches of Christ (I Cor. 1:2; Gal. 1:2).

The Church Appears at Times to Be Extinct. Yes, and it sometimes happens that God in his just judgment allows the truth of his Word, and the catholic faith, and the proper worship of God to be so obscured and overthrown that the Church seems amost extinct, and no more to exist, as we see to have happened in the days of Elijah (I Kings 19:10, 14), and at other times. Meanwhile God has in this world and in this darkness his true worshippers, and those not a few, but even seven thousand and more (I Kings 19:18; Rev. 7:3 ff.).

For the apostle exclaims: " God's firm foundation stands, bearing this seal, ' The Lord knows those who are his,' " etc. (II Tim. 2:19.) Whence the Church of God may be termed invisible; not because the men from whom the Church is gathered are invisible, but because, being hidden from our eyes and known only to God, it often secretly escapes human judgment.

Not All Who Are in the Church Are of the Church. Again, not all that are reckoned in the number of the Church are saints, and living and true members of the Church. For there are many hypocrites, who outwardly hear the Word of God, and publicly receive the sacraments, and seem to pray to God through Christ alone, to confess Christ to be their only righteousness, and to worship God, and to exercise the duties of charity, and for a time to endure with patience in misfortune. And yet they are inwardly desitute of true illumination of the Spirit, of faith and sincerity of heart, and of perseverance to the end. But eventually the character of these men, for the most part, will be disclosed. For the apostle John says: " They went out from us, but they were not of us; for if they had been of us, they would indeed have continued with us." (I John 2:19.) And although while they simulate piety they are not of the Church, yet they are considered to be in the Church, just as traitors in a state are numbered among its citizens before they are discovered; and as the tares or darnel and chaff are found among the wheat, and as swellings and tumors are found in a sound body, when they are rather diseases and deformities than true members of the body. And therefore the Church of God is rightly compared to a net which catches fish of all kinds, and to a field, in which both wheat and tares are found (Matt. 13:24 ff., 47 ff.).

We Must Not Judge Rashly or Prematurely. Hence we must be very careful not to judge before the time, nor undertake to exclude, reject or cut off those whom the Lord does not want to have excluded or rejected, and those whom we cannot eliminate without loss to the Church. On the other hand, we must be vigilant lest while the pious snore the wicked gain ground and do harm to the Church.

The Unity of the Church Is Not in External Rites. Furthermore, we diligently teach that care is to be taken wherein the truth and unity of the Church chiefly lies, lest we rashly provoke and foster schisms in the Church. Unity consists not in outward rites and ceremonies, but rather in the truth and unity of the catholic faith. This catholic faith is not given to us by human laws, but by Holy Scriptures, of which the Apostles' Creed is a compendium. And, therefore, we read in the ancient writers that there was a manifold diversity of rites, but that they were free, and no one ever thought that the unity of the Church was thereby dissolved. So we teach that the true harmony of the Church consists in doctrines and in the true and harmonious preaching of the Gospel of Christ, and in rites that have been expressly delivered by the Lord. And here we especially urge that saying of the apostle: " Let those of us who are perfect have this mind; and if in any thing you are otherwise minded, God will reveal that also to you. Nevertheless let us walk by the same rule according to what we have attained, and let us be of the same mind " (Phil. 3:15 f.) .

Chapter XVIII. Of the Ministers of the Church, Their Institution and Duties

God Uses Ministers in the Building of the Church. God has always used ministers for the gathering or establishing of a Church for himself, and for the governing and preservation of the same; and still he does, and always will, use them so long as the Church remains on earth. Therefore, the first beginning, institution, and office of ministers is a most ancient arrangement of God himself, and not a new one of men. *Institution and Origin of Ministers.* It is true that God can, by his power, without any means join to himself a Church from among men; but he preferred to deal with men by the ministry of men. Therefore ministers are to be regarded, not as ministers by themselves alone, but as the ministers of God, inasmuch as God effects the salvation of men through them.

The Ministry Is Not to Be Despised. Hence we warn men to beware lest we attribute what has to do with our conversion and instruction to the secret power of the Holy Spirit in such a way that we make void the ecclesiastical ministry. For it is fitting that we always have in mind the words of the apostle: " How are they to believe in him of whom they have not heard? And how are they to hear without a preacher? So faith comes from hearing, and hearing comes by the word of God " (Rom. 10:14, 17) . And also what the Lord said in the Gospel: " Truly, truly, I say to you, he who receives any one whom I send receives me; and he who receives me receives him who sent me " (John 13:20) . Likewise a man of Macedonia, who appeared to Paul in a vision while he was in Asia, secretly admonished him, saying: " Come over to Macedonia and help us " (Acts 16:9). And in another place the same apostle said: "We are fellow workmen for God; you are God's tillage, God's building " (I Cor. 3:9).

Yet, on the other hand, we must beware that we do not attribute too much to ministers and the ministry; remembering here also the words of the Lord in the Gospel: " No one can come to me unless my Father draws him " (John 6:44), and the words of the apostle: " What then is Paul? What is Apollos? Servants through whom you believed, as the Lord assigned to each. I planted, Apollos watered, but only God gives the growth " (I Cor. 3:5 ff.). *God Moves the Hearts of Men.* Therefore, let us believe that God teaches us by his word, outwardly through his ministers, and inwardly moves the hearts of his elect to faith by the Holy Spirit; and that therefore we ought to render all glory unto God for this whole favor. But this matter has been dealt with in the first chapter of this Exposition.

Who the Ministers Are and of What Sort God Has Given to the World. And even from the beginning of the world God has used the most excellent men in the whole world (even if many of them were simple in worldly wisdom or philosophy, but were outstanding in true theology), namely, the patriarchs, with whom he frequently spoke by angels. For the patriarchs were the prophets or teachers of their age whom God for this reason wanted to live for several centuries, in order that they might be, as it were, fathers and lights of the world. They were followed by Moses and the prophets renowned throughout all the world.

Christ the Teacher. After these the heavenly Father even sent his only-begotten Son, the most perfect teacher of the world; in whom is hidden the wisdom of God, and which has come to us through the most holy, simple, and most perfect doctrine of all. For he chose disciples for himself whom he made apostles. These went out into the whole world, and everywhere gathered together churches by the preaching of the Gospel, and then throughout all the churches in the world they appointed pastors or teachers [7] according to Christ's command; through their successors he has taught and governed the Church unto this day. Therefore, as God gave unto his ancient people the patriarchs, together with Moses and

[7] *Ordinarunt pastores, atque doctores.*

the prophets, so also to his people of the New Testament he sent his only-begotten Son, and, with him, the apostles and teachers of the Church.

Ministers of the New Testament. Furthermore, the ministers of the new people are called by various names. For they are called apostles, prophets, evangelists, bishops, elders, pastors, and teachers (I Cor. 12:28; Eph. 4:11). *The Apostles.* The apostles did not stay in any particular place, but throughout the world gathered together different churches. When they were once established, there ceased to be apostles, and pastors took their place, each in his church. *Prophets.* In former times the prophets were seers, knowing the future; but they also interpreted the Scriptures. Such men are also found still today. *Evangelists.* The writers of the history of the Gospel were called Evangelists; but they also were heralds of the Gospel of Christ; as Paul also commended Timothy: " Do the work of an evangelist " (II Tim. 4:5). *Bishops.* Bishops are the overseers and watchmen of the Church, who administer the food and needs of the life of the Church. *Presbyters.* The presbyters are the elders and, as it were, senators and fathers of the Church, governing it with wholesome counsel. *Pastors.* The pastors both keep the Lord's sheepfold, and also provide for its needs. *Teachers.* The teachers instruct and teach the true faith and godliness. Therefore, the ministers of the churches may now be called bishops, elders, pastors, and teachers.

Papal Orders. Then in subsequent times many more names of ministers in the Church were introduced into the Church of God. For some were appointed patriarchs, others archbishops, others suffragans; also, metropolitans, archdeacons, deacons, subdeacons, acolytes, exorcists, cantors, porters, and I know not what others, as cardinals, provosts, and priors; greater and lesser fathers, greater and lesser orders. But we are not troubled about all these, about how they once were and are now. For us the apostolic doctrine concerning ministers is sufficient.

Concerning Monks. Since we assuredly know that monks, and the orders or sects of monks, are instituted neither by Christ nor by the apostles, we teach that they are of no use to the Church of God, nay rather, are pernicious. For, although in former times they were tolerable (when they were hermits, earning their living with their own hands, and were not a burden to anyone, but like the laity were everywhere obedient to the pastors of the churches), yet now the whole world sees and knows what they are like. They formulate I know not what vows; but they lead a life quite contrary to their vows, so that the best of them deserves to be numbered among those of whom the apostle said: " We hear that some of you are living an irregular life, mere busybodies, not doing any work " etc. (II Thess. 3:11). Therefore, we neither have such in our churches, nor do we teach that they should be in the churches of Christ.

Ministers Are to Be Called and Elected. Furthermore, no man ought to usurp the honor of the ecclesiastical ministry; that is, to seize it for himself by bribery or any deceits, or by his own free choice. But let the ministers of the Church be called and chosen by lawful and ecclesiastical election; that is to say, let them be carefully chosen by the Church or by those delegated from the Church for that purpose in a proper order without any uproar, dissension and rivalry. Not any one may be elected, but capable men distinguished by sufficient consecrated learning, pious eloquence, simple wisdom, lastly, by moderation and an honorable reputation, according to that apostolic rule which is compiled by the apostle in I Tim., ch. 3, and Titus, ch. 1.

Ordination. And those who are elected are to be ordained by the elders with public prayer and laying on of hands. Here we condemn all those who go off of their own accord, being neither chosen, sent, nor ordained (Jer., ch. 23). We condemn unfit ministers and those not furnished with the necessary gifts of a pastor.

In the meantime we acknowledge that the harmless simplicity of some pastors in the primitive Church sometimes profited the Church more than the many-sided, refined and fastidious, but a little too esoteric learning of others. For this reason we do not reject even today the honest, yet by no means ignorant, simplicity of some.

Priesthood of All Believers. To be sure, Christ's apostles call all who believe in Christ " priests," but not on account of an office, but because, all the faithful having been made kings and priests, we are able to offer up spiritual sacrifices to God through Christ (Ex. 19:6; I Peter 2:9; Rev. 1:6). Therefore, the priesthood and the ministry are very different from one another. For the priesthood, as we have just said, is common to all Christians; not so is the ministry. Nor have we abolished the ministry of the Church because we have repudiated the papal priesthood from the Church of Christ.

Priests and Priesthood. Surely in the new covenant of Christ there is no longer any such priesthood as was under the ancient people; which had an external anointing, holy garments, and very many ceremonies which were types of Christ, who abolished them all by his coming and fulfilling them. But he himself remains the only priest forever, and lest we derogate anything from him, we do not impart the name of priest to any minister. For the Lord himself did not appoint any priests in the Church of the New Testament who, having received authority from the suffragan, may daily offer up the sacrifice, that is, the very flesh and blood of the Lord, for the living and the dead, but ministers who may teach and administer the sacraments.

The Nature of the Ministers of the New Testament. Paul explains simply and briefly what we are to think of the ministers of the New Testament or of the Christian Church, and what we are to attribute to them. " This is how one should regard us, as servants of Christ and stewards of the mysteries of God " (I Cor. 4:1). Therefore, the apostle wants us to think of ministers as ministers. Now the apostle calls them ὑπηρέτας, rowers, who have their eyes fixed on the coxswain, and so men who do not live for themselves or according to their own will, but for others — namely, their masters, upon whose command they altogether depend. For in all his duties every minister of the Church is commanded to carry out only what he has received in commandment from his Lord, and not to indulge his own free choice. And in this case it is expressly declared who is the Lord, namely, Christ; to whom the ministers are subject in all the affairs of the ministry.

Ministers as Stewards of the Mysteries of God. Moreover, to the end that he might expound the ministry more fully, the apostle adds that ministers of the Church are administrators and stewards of the mysteries of God. Now in many passages, especially in Eph., ch. 3, Paul called the mysteries of God the Gospel of Christ. And the sacraments of Christ are also called mysteries by the ancient writers. Therefore for this purpose are the ministers of the Church called — namely, to preach the Gospel of Christ to the faithful, and to administer the sacraments. We read, also, in another place in the Gospel, of " the faithful and wise steward," whom " his master will set over his household, to give them their portion of food at the proper time " (Luke 12:42). Again, elsewhere in the Gospel a man takes a journey in a foreign country and, leaving his house, gives his substance and authority over it to his servants, and to each his work.

The Power of Ministers of the Church. Now, therefore, it is fitting that we also say something about the power and duty of the ministers of the Church. Concerning this power some have argued industriously, and to it have subjected everything on earth, even the greatest things, and they have done so contrary to the commandment of the Lord who has prohibited dominion for his disciples and has highly commended humility (Luke 22:24 ff.; Matt. 18:3 f.; 20:25 ff.). There is, indeed, another power that is pure and absolute, which is called the power of right. According to this power all things in the whole world are subject to Christ, who is Lord of all, as he himself has testified when he said: " All authority in heaven and on earth has been given to me " (Matt. 28:18), and again, " I am the first and the last, and behold I am alive for evermore, and I have the keys of Hades and Death " (Rev. 1:18); also, " He has the key of David, which opens and no one shall shut, who shuts and no one opens " (Rev. 3:7).

The Lord Reserves True Power for Himself. This power the Lord reserves to himself, and does not transfer it to any other, so that he might stand idly by as a spectator while his ministers work. For Isaiah says, " I will place on his shoulder the key of the house of David " (Isa. 22:22), and again, " The government will be upon his shoulders " (Isa. 9:6). For he does not lay the government on other men's shoulders, but still keeps and uses his own power, governing all things.

The Power of the Office and of the Minister. Then there is another power of an office or of ministry limited by him who has full and absolute power. And this is more like a service than a dominion. *The Keys.* For a lord gives up his power to the steward in his house, and for that cause gives him the keys, that he may admit into or exclude from the house those whom his lord will have admitted or excluded. In virtue of this power the minister, because of his office, does that which the Lord has commanded him to do; and the Lord confirms what he does, and wills that what his servant has done will be so regarded and acknowledged, as if he himself had done it. Undoubtedly, it is to this that these evangelical sentences refer: " I will give you the keys of the kingdom of heaven, and whatever you bind on earth shall be bound in heaven, and whatever you loose on earth shall be loosed in heaven" (Matt. 16:19). Again, " If you forgive the sins of any, they are forgiven; if you retain the sins of any, they are retained" (John 20:23). But if the minister does not carry out everything as the Lord has commanded him, but transgresses the bounds of faith, then the Lord certainly makes void what he has done. Wherefore the ecclesiastical power of the ministers of the Church is that function whereby they indeed govern the Church of God, but yet so do all things in the Church as the Lord has prescribed in his Word. When those things are done, the faithful esteem them as done by the Lord himself. But mention has already been made of the keys above.

The Power of Ministers Is One and the Same, and Equal. Now the one and an equal power or function is given to all ministers in the Church. Certainly, in the beginning, the bishops or presbyters governed the Church in common; no man lifted up himself above another, none usurped greater power or authority over his fellow-bishops. For remembering the words of the Lord: " Let the leader among you become as one who serves" (Luke 22:26), they kept themselves in humility, and by mutual services they helped one another in the governing and preserving of the Church.

Order to Be Preserved. Nevertheless, for the sake of preserving order some one of the ministers called the assembly together, proposed matters to be laid before it, gathered the opinions of the others, in short, to the best of man's ability took precaution lest any confusion should arise. Thus did St. Peter, as we read in The Acts of the Apostles, who nevertheless was not on that account preferred to the others, nor endowed with greater authority than the rest. Rightly then does Cyprian the Martyr say, in his *De Simplicitate Clericorum:* " The other apostles were assuredly what Peter was, endowed with a like fellowship of honor and power; but [his] primacy proceeds from unity in order that the Church may be shown to be one."

When and How One Was Placed Before the Others. St. Jerome also in his commentary upon The Epistle of Paul to Titus, says something not unlike this: " Before attachment to persons in religion was begun at the instigation of the devil, the churches were governed by the common consultation of the elders; but after every one thought that those whom he had baptized were his own, and not Christ's, it was decreed that one of the elders should be chosen, and set over the rest, upon whom should fall the care of the whole Church, and all schismatic seeds should be removed." Yet St. Jerome does not recommend this decree as divine; for he immediately adds: " As the elders knew from the custom of the Church that they were subject to him who was set over them, so the bishops knew that they were above the elders, more from custom than from the truth of an arrangement by the Lord, and that they ought to rule the Church in common with them." Thus far St. Jerome. Hence no one can rightly forbid a return to the ancient constitution of the Church of God, and to have recourse to it before human custom.

The Duties of Ministers. The duties of ministers are various; yet for the most part they are restricted to two, in which all the rest are comprehended: to the teaching of the Gospel of Christ, and to the proper administration of the sacraments. For it is the duty of the ministers to gather together an assembly for worship in which to expound God's Word and to apply the whole doctrine to the care and use of the Church, so that what is taught may benefit the hearers and edify the faithful. It falls to ministers, I say, to teach the ignorant, and to exhort; and to urge the idlers and lingerers to make progress in the way of the Lord. Moreover, they are to comfort and to strengthen the fainthearted, and to arm them against the manifold temptations of Satan; to rebuke offenders; to recall the erring into the way; to raise the fallen; to convince the gainsayers to drive the wolf away from the sheepfold of the Lord; to rebuke wickedness and wicked men wisely and severely; not to wink at nor to pass over great wickedness. And, besides, they are to administer the sacraments, and to commend the right use of them, and to prepare all men by wholesome doctrine to receive them; to preserve the faithful in a holy unity; and to check schisms; to catechize the unlearned, to commend the needs of the poor to the Church, to visit, instruct, and keep in the way of life the sick and those afflicted with various temptations. In addition, they are to attend to public prayers or supplications in times of need, together with common fasting, that is, a holy abstinence; and as diligently as possible to see to everything that pertains to the tranquillity, peace and welfare of the churches.

But in order that the minister may perform all these things better and more easily, it is especially required of him that he fear God, be constant in prayer, attend to spiritual reading, and in all things and at all times be watchful, and by a purity of life to let his light to shine before all men.

Discipline. And since discipline is an absolute necessity in the Church and excommunication was once used in the time of the early fathers, and there were ecclesiastical judgments among the people of God, wherein this discipline was exercised by wise and godly men, it also falls to ministers to regulate this discipline for edification, according to the circumstances of the time, public state, and necessity. At all times and in all places the rule is to be observed that everything is to be done for edification, decently and honorably, without oppression and strife. For the apostle testifies that authority in the Church was given to him by the Lord for building up and not for destroying (II Cor. 10:8). And the Lord himself forbade the weeds to be plucked up in the Lord's field, because there would be danger lest the wheat also be plucked up with it (Matt. 13:29 f.).

Even Evil Ministers Are to Be Heard. Moreover, we strongly detest the error of the Donatists who esteem the doctrine and administration of the sacraments to be either effectual or not effectual, according to the good or evil life of the ministers. For we know that the voice of Christ is to be heard, though it be out of the mouths of evil ministers; because the Lord himself said: " Practice and observe whatever they tell you, but not what they do " (Matt. 23:3). We know that the sacraments are sanctified by the institution and the word of Christ, and that they are effectual to the godly, although they be administered by unworthy ministers. Concerning this matter, Augustine, the blessed servant of God, many times argued from the Scriptures against the Donatists.

Synods. Nevertheless, there ought to be proper discipline among ministers. In synods the doctrine and life of ministers is to be carefully examined. Offenders who can be cured are to be rebuked by the elders and restored to the right way, and if they are incurable, they are to be deposed, and like wolves driven away from the flock of the Lord by the true shepherds. For, if they be false teachers, they are not to be tolerated at all. Neither do we disapprove of ecumenical councils, if they are convened according to the example of the apostles, for the welfare of the Church and not for its destruction.

The Worker Is Worthy of His Reward. All faithful ministers, as good workmen, are also worthy of their reward, and do not sin when they receive a stipend, and all things that be necessary for themselves and their family. For the apostle shows in I Cor., ch. 9, and in I Tim., ch. 5, and elsewhere that these things may rightly be given by the Church and received by ministers. The Anabaptists, who condemn and defame ministers who live from their ministry are also refuted by the apostolic teaching.

Chapter XIX. OF THE SACRAMENTS OF THE CHURCH OF CHRIST

The Sacraments [Are] Added to the Word and What They Are. From the beginning, God added to the preaching of his Word in his Church sacraments or sacramental signs. For thus does all Holy Scripture clearly testify. Sacraments are mystical symbols, or holy rites, or sacred actions, instituted by God himself, consisting of his Word, of signs and of things signified, whereby in the Church he keeps in mind and from time to time recalls the great benefits he has shown to men; whereby also he seals his promises, and outwardly represents, and, as it were, offers unto our sight those things which inwardly he performs for us, and so strengthens and increases our faith through the working of God's Spirit in our hearts. Lastly, he thereby distinguishes us from all other people and religions, and consecrates and binds us wholly to himself, and signifies what he requires of us.

Some Are Sacraments of the Old, Others of the New, Testament. Some sacraments are of the old, others of the new, people. The sacraments of the ancient people were circumcision, and the Paschal Lamb, which was offered up; for that reason it is referred to the sacrifices which were practiced from the beginning of the world.

The Number of Sacraments of the New People. The sacraments of the new people are Baptism and the Lord's Supper. There are some who count seven sacraments of the new people. Of these we acknowledge that repentance, the ordination of ministers (not indeed the papal but apostolic ordination), and matrimony are profitable ordinances of God, but not sacraments. Confirmation and extreme unction are human inventions which the Church can dispense with without any loss, and indeed, we do not have them in our churches. For they contain some things of which we can by no means approve. Above all we detest all the trafficking in which the Papists engage in dispensing the sacraments.

The Author of the Sacraments. The author of all sacraments is not any man, but God alone. Men cannot institute sacraments. For they pertain to the worship of God, and it is not for man to appoint and prescribe a worship of God, but to accept and preserve the one he has received from God. Besides, the symbols have God's promises annexed to them, which require faith. Now faith rests only upon the Word of God; and the Word of God is like papers or letters, and the sacraments are like seals which only God appends to the letters.

Christ Still Works in Sacraments. And as God is the author of the sacraments, so he continually works in the Church in which they are rightly carried out; so that the faithful, when they receive them from the ministers, know that God works in his own ordinance, and therefore they receive them as from the hand of God; and the minister's faults (even if they be very great) cannot affect them, since they acknowledge the integrity of the sacraments to depend upon the institution of the Lord.

The Author and the Ministers of the Sacraments to Be Distinguished. Hence in the administration of the sacraments they also clearly distinguish between the Lord himself and the ministers of the Lord, confessing that the substance of the sacraments is given them by the Lord, and the outward signs by the ministers of the Lord.

The Substance or Chief Thing in the Sacraments. But the principal thing which God promises in all sacraments and to which all the godly in all ages direct their attention (some call it the substance and matter of the sacraments) is Christ the Savior — that only sacrifice, and that Lamb of God slain from the foundation of the world; that rock, also, from which all our fathers drank, by whom all the elect are circumcised without hands through the Holy Spirit, and are washed from all their sins, and are nourished with the very body and blood of Christ unto eternal life.

The Similarity and Difference in the Sacraments of Old and New Peoples. Now, in respect of that which is the principal thing and the matter itself in the sacraments, the sacraments of both peoples are equal. For Christ, the only Mediator and Savior of the faithful, is the chief thing and very substance of the sacraments in both; for the one God is the author of them both. They were given to both peoples as signs and seals of the grace and promises of God, which should call to mind and renew the memory of God's great benefits, and should distinguish the faithful from all the religions in the world; lastly, which should be received spiritually by faith, and should bind the receivers to the Church, and admonish them of their duty. In these and similar respects, I say, the sacraments of both peoples are not dissimilar, although in the outward signs they are different. And, indeed, with respect to the signs we make a great difference. For ours are more firm and lasting, inasmuch as they will never be changed to the end of the world. Moreover, ours testify that both the substance and the promise have been fulfilled or perfected in Christ; the former signified what was to be fulfilled. Ours are also more simple and less laborious, less sumptuous and involved with ceremonies. Moreover, they belong to a more numerous people, one that is dispersed throughout the whole earth. And since they are more excellent, and by the Holy Spirit kindle greater faith, a greater abundance of the Spirit also ensues.

Our Sacraments Succeed the Old Which Are Abrogated. But now since Christ the true Messiah is exhibited unto us, and the abundance of grace is poured forth upon the people of the New Testament, the sacraments of the old people are surely abrogated and have ceased; and in their stead the symbols of the New Testament are placed — Baptism in the place of circumcision, the Lord's Supper in place of the Paschal Lamb and sacrifices.

In What the Sacraments Consist. And as formerly the sacraments consisted of the word, the sign, and the thing signified; so even now they are composed, as it were, of the same parts. For the Word of God makes them sacraments, which before they were not. *The Consecration of the Sacraments.* For they are consecrated by the Word, and shown to be sanctified by him who instituted them. To sanctify or consecrate anything to God is to dedicate it to holy uses; that is, to take it from the common and ordinary use, and to appoint it to a holy use. For the signs in the sacraments are drawn from common use, things external and visible. For in baptism the sign is the element of water, and that visible washing which is done by the minister; but the thing signified is regeneration and the cleansing from sins. Likewise, in the Lord's Supper, the outward sign is bread and wine, taken from things commonly used for meat and drink; but the thing signified is the body of Christ which was given, and his blood which was shed for us, or the communion of the body and blood of the Lord. Wherefore, the water, bread, and wine, according to their nature and apart from the divine institution and sacred use, are only that which they are called and we experience. But when the Word of God is added to them, together with invocation of the divine name, and the renewing of their first institution and sanctification, then these signs are consecrated, and shown to be sanctified by Christ. For Christ's first institution and consecration of the sacraments remains always effectual in the Church of God, so that those who do not celebrate the sacraments in any other way than the Lord himself instituted from the beginning still today enjoy that first and all-surpassing consecration. And hence in the celebration of the sacraments the very words of Christ are repeated.

Signs Take Name of Things Signified. And as we learn out of the Word of God that these signs were instituted for another purpose than the usual use, therefore we teach that they now, in their holy use, take upon them the names of things signified, and are no longer called mere water, bread or wine, but also regeneration or the washing of water, and the body and blood of the Lord or symbols and sacraments of the Lord's body and blood. Not that the symbols are changed into the things signified, or cease to be what they are in their own nature. For otherwise they would not be sacraments. If they were only the thing signified, they would not be signs.

The Sacramental Union. Therefore the signs acquire the names of things because they are mystical signs of sacred things, and because the signs and the things signified are sacramentally joined together; joined together, I say, or united by a mystical signification, and by the purpose or will of him who instituted the sacraments. For the water, bread, and wine are not common, but holy signs. And he that instituted water in baptism did not institute it with the will and intention that the faithful should only be sprinkled by the water of baptism; and he who commanded the bread to be eaten and the wine to be drunk in the supper did not want the faithful to receive only bread and wine without any mystery as they eat bread in their homes; but that they should spiritually partake of the things signified, and by faith be truly cleansed from their sins, and partake of Christ.

The Sects. And, therefore, we do not at all approve of those who attribute the sanctification of the sacraments to I know not what properties and formula or to the power of words pronounced by one who is consecrated and who has the intention of consecrating, and to other accidental things which neither Christ or the apostles delivered to us by word or example. Neither do we approve of the doctrine of those who speak of the sacraments just as common signs, not sanctified and effectual. Nor do we approve of those who despise the visible aspect of the sacraments because of the invisible, and so believe the signs to be superfluous because they think they already enjoy the things themselves, as the Messalians are said to have held.

The Thing Signified Is Neither Included in or Bound to the Sacraments. We do not approve of the doctrine of those who teach that grace and the things signified are so bound to and included in the signs that whoever participate outwardly in the signs, no matter what sort of persons they be, also inwardly participate in the grace and things signified.

However, as we do not estimate the value of the sacraments by the worthiness or unworthiness of the ministers, so we do not estimate it by the condition of those who receive them. For we know that the value of the sacraments depends upon faith and upon the truthfulness and pure goodness of God. For as the Word of God remains the true Word of God, in which, when it is preached, not only bare words are repeated, but at the same time the things signified or announced in words are offered by God, even if the ungodly and unbelievers hear and understand the words yet do not enjoy the things signified, because they do not receive them by true faith; so the sacraments, which by the Word consist of signs and the things signified, remain true and inviolate sacraments, signifying not only sacred things, but, by God offering, the things signified, even if unbelievers do not receive the things offered. This is not the fault of God who gives and offers them, but the fault of men who receive them without faith and illegitimately; but whose unbelief does not invalidate the faithfulness of God (Rom. 3:3 f.).

The Purpose for Which Sacraments Were Instituted. Since the purpose for which sacraments were instituted was also explained in passing when right at the beginning of our exposition it was shown what sacraments are, there is no need to be tedious by repeating what once has been said. Logically, therefore, we now speak severally of the sacraments of the new people.

Chapter XX. OF HOLY BAPTISM

The Institution of Baptism. Baptism was instituted and consecrated by God. First John baptized, who dipped Christ in the water in Jordon. From him it came to the apostles, who also baptized with water. The Lord expressly commanded them to preach the Gospel and to baptize " in the name of the Father and of the Son and of the Holy Spirit " (Matt. 28:19). And in The Acts, Peter said to the Jews who inquired what they ought to do: " Be baptized every one of you in the name of Jesus Christ for the forgiveness of your sins; and you shall receive the gift of the Holy Spirit " (Acts 2:37 f.). Hence by some baptism is called a sign of initiation for God's people, since by it the elect of God are consecrated to God.

One Baptism. There is but one baptism in the Church of God; and it is sufficient to be once baptized or consecrated unto God. For baptism once received continues for all of life, and is a perpetual sealing of our adoption.

What It Means to Be Baptized. Now to be baptized in the name of Christ is to be enrolled, entered, and received into the covenant and family, and so into the inheritance of the sons of God; yes, and in this life to be called after the name of God; that is to say, to be called a son of God; to be cleansed also from the filthiness of sins, and to be granted the manifold grace of God, in order to lead a new and innocent life. Baptism, therefore, calls to mind and renews the great favor God has shown to the race of mortal men. For we are all born in the pollution of sin and are the children of wrath. But God, who is rich in mercy, freely cleanses us from our sins by the blood of his Son, and in him adopts us to be his sons, and by a holy covenant joins us to himself, and enriches us with various gifts, that we might live a new life. All these things are assured by baptism. For inwardly we are regenerated, purified, and renewed by God through the Holy Spirit; and outwardly we receive the assurance of the greatest gifts in the water, by which also those great benefits are represented, and, as it were, set before our eyes to be beheld.

We Are Baptized with Water. And therefore we are baptized, that is, washed or sprinkled with visible water. For the water washes dirt away, and cools and refreshes hot and tired bodies. And the grace of God performs these things for souls, and does so invisibly or spiritually.

The Obligation of Baptism. Moreover, God also separates us from all strange religions and peoples by the symbol of baptism, and consecrates us to himself as his property. We, therefore, confess our faith when we are baptized, and obligate ourselves to God for obedience, mortification of the flesh, and newness of life. Hence, we are enlisted in the holy military service of Christ that all our life long we should fight against the world, Satan, and our own flesh. Moreover, we are baptized into one body of the Church, that with all members of the Church we might beautifully concur in the one religion and in mutual services.

The Form of Baptism. We believe that the most perfect form of baptism is that by which Christ was baptized, and by which the apostles baptized. Those things, therefore, which by man's device were added afterwards and used in the Church we do not consider necessary to the perfection of baptism. Of this kind is exorcism, the use of burning lights, oil, salt, spittle, and such other things as that baptism is to be celebrated twice every year with a multitude of ceremonies. For we believe that one baptism of the Church has been sanctified in God's first institution, and that it is consecrated by the Word and is also effectual today in virtue of God's first blessing.

The Minister of Baptism. We teach that baptism should not be administered in the Church by women or midwives. For Paul deprived women of ecclesiastical duties, and baptism has to do with these.

Anabaptists. We condemn the Anabaptists, who deny that newborn infants of the faithful are to be baptized. For according to evangelical teaching, of such is the Kingdom of God, and they are in the covenant of God. Why, then, should the sign of God's covenant not be given to them? Why should those who belong to God and are in his Church not be initiated by holy baptism? We condemn also the Anabaptists in the rest of their peculiar doctrines which they hold contrary to the Word of God. We therefore are not Anabaptists and have nothing in common with them.

Chapter XXI. OF THE HOLY SUPPER OF THE LORD

The Supper of the Lord. The Supper of the Lord, (which is called the Lord's Table, and the Eucharist, that is, a Thanksgiving) is, therefore, usually called a supper, because it was instituted by Christ at his last supper, and still represents it, and because in it the faithful are spiritually fed and given drink.

The Author and Consecrator of the Supper. For the author

of the Supper of the Lord is not an angel or any man, but the Son of God himself, our Lord Jesus Christ, who first consecrated it to his Church. And the same consecration or blessing still remains among all those who celebrate no other but that very Supper which the Lord instituted, and at which they repeat the words of the Lord's Supper, and in all things look to the one Christ by a true faith, from whose hands they receive, as it were, what they receive through the ministry of the ministers of the Church.

A Memorial of God's Benefits. By this sacred rite the Lord wishes to keep in fresh remembrance that greatest benefit which he showed to mortal men, namely, that by having given his body and shed his blood he has pardoned all our sins, and redeemed us from eternal death and the power of the devil, and now feeds us with his flesh, and gives us his blood to drink, which, being received spiritually by true faith, nourish us to eternal life. And this so great a benefit is renewed as often as the Lord's Supper is celebrated. For the Lord said: "Do this in remembrance of me." This holy Supper also seals to us that the very body of Christ was truly given for us, and his blood shed for the remission of our sins, lest our faith should in any way waver.

The Sign and Thing Signified. And this is visibly represented by this sacrament outwardly through the ministers, and, as it were, presented to our eyes to be seen, which is invisibly wrought by the Holy Spirit inwardly in the soul. Bread is outwardly offered by the minister, and the words of the Lord are heard: "Take, eat; this is my body"; and, "Take and divide among you. Drink of it, all of you; this is my blood." Therefore the faithful receive what is given by the ministers of the Lord, and they eat the bread of the Lord and drink of the Lord's cup. At the same time by the work of Christ through the Holy Spirit they also inwardly receive the flesh and blood of the Lord, and are thereby nourished unto life eternal. For the flesh and blood of Christ is the true food and drink unto life eternal; and Christ himself, since he was given for us and is our Savior, is the principal thing in the Supper, and we do not permit anything else to be substituted in his place.

But in order to understand better and more clearly how the flesh and blood of Christ are the food and drink of the faithful, and are received by the faithful unto eternal life, we would add these few things. There is more than one kind of eating. There is corporeal eating whereby food is taken into the mouth, is chewed with the teeth, and swallowed into the stomach. In times past the Capernaites thought that the flesh of the Lord should be eaten in this way, but they are refuted by him in John, ch. 6. For as the flesh of Christ cannot be eaten corporeally without infamy and savagery, so it is not food for the stomach. All men are forced to admit this. We therefore disapprove of that canon in the Pope's decrees, *Ego Berengarius* (*De Consecrat.,* Dist. 2). For neither did godly antiquity believe, nor do we believe, that the body of Christ is to be eaten corporeally and essentially with a bodily mouth.

Spiritual Eating of the Lord. There is also a spiritual eating of Christ's body; not such that we think that thereby the food itself is to be changed into spirit, but whereby the body and blood of the Lord, while remaining in their own essence and property, are spiritually communicated to us, certainly not in a corporeal but in a spiritual way, by the Holy Spirit, who applies and bestows upon us these things which have been prepared for us by the sacrifice of the Lord's body and blood for us, namely, the remission of sins, deliverance, and eternal life; so that Christ lives in us and we live in him, and he causes us to receive him by true faith to this end that he may become for us such spiritual food and drink, that is, our life.

Christ as Our Food Sustains Us in Life. For even as bodily food and drink not only refresh and strengthen our bodies, but also keeps them alive, so the flesh of Christ delivered for us, and his blood shed for us, not only refresh and strengthen our souls, but also preserve them alive, not in so far as they are corporeally eaten and drunken, but in so far as they are communicated unto us spiritually by the Spirit of God, as the Lord said: " The bread which I shall give for the life of the world is my flesh " (John 6:51), and " the flesh " (namely what is eaten bodily) " is of no avail; it is the spirit that gives life " (v. 63). And: " The words that I have spoken to you are spirit and life."

Christ Received by Faith. And as we must by eating receive food into our bodies in order that it may work in us, and prove its efficacy in us — since it profits us nothing when it remains outside us — so it is necessary that we receive Christ by faith, that he may become ours, and he may live in us and we in him. For he says: " I am the bread of life; he who comes to me shall not hunger, and he who believes in me shall never thirst " (John 6:35); and also, " He who eats me

will live because of me . . . he abides in me, I in him "
(vs. 57, 56) .

Spiritual Food. From all this it is clear that by spiritual
food we do not mean some imaginary food I know not what,
but the very body of the Lord given to us, which nevertheless
is received by the faithful not corporeally, but spiritually by
faith. In this matter we follow the teaching of the Savior himself, Christ the Lord, according to John, ch. 6.

Eating Necessary for Salvation. And this eating of the flesh
and drinking of the blood of the Lord is so necessary for
salvation that without it no man can be saved. But this spiritual eating and drinking also occurs apart from the Supper
of the Lord, and as often and wherever a man believes in
Christ. To which that sentence of St. Augustine's perhaps
applies: " Why do you provide for your teeth and your
stomach? Believe, and you have eaten."

Sacramental Eating of the Lord. Besides the higher spiritual
eating there is also a sacramental eating of the body of the
Lord by which not only spiritually and internally the believer
truly participates in the true body and blood of the Lord,
but also, by coming to the Table of the Lord, outwardly receives the visible sacrament of the body and blood of the
Lord. To be sure, when the believer believed, he first received the life-giving food, and still enjoys it. But therefore,
when he now receives the sacrament, he does not receive
nothing. For he progresses in continuing to communicate in
the body and blood of the Lord, and so his faith is kindled
and grows more and more, and is refreshed by spiritual food.
For while we live, faith is continually increased. And he who
outwardly receives the sacrament by true faith, not only receives the sign, but also, as we said, enjoys the thing itself.
Moreover, he obeys the Lord's institution and commandment, and with a joyful mind gives thanks for his redemption
and that of all mankind, and makes a faithful memorial to
the Lord's death, and gives a witness before the Church, of
whose body he is a member. Assurance is also given to those
who receive the sacrament that the body of the Lord was given
and his blood shed, not only for men in general, but particularly for every faithful communicant, to whom it is food
and drink unto eternal life.

Unbelievers Take the Sacrament to Their Judgment. But
he who comes to this sacred Table of the Lord without faith,
communicates only in the sacrament and does not receive the

substance of the sacrament whence comes life and salvation; and such men unworthily eat of the Lord's Table. Whoever eats the bread or drinks the cup of the Lord in an unworthy manner will be guilty of the body and blood of the Lord, and eats and drinks judgment upon himself (I Cor. 11:26-29). For when they do not approach with true faith, they dishonor the death of Christ, and therefore eat and drink condemnation to themselves.

The Presence of Christ in the Supper. We do not, therefore, so join the body of the Lord and his blood with the bread and wine as to say that the bread itself is the body of Christ except in a sacramental way; or that the body of Christ is hidden corporeally under the bread, so that it ought to be worshipped under the form of bread; or yet that whoever receives the sign, receives also the thing itself. The body of Christ is in heaven at the right hand of the Father; and therefore our hearts are to be lifted up on high, and not to be fixed on the bread, neither is the Lord to be worshipped in the bread. Yet the Lord is not absent from his Church when she celebrates the Supper. The sun, which is absent from us in the heavens, is notwithstanding effectually present among us. How much more is the Sun of Righteousness, Christ, although in his body he is absent from us in heaven, present with us, not corporeally, but spiritually, by his vivifying operation, and as he himself explained at his Last Supper that he would be present with us (John, chs. 14; 15; and 16). Whence it follows that we do not have the Supper without Christ, and yet at the same time have an unbloody and mystical Supper, as it was universally called by antiquity.

Other Purposes of the Lord's Supper. Moreover, we are admonished in the celebration of the Supper of the Lord to be mindful of whose body we have become members, and that, therefore, we may be of one mind with all the brethren, live a holy life, and not pollute ourselves with wickedness and strange religions; but, persevering in the true faith to the end of our life, strive to excel in holiness of life.

Preparation for the Supper. It is therefore fitting that when we would come to the Supper, we first examine ourselves according to the commandment of the apostle, especially as to the kind of faith we have, whether we believe that Christ has come to save sinners and to call them to repentance, and whether each man believes that he is in the number of those who have been delivered by Christ and saved; and whether he is determined to change his wicked life, to lead a holy life, and with the Lord's help to persevere in the true religion and in harmony with the brethren, and to give due thanks to God for his deliverance.

The Observance of the Supper with Both Bread and Wine. We think that rite, manner, or form of the Supper to be the most simple and excellent which comes nearest to the first institution of the Lord and to the apostles' doctrine. It consists in proclaiming the Word of God, in godly prayers, in the action of the Lord himself, and its repetition, in the eating of the Lord's body and drinking of his blood; in a fitting remembrance of the Lord's death, and a faithful thanksgiving; and in a holy fellowship in the union of the body of the Church.

We therefore disapprove of those who have taken from the faithful one species of the sacrament, namely, the Lord's cup. For these seriously offend against the institution of the Lord who says: " Drink ye all of this "; which he did not so expressly say of the bread.

We are not now discussing what kind of mass once existed among the fathers, whether it is to be tolerated or not. But this we say freely that the mass which is now used throughout the Roman Church has been abolished in our churches for many and very good reasons which, for brevity's sake, we do not now enumerate in detail. We certainly could not approve of making a wholesome action into a vain spectacle and a means of gaining merit, and of celebrating it for a price. Nor could we approve of saying that in it the priest is said to effect the very body of the Lord, and really to offer it for the remission of the sins of the living and the dead, and in addition, for the honor, veneration and remembrance of the saints in heaven, etc.

Chapter XXII. OF RELIGIOUS AND ECCLESIASTICAL MEETINGS

What Ought to Be Done in Meetings for Worship. Although it is permitted all men to read the Holy Scriptures privately at home, and by instruction to edify one another in the true religion, yet in order that the Word of God may be properly preached to the people, and prayers and supplication publicly made, also that the sacraments may be rightly administered, and that collections may be made for the poor and to pay the cost of all the Church's expenses, and in order to maintain social intercourse, it is most necessary that religious or Church gatherings be held. For it is certain that in the apostolic and primitive Church, there were such assemblies frequented by all the godly.

Meetings for Worship Not to Be Neglected. As many as spurn such meetings and stay away from them, despise true religion, and are to be urged by the pastors and godly magistrates to abstain from stubbornly absenting themselves from sacred assemblies.

Meetings Are Public. But Church meetings are not to be secret and hidden, but public and well attended, unless persecution by the enemies of Christ and the Church does not permit them to be public. For we know how under the tyranny of the Roman emperors the meetings of the primitive Church were held in secret places.

Decent Meeting Places. Moreover, the places where the faithful meet are to be decent, and in all respects fit for God's Church. Therefore, spacious buildings or temples are to be chosen, but they are to be purged of everything that is not fitting for a church. And everything is to be arranged for decorum, necessity, and godly decency, lest anything be lacking that is required for worship and the necessary works of the Church.

Modesty and Humility to Be Observed in Meetings. And as we believe that God does not dwell in temples made with hands, so we know that on account of God's Word and sacred use places dedicated to God and his worship are not profane, but holy, and that those who are present in them are to conduct themselves reverently and modestly, seeing that they are in a sacred place, in the presence of God and his holy angels.

The True Ornamentation of Sanctuaries. Therefore, all luxurious attire, all pride, and everything unbecoming to Christian humility, discipline and modesty, are to be banished from the sanctuaries and places of prayer of Christians. For the true ornamentation of churches does not consist in ivory, gold, and precious stones, but in the frugality, piety, and virtues of those who are in the Church. Let all things be done decently and in order in the church, and finally, let all things be done for edification.

Worship in the Common Language. Therefore, let all strange tongues keep silence in gatherings for worship, and let all things be set forth in a common language which is understood by the people gathered in that place.

Chapter XXIII. OF THE PRAYERS OF THE CHURCH, OF SINGING, AND OF CANONICAL HOURS

Common Language. It is true that a man is permitted to pray privately in any language that he understands, but public prayers in meetings for worship are to be made in the common language known to all. *Prayer.* Let all the prayers of the faithful be poured forth to God alone, through the mediation of Christ only, out of faith and love. The priesthood of Christ the Lord and true religion forbid the invocation of saints in heaven or to use them as intercessors. Prayer is to be made for magistracy, for kings, and all that are placed in authority, for ministers of the Church, and for all needs of churches. In calamities, especially of the Church, unceasing prayer is to be made both privately and publicly.

Free Prayer. Moreover, prayer is to be made voluntarily, without constraint or for any reward. Nor is it proper for prayer to be superstitiously restricted to one place, as if it were not permitted to pray anywhere except in a sanctuary. Neither is it necessary for public prayers to be the same in all churches with respect to form and time. Each Church is to exercise its own freedom. Socrates, in his history, says, " In all regions of the world you will not find two churches which wholly agree in prayer." (*Hist. ecclesiast.* V.22, 57.) The authors of this difference, I think, were those who were in charge of the Churches at particular times. Yet if they agree, it is to be highly commended and imitated by others.

The Method to Be Employed in Public Prayers. As in everything, so also in public prayers there is to be a standard lest they be excessively long and irksome. The greater part of meetings for worship is therefore to be given to evangelical teaching, and care is to be taken lest the congregation is wearied by too lengthy prayers and when they are to hear the preaching of the Gospel they either leave the meeting or, having been exhausted, want to do away with it altogether. To such people the sermon seems to be overlong, which otherwise is brief enough. And therefore it is appropriate for preachers to keep to a standard.

Singing. Likewise moderation is to be exercised where singing is used in a meeting for worship. That song which they call the Gregorian Chant has many foolish things in it; hence it is rightly rejected by many of our churches. If there are churches which have a true and proper sermon [8] but no singing, they ought not to be condemned. For all churches do not have the advantage of singing. And it is well known from testimonies of antiquity that the custom of singing is very old in the Eastern Churches whereas it was late when it was at length accepted in the West.

Canonical Hours. Antiquity knew nothing of canonical hours, that is, prayers arranged for certain hours of the day, and sung or recited by the Papists, as can be proved from their breviaries and by many arguments. But they also have not a few absurdities, of which I say nothing else; accordingly they are rightly omitted by churches which substitute in their place things that are beneficial for the whole Church of God.

Chapter XXIV. Of Holy Days, Fasts and the Choice of Foods

The Time Necessary for Worship. Although religion is not bound to time, yet it cannot be cultivated and exercised without a proper distribution and arrangement of time. Every Church, therefore, chooses for itself a certain time for public prayers, and for the preaching of the Gospel, and for the celebration of the sacraments; and no one is permitted to overthrow this appointment of the Church at his own pleasure. For unless some due time and leisure is given for the outward exercise of religion, without doubt men would be drawn away from it by their own affairs.

The Lord's Day. Hence we see that in the ancient churches there were not only certain set hours in the week appointed for meetings, but that also the Lord's Day itself, ever since the apostles' time, was set aside for them and for a holy rest, a practice now rightly preserved by our Churches for the sake of worship and love.

Superstition. In this connection we do not yield to the Jewish observance and to superstitions. For we do not believe that one day is any holier than another, or think that rest in itself is acceptable to God. Moreover, we celebrate the Lord's Day and not the Sabbath as a free observance.

The Festivals of Christ and the Saints. Moreover, if in Christian liberty the churches religiously celebrate the mem-

---

[8] The Latin has *orationem* which has been rendered as "prayer." But from the context it would seem that the word should be given its usual classical meaning of a "speech."

ory of the Lord's nativity, circumcision, passion, resurrection, and of his ascension into heaven, and the sending of the Holy Spirit upon his disciples, we approve of it highly. But we do not approve of feasts instituted for men and for saints. Holy days have to do with the first Table of the Law and belong to God alone. Finally, holy days which have been instituted for the saints and which we have abolished, have much that is absurd and useless, and are not to be tolerated. In the meantime, we confess that the remembrance of saints, at a suitable time and place, is to be profitably commended to the people in sermons, and the holy examples of the saints set forth to be imitated by all.

Fasting. Now, the more seriously the Church of Christ condemns surfeiting, drunkenness, and all kinds of lust and intemperance, so much the more strongly does it commend to us Christian fasting. For fasting is nothing else than the abstinence and moderation of the godly, and a discipline, care and chastisement of our flesh undertaken as a necessity for the time being, whereby we are humbled before God, and we deprive the flesh of its fuel so that it may the more willingly and easily obey the Spirit. Therefore, those who pay no attention to such things do not fast, but imagine that they fast if they stuff their stomachs once a day, and at a certain or prescribed time abstain from certain foods, thinking that by having done this work they please God and do something good. Fasting is an aid to the prayers of the saints and for all virtues. But as is seen in the books of the prophets, the fast of the Jews who fasted from food but not from wickedness did not please God.

Public and Private Fasting. Now there is a public and a private fasting. In olden times they celebrated public fasts in calamitous times and in the affliction of the Church. They abstained altogether from food till the evening, and spent all that time in holy prayers, the worship of God, and repentance. These differed little from mourning, and there is frequent mention of them in the Prophets and especially by Joel in ch. 2. Such a fast should be kept at this day, when the Church is in distress. Private fasts are undertaken by each one of us, as he feels himself withdrawn from the Spirit. For in this manner he withdraws the flesh from its fuel.

Characteristics of Fasting. All fasts ought to proceed from a free and willing spirit, and from genuine humility, and not feigned to gain the applause or favor of men, much less that a man should wish to merit righteousness by them. But let every one fast to this end, that he may deprive the flesh of its fuel in order that he may the more zealously serve God.

Lent. The fast of Lent is attested by antiquity but not at all in the writings of the apostles. Therefore it ought not, and cannot, be imposed on the faithful. It is certain that formerly there were various forms and customs of fasting. Hence, Irenaeus, a most ancient writer, says: " Some think that a fast should be observed one day only, others two days, but others more, and some forty days. This diversity in keeping this fast did not first begin in our times, but long before us by those, as I suppose, who did not simply keep to what had been delivered to them from the beginning, but afterwards fell into another custom either through negligence or ignorance " (*Fragm.* 3, ed. Stieren, I. 824 f.). Moreover, Socrates, the historian, says: " Because no ancient text is found concerning this matter, I think the apostles left this to every man's own judgment, that every one might do what is good without fear or constraint " (*Hist. ecclesiast.* V.22, 40).

Choice of food. Now concerning the choice of foods, we think that in fasting all things should be denied to the flesh whereby the flesh is made more insolent, and by which it is greatly pleased, and by which it is inflamed with desire whether by fish or meat or spices or delicacies and excellent wines. Moreover, we know that all the creatures of God were made for the use and service of men. All things which God made are good, and without distinction are to be used in the fear of God and with proper moderation (Gen. 2:15 f.). For the apostle says: " To the pure all things are pure " (Titus 1:15), and also: " Eat whatever is sold in the meat market without raising any question on the ground of conscience " (I Cor. 10:25). The same apostle calls the doctrine of those who teach to abstain from meats " the doctrine of demons "; for " God created foods to be received with thanksgiving by those who believe and know this truth that everything created by God is good, and nothing is to be rejected if it is received with thanksgiving " (I Tim. 4:1 ff.). The same apostle, in the epistle to the Colossians, reproves those who want to acquire a reputation for holiness by excessive abstinence (Col. 2:18 ff.).

Sects. Therefore we entirely disapprove of the Tatians and the Encratites, and all the disciples of Eustathius, against whom the Gangrian Synod was called.

Chapter XXV. OF CATECHIZING AND OF COMFORTING
AND VISITING THE SICK

Youth to Be Instructed in Godliness. The Lord enjoined
his ancient people to exercise the greatest care that young
people, even from infancy, be properly instructed. Moreover,
he expressly commanded in his law that they should teach
them, and that the mysteries of the sacraments should be explained. Now since it is well known from the writings of the
Evangelists and apostles that God has no less concern for the
youth of his new people, when he openly testifies and says:
" Let the children come to me; for to such belongs the kingdom of heaven " (Mark 10:14) , the pastors of the churches act
most wisely when they early and carefully catechize the youth,
laying the first grounds of faith, and faithfully teaching the
rudiments of our religion by expounding the Ten Commandments, the Apostles' Creed, the Lord's Prayer, and the doctrine of the sacraments, with other such principles and chief
heads of our religion. Here let the Church show her faith and
diligence in bringing the children to be catechized, desirous
and glad to have her children well instructed.

The Visitation of the Sick. Since men are never exposed to
more grievous temptations than when they are harassed by
infirmities, are sick and are weakened by diseases of both soul
and body, surely it is never more fitting for pastors of churches
to watch more carefully for the welfare of their flocks than in
such diseases and infirmities. Therefore let them visit the
sick soon, and let them be called in good time by the sick, if
the circumstance itself would have required it. Let them
comfort and confirm them in the true faith, and then arm
them against the dangerous suggestions of Satan. They should
also hold prayer for the sick in the home and, if need be,
prayers should also be made for the sick in the public meeting; and they should see that they happily depart this life.
We said above that we do not approve of the Popish visitation
of the sick with extreme unction because it is absurd and is
not approved by canonical Scriptures.

Chapter XXVI. OF THE BURIAL OF THE FAITHFUL,
AND OF THE CARE TO BE SHOWN FOR THE DEAD;
OF PURGATORY, AND THE APPEARING OF SPIRITS

The Burial of Bodies. As the bodies of the faithful are the
temples of the Holy Spirit which we truly believe will rise

again at the Last Day, Scriptures command that they be honorably and without superstition committed to the earth, and also that honorable mention be made of those saints who have fallen asleep in the Lord, and that all duties of familial piety be shown to those left behind, their widows and orphans. We do not teach that any other care be taken for the dead. Therefore, we greatly disapprove of the Cynics, who neglected the bodies of the dead or most carelessly and disdainfully cast them into the earth, never saying a good word about the deceased, or caring a bit about those whom they left behind them.

The Care for the Dead. On the other hand, we do not approve of those who are overly and absurdly attentive to the deceased; who, like the heathen, bewail their dead (although we do not blame that moderate mourning which the apostle permits in I Thess. 4:13, judging it to be inhuman not to grieve at all); and who sacrifice for the dead, and mumble certain prayers for pay, in order by such ceremonies to deliver their loved ones from the torments in which they are immersed by death, and then think they are able to liberate them by such incantations.

The State of the Soul Departed from the Body. For we believe that the faithful, after bodily death, go directly to Christ, and, therefore, do not need the eulogies and prayers of the living for the dead and their services. Likewise we believe that unbelievers are immediately cast into hell from which no exit is opened for the wicked by any services of the living.

Purgatory. But what some teach concerning the fire of purgatory is opposed to the Christian faith, namely, " I believe in the forgiveness of sins, and the life everlasting," and to the perfect purgation through Christ, and to these words of Christ our Lord: " Truly, truly, I say to you, he who hears my word and believes him who sent me, has eternal life; he shall not come into judgment, but has passed from death to life " (John 5:24). Again: " He who has bathed does not need to wash, except for his feet, but he is clean all over, and you are clean " (John 13:10).

The Apparition of Spirits. Now what is related of the spirits or souls of the dead sometimes appearing to those who are alive, and begging certain duties of them whereby they may be set free, we count those apparitions among the laughingstocks, crafts, and deceptions of the devil, who, as he can transform himself into an angel of light, so he strives either to overthrow the true faith or to call it into doubt. In the Old Testament the Lord forbade the seeking of the truth from the dead, and any sort of commerce with spirits. (Deut. 18:11.) Indeed, as evangelical truth declares, the glutton, being in torment, is denied a return to his brethren, as the divine oracle declares in the words: " They have Moses and the prophets; let them hear them. If they hear not Moses and the prophets, neither will they be convinced if some one should rise from the dead " (Luke 16:29 ff.).

Chapter XXVII. Of Rites, Ceremonies and Things Indifferent

Ceremonies and Rites. Unto the ancient people were given at one time certain ceremonies, as a kind of instruction for those who were kept under the law, as under a schoolmaster or tutor. But when Christ, the Deliverer, came and the law was abolished, we who believe are no more under the law (Rom. 6:14), and the ceremonies have disappeared; hence the apostles did not want to retain or to restore them in Christ's Church to such a degree that they openly testified that they did not wish to impose any burden upon the Church. Therefore, we would seem to be bringing in and restoring Judaism if we were to increase ceremonies and rites in Christ's Church according to the custom in the ancient Church. Hence, we by no means approve of the opinion of those who think that the Church of Christ must be held in check by many different rites, as if by some kind of training. For if the apostles did not want to impose upon Christian people ceremonies or rites which were appointed by God, who, I pray, in his right mind would obtrude upon them the inventions devised by man? The more the mass of rites is increased in the Church, the more is detracted not only from Christian liberty, but also from Christ, and from faith in him, as long as the people seek those things in ceremonies which they should seek in the only Son of God, Jesus Christ, through faith. Wherefore a few moderate and simple rites, that are not contrary to the Word of God, are sufficient for the godly.

Diversity of Rites. If different rites are found in churches, no one should think that for this reason the churches disagree. Socrates says: " It would be impossible to put together in writing all the rites of churches throughout cities and countries. No religion observes the same rites, even though it embraces the same doctrine concerning them. For those who are of the same faith disagree among themselves about rites." (*Hist. ecclesiast.* V.22, 30, 62.) This much says Socrates. And we, today, having in our churches different rites in the celebration of the Lord's Supper and in some other things, nevertheless do not disagree in doctrine and faith; nor is the unity and fellowship of our churches thereby rent asunder. For the churches have always used their liberty in such rites, as being things indifferent. We also do the same thing today.

Things Indifferent. But at the same time we admonish men to be on guard lest they reckon among things indifferent what are in fact not indifferent, as some are wont to regard the mass and the use of images in places of worship as things indifferent. " Indifferent," wrote Jerome to Augustine, " is that which is neither good nor bad, so that, whether you do it or not, you are neither just nor unjust." Therefore, when things indifferent are wrested to the confession of faith, they cease to be free; as Paul shows that it is lawful for a man to eat flesh if someone does not remind him that it was offered to idols; for then it is unlawful, because he who eats it seems to approve idolatry by eating it (I Cor. 8:9 ff.; 10:25 ff.).

Chapter XXVIII. Of the Possessions of the Church

The Possessions of the Church and Their Proper Use. The Church of Christ possesses riches through the munificence of princes and the liberality of the faithful who have given their means to the Church. For the Church has need of such resources and from ancient time has had resources for the maintenance of things necessary for the Church. Now the true use of the Church's wealth was, and is now, to maintain teaching in schools and in religious meetings, along with all the worship, rites, and buildings of the Church; finally, to maintain teachers, scholars, and ministers, with other necessary things, and especially for the succor and relief of the poor. *Management.* Moreover, God-fearing and wise men, noted for the management of domestic affairs, should be chosen to administer properly the Church's possessions.

The Misuse of the Church's Possessions. But if through misfortune or through the audacity, ignorance or avarice of some persons the Church's wealth is abused, it is to be restored to a sacred use by godly and wise men. For neither is an abuse, which is the greatest sacrilege, to be winked at.

Therefore, we teach that schools and institutions which have been corrupted in doctrine, worship and morals must be reformed, and that the relief of the poor must be arranged dutifully, wisely, and in good faith.

Chapter XXIX. OF CELIBACY, MARRIAGE AND THE MANAGEMENT OF DOMESTIC AFFAIRS

Single People. Those who have the gift of celibacy from heaven, so that from the heart or with their whole soul are pure and continent and are not aflame with passion, let them serve the Lord in that calling, as long as they feel endued with that divine gift; and let them not lift up themselves above others, but let them serve the Lord continuously in simplicity and humility (I Cor. 7:7 ff.). For such are more apt to attend to divine things than those who are distracted with the private affairs of a family. But if, again, the gift be taken away, and they feel a continual burning, let them call to mind the words of the apostle: " It is better to marry than to be aflame " (I Cor. 7:9).

Marriage. For marriage (which is the medicine of incontinency, and continency itself) was instituted by the Lord God himself, who blessed it most bountifully, and willed man and woman to cleave one to the other inseparably, and to live together in complete love and concord (Matt. 19:4 ff.). Whereupon we know that the apostle said: " Let marriage be held in honor among all, and let the marriage bed be undefiled." (Heb. 13:4.) And again: " If a girl marries, she does not sin " (I Cor. 7:28). *The sects.* We therefore condemn polygamy, and those who condemn second marriages.

How Marriages Are to Be Contracted. We teach that marriages are to be lawfully contracted in the fear of the Lord, and not against the laws which forbid certain degrees of consanguinity, lest the marriages should be incestuous. Let marriages be made with consent of the parents, or of those who take the place of parents, and above all for that purpose for which the Lord instituted marriages. Moreover, let them be kept holy with the utmost faithfulness, piety, love and purity of those joined together. Therefore let them guard against quarrels, dissensions, lust and adultery.

Matrimonial Forum. Let lawful courts be established in the Church, and holy judges who may care for marriages, and may repress all unchastity and shamefulness, and before whom matrimonial disputes may be settled.

The Rearing of Children. Children are to be brought up by the parents in the fear of the Lord; and parents are to provide for their children, remembering the saying of the apostle: " If anyone does not provide for his relatives, he has disowned the faith and is worse than an unbeliever " (I Tim. 5:8). But especially they should teach their children honest trades or professions by which they may support themselves. They should keep them from idleness and in all these things instill in them true faith in God, lest through a lack of confidence or too much security or filthy greed they become dissolute and achieve no success.

And it is most certain that those works which are done by parents in true faith by way of domestic duties and the management of their households are in God's sight holy and truly good works. They are no less pleasing to God than prayers, fasting and almsgiving. For thus the apostle has taught in his epistles, especially in those to Timothy and Titus. And with the same apostle we account the doctrine of those who forbid marriage or openly castigate or indirectly discredit it, as if it were not holy and pure, among the doctrine of demons.

We also detest an impure single life, the secret and open lusts and fornications of hypocrites pretending to be continent when they are the most incontinent of all. All these God will judge. We do not disapprove of riches or rich men, if they be godly and use their riches well. But we reject the sect of the Apostolicals, etc.[9]

Chapter XXX. Of the Magistracy

The Magistracy Is from God. Magistracy of every kind is instituted by God himself for the peace and tranquillity of the human race, and thus it should have the chief place in the world. If the magistrate is opposed to the Church, he can hinder and disturb it very much; but if he is a friend and even a member of the Church, he is a most useful and excellent member of it, who is able to benefit it greatly, and to assist it best of all.

The Duty of the Magistrate. The chief duty of the magistrate is to secure and preserve peace and public tranquillity. Doubtless he will never do this more successfully than when he is truly God-fearing and religious; that is to say, when,

---

9 The Apostolicals were followers of a religious fanatic, Gherardo Segarelli, of Parma, who in the thirteenth century wanted to restore the poverty of the apostolic life.

according to the example of the most holy kings and princes of the people of the Lord, he promotes the preaching of the truth and sincere faith, roots out lies and all superstition, together with all impiety and idolatry, and defends the Church of God. We certainly teach that the care of religion belongs especially to the holy magistrate.

Let him, therefore, hold the Word of God in his hands, and take care lest anything contrary to it is taught. Likewise let him govern the people entrusted to him by God with good laws made according to the Word of God, and let him keep them in discipline, duty and obedience. Let him exercise judgment by judging uprightly. Let him not respect any man's person or accept bribes. Let him protect widows, orphans and the afflicted. Let him punish and even banish criminals, impostors and barbarians. For he does not bear the sword in vain. (Rom. 13:4.)

Therefore, let him draw this sword of God against all malefactors, seditious persons, thieves, murderers, oppressors, blasphemers, perjured persons, and all those whom God has commanded him to punish and even to execute. Let him suppress stubborn heretics (who are truly heretics), who do not cease to blaspheme the majesty of God and to trouble, and even to destroy the Church of God.

War. And if it is necessary to preserve the safety of the people by war, let him wage war in the name of God; provided he has first sought peace by all means possible, and cannot save his people in any other way except by war. And when the magistrate does these things in faith, he serves God by those very works which are truly good, and receives a blessing from the Lord.

We condemn the Anabaptists, who, when they deny that a Christian may hold the office of a magistrate, deny also that a man may be justly put to death by the magistrate, or that the magistrate may wage war, or that oaths are to be rendered to a magistrate, and such like things.

The Duty of Subjects. For as God wants to effect the safety of his people by the magistrate, whom he has given to the world to be, as it were, a father, so all subjects are commanded to acknowledge this favor of God in the magistrate. Therefore let them honor and reverence the magistrate as the minister of God; let them love him, favor him, and pray for him as their father; and let them obey all his just and fair commands. Finally, let them pay all customs and taxes, and all other such dues faithfully and willingly. And if the public safety of the country and justice require it, and the magistrate of necessity wages war, let them even lay down their life and pour out their blood for the public safety and that of the magistrate. And let them do this in the name of God willingly, bravely and cheerfully. For he who opposes the magistrate provokes the severe wrath of God against himself.

Sects and Seditions. We, therefore, condemn all who are contemptuous of the magistrate — rebels, enemies of the state, seditious villains, finally, all who openly or craftily refuse to perform whatever duties they owe.

We beseech God, our most merciful Father in heaven, that he will bless the rulers of the people, and us, and his whole people, through Jesus Christ, our only Lord and Savior; to whom be praise and glory and thanksgiving, for all ages. Amen.

APPENDIX

THE NICENE CREED

WE BELIEVE in one God the Father Almighty, Maker of heaven and earth, and of all things visible and invisible;

And in one Lord Jesus Christ, the only-begotten Son of God, begotten of the Father before all worlds, God of God, Light of Light, Very God of Very God, begotten, not made, being of one substance with the Father by whom all things were made; who for us men, and for our salvation, came down from heaven, and was incarnate by the Holy Spirit of the Virgin Mary, and was made man, and was crucified also for us under Pontius Pilate. He suffered and was buried, and the third day he rose again according to the Scriptures, and ascended into heaven, and sitteth on the right hand of the Father. And he shall come again with glory to judge both the quick and the dead, whose kingdom shall have no end.

And we believe in the Holy Spirit, the Lord and Giver of Life, who proceedeth from the Father and the Son, who with the Father and the Son together is worshipped and glorified, who spoke by the prophets. And we believe one holy catholic and apostolic Church. We acknowledge one baptism for the remission of sins. And we look for the resurrection of the dead, and the life of the world to come. Amen.

THE APOSTLES' CREED

I BELIEVE in God the Father Almighty, Maker of heaven and earth;

And in Jesus Christ his only Son our Lord; who was conceived by the Holy Ghost, born of the Virgin Mary, suffered under Pontius Pilate, was crucified, dead, and buried; he descended into hell; the third day he rose again from the dead; he ascended into heaven, and sitteth on the right hand of God the Father Almighty; from thence he shall come to judge the quick and the dead.

I believe in the Holy Ghost; the holy catholic Church; the communion of saints; the forgiveness of sins; the resurrection of the body; and the life everlasting. Amen.

THE HEIDELBERG CATECHISM, 1563

Q. 1. *What is your only comfort, in life and in death?*

A. That I belong — body and soul, in life and in death — not to myself but to my faithful Savior, Jesus Christ, who at the cost of his own blood has fully paid for all my sins and has completely freed me from the dominion of the devil; that he protects me so well that without the will of my Father in heaven not a hair can fall from my head; indeed, that everything must fit his purpose for my salvation. Therefore, by his Holy Spirit, he also assures me of eternal life, and makes me wholeheartedly willing and ready from now on to live for him.

Q. 2. *How many things must you know that you may live and die in the blessedness of this comfort?*

A. Three. First, the greatness of my sin and wretchedness. Second, how I am freed from all my sins and their wretched consequences. Third, what gratitude I owe to God for such redemption.

Part I

OF MAN'S MISERY

Q. 3. *Where do you learn of your sin and its wretched consequences?*

A. From the Law of God.

Q. 4. *What does the Law of God require of us?*

A. Jesus Christ teaches this in a summary in Matthew 22:37-40:

"You shall love the Lord your God with all your heart, and with all your soul, and with all your mind. This is the great and first commandment. And a second is like it, you shall love your neighbor as yourself. On these two commandments depend all the law and the prophets." (Cf. Luke 10:27.)

Q. 5. *Can you keep all this perfectly?*

A. No, for by nature I am prone to hate God and my neighbor.

Q. 6. *Did God create man evil and perverse like this?*
A. No. On the contrary, God created man good and in his image, that is, in true righteousness and holiness, so that he might rightly know God his Creator, love him with his whole heart, and live with him in eternal blessedness, praising and glorifying him.

Q. 7. *Where, then, does this corruption of human nature come from?*
A. From the fall and disobedience of our first parents, Adam and Eve, in the Garden of Eden; whereby our human life is so poisoned that we are all conceived and born in the state of sin.

Q. 8. *But are we so perverted that we are altogether unable to do good and prone to do evil?*
A. Yes, unless we are born again through the Spirit of God.

Q. 9. *Is not God unjust in requiring of man in his Law what he cannot do?*
A. No, for God so created man that he could do it. But man, upon the instigation of the devil, by deliberate disobedience, has cheated himself and all his descendants out of these gifts.

Q. 10. *Will God let man get by with such disobedience and defection?*
A. Certainly not, for the wrath of God is revealed from heaven, both against our inborn sinfulness and our actual sins, and he will punish them according to his righteous judg-man, upon the instigation of the devil, by deliberate dis-everyone who does not abide by all things written in the book of the Law, and do them."

Q. 11. *But is not God also merciful?*
A. God is indeed merciful and gracious, but he is also righteous. It is his righteousness which requires that sin committed against the supreme majesty of God be punished with extreme, that is, with eternal punishment of body and soul.

Part II

Of Man's Redemption

Q. 12. *Since, then, by the righteous judgment of God we have deserved temporal and eternal punishment, how may we escape this punishment, come again to grace, and be reconciled to God?*

A. God wills that his righteousness be satisfied; therefore, payment in full must be made to his righteousness, either by ourselves or by another.

Q. 13. *Can we make this payment ourselves?*

A. By no means. On the contrary, we increase our debt each day.

Q. 14. *Can any mere creature make the payment for us?*

A. No one. First of all, God does not want to punish any other creature for man's debt. Moreover, no mere creature can bear the burden of God's eternal wrath against sin and redeem others from it.

Q. 15. *Then, what kind of mediator and redeemer must we seek?*

A. One who is a true and righteous man and yet more powerful than all creatures, that is, one who is at the same time true God.

Q. 16. *Why must he be a true and righteous man?*

A. Because God's righteousness requires that man who has sinned should make reparation for sin, but the man who is himself a sinner cannot pay for others.

Q. 17. *Why must he at the same time be true God?*

A. So that by the power of his divinity he might bear as a man the burden of God's wrath, and recover for us and restore to us righteousness and life.

Q. 18. *Who is this mediator who is at the same time true God and a true and perfectly righteous man?*

A. Our Lord Jesus Christ, who is freely given to us for complete redemption and righteousness.

Q. 19. *Whence do you know this?*
A. From the holy gospel, which God himself revealed in the beginning in the Garden of Eden, afterward proclaimed through the holy patriarchs and prophets and foreshadowed through the sacrifices and other rites of the Old Covenant, and finally fulfilled through his own well-beloved Son.

LORD'S DAY 7

Q. 20. *Will all men, then, be saved through Christ as they became lost through Adam?*
A. No. Only those who, by true faith, are incorporated into him and accept all his benefits.

Q. 21. *What is true faith?*
A. It is not only a certain knowledge by which I accept as true all that God has revealed to us in his Word, but also a wholehearted trust which the Holy Spirit creates in me through the gospel, that, not only to others, but to me also God has given the forgiveness of sins, everlasting righteousness and salvation, out of sheer grace solely for the sake of Christ's saving work.

Q. 22. *What, then, must a Christian believe?*
A. All that is promised us in the gospel, a summary of which is taught us in the articles of the Apostles' Creed, our universally acknowledged confession of faith.

Q. 23. *What are these articles?*
A. I believe in God the Father Almighty, Maker of heaven and earth;

And in Jesus Christ, his only-begotten Son, our Lord; who was conceived by the Holy Spirit, born of the Virgin Mary; suffered under Pontius Pilate, was crucified, dead, and buried; he descended into hell; the third day he rose again from the dead; he ascended into heaven, and sits at the right hand of God the Father Almighty; from thence he shall come to judge the living and the dead.

I believe in the Holy Spirit; the holy catholic Church; the communion of saints; the forgiveness of sins; the resurrection of the body; and the life everlasting.

Q. 24. *How are these articles divided?*

A. Into three parts: The first concerns God *the Father* and our *creation;* the second, God *the Son* and our *redemption;* and the third, God *the Holy Spirit* and our *sanctification.*

Q. 25. *Since there is only one Divine Being, why do you speak of three, Father, Son, and Holy Spirit?*

A. Because God has thus revealed himself in his Word, that these three distinct persons are the one, true, eternal God.

OF GOD THE FATHER

Q. 26. *What do you believe when you say: " I believe in God the Father Almighty, Maker of heaven and earth "?*

A. That the eternal Father of our Lord Jesus Christ, who out of nothing created heaven and earth with all that is in them, who also upholds and governs them by his eternal counsel and providence, is for the sake of Christ his Son my God and my Father. I trust in him so completely that I have no doubt that he will provide me with all things necessary for body and soul. Moreover, whatever evil he sends upon me in this troubled life he will turn to my good, for he is able to do it, being almighty God, and is determined to do it, being a faithful Father.

Q. 27. *What do you understand by the providence of God?*

A. The almighty and ever-present power of God whereby he still upholds, as it were by his own hand, heaven and earth together with all creatures, and rules in such a way that leaves and grass, rain and drought, fruitful and unfruitful years, food and drink, health and sickness, riches and poverty, and everything else, come to us not by chance but by his fatherly hand.

Q. 28. *What advantage comes from acknowledging God's creation and providence?*

A. We learn that we are to be patient in adversity, grateful in the midst of blessing, and to trust our faithful God and Father for the future, assured that no creature shall separate

us from his love, since all creatures are so completely in his
hand that without his will they cannot even move.

OF GOD THE SON

Q. 29. *Why is the Son of God called* JESUS, *which means*
SAVIOR?
A. Because he saves us from our sins, and because salva-
tion is to be sought or found in no other.

Q. 30. *Do those who seek their salvation and well-being
from saints, by their own efforts, or by other means really believe in the only Savior Jesus?*
A. No. Rather, by such actions they deny Jesus, the only
Savior and Redeemer, even though they boast of belonging to
him. It therefore follows that either Jesus is not a perfect
Savior, or those who receive this Savior with true faith must
possess in him all that is necessary for their salvation.

Q. 31. *Why is he called* CHRIST, *that is, the* ANOINTED ONE?
A. Because he is ordained by God the Father and anointed
with the Holy Spirit to be *our chief Prophet* and *Teacher,*
fully revealing to us the secret purpose and will of God concerning our redemption; to be *our only High Priest,* having
redeemed us by the one sacrifice of his body and ever inter-
ceding for us with the Father; and to be *our eternal King,*
governing us by his Word and Spirit, and defending and sus-
taining us in the redemption he has won for us.

Q. 32. *But why are you called a Christian?*
A. Because through faith I share in Christ and thus in his
anointing, so that I may confess his name, offer myself a living sacrifice of gratitude to him, and fight against sin and the
devil with a free and good conscience throughout this life
and hereafter rule with him in eternity over all creatures.

Q. 33. *Why is he called* GOD'S ONLY-BEGOTTEN SON, *since
we also are God's children?*

A. Because Christ alone is God's own eternal Son, whereas we are accepted for his sake as children of God by grace.

Q. 34. *Why do you call him* OUR LORD?
A. Because, not with gold or silver but at the cost of his blood, he has redeemed us body and soul from sin and all the dominion of the devil, and has bought us for his very own.

[handwritten: Follows the Lutheran Larger Catechism here (cf. Second Article)]

LORD'S DAY 14

Q. 35. *What is the meaning of: " Conceived by the Holy Spirit, born of the Virgin Mary "*?
A. That the eternal Son of God, who is and remains true and eternal God, took upon himself our true manhood from the flesh and blood of the Virgin Mary through the action of the Holy Spirit, so that he might also be the true seed of David, like his fellow men in all things, except for sin.

Q. 36. *What benefit do you receive from the holy conception and birth of Christ?*
A. That he is our Mediator, and that, in God's sight, he covers over with his innocence and perfect holiness the sinfulness in which I have been conceived.

LORD'S DAY 15

Q. 37. *What do you understand by the word " suffered "?*
A. That throughout his life on earth, but especially at the end of it, he bore in body and soul the wrath of God against the sin of the whole human race, so that by his suffering, as the only expiatory sacrifice, he might redeem our body and soul from everlasting damnation, and might obtain for us God's grace, righteousness, and eternal life.

[handwritten: His life was one of suffering?]

Q. 38. *Why did he suffer " under Pontius Pilate " as his judge?*
A. That he, being innocent, might be condemned by an earthly judge, and thereby set us free from the judgment of God which, in all its severity, ought to fall upon us.

Q. 39. *Is there something more in his having been crucified than if he had died some other death?*

A. Yes, for by this I am assured that he took upon himself the curse which lay upon me, because the death of the cross was cursed by God.

LORD'S DAY 16

Q. 40. *Why did Christ have to suffer " death "?*
A. Because the righteousness and truth of God are such that nothing else could make reparation for our sins except the death of the Son of God.

Q. 41. *Why was he " buried "?*
A. To confirm the fact that he was really dead.

Q. 42. *Since, then, Christ died for us, why must we also die?*
A. Our death is not a reparation for our sins, but only a dying to sin and an entering into eternal life.

This Conflicts with the 2nd Helvetic?

Q. 43. *What further benefit do we receive from the sacrifice and death of Christ on the cross?*
A. That by his power our old self is crucified, put to death, and buried with him, so that the evil passions of our mortal bodies may reign in us no more, but that we may offer ourselves to him as a sacrifice of thanksgiving.

Q. 44. *Why is there added: " He descended into hell "?*
A. That in my severest tribulations I may be assured that Christ my Lord has redeemed me from hellish anxieties and torment by the unspeakable anguish, pains, and terrors which he suffered in his soul both on the cross and before.

So Christ did not go to Hell, but experienced Hell on earth.

LORD'S DAY 17

Q. 45. *What benefit do we receive from " the resurrection " of Christ?*
A. First, by his resurrection he has overcome death that he might make us share in the righteousness which he has obtained for us through his death. Second, we too are now raised by his power to a new life. Third, the resurrection of Christ is a sure pledge to us of our blessed resurrection.

LORD'S DAY 18

Q. 46. *How do you understand the words: " He ascended into heaven "?*

A. That Christ was taken up from the earth into heaven before the eyes of his disciples and remains there on our behalf until he comes again to judge the living and the dead.

Q. 47. *Then, is not Christ with us unto the end of the world, as he has promised us?*
A. Christ is true man and true God. As a man he is no longer on earth, but in his divinity, majesty, grace, and Spirit, he is never absent from us.

[handwritten: Lutherans would dispute this]

Q. 48. *But are not the two natures in Christ separated from each other in this way, if the humanity is not wherever the divinity is?*
A. Not at all; for since divinity is incomprehensible and everywhere present, it must follow that the divinity is indeed beyond the bounds of the humanity which it has assumed, and is nonetheless ever in that humanity as well, and remains personally united to it.

[handwritten: Reformed Response to the Lutherans]

Q. 49. *What benefit do we receive from Christ's ascension into heaven?*
A. First, that he is our Advocate in the presence of his Father in heaven. Second, that we have our flesh in heaven as a sure pledge that he, as the Head, will also take us, his members, up to himself. Third, that he sends us his Spirit as a counterpledge by whose power we seek what is above, where Christ is, sitting at the right hand of God, and not things that are on earth.

LORD'S DAY 19

Q. 50. *Why is there added: " And sits at the right hand of God "?*
A. Because Christ ascended into heaven so that he might manifest himself there as the Head of his Church, through whom the Father governs all things.

Q. 51. *What benefit do we receive from this glory of Christ, our Head?*
A. First, that through his Holy Spirit he pours out heavenly gifts upon us, his members. Second, that by his power he defends and supports us against all our enemies.

Q. 52. *What comfort does the return of Christ " to judge the living and the dead " give you?*

A. That in all affliction and persecution I may await with head held high the very Judge from heaven who has already submitted himself to the judgment of God for me and has removed all the curse from me; that he will cast all his enemies and mine into everlasting condemnation, but he shall take me, together with all his elect, to himself into heavenly joy and glory.

The Holy Spirit

lord's day 20

Q. 53. *What do you believe concerning "the Holy Spirit"?*

A. First, that, with the Father and the Son, he is equally eternal God; second, that God's Spirit is also given to me, preparing me through a true faith to share in Christ and all his benefits, that he comforts me and will abide with me forever.

lord's day 21

Q. 54. *What do you believe concerning "the Holy Catholic Church"?*

A. I believe that, from the beginning to the end of the world, and from among the whole human race, the Son of God, by his Spirit and his Word, gathers, protects, and preserves for himself, in the unity of the true faith, a congregation chosen for eternal life. Moreover, I believe that I am and forever will remain a living member of it.

Q. 55. *What do you understand by "the communion of saints"?*

A. First, that believers one and all, as partakers of the Lord Christ, and all his treasures and gifts, shall share in one fellowship. Second, that each one ought to know that he is obliged to use his gifts freely and with joy for the benefit and welfare of other members.

Q. 56. *What do you believe concerning "the forgiveness of sins"?*

A. That, for the sake of Christ's reconciling work, God will no more remember my sins or the sinfulness with which I have to struggle all my life long; but that he graciously imparts to me the righteousness of Christ so that I may never come into condemnation.

Q. 57. *What comfort does " the resurrection of the body "
give you?*

A. That after this life my soul shall be immediately taken
up to Christ, its Head, and that this flesh of mine, raised by
the power of Christ, shall be reunited with my soul, and be
conformed to the glorious body of Christ.

Q. 58. *What comfort does the article concerning " the life
everlasting " give you?*

A. That, since I now feel in my heart the beginning of
eternal joy, I shall possess, after this life, perfect blessedness,
which no eye has seen, nor ear heard, nor the heart of man
conceived, and thereby praise God forever.

Q. 59. *But how does it help you now that you believe all
this?*

A. That I am righteous in Christ before God, and an heir
of eternal life.

Q. 60. *How are you righteous before God?*

A. Only by true faith in Jesus Christ. In spite of the fact
that my conscience accuses me that I have grievously sinned
against all the commandments of God, and have not kept any
one of them, and that I am still ever prone to all that is evil,
nevertheless, God, without any merit of my own, out of pure
grace, grants me the benefits of the perfect expiation of
Christ, imputing to me his righteousness and holiness as if I
had never committed a single sin or had ever been sinful,
having fulfilled myself all the obedience which Christ has carried out for me, if only I accept such favor with a trusting
heart.

Q. 61. *Why do you say that you are righteous by faith
alone?*

A. Not because I please God by virtue of the worthiness
of my faith, but because the satisfaction, righteousness, and
holiness of Christ alone are my righteousness before God,
and because I can accept it and make it mine in no other way
than by faith alone.

Q. 62. *But why cannot our good works be our righteousness before God, or at least a part of it?*

A. Because the righteousness which can stand before the judgment of God must be absolutely perfect and wholly in conformity with the divine Law. But even our best works in this life are all imperfect and defiled with sin.

Q. 63. *Will our good works merit nothing, even when it is God's purpose to reward them in this life, and in the future life as well?*

A. This reward is not given because of merit, but out of grace.

Q. 64. *But does not this teaching make people careless and sinful?*

A. No, for it is impossible for those who are ingrafted into Christ by true faith not to bring forth the fruit of gratitude.

THE HOLY SACRAMENTS

Q. 65. *Since, then, faith alone makes us share in Christ and all his benefits, where does such faith originate?*

A. The Holy Spirit creates it in our hearts by the preaching of the holy gospel, and confirms it by the use of the holy Sacraments.

Q. 66. *What are the Sacraments?*

A. They are visible, holy signs and seals instituted by God in order that by their use he may the more fully disclose and seal to us the promise of the gospel, namely, that because of the one sacrifice of Christ accomplished on the cross he graciously grants us the forgiveness of sins and eternal life.

Q. 67. *Are both the Word and the Sacraments designed to direct our faith to the one sacrifice of Jesus Christ on the cross as the only ground of our salvation?*

A. Yes, indeed, for the Holy Spirit teaches in the gospel and confirms by the holy Sacraments that our whole salvation is rooted in the one sacrifice of Christ offered for us on the cross.

Q. 68. *How many Sacraments has Christ instituted in the New Testament?*

A. Two, holy Baptism and the holy Supper.

HOLY BAPTISM

LORD'S DAY 26

Q. 69. *How does holy Baptism remind and assure you that the one sacrifice of Christ on the cross avails for you?*

A. In this way: Christ has instituted this external washing with water and by it has promised that I am as certainly washed with his blood and Spirit from the uncleanness of my soul and from all my sins, as I am washed externally with water which is used to remove the dirt from my body.

Q. 70. *What does it mean to be washed with the blood and Spirit of Christ?*

A. It means to have the forgiveness of sins from God, through grace, for the sake of Christ's blood which he shed for us in his sacrifice on the cross, and also to be renewed by the Holy Spirit and sanctified as members of Christ, so that we may more and more die unto sin and live in a consecrated and blameless way.

Q. 71. *Where has Christ promised that we are as certainly washed with his blood and Spirit as with the water of baptism?*

A. In the institution of Baptism which runs thus: " Go therefore and make disciples of all nations, baptizing them in the name of the Father and of the Son and of the Holy Spirit." " He who believes and is baptized will be saved: but he who does not believe will be condemned." This promise is also repeated where the Scriptures call baptism " the water of rebirth " and the washing away of sins.

LORD'S DAY 27

Q. 72. *Does merely the outward washing with water itself wash away sins?*

A. No; for only the blood of Jesus Christ and the Holy Spirit cleanse us from all sins.

Q. 73. *Then why does the Holy Spirit call baptism the water of rebirth and the washing away of sins?*

A. God does not speak in this way except for a strong reason. Not only does he teach us by Baptism that just as the dirt of the body is taken away by water, so our sins are removed by the blood and Spirit of Christ; but more important still, by the divine pledge and sign he wishes to assure us that we are just as truly washed from our sins spiritually as our bodies are washed with water.

Q. 74. *Are infants also to be baptized?*

A. Yes, because they, as well as their parents, are included in the covenant and belong to the people of God. Since both redemption from sin through the blood of Christ and the gift of faith from the Holy Spirit are promised to these children no less than to their parents, infants are also by baptism, as a sign of the covenant, to be incorporated into the Christian church and distinguished from the children of unbelievers. This was done in the Old Covenant by circumcision. In the New Covenant baptism has been instituted to take its place.

The Holy Supper

LORD'S DAY 28

Q. 75. *How are you reminded and assured in the holy Supper that you participate in the one sacrifice of Christ on the cross and in all his benefits?*

A. In this way: Christ has commanded me and all believers to eat of this broken bread, and to drink of this cup in remembrance of him. He has thereby promised that his body was offered and broken on the cross for me, and his blood was shed for me, as surely as I see with my eyes that the bread of the Lord is broken for me, and that the cup is shared with me. Also, he has promised that he himself as certainly feeds and nourishes my soul to everlasting life with his crucified body and shed blood as I receive from the hand of the minister and actually taste the bread and the cup of the Lord which are given to me as sure signs of the body and blood of Christ.

Q. 76. *What does it mean to eat the crucified body of Christ and to drink his shed blood?*

A. It is not only to embrace with a trusting heart the whole passion and death of Christ, and by it to receive the forgiveness of sins and eternal life. In addition, it is to be so united more and more to his blessed body by the Holy Spirit dwelling both in Christ and in us that, although he is in heaven and we are on earth, we are nevertheless flesh of his flesh and bone of his bone, always living and being governed by one Spirit, as the members of our bodies are governed by one soul.

Q. 77. *Where has Christ promised that he will feed and nourish believers with his body and blood just as surely as they eat of this broken bread and drink of this cup?*
A. In the institution of the holy Supper which reads: The Lord Jesus on the night when He was betrayed took bread, and when He had given thanks, He broke it, and said, " this is My body which is for you. Do this in remembrance of Me." In the same way also the cup, after supper, saying, " this cup is the new covenant in My blood. Do this, as often as you drink it, in remembrance of Me." For as often as you eat this bread and drink the cup, you proclaim the Lord's death until He comes.
This promise is also repeated by the apostle Paul: When we bless " the cup of blessing," is it not a means of sharing in the blood of Christ? When we break the bread, is it not a means of sharing the body of Christ? Because there is one loaf, we, many as we are, are one body; for it is one loaf of which we all partake.

LORD'S DAY 29

Q. 78. *Do the bread and wine become the very body and blood of Christ?*
A. No, for as the water in baptism is not changed into the blood of Christ, nor becomes the washing away of sins by itself, but is only a divine sign and confirmation of it, so also in the Lord's Supper the sacred bread does not become the body of Christ itself, although, in accordance with the nature and usage of sacraments, it is called the body of Christ.

Q. 79. *Then why does Christ call the bread his body, and the cup his blood, or the New Covenant in his blood, and why does the apostle Paul call the Supper " a means of sharing " in the body and blood of Christ?*
A. Christ does not speak in this way except for a strong reason. He wishes to teach us by it that as bread and wine sus-

tain this temporal life so his crucified body and shed blood are the true food and drink of our souls for eternal life. Even more, he wishes to assure us by this visible sign and pledge that we come to share in his true body and blood through the working of the Holy Spirit as surely as we receive with our mouth these holy tokens in remembrance of him, and that all his sufferings and his death are our own as certainly as if we had ourselves suffered and rendered satisfaction in our own persons.

LORD'S DAY 30

Q. 80. *What difference is there between the Lord's Supper and the papal Mass?*
A. The Lord's Supper testifies to us that we have complete forgiveness of all our sins through the one sacrifice of Jesus Christ which he himself has accomplished on the cross once for all; and that through the Holy Spirit we are incorporated into Christ, who is now in heaven with his true body at the right hand of the Father and is there to be worshiped. But the Mass teaches that the living and the dead do not have forgiveness of sins through the sufferings of Christ unless Christ is again offered for them daily by the priest; (and that Christ is bodily under the form of bread and wine and is therefore to be worshiped in them). Therefore the Mass is fundamentally a complete denial of the once for all sacrifice and passion of Jesus Christ (and as such an idolatry to be condemned).
NOTE: This question is omitted in the first edition. The sections in parentheses were added for the first time in the third edition.

Q. 81. *Who ought to come to the table of the Lord?*
A. Those who are displeased with themselves for their sins, and who nevertheless trust that these sins have been forgiven them and that their remaining weakness is covered by the passion and death of Christ, and who also desire more and more to strengthen their faith and improve their life. The impenitent and hypocrites, however, eat and drink judgment to themselves.

Q. 82. *Should those who show themselves to be unbelievers and enemies of God by their confession and life be admitted to this Supper?*

A. No, for then the covenant of God would be profaned and his wrath provoked against the whole congregation. According to the ordinance of Christ and his apostles, therefore, the Christian church is under obligation, by the office of the keys, to exclude such persons until they amend their lives.

Q. 83. *What is the office of the keys?*
A. The preaching of the holy gospel and Christian discipline. By these two means the kingdom of heaven is opened to believers and shut against unbelievers.

Q. 84. *How is the kingdom of heaven opened and shut by the preaching of the holy gospel?*
A: In this way: The kingdom of heaven is opened when it is proclaimed and openly testified to believers, one and all, according to the command of Christ, that as often as they accept the promise of the gospel with true faith all their sins are truly forgiven them by God for the sake of Christ's gracious work. On the contrary, the wrath of God and eternal condemnation fall upon all unbelievers and hypocrites as long as they do not repent. It is according to this witness of the gospel that God will judge the one and the other in this life and in the life to come.

Q. 85. *How is the kingdom of heaven shut and opened by Christian discipline?*
A. In this way: Christ commanded that those who bear the Christian name in an unchristian way either in doctrine or in life should be given brotherly admonition. If they do not give up their errors or evil ways, notification is given to the church or to those ordained for this by the church. Then, if they do not change after this warning, they are forbidden to partake of the holy Sacraments and are thus excluded from the communion of the church and by God himself from the kingdom of Christ. However, if they promise and show real amendment, they are received again as members of Christ and of the church.

Part III

THANKFULNESS

Q. 86. *Since we are redeemed from our sin and its
wretched consequences by grace through Christ without any
merit of our own, why must we do good works?*

A. Because just as Christ has redeemed us with his blood
he also renews us through his Holy Spirit according to his
own image, so that with our whole life we may show ourselves grateful to God for his goodness and that he may be
glorified through us; and further, so that we ourselves may
be assured of our faith by its fruits and by our reverent be-
havior may win our neighbors to Christ.

Q. 87. *Can those who do not turn to God from their ungrateful, impenitent life be saved?*

A. Certainly not! Scripture says, " Surely you know that
the unjust will never come into possession of the kingdom of
God. Make no mistake; no fornicator or idolater, none who
are guilty either of adultery or of homosexual perversion, no
thieves or grabbers or drunkards or slanderers or swindlers,
will possess the kingdom of God."

Q. 88. *How many parts are there to the true repentance
or conversion of man?*

A. Two: the dying of the old self and the birth of the new.

Q. 89. *What is the dying of the old self?*

A. Sincere sorrow over our sins and more and more to
hate them and to flee from them.

Q. 90. *What is the birth of the new man?*

A. Complete joy in God through Christ and a strong desire to live according to the will of God in all good works.

Q. 91. *But what are good works?*

A. Only those which are done out of true faith, in accordance with the Law of God, and for his glory, and not those
based on our own opinion or on the traditions of men.

Q. 92. *What is the Law of God?*
A. God spoke all these words saying:

FIRST COMMANDMENT

" I am the Lord your God, who brought you out of the land of Egypt, out of the house of bondage. You shall have no other gods before Me."

SECOND COMMANDMENT

" You shall not make yourself a graven image, or any likeness of anything that is in heaven above, or that is in the earth beneath, or that is in the water under the earth; you shall not bow down to them or serve them; for I the Lord your God am a jealous God, visiting the iniquity of the fathers upon the children to the third and the fourth generation of those who hate Me, but showing steadfast love to thousands of those who love Me and keep My commandments."

THIRD COMMANDMENT

" You shall not take the name of the Lord your God in vain; for the Lord will not hold him guiltless who takes His name in vain."

FOURTH COMMANDMENT

" Remember the sabbath day, to keep it holy. Six days you shall labor, and do all your work; but the seventh day is a sabbath to the Lord your God; in it you shall not do any work, you, or your son, or your daughter, your manservant, or your maidservant, or your cattle, or the sojourner who is within your gates; for in six days the Lord made heaven and earth, the sea, and all that is in them, and rested the seventh day; therefore the Lord blessed the sabbath day and hallowed it."

FIFTH COMMANDMENT

" Honor your father and your mother, that your days may be long in the land which the Lord your God gives you."

SIXTH COMMANDMENT

" You shall not kill."

SEVENTH COMMANDMENT

" You shall not commit adultery."

EIGHTH COMMANDMENT

" You shall not steal."

" You shall not bear false witness against your neighbor."

"You shall not covet your neighbor's house; you shall not
covet your neighbor's wife, or his manservant, or his maidservant, or his ox, or his ass, or anything that is your neighbor's."

Q. 93. *How are these commandments divided?*
A. Into two tables, the first of which teaches us in four
commandments how we ought to live in relation to God; the
other, in six commandments, what we owe to our neighbor.

Q. 94. *What does the Lord require in the first commandment?*
A. That I must avoid and flee all idolatry, sorcery, en-
chantments, invocation of saints or other creatures because
of the risk of losing my salvation. Indeed, I ought properly to
acknowledge the only true God, trust in him alone, in humility and patience expect all good from him only, and love,
fear and honor him with my whole heart. In short, I should
rather turn my back on all creatures than do the least thing
against his will.

Q. 95. *What is idolatry?*
A. It is to imagine or possess something in which to put
one's trust in place of or beside the one true God who has revealed himself in his Word.

LORD'S DAY 35

Q. 96. *What does God require in the second commandment?*
A. That we should not represent him or worship him in
any other manner than he has commanded in his Word.

Q. 97. *Should we, then, not make any images at all?*
A. God cannot and should not be pictured in any way. As
for creatures, although they may indeed be portrayed, God
forbids making or having any likeness of them in order to
worship them, or to use them to serve him.

Q. 98. *But may not pictures be tolerated in churches in
place of books for unlearned people?*

A. No, for we must not try to be wiser than God who does not want his people to be taught by means of lifeless idols, but through the living preaching of his Word.

LORD'S DAY 36

Q. 99. *What is required in the third commandment?*
A. That we must not profane or abuse the name of God by cursing, by perjury, or by unnecessary oaths. Nor are we to participate in such horrible sins by keeping quiet and thus giving silent consent. In a word, we must not use the holy name of God except with fear and reverence so that he may be rightly confessed and addressed by us, and be glorified in all our words and works.

Q. 100. *Is it, therefore, so great a sin to blaspheme God's name by cursing and swearing that God is also angry with those who do not try to prevent and forbid it as much as they can?*
A. Yes, indeed; for no sin is greater or provokes his wrath more than the profaning of his name. That is why he commanded it to be punished with death.

LORD'S DAY 37

Q. 101. *But may we not swear oaths by the name of God in a devout manner?*
A. Yes, when the civil authorities require it of their subjects, or when it is otherwise needed to maintain and promote fidelity and truth, to the glory of God and the welfare of our neighbor. Such oath-taking is grounded in God's Word and has therefore been rightly used by God's people under the Old and New Covenants.

Q. 102. *May we also swear by the saints or other creatures?*
A. No; for a lawful oath is a calling upon God, as the only searcher of hearts, to bear witness to the truth, and to punish me if I swear falsely. No creature deserves such honor.

LORD'S DAY 38

Q. 103. *What does God require in the fourth commandment?*
A. First, that the ministry of the gospel and Christian education be maintained, and that I diligently attend church, es-

pecially on the Lord's day, to hear the Word of God, to participate in the holy Sacraments, to call publicly upon the Lord, and to give Christian service to those in need. Second, that I cease from my evil works all the days of my life, allow the Lord to work in me through his Spirit, and thus begin in this life the eternal Sabbath.

LORD'S DAY 39

Q. 104. *What does God require in the fifth commandment?*

A. That I show honor, love, and faithfulness to my father and mother and to all who are set in authority over me; that I submit myself with respectful obedience to all their careful instruction and discipline; and that I also bear patiently their failures, since it is God's will to govern us by their hand.

LORD'S DAY 40

Q. 105. *What does God require in the sixth commandment?*

A. That I am not to abuse, hate, injure, or kill my neighbor, either with thought, or by word or gesture, much less by deed, whether by myself or through another, but to lay aside all desire for revenge; and that I do not harm myself or willfully expose myself to danger. This is why the authorities are armed with the means to prevent murder.

Q. 106. *But does this commandment speak only of killing?*

A. In forbidding murder God means to teach us that he abhors the root of murder, which is envy, hatred, anger, and desire for revenge, and that he regards all these as hidden murder.

Q. 107. *Is it enough, then, if we do not kill our neighbor in any of these ways?*

A. No; for when God condemns envy, hatred, and anger, he requires us to love our neighbor as ourselves, to show patience, peace, gentleness, mercy and friendliness toward him, to prevent injury to him as much as we can, also to do good to our enemies.

LORD'S DAY 41

Q. 108. *What does the seventh commandment teach us?*

A. That all unchastity is condemned by God, and that we

should therefore detest it from the heart, and live chaste and disciplined lives, whether in holy wedlock or in single life.

Q. 109. *Does God forbid nothing more than adultery and such gross sins in this commandment?*

A. Since both our body and soul are a temple of the Holy Spirit, it is his will that we keep both pure and holy. Therefore he forbids all unchaste actions, gestures, words, thoughts, desires, and whatever may excite another person to them.

LORD'S DAY 42

Q. 110. *What does God forbid in the eighth commandment?*

A. He forbids not only the theft and robbery which civil authorities punish, but God also labels as theft all wicked tricks and schemes by which we seek to get for ourselves our neighbor's goods, whether by force or under the pretext of right, such as false weights and measures, deceptive advertising or merchandising, counterfeit money, exorbitant interest, or any other means forbidden by God. He also forbids all greed and misuse and waste of his gifts.

Q. 111. *But what does God require of you in this commandment?*

A. That I work for the good of my neighbor wherever I can and may, deal with him as I would have others deal with me, and do my work well so that I may be able to help the poor in their need.

LORD'S DAY 43

Q. 112. *What is required in the ninth commandment?*

A. That I do not bear false witness against anyone, twist anyone's words, be a gossip or a slanderer, or condemn anyone lightly without a hearing. Rather I am required to avoid, under penalty of God's wrath, all lying and deceit as the works of the devil himself. In judicial and all other matters I am to love the truth, and to speak and confess it honestly. Indeed, insofar as I am able, I am to defend and promote my neighbor's good name.

LORD'S DAY 44

Q. 113. *What is required in the tenth commandment?*

A. That there should never enter our heart even the least

inclination or thought contrary to any commandment of God, but that we should always hate sin with our whole heart and find satisfaction and joy in all righteousness.

Q. 114. *But can those who are converted to God keep these commandments perfectly?*
A. No, for even the holiest of them make only a small beginning in obedience in this life. Nevertheless, they begin with serious purpose to conform not only to some, but to all the commandments of God.

Q. 115. *Why, then, does God have the ten commandments preached so strictly since no one can keep them in this life?*
A. First, that all our life long we may become increasingly aware of our sinfulness, and therefore more eagerly seek forgiveness of sins and righteousness in Christ. Second, that we may constantly and diligently pray to God for the grace of the Holy Spirit, so that more and more we may be renewed in the image of God, until we attain the goal of full perfection after this life.

PRAYER

LORD'S DAY 45

Q. 116. *Why is prayer necessary for Christians?*
A. Because it is the chief part of the gratitude which God requires of us, and because God will give his grace and Holy Spirit only to those who sincerely beseech him in prayer without ceasing, and who thank him for these gifts.

Q. 117. *What is contained in a prayer which pleases God and is heard by him?*
A. First, that we sincerely call upon the one true God, who has revealed himself to us in his Word, for all that he has commanded us to ask of him. Then, that we thoroughly acknowledge our need and evil condition so that we may humble ourselves in the presence of his majesty. Third, that we rest assured that, in spite of our unworthiness, he will certainly hear our prayer for the sake of Christ our Lord, as he has promised us in his Word.

Q. 118. *What has God commanded us to ask of him?*
A. All things necessary for soul and body which Christ the Lord has included in the prayer which he himself taught us.

Q. 119. *What is the Lord's Prayer?*
A. " Our father who art in heaven, hallowed be thy name.
Thy kingdom come, thy will be done, on earth as it is in
heaven. Give us this day our daily bread; and forgive us our
debts, as we also have forgiven our debtors; and lead us not
into temptation, but deliver us from evil, for thine is the
kingdom and the power and the glory, forever. Amen."

OUR LORD'S PRAYER

LORD'S DAY 46

Q. 120. *Why has Christ commanded us to address God:
" Our Father "?*
A. That at the very beginning of our prayer he may
awaken in us the childlike reverence and trust toward God
which should be the motivation of our prayer, which is that
God has become our Father through Christ and will much
less deny us what we ask him in faith than our human fathers
will refuse us earthly things.

Q. 121. *Why is there added: " who art in heaven "?*
A. That we may have no earthly conception of the heavenly majesty of God, but that we may expect from his almighty power all things that are needed for body and soul.

LORD'S DAY 47

Q. 122. *What is the first petition?*
A. " Hallowed be thy name." That is: help us first of all to
know thee rightly, and to hallow, glorify, and praise thee in
all thy works through which there shine thine almighty
power, wisdom, goodness, righteousness, mercy, and truth.
And so order our whole life in thought, word, and deed that
thy name may never be blasphemed on our account, but may
always be honored and praised.

LORD'S DAY 48

Q.123. *What is the second petition?*
A. " Thy kingdom come." That is: so govern us by thy
Word and Spirit that we may more and more submit ourselves unto thee. Uphold and increase thy church. Destroy
the works of the devil, every power that raises itself against
thee, and all wicked schemes thought up against thy holy

Word, until the full coming of thy kingdom in which thou shalt be all in all.

Q. 124. *What is the third petition?*
A. " Thy will be done, on earth, as it is in heaven." That is: grant that we and all men may renounce our own will and obey thy will, which alone is good, without grumbling, so that everyone may carry out his office and calling as willingly and faithfully as the angels in heaven.

Q. 125. *What is the fourth petition?*
A. " Give us this day our daily bread." That is: be pleased to provide for all our bodily needs so that thereby we may acknowledge that thou art the only source of all that is good, and that without thy blessing neither our care and labor nor thy gifts can do us any good. Therefore, may we withdraw our trust from all creatures and place it in thee alone.

Q. 126. *What is the fifth petition?*
A. " And forgive us our debts, as we also have forgiven our debtors." That is: be pleased, for the sake of Christ's blood, not to charge to us, miserable sinners, our many transgressions, nor the evil which still clings to us. We also find this witness of thy grace in us, that it is our sincere intention heartily to forgive our neighbor.

Q. 127. *What is the sixth petition?*
A. " And lead us not into temptation, but deliver us from evil." That is: since we are so weak that we cannot stand by ourselves for one moment, and besides, since our sworn enemies, the devil, the world, and our own sin, ceaselessly assail us, be pleased to preserve and strengthen us through the power of thy Holy Spirit so that we may stand firm against them, and not be defeated in this spiritual warfare, until at last we obtain complete victory.

Q. 128. *How do you close this prayer?*
A. " For thine is the kingdom and the power and the glory,

forever." That is: we ask all this of thee because, as our King, thou art willing and able to give us all that is good since thou hast power over all things, and that by this not we ourselves but thy holy name may be glorified forever.

Q. 129. *What is the meaning of the little word " Amen "?*
A. Amen means: this shall truly and certainly be. For my prayer is much more certainly heard by God than I am persuaded in my heart that I desire such things from him.

THE THEOLOGICAL DECLARATION OF BARMEN, 1934

I. An Appeal to the Evangelical Congregations and Christians in Germany

The Confessional Synod of the German Evangelical Church met in Barmen, May 29–31, 1934. Here representatives from all the German Confessional Churches met with one accord in a confession of the one Lord of the one, holy, apostolic Church. In fidelity to their Confession of Faith, members of Lutheran, Reformed, and United Churches sought a common message for the need and temptation of the Church in our day. With gratitude to God they are convinced that they have been given a common word to utter. It was not their intention to found a new Church or to form a union. For nothing was farther from their minds than the abolition of the confessional status of our Churches. Their intention was, rather, to withstand in faith and unanimity the destruction of the Confession of Faith, and thus of the Evangelical Church in Germany. In opposition to attempts to establish the unity of the German Evangelical Church by means of false doctrine, by the use of force and insincere practices, the Confessional Synod insists that the unity of the Evangelical Churches in Germany can come only from the Word of God in faith through the Holy Spirit. Thus alone is the Church renewed.

Therefore the Confessional Synod calls upon the congregations to range themselves behind it in prayer, and steadfastly to gather around those pastors and teachers who are loyal to the Confessions.

Be not deceived by loose talk, as if we meant to oppose the unity of the German nation! Do not listen to the seducers who pervert our intentions, as if we wanted to break up the unity of the German Evangelical Church or to forsake the Confessions of the Fathers!

Try the spirits whether they are of God! Prove also the words of the Confessional Synod of the German Evangelical Church to see whether they agree with Holy Scripture and with the Confessions of the Fathers. If you find that we are speaking contrary to Scripture, then do not listen to us! But if you find that we are taking our stand upon Scripture, then let no fear or temptation keep you from treading with us the path of faith and obedience to the Word of God, in order that God's people be of one mind upon earth and that we in faith experience what he himself has said: " I will never leave you, nor forsake you." Therefore, " Fear not, little flock, for it is your Father's good pleasure to give you the kingdom."

II. Theological Declaration Concerning the Present Situation of the German Evangelical Church

According to the opening words of its constitution of July 11, 1933, the German Evangelical Church is a federation of Confessional Churches that grew out of the Reformation and that enjoy equal rights. The theological basis for the unification of these Churches is laid down in Article 1 and Article 2 (1) of the constitution of the German Evangelical Church that was recognized by the Reich Government on July 14, 1933:

> Article 1. The inviolable foundation of the German Evangelical Church is the gospel of Jesus Christ as it is attested for us in Holy Scripture and brought to light again in the Confessions of the Reformation. The full powers that the Church needs for its mission are hereby determined and limited.

> Article 2 (1). The German Evangelical Church is divided into member Churches (*Landeskirchen*).

We, the representatives of Lutheran, Reformed, and United Churches, of free synods, Church assemblies, and parish organizations united in the Confessional Synod of the German Evangelical Church, declare that we stand together on the ground of the German Evangelical Church as a federation of German Confessional Churches. We are bound together by the confession of the one Lord of the one, holy, catholic, and apostolic Church.

We publicly declare before all evangelical Churches in Germany that what they hold in common in this Confession is grievously imperiled, and with it the unity of the German Evangelical Church. It is threatened by the teaching methods and actions of the ruling Church party of the " German Christians " and of the Church administration carried on by them. These have become more and more apparent during the first year of the existence of the German Evangelical Church. This threat consists in the fact that the theological basis, in which the German Evangelical Church is united, has been continually and systematically thwarted and rendered ineffective by alien principles, on the part of the leaders and spokesmen of the " German Christians " as well as on the part of the Church administration. When these principles are held to be valid, then, according to all the Confessions in force among us, the Church ceases to be the Church and the German Evangelical Church, as a federation of Confessional Churches, becomes intrinsically impossible.

As members of Lutheran, Reformed, and United Churches we may and must speak with one voice in this matter today. Precisely because we want to be and to remain faithful to our various Confessions, we may not keep silent, since we believe that we have been given a common message to utter in a time of common need and temptation. We commend to God what this may mean for the interrelations of the Confessional Churches.

In view of the errors of the " German Christians " of the present Reich Church government which are devastating the Church and are also thereby breaking up the unity of the German Evangelical Church, we confess the following evangelical truths:

1. " *I am the way, and the truth, and the life; no one comes to the Father, but by me.*" (John 14:6.) " *Truly, truly, I say to you, he who does not enter the sheepfold by the door but climbs in by another way, that man is a thief and a robber. . . . I am the door; if anyone enters by me, he will be saved.*" (John 10:1, 9.)

Jesus Christ, as he is attested for us in Holy Scripture, is the one Word of God which we have to hear and which we have to trust and obey in life and in death.

We reject the false doctrine, as though the Church could and would have to acknowledge as a source of its proclamation, apart from and besides this one Word of God, still other events and powers, figures and truths, as God's revelation.

2. " *Christ Jesus, whom God made our wisdom, our righteousness and sanctification and redemption.*" (I Cor. 1:30.)

As Jesus Christ is God's assurance of the forgiveness of all our sins, so in the same way and with the same seriousness he is also God's mighty claim upon our whole life. Through him befalls us a joyful deliverance from the godless fetters of this world for a free, grateful service to his creatures.

We reject the false doctrine, as though there were areas of our life in which we would not belong to Jesus Christ, but to other lords — areas in which we would not need justification and sanctification through him.

3. " *Rather, speaking the truth in love, we are to grow up in every way into him who is the head, into Christ, from whom the whole body [is] joined and knit together.*" (Eph. 4:15, 16.)

The Christian Church is the congregation of the brethren in which Jesus Christ acts presently as the Lord in Word and sacrament through the Holy Spirit. As the Church of pardoned sinners, it has to testify in the midst of a sinful world, with its faith as with its obedience, with its message as with its order, that it is solely his property, and that it lives and wants to live solely from his comfort and from his direction in the expectation of his appearance.

We reject the false doctrine, as though the Church were permitted to abandon the form of its message and order to its own pleasure or to changes in prevailing ideological and political convictions.

4. " *You know that the rulers of the Gentiles lord it over them, and their great men exercise authority over them. It shall not be so among you; but whoever would be great among you must be your servant.*" (Matt. 20:25, 26.)

The various offices in the Church do not establish a dominion of some over the others; on the contrary, they are for the exercise of the ministry entrusted to and enjoined upon the whole congregation.

We reject the false doctrine, as though the Church, apart from this ministry, could and were permitted to give to itself, or allow to be given to it, special leaders vested with ruling powers.

5. "*Fear God. Honor the emperor.*" (I Peter 2:17.)

Scripture tells us that, in the as yet unredeemed world in which the Church also exists, the State has by divine appointment the task of providing for justice and peace. [It fulfills this task] by means of the threat and exercise of force, according to the measure of human judgment and human ability. The Church acknowledges the benefit of this divine appointment in gratitude and reverence before him. It calls to mind the Kingdom of God, God's commandment and righteousness, and thereby the responsibility both of rulers and of the ruled. It trusts and obeys the power of the Word by which God upholds all things.

We reject the false doctrine, as though the State, over and beyond its special commission, should and could become the single and totalitarian order of human life, thus fulfilling the Church's vocation as well.

We reject the false doctrine, as though the Church, over and beyond its special commission, should and could appropriate the characteristics, the tasks, and the dignity of the State, thus itself becoming an organ of the State.

6. *"Lo, I am with you always, to the close of the age."* (Matt. 28:20.)
"The Word of God is not fettered." (II Tim. 2:9.)

The Church's commission, upon which its freedom is founded, consists in delivering the message of the free grace of God to all people in Christ's stead, and therefore in the ministry of his own Word and work through sermon and sacrament.

We reject the false doctrine, as though the Church in human arrogance could place the Word and work of the Lord in the service of any arbitrarily chosen desires, purposes, and plans.

The Confessional Synod of the German Evangelical Church declares that it sees in the acknowledgment of these truths and in the rejection of these errors the indispensable theological basis of the German Evangelical Church as a federation of Confessional Churches. It invites all who are able to accept its declaration to be mindful of these theological principles in their decisions in Church politics. It entreats all whom it concerns to return to the unity of faith, love, and hope.